THE ETHNIC IMAGE IN MODERN AMERICAN LITERATURE: 1900–1950

Volume I

THE ETHNIC IMAGE IN MODERN AMERICAN LITERATURE: 1900–1950

Volume I

Edited by
PHILIP BUTCHER

HOWARD UNIVERSITY PRESS
Washington, D.C.   1984

Library of Congress Cataloging in Publication Data

Main entry under title:

The Ethnic image in modern American literature, 1900–1950.

   Includes index.
   1. American literature—20th century.   2. Minorities—
United States—Literary collections.   3. United States—
Ethnic relations—Literary collections.   4. American
literature—Minority authors.   I. Butcher, Philip,
1918–
PS509.M5E86   1984   810'.9'3520693   83–8440
ISBN 0–88258–110–4 (set)
ISBN 0–88258–119–8 (v. 1)
ISBN 0–88258–120–1 (v. 2)

To Jennie
and her generation

Contents

THE DARK PAST
The Burden of Bondage

ON THE FRONTIER
Cultures in Conflict

SERVANT AND MASTER
The Pecking Order

ETHNIC PRIDE
Ethnic Heroes

THE SOUTHERN SCENE

Preface

This anthology is intended to enlighten and entertain the general reader and to instruct the student, for whom it can serve as a text or reference in a variety of academic situations. The selections have been chosen to portray the realities of ethnic participation in American culture as well as the stereotypes that have stigmatized, at one time or another, all Americans of ancestry other than white Anglo-Saxon Protestant (WASP). The collection constitutes a significant survey of our literature and social history over a fifty-year span (1900–1950), a period not treated in my earlier anthology, *The Minority Presence in American Literature, 1600–1900* (2 vols., 1977), and one rich in representations of the multicultural character of our society.

During the first half of the twentieth century many ethnic groups moved toward or achieved assimilation, while new arrivals, refugees or immigrants to the Promised Land, took their place in the lower ranks of the national hierarchy. Others, although hindered by their high visibility, improved their image in literature and their status in the social order. Charles M. Sheldon, whose *In His Steps* (1896) sold twenty million copies, began *Richard Bruce* (1892) with the claim that the hero of the novel was "a typical American" whose grandfather and grandmother were born in the heart of New England "of what we call Anglo-Saxon ancestry." Fifty years later, so effective had the Americanization process been and so much had the social order changed, the concept of American identity could not be restricted to so narrow a definition.

In publishing without comment writing that expresses a variety of attitudes toward those Americans who were once placed beyond the pale because they were "different" and, at the same time, were disparaged as being "all alike," an editor may appear to approve of bigotry and chauvinism, stereotyping and gratuitous insults. But I depend on the reader to appraise each selection on the basis of its integrity in depicting ethnic life and character as well as on its merits as literature. An author who does not grant to characters of a race or

xiii

religion or culture other than his own their full stature and an equal claim to the rights of all human beings will not escape detection.

The readings are assembled under thematic headings and are arranged within these groups in chronological order. In some instances excerpts from a single work may be found in more than one classification. An index is provided, but space limitations and other considerations account for the omission of bibliography, chronology, and author biographies. Mounting interest in the ethnic experience has made available an abundance of reference books and other guides which the reader may consult, along with the standard literary and historical sources, as needed.

Every anthology may be charged with neglecting items that ought to be included, and this work is no exception. Some pieces have been omitted because permission to reprint could not be arranged with copyright owners. It may seem that particular ethnic groups have been overlooked. Why is there nothing about Puerto Ricans, Hungarians, Vietnamese? In general, the explanation for unrepresented and underrepresented groups is either their slight literary impact by the 1950 cut-off date or their recent arrival on the American scene.

Inevitably there will be laments about what is included as well as about what is not. Why reprint the work of authors once popular but no longer accepted as artists of consequence? Their one-time popularity, it may be argued in rebuttal, attests to their value as spokesmen for their time and as recorders of—perhaps even influencers of—the prevailing ethnic image. Why resurrect the work of serious but obscure writers now remembered only by scholars? Neglected pieces that present the realities of the ethnic predicament and ethnic feeling must not be ignored in a survey of the ethnic presence in American writing. Why bother with fragments extracted from works dealing with that presence only in a peripheral way? The casual epithet and incidental attention to groups that are "foreign" or "alien" can be as illuminating as a tract on the democratic ideal or a tome on the status of minorities in the United States.

This collection provides material likely to interest some readers for other than literary reasons, but it is essentially an anthology of American writing of a restricted period. The authors, many concerned about the underdog and some especially interested in their own ethnic group, are among the most important of their time, but the focus of this anthology is on the ethnic image, not on the identity of the writers. American literature began as reports about the New World by transplanted Englishmen. Now it is multi-ethnic writing about a complex multi-cultural society that still is more like a mosaic than a melting pot. Here is a rich sample of our literary heritage—a record of where we have been and a guide, perhaps, to where we are going.

PHILIP BUTCHER

Acknowledgments

The copyrighted selections reprinted in this book are used by permission of and special arrangement with the proprietors of their respective copyrights. Apologies are offered to any copyright holder we were unable to locate.

Grateful acknowledgment is made to the following:

Houghton Mifflin Company for selections from *The Promised Land* by Mary Antin (Copyright 1912 by Houghton Mifflin Company. Copyright renewed 1940 by Mary Antin); "Burying Ground by the Ties" and "Wildwest" from *New and Collected Poems 1917–1976* by Archibald MacLeish (Copyright © 1976 by Archibald MacLeish); *The Street* by Ann Petry (Copyright 1946. Copyright © renewed 1974 by Ann Petry); *The Member of the Wedding* by Carson McCullers (Copyright 1946 by Carson McCullers. Copyright © renewed 1974 by Floria V. Lasky); *Laughing Boy* by Oliver LaFarge (Copyright 1929, and copyright © renewed 1957 by Oliver LaFarge); and *Let Us Now Praise Famous Men* by James Agee and Walker Evans (Copyright 1941 by James Agee and Walker Evans. Copyright © renewed 1969 by Mia Fritsch Agee); all reprinted by permission of Houghton Mifflin Company.

Harper & Row, Publishers, Inc. for selections from *The Rise of David Levinsky* by Abraham Cahan (Copyright, 1917, by Harper & Row, Publishers, Inc. Renewed, 1945, by Abraham Cahan); *Giants in the Earth* by O. E. Rölvaag (Copyright, 1927, by Harper & Row, Publishers, Inc. Renewed © 1955, by Jennie Marie Berdahl Rölvaag); "The First Day" from *Anything Can Happen* by George and Helen Papashvily (Copyright 1943, © 1972 by George and Helen Waite Papashvily); "Heritage" and "For a Lady I Know" from *On These I Stand* by Countee Cullen (Copyright, 1925, by Harper & Row, Publishers, Inc. Renewed, 1953, by Ida M. Cullen); *Mules and Men* by Zora Neale Hurston (J. B. Lippincott) (Copyright, 1935, by Zora Neale Hurston. Renewed © 1965 by John C. Hurston and Joel Hurston); "Let's Go to Hinky-Dink's" in *Awake and Rehearse* by Louis Bromfield (Copyright, 1927, © 1955 by Louis Bromfield); *A Tree Grows in Brooklyn* by Betty Smith (Copyright, 1948, by Betty Smith); *Kitty Foyle* by Christopher Morley (J. B. Lippincott, Publishers) (Copyright, 1939, by Christopher Morley); *You Can't Go Home Again* by Thomas Wolfe (Copyright, 1934, 1937, 1938, 1939, 1940 by Maxwell Perkins as executor. Renewed © 1968 by Paul Gitlin); and abridgement of "On a Florida Key" from *Essays of E. B. White* by E. B. White (Copyright, 1941, by E. B. White); all reprinted by permission of Harper & Row, Publishers, Inc.

Charles Scribner's Sons for selections from *The Americanization of Edward Bok* by Edward Bok (Copyright 1920 Charles Scribner's Sons; copyright renewed 1948 Mary Louise Curtis Zimbalist) and *So Red the Rose* by Stark Young (Copyright 1934 Charles Scribner's Sons; copyright renewed 1962 Stark Young), reprinted by permission of Charles Scribner's Sons.

Perina Panunzio for permission to reprint the selection from *The Soul of an Immigrant* by Constantine M. Panunzio.

Harriet F. Pilpel for permission to reprint excerpts from "Every Other Thursday" in *One*

Basket: Thirty-One Short Stories by Edna Ferber (Copyright © 1947 by Edna Ferber. Copyright © renewed 1975 by Harriet F. Pilpel, Executrix) and *American Beauty* by Edna Ferber (Copyright © 1931 by Edna Ferber, Copyright © renewed 1959 by Edna Ferber), All Rights Reserved.

Vanguard Press, Inc., the publisher, for permission to reprint the selection from "The Benefits of American Life" in *The Short Stories of James T. Farrell* (Copyright © 1934, 1935, 1937 by Vanguard Press, Inc. Copyright © renewed 1961, 1962, 1964 by James T. Farrell).

Dodd, Mead & Company, Inc. for selections from *Gold in the Streets* by Mary Vardoulakis; "Dark Symphony" in *Rendezvous with America* by Melvin B. Tolson; *Toucoutou* by Edward Laroque Tinker; and "A Summer Tragedy" from *The Old South* by Arna Bontemps (Copyright 1933 by Arna Bontemps. Copyright renewed 1961 by Arna Bontemps. Copyright 1973 by Alberta Bontemps, Executrix); all published by and reprinted by permission of Dodd, Mead & Company, Inc.

Harcourt Brace Jovanovich, Inc. for selections from *The Autobiography of Lincoln Steffens* (Copyright 1931 by Harcourt Brace Jovanovich, Inc.; renewed 1959 by Peter Steffens); "Mr. K*A*P*L*A*N, the Comparative, and the Superlative" from *The Education of Hyman Kaplan* by Leonard Q. Ross (Copyright 1937 by Harcourt Brace Jovanovich, Inc.; copyright 1965 by Leo Rosten); "My Cousin Dikran, the Orator" from *My Name Is Aram* by William Saroyan (Copyright 1938, 1966 by William Saroyan); *Mama's Bank Account* by Kathryn Forbes (Copyright 1943 by Kathryn Forbes; renewed 1971 by Richard E. McLean and Robert M. McLean); *Boston Adventure* by Jean Stafford (Copyright 1942 by Harcourt Brace Jovanovich, Inc.; copyright 1970 by Jean Stafford); "Nigger," and "Child of the Romans" from *Chicago Poems* by Carl Sandburg (Copyright 1916 by Holt, Rinehart and Winston, Inc.; copyright 1944 by Carl Sandburg); "The Negro Migration" from *The Chicago Race Riots* by Carl Sandburg (Copyright 1919 by Harcourt, Brace & Howe, Inc.; renewed 1947 by Carl Sandburg); "The Witness" from *The Leaning Tower and Other Stories* by Katherine Anne Porter (Copyright 1935, 1963 by Katherine Anne Porter); "Powerhouse" from *A Curtain of Green and Other Stories* by Eudora Welty (Copyright 1941, 1969 by Eudora Welty); and *The Seven Storey Mountain* by Thomas Merton (Copyright 1948 by Harcourt Brace Jovanovich, Inc.; renewed 1976 by The Trustees of the Merton Legacy Trust); all reprinted by permission of Harcourt Brace Jovanovich, Inc.

Liveright Publishing Corporation:

Selections are reprinted from *Fig Tree John* by Edwin Corle, by permission of Liveright Publishing Corporation. Copyright 1935 by Edwin Corle. Copyright renewed 1963 by Mrs. Jean Corle.

"Black Tambourine" and "The Sad Indian" are reprinted from *The Complete Poems and Selected Letters and Prose of Hart Crane,* Edited by Brom Weber, with the permission of Liveright Publishing Corporation. Copyright 1933, © 1958, 1966 by Liveright Publishing Corporation.

Selection from *The Enormous Room* by E. E. Cummings is reprinted by permission of Liveright Publishing Corporation. Copyright 1922 by Boni & Liveright, Inc. Copyright renewed 1950 by E. E. Cummings. Copyright © 1978 by the Trustees for the E. E. Cummings Trust. Copyright © 1978 by George James Firmage.

"Frederick Douglass" is reprinted from *Angle of Ascent, New and Selected Poems* by Robert Hayden, by permission of Liveright Publishing Corporation. Copyright © 1975, 1972, 1970, 1966 by Robert Hayden.

Antoinette McNickle Vogel, P.R. for the Estate of D'Arcy McNickle, for permission to reprint selections from *The Surrounded* by D'Arcy McNickle.

Scott Meredith Literary Agency, Inc. for permission to reprint the selection from *Christ in Concrete* by Pietro Di Donato.

Random House, Inc./Alfred A. Knopf, Inc. for selections from *The Free Man* by Conrad Richter (Copyright 1943 by Conrad Richter); *Nigger Heaven* by Carl Van Vechten (Copyright 1926 by Alfred A. Knopf, Inc. and renewed 1954 by Carl Van Vechten); "The Strong Swimmer" from *Day of Deliverance: A Book of Poems in Wartime* by William Rose Benét (Copyright 1944 by William Rose Benét and renewed 1972 by James Benét and Mrs. Richard S. Dawson); *The Autobiography of an Ex-Coloured Man* by James Weldon Johnson (Copyright 1927 by Alfred A. Knopf, Inc. Renewal Copyright © 1955 by Carl Van Vechten); and "The Sahara of the Bozart" by H. L. Mencken (Copyright 1920 by Alfred A. Knopf, Inc. and renewed 1948 by H. L. Mencken. Reprinted from *A Mencken Chrestomathy* by H. L. Mencken); all reprinted by permission of Alfred A. Knopf, Inc.

Random House, Inc./Alfred A. Knopf, Inc. for selections from "Melanctha" and "The Gentle Lena" from *Three Lives* by Gertrude Stein (Copyright 1909 and renewed 1937 by Gertrude Stein); *Other Voices, Other Rooms* by Truman Capote (Copyright 1948 by Truman Capote); "The

Way It Is'' by Ralph Ellison (Copyright 1942 by Weekly Masses Co., Inc. Reprinted from *Shadow and Act* by Ralph Ellison); ''I Thought about this Girl'' by Jerome Weidman (Copyright 1938 and renewed 1966 by Jerome Weidman. Reprinted from *My Father Sits in the Dark and Other Stories* by Jerome Weidman. Originally appeared in *The New Yorker*); *Cass Timberlane* by Sinclair Lewis (Copyright 1945 by Sinclair Lewis); ''Jew'' by Karl Shapiro (Copyright 1943 by Karl Shapiro. Reprinted from *Collected Poems 1940–1978* by Karl Shapiro); and *The Sound and the Fury* by William Faulkner (Copyright 1929 and renewed 1957 by William Faulkner); all reprinted by permission of Random House, Inc.

Russell & Volkening, Inc. for permission to reprint ''Papa, Mama and Economics'' from *We Ride a White Donkey* by George Panetta (Copyright © 1944 by George Panetta, renewed 1972 by George Panetta).

Viking Penguin Inc. for permission to reprint Chapter 1 from *Cannery Row* by John Steinbeck (Copyright 1945 by John Steinbeck. Copyright renewed 1973 by Elaine Steinbeck, John Steinbeck IV, and Thom Steinbeck) and ''O Black and Unknown Bards'' from *St. Peter Relates an Incident of Resurrection Day* by James Weldon Johnson (Copyright 1935 by James Weldon Johnson. Copyright renewed 1963 by Grace Nail Johnson).

Farrar, Straus & Giroux, Inc. for permission to reprint excerpts from ''The Mohawks in High Steel'' by Joseph Mitchell, collected in *Apologies to the Iroquois* by Edmund Wilson (Copyright © 1949 by Joseph Mitchell. This essay originally appeared in *The New Yorker*) and from ''A Wife of Nashville'' from *The Collected Stories of Peter Taylor* (Copyright © 1949, 1969 by Peter Taylor. This story originally appeared in *The New Yorker*).

Brandt & Brandt Literary Agents, Inc. for permission to reprint selections from *John Brown's Body* and ''Freedom's a Hard-Bought Thing'' by Stephen Vincent Benét from *The Selected Works of Stephen Vincent Benét* (Holt, Rinehart & Winston, Inc.) (Copyright 1940 by Stephen Vincent Benét. Copyright renewed 1955, 1956 by Rosemary Carr Benét. Copyright renewed © 1968 by Thomas C. Benét, Rachel Lewis and Stephanie B. Mahin) and from *Penrod, His Complete Story* by Booth Tarkington (Copyright 1913, 1941 by Booth Tarkington).

Howard Fast for permission to reprint the selection from *Freedom Road* by Howard Fast.

Constance Garland Doyle for permission to reprint a selection from *The Book of the American Indian* by Hamlin Garland.

The John G. Neihardt Trust for permission to reprint ''The Last Thunder Song'' from *Indian Tales and Others* by John G. Neihardt (Copyright by the John G. Neihardt Trust).

William Morrow & Company, Inc. for permission to reprint selections from *Wolf Song* by Harvey Fergusson (Copyright © 1927; renewed 1955, by Harvey Fergusson) and *Inchin' Along* by Welbourn Kelley (Copyright 1932 by Welbourn Kelley).

The Witter Bynner Foundation for Poetry, Inc. for permission to reprint ''Indian Earth'' from *Indian Earth* by Witter Bynner (Copyright © 1929 by Alfred A. Knopf, Inc. Copyright renewed 1957 by Witter Bynner).

Curtis Brown, Ltd. for permission to reprint the selection from *Children of God* by Vardis Fisher (Copyright © 1939 by Vardis Fisher).

Holt, Rinehart and Winston, Publishers, for permission to reprint the selection from *The Forest and the Fort* by Hervey Allen (Copyright 1943 by Hervey Allen. Copyright © 1971 by Ann Andrews Allen).

Doubleday & Company, Inc. for permission to reprint excerpts from *Rabble in Arms* by Kenneth Roberts (Copyright 1933, 1947 by Kenneth Roberts); ''How the Devil Came Down Division Street'' from *The Neon Wilderness* by Nelson Algren (Copyright 1944 by Nelson Algren. Copyright © 1947 The Hearst Corporation. Courtesy of *Harper's Bazaar*); *Mamba's Daughters* by Dubose Heyward (Copyright 1929 by Dubose Heyward); and *Following the Color Line* by Ray Stannard Baker (Copyright 1904, 1905 by S. S. McClure Company. Copyright 1907, 1908 by The Phillips Publishing Company. Copyright 1908 by Doubleday & Company, Inc.).

Virginia E. Whitbeck and Eleanor E. Mensel for permission to reprint a selection from *The Soul of the Indian* by Charles A. Eastman.

Dr. Loren Grey, President, Zane Grey, Inc. for permission to reprint an excerpt from *The Rainbow Trail* by Zane Grey.

E. P. Dutton, Inc. for permission to reprint ''Indian Sky'' from *Selected Poems* by Alfred Kreymborg (Copyright, 1945, by Alfred Kreymborg. Renewal, 1973, by Dorothy Kreymborg), the selection from *Knock on Any Door* by Willard Motley (Copyright 1947, by Willard Motley. Renewal, 1975, by Frederica Westbrooke) and the selection from *Birthright* by T. S. Stribling (Copyright, 1922, 1950, by T. S. Stribling).

New Directions Publishing Corporation for permission to reprint "Advent of the Slaves" from *In the American Grain* by William Carlos Williams (Copyright 1933 by William Carlos Williams).

The Atlantic Monthly Company, Boston, Mass., for permission to reprint "Black Troubadour" by David L. Cohn (Copyright © 1938 ® 1966).

Evelyn Singer Literary Agency for permission to reprint the selection from *Jews without Money* by Michael Gold.

Daniel Fuchs for permission to reprint the selection from *Summer in Williamsburg* by Daniel Fuchs.

Elizabeth H. Dos Passos for permission to reprint the excerpt from from *The Big Money* by John Dos Passos.

Sophie M. Appel for permission to reprint the selection from *The Dark Stain* by Benjamin Appel.

Harold Orenstein for permission to reprint the selection from *East River* by Sholem Asch.

Helen Thurber for permission to reprint "A Sequence of Servants" from *My Life and Hard Times* by James Thurber (Harper & Row) (Copyright © 1933, 1961 by James Thurber).

Andrew Lytle for permission to reprint "Mister McGregor" by Andrew Lytle, first published in *Virginia Quarterly Review*.

The New Yorker for permission to reprint "Boogie-Woogie Ballads: The Touchin' Case of Mr. and Mrs. Massa" by St. Clair McKelway (Copyright © 1943, 1971 by The New Yorker Magazine, Inc.).

Macmillan Publishing Co., Inc. for permission to reprint an excerpt from "The Chinese Nightingale" in *Collected Poems* by Vachel Lindsay (Copyright 1917 by Macmillan Publishing Co., Inc., renewed 1945 by Elizabeth C. Lindsay).

G. K. Hall & Co. for permission to reprint "To the White Fiends" from *Selected Poems* by Claude McKay (Copyright 1981 by Twayne Publishers, Inc., and reprinted with the permission of Twayne Publishers, Inc., a division of G. K. Hall & Co., Boston).

International Creative Management, Inc. for permission to reprint an excerpt from "Letter to the Front" in *Collected Poems* by Muriel Rukeyser (McGraw-Hill) (Copyright © 1944, 1978).

University of South Carolina Press for permission to reprint "The Merry-go-Round" from *Collected Short Stories of Julia Peterkin*, selected and edited with an introduction by Frank Durham (Copyright © 1970 by the University of South Carolina Press).

Harold Ober Associates Incorporated for permission to reprint an excerpt from "Harlem" in *Man Possessed* by William Rose Benét (Copyright © 1927 by William Rose Benét. All rights reserved) and "Runagate Niggers" by William March (Copyright 1938 by Esquire-Coronet Inc. Renewed © 1966 by the Merchants National Bank of Mobile as Trustees for the Estate of William Campbell).

Sterling A. Brown for permission to reprint "And/Or" by Sterling A. Brown.

THE ETHNIC IMAGE IN MODERN AMERICAN LITERATURE: 1900–1950

Volume I

DISCOVERING AMERICA
The Promised Land

"Give me your tired, your poor,
Your huddled masses yearning to breathe free,
The wretched refuse of your teeming shore.
Send these, the homeless, tempest-tost to me:
I lift my lamp beside the golden door!"

Emma Lazarus
The New Colossus

All of us . . . are descended from immigrants and revolutionists.

Franklin D. Roosevelt
Remarks to the Daughters of
the American Revolution

Immigrants! My family's been having trouble with immigrants ever since we came to this country.

E.Y. Harburg and Fred Saidy
Finian's Rainbow

IMMIGRATION

by Finley Peter Dunne

"Well, I see Congress has got to wurruk again," said Mr. Dooley.

"The Lord save us fr'm harm," said Mr. Hennessy.

"Yes, sir," said Mr. Dooley, "Congress has got to wurruk again, an' manny things that seems important to a Congressman 'll be brought up befure thim. 'Tis sthrange that what's a big thing to a man in Wash'nton, Hinnissy, don't seem much account to me. Divvle a bit do I care whether they dig th' Nicaragoon Canal or cross th' Isthmus in a balloon; or whether th' Monroe docthrine is enfoorced or whether it ain't; or whether th' thrusts is abolished as Teddy Rosenfelt wud like to have thim or encouraged to go on with their nee-faryous but magnificent entherprises as th' Prisidint wud like; or whether th' water is poured into th' ditches to reclaim th' arid lands iv th' West or th' money fr thim to fertilize th' arid pocket-books iv th' conthractors; or whether th' Injun is threated like a depindant an' miserable thribesman or like a free an' in-depindant dog; or whether we restore th' merchant marine to th' ocean or whether we lave it to restore itsilf. None iv these here questions inthrests me, an' be me I mane you an' be you I mane ivrybody. What we want to know is, ar-re we goin' to have coal enough in th' hod whin th' cold snap comes, will th' plumbin' hold out, an' will th' job last.

"But they'se wan question that Congress is goin' to take up that you an' me are intherested in. As a pilgrim father that missed th' first boats, I must raise me claryon voice again' th' invasion iv this fair land be th' paupers an' arnychists iv effete Europe. Ye bet I must—because I'm here first. 'Twas diff'rent whin I was dashed high on th' stern an' rockbound coast. In thim days America was th' refuge iv th' oppressed iv all th' wurruld. They cud come over here an' do a good job iv oppressin' thimsilves. As I told ye I come a little late. Th' Rosenfelts an' th' Lodges bate me be at laste a boat length, an' be th' time I got here they was stern an' rockbound thimsilves. So I got a gloryous raycip-tion as soon as I was towed off th' rocks. Th' stars an' sthripes whispered a welcome in th' breeze an' a shovel was thrust into me hand an' I was pushed into a sthreet excyvatin' as though I'd been born here. Th' pilgrim father who bossed th' job was a fine ol' puritan be th' name iv Doherty, who come over in th' Mayflower about th' time iv th' potato rot in Wexford, an' he made me think they was a hole in th' breakwather iv th' haven iv refuge an' some iv th' wash iv th' seas iv opprission had got through. He was a stern an' rockbound la-ad himsilf, but I was a good hand at loose stones an' wan day—but I'll tell ye about that another time.

"Annyhow, I was rayceived with open arms that sometimes ended in a clinch. I was afraid I wasn't goin' to assimilate with th' airlyer pilgrim fathers an' th' instichoochions iv th' counthry, but I soon found that a long swing iv th' pick made me as good as another man an' it didn't require a gr-reat intellect, or sometimes anny at all, to vote th' dimmycrat ticket, an' befure I was here a month, I felt enough like a native born American to burn a witch. Wanst in a while a mob iv intilligint collajeens, whose grandfathers had bate me to th' dock, wud take a shy at me Pathrick's Day procission or burn down wan iv me churches, but they got tired iv that befure long; 'twas too much like wurruk.

"But as I tell ye, Hinnissy, 'tis diff'rent now. I don't know why 'tis diff'rent but 'tis diff'rent. 'Tis time we put our back again' th' open dure an' keep out th' savage horde. If that cousin iv ye'ers expects to cross, he'd better tear f'r th' ship. In a few minyits th' gates 'll be down an' whin th' oppressed wurruld comes hikin' acrost to th' haven iv refuge, they'll do well to put a couplin' pin undher their hats, f'r th' Goddess iv Liberty 'll meet thim at th' dock with an axe in her hand. Congress is goin' to fix it. Me frind Shaughnessy says so. He was in yisterdah an' says he: ''Tis time we done something to make th' immigration laws sthronger,' says he. 'Thrue f'r ye, Miles Standish,' says I; 'but what wud ye do?' 'I'd keep out th' offscourin's iv Europe,' says he. 'Wud ye go back?' says I. 'Have ye'er joke,' says he. ''Tis not so seeryus as it was befure ye come,' says I. 'But what ar-re th' immygrants doin' that's roonous to us?' I says. 'Well,' says he, 'they're arnychists,' he says; 'they don't assymilate with th' counthry,' he says. 'Maybe th' counthry's digestion has gone wrong fr'm too much rich food,' says I; 'perhaps now if we'd lave off thryin' to digest Rockyfellar an' thry a simple diet like Schwartzmeister, we wudden't feel th' effects iv our vittels,' I says. 'Maybe if we'd season th' immygrants a little or cook thim thurly, they'd go down betther,' I says.

" 'They're arnychists, like Parsons,' he says. 'He wud've been an immygrant if Texas hadn't been admitted to th' Union,' I says. 'Or Snolgosh,' he says. 'Has Mitchigan seceded?' I says. 'Or Gittoo,' he says. 'Who come fr'm th' effete monarchies iv Chicago, west iv Ashland Av'noo,' I says. 'Or what's-his-name, Wilkes Booth,' he says. 'I don't know what he was—maybe a Boolgharyen,' says I. 'Well, annyhow,' says he, 'they're th' scum iv th' earth.' 'They may be that,' says I; 'but we used to think they was th' cream iv civilization,' I says. 'They're off th' top annyhow. I wanst believed 'twas th' best men iv Europe come here, th' la-ads that was too sthrong and indepindant to be kicked around be a boorgomasther at home an' wanted to dig out f'r a place where they cud get a chanst to make their way to th' money. I see their sons fightin' into politics an' their daughters tachin' young American idee how to shoot too high in th' public school, an' I thought they was all right. But I see

I was wrong. Thim boys out there towin' wan heavy foot afther th' other to th' rowlin' mills is all arnychists. There's warrants out f'r all names endin' in 'inski, an' I think I'll board up me windows, f'r,' I says, 'if immygrants is as dangerous to this counthry as ye an' I an' other pilgrim fathers believe they are, they'se enough iv thim sneaked in already to make us aborigines about as infloointial as the prohibition vote in th' Twinty-ninth Ward. They'll dash again' our stern an' rockbound coast till they bust it,' says I.

" 'But I ain't so much afraid as ye ar-re. I'm not afraid iv me father an' I'm not afraid iv mesilf. An' I'm not afraid iv Schwartzmeister's father or Hinnery Cabin Lodge's grandfather. We all come over th' same way, an' if me ancestors were not what Hogan calls rigicides, 'twas not because they were not ready an' willin', on'y a king niver come their way. I don't believe in killin' kings, mesilf. I niver wud've sawed th' block off that curlyheaded potintate that I see in th' pitchers down town, but, be hivins, Presarved Codfish Shaughnessy, if we'd begun a few years ago shuttin' out folks that wudden't mind handin' a bomb to a king, they wudden't be enough people in Mattsachoosetts to make a quorum f'r th' Anti-Impeeryal S'ciety,' says I. 'But what wud ye do with th' offscourin' iv Europe?' says he. 'I'd scour thim some more,' says I.

"An' so th' meetin' iv th' Plymouth Rock Assocyation come to an end. But if ye wud like to get it together, Deacon Hinnissy, to discuss th' immigration question, I'll sind out a hurry call f'r Schwartzmeister an' Mulcahey an' Ignacio Sbarbaro an' Nels Larsen an' Petrus Gooldvink, an' we 'll gather tonight at Fanneilnoviski Hall at th' corner iv Sheridan an' Sigel sthreets. All th' pilgrim fathers is rayquested f'r to bring interpreters."

"Well," said Mr. Hennessy, "divvle th' bit I care, on'y I'm here first, an' I ought to have th' right to keep th' bus fr'm bein' overcrowded."

"Well," said Mr. Dooley, "as a pilgrim father on me gran' nephew's side, I don't know but ye're right. An' they'se wan sure way to keep thim out."

"What's that?" asked Mr. Hennessy.

"Teach thim all about our instichoochions befur they come," said Mr. Dooley.

(1902)

From

THE BREAKER BOY

by Clarence Darrow

Johnny McCaffery was eleven years old when he became a man.

Five years before this, his father and mother, with their four children and steerage tickets sailed out of the Queenstown Harbor, bound for the United States. They had heard of America—all Irishmen had—they knew that America had no English landlords; no rack-rented tenants; no hopeless men and ragged women and hungry boys and girls. So, as they stood on the steerage deck and looked through the wire netting of the fading white houses and green fields of their native land, Owen and Bridget were light of heart. Beyond the great turbulent ocean, were contentment, equality, and wealth; a home for themselves and a brilliant future for the four children, who half in fear and half in wonder, were looking out at the white gulls and the white crested waves.

Two weeks later, they landed in New York, were rushed through Castle Garden and hurried to the railway station where they set out for Scranton, Pennsylvania.

Within a few days, Owen had found a job in the mines, opened an account with a "company" store, and rented a "company" house, with a kitchen and parlor below and two little bedrooms above. Down under the kitchen floor was a hole in the ground which they called a cellar, and some rough wooden steps led to the bottom from the side of the house. The hut was closed with boards which ran up and down; the inside was without paper or even plaster; while, here and there, the cracks let in the daylight, and, through the winter, the wind and sifting snow.

Owen and Bridget were a trifle disappointed in their home. In their little stone hut in their far-off island, they had never dreamed that a house like this could be found in a land so rich and free. But they were starting life in a new and strange world; so,—with strong hopes and brave hearts, they set to work to make the best of what they had, never doubting that the looked-for mansion would soon be theirs.

Owen went to work in the coal mines—five hundred feet beneath the ground. Every morning he stepped on board a car, grasped his dinner pail in one hand, while he clutched the iron rail in his other, and held his breath until he was dropped to the bottom; then, at night, he went back to the foot of the pit, and boarded the car to be taken again to the top of the earth.

But this story is about Johnny. There is no time to tell more of Owen, except that one day a great piece of rock broke off from the roof of the chamber where he worked and fell squarely upon him, crushing him to death.

The miners took him to the top of the shaft and back to the little hut, and consoled the helpless widow and children as best they could. Then they followed him to the grave, and the story of his hopes and struggles was told.

Johnny was almost eleven when they laid his father in the little consecrated ground and put the white wooden cross above his head. He was at school the day the rock came down, and had done so well that he was in the third reader, and had reached division in the arithmetic.

Johnny's older brother was already tending a door in the mine, and his sisters were in the public school. Some years before, a wise good man, seeing how scant was the miner's income, had built a lace mill so that his girls could earn something to help the family along. So one night the older sister carefully packed up her books and slate and took them home, and the next day, went to the mill.

Bridget planned and saved the best she could. She had great hopes for little Johnny. He would surely be a scholar and make famous the McCaffery name. But Owen's funeral had left them hopelessly in debt, and the earning of the older boy and girl could not keep the family alive. So there was really nothing left to do but send Johnny to the breaker.

*　　*　　*　　*　　*

It will not do to imagine that Johnny had no fun. He learned to chew plug tobacco and often went to the saloon at night. To be sure, he was pretty young for this—still a boy who is old enough to go to a breaker, is old enough to go to a saloon. When one is old enough to do manly work, he is old enough to have manly sport.

He used to go home at night so black that his closest friends could not have told his name. Then he washed himself in a tub of water in the parlor, changed all his clothes, got his supper, and went out with the rest of the boys to play. There were the ordinary games for boys; there were cats to stone; there was a great cave where a house had gone down into an old worked-out mine, and where the boys gathered at night and built a fire from old rubbish, and where one boy who had gone as far as the fourth grade, read to the rest wonderful stories from the nickel novels that they managed somehow to get. Then, there was the night school kept up for miners' boys and girls—but they could not study much after the day's work at the mill. Sometimes Johnny went to the night school, but he often fell asleep when he tried to study; so he never got past the third reader, after all.

In this way Johnny went on until his fourteenth year. There was really nothing to tell after that time and very little before. In fact, it is rather absurd to write a story about a breaker-boy; nothing happens to a breaker-boy. There must be some dramatic situation to make a story, and there is nothing dramatic in a life of endless toil. Strange as it may seem, Johnny never had an unknown rich uncle who died and left him a fortune. Mr. Fox never looked at his swiftly moving fingers and took a fancy to him and invited him to his home and married him to his daughter. In fact, Mr. Fox never even saw him in the dust and gloom.

Almost all of his life must be skipped because it is so dull. In writing biography, one cannot dwell long on the parts that are very dull, and one must entirely omit the parts that are very interesting, and so biography is not biography after all. Anyhow Johnny left the breaker when he was fourteen and was promoted to the place of door-keeper in the mine.

All of this was over forty years ago and forty years makes a great change in any one who lives upon the earth. But it makes a greater change in the miner than in most other men. Fifty-four is not so very old, so at least most of us think who cling tenaciously to the forties, and still more those who watch anxiously while the fifties are checked off. But, at fifty-four, the man who has money and can have leisure still feels that he is young. He can eat and drink; can laugh, and dance and play; he can marry and travel and write; in fact, can still chase all the fantasies and bubbles that make us forget the waiting open grave.

Forty years entirely transformed Johnny. Even his name was changed; he was now John; generally Uncle John. He had been a door boy, a driver, a helper, a miner, and he had now come up out of the earth to spend his last few years above the ground. His face was scarred and one ear was missing. This came not from war, but from powder all the same. A belated fuse exploded when he thought it had gone out. But still he counted this as luck for his life was saved. One arm was crippled from a falling rock and his right hip was never free from pain, but this was only the rheumatism that he caught while working in the ground. Except for the asthma, he could still have stayed a number of years inside the earth before the last time that he should be lowered down to come up no more.

But his old valves were growing more and more rusty every year. He wheezed instead of breathed, and he could walk but a very little way, and could stand upon his feet only a few minutes at a time. His strength was almost gone. Some doctors would have advised rest and travel and a higher altitude, but his did not. In fact, he had no doctor. Every one in the mine knew all about asthma, the black shadow that hangs always above a miner's life.

John did not live in the same house where his father first placed him when he came from Ireland so long ago, but he lived very near the spot, still in a ''company'' house. The miners, and the mules, and machinery, had changed from time to time, but the breaker, the black culm pile, and the ''company'' houses still remained.

In forty years, John had buried his mother; had married, raised a family and traveled back and forth along the short path from his hut to the open mouth of the mine day after day, and this was all. As the years had passed, his one ambition had been to go back to Ireland, even for a short time, as his father's had been to come to the United States, but this ambition he had buried in the mines long years ago. He had left the valley once in forty years. Then he had gone to Philadelphia, and his ticket had cost him $5.40. This was a quarter of a century ago, but he remembered the exact amount that he gave in exchange for the little pasteboard at the station window.

John really had earned the right to rest, but then, he and his family must live—at least he thought they must, and so they must, else the rich man's coal could never get dug up. The mine boss was really not unkind, so when John told him that he could not go down the shaft again, the boss promised him an easier job. The boss took John to the breaker, up the long flight of stairs, down the ladder of little boards nailed across the chute, and sat him down on the old board that he had left forty years ago. John was not a poet or a dreamer. In fact, he had never had a great deal of imagination, and what he had was buried long ago in the deep, black mine. He did not seem to think of the strange fate that sat him down on the narrow board after the circle of his life was done. He thought no more about it than do the rest of us of the everlasting turning of the great wheel to which all of us are strapped.

This is about all of John's story. It is really up to date. The other morning, he walked up the slope to the great black mill. As he went up the hill, his wheezing could be heard a hundred feet away. Every few rods he stopped to rest. In his right hand, he carried the everlasting dinner pail. In his mouth was a black briar pipe. Thank God, he could smoke. He reached the breaker and started up the steps. At the first landing, he stopped to rest. The boys rushed past, calling out, "Hellow, Uncle John!" At the second landing he stopped again, and so on at each landing to the top. Then he took a good long wait until he fully got his breath, before he started down the ladder to his seat. Slowly and deliberately, he sat down upon the rough, hard board. Mechanically, he took his tobacco pouch from his pockets, knocked the ashes from his pipe, filled it full of fresh tobacco, put it in his mouth, struck a match upon the sheet iron lining of the chute, drew in his wheezy breath and commenced to smoke. Then he took his rheumatic leg in his hand, raised his foot until it rested on the right hand side of the long chute; then he raised his left foot to the other side, bent over and looked at the black, iron trough and waited for the coal to tumble down.

(1902)

From

THE PROMISED LAND
by Mary Antin

Now I was not exactly an infant when I was set down, on a May day some fifteen years ago, in this pleasant nursery of America. I had long since acquired the use of my faculties, and had collected some bits of experience, practical and emotional, and had even learned to give an account of them. Still, I had very little perspective, and my observations and comparisons were superficial. I was too much carried away to analyze the forces that were moving me. My Polotzk I knew well before I began to judge it and experiment with it. America was bewilderingly strange, unimaginably complex, delightfully unexplored. I rushed impetuously out of the cage of my provincialism and looked eagerly about the brilliant universe. My question was, What have we here?—not, What does this mean? That query came much later. When I now become retrospectively introspective, I fall into the predicament of the centipede in the rhyme, who got along very smoothly until he was asked which leg came after which, whereupon he became so rattled that he couldn't take a step. I know I have come on a thousand feet, on wings, winds, and American machines,—I have leaped and run and climbed and crawled,—but to tell which step came after which I find a puzzling matter. Plenty of maiden aunts were present during my second infancy, in the guise of immigrant officials, school-teachers, settlement workers, and sundry other unprejudiced and critical observers. Their statistics I might properly borrow to fill the gaps in my recollections, but I am prevented by my sense of harmony. The individual, we know, is a creature unknown to the statistician, whereas I undertook to give the personal view of everything. So I am bound to unravel, as well as I can, the tangle of events, outer and inner, which made up the first breathless years of my American life.

During his three years of probation, my father had made a number of false starts in business. His history for that period is the history of thousands who come to America, like him, with pockets empty, hands untrained to the use of tools, minds cramped by centuries of repression in their native land. Dozens of these men pass under your eyes every day, my American friend, too absorbed in their honest affairs to notice the looks of suspicion which you cast at them, the repugnance with which you shrink from their touch. You see them shuffle from door to door with a basket of spools and buttons, or bending over the sizzling irons in a basement tailor shop, or rummaging in your ash can, or moving a pushcart from curb to curb, at the command of the burly policeman.

"The Jew peddler!" you say, and dismiss him from your premises and from your thoughts, never dreaming that the sordid drama of his days may have a moral that concerns you. What if the creature with the untidy beard carries in his bosom his citizenship papers? What if the cross-legged tailor is supporting a boy in college who is one day going to mend your state constitution for you? What if the ragpicker's daughters are hastening over the ocean to teach your children in the public schools? Think, every time you pass the greasy alien on the street, that he was born thousands of years before the oldest native American; and he may have something to communicate to you, when you two shall have learned a common language. Remember that his very physiognomy is a cipher the key to which it behooves you to search for most diligently.

By the time we joined my father, he had surveyed many avenues of approach toward the coveted citadel of fortune. One of these, heretofore untried, he now proposed to essay, armed with new courage, and cheered on by the presence of his family. In partnership with an energetic little man who had an English chapter in his history, he prepared to set up a refreshment booth on Crescent Beach. But while he was completing arrangements at the beach we remained in town, where we enjoyed the educational advantages of a thickly populated neighborhood; namely, Wall Street, in the West End of Boston.

Anybody who knows Boston knows that the West and North Ends are the wrong ends of that city. They form the tenement district, or, in the newer phrase, the slums of Boston. Anybody who is acquainted with the slums of any American metropolis knows that that is the quarter where poor immigrants foregather, to live, for the most part, as unkempt, half-washed, toiling, unaspiring foreigners; pitiful in the eyes of social missionaries, the despair of boards of health, the hope of ward politicians, the touchstone of American democracy. The well-versed metropolitan knows the slums as a sort of house of detention for poor aliens, where they live on probation till they can show a certificate of good citizenship.

He may know all this and yet not guess how Wall Street, in the West End, appears in the eyes of a little immigrant from Polotzk. What would the sophisticated sight-seer say about Union Place, off Wall Street, where my new home waited for me? He would say that it is no place at all, but a short box of an alley. Two rows of three-story tenements are its sides, a stingy strip of sky is its lid, a littered pavement is the floor, and a narrow mouth its exit.

But I saw a very different picture on my introduction to Union Place. I saw two imposing rows of brick buildings, loftier than any dwelling I had ever lived in. Brick was even on the ground for me to tread on, instead of common earth or boards. Many friendly windows stood open, filled with uncovered heads of women and children. I thought the people were interested in us, which was very neighborly. I looked up to the topmost row of windows, and my eyes were filled with the May blue of an American sky!

In our days of affluence in Russia we had been accustomed to upholstered parlors, embroidered linen, silver spoons and candlesticks, goblets of gold, kitchen shelves shining with copper and brass. We had featherbeds heaped halfway to the ceiling; we had clothes presses dusky with velvet and silk and fine woollen. The three small rooms into which my father now ushered us, up one flight of stairs, contained only the necessary beds, with lean mattresses; a few wooden chairs; a table or two; a mysterious iron structure, which later turned out to be a stove; a couple of unornamental kerosene lamps; and a scanty array of cooking-utensils and crockery. And yet we were all impressed with our new home and its furniture. It was not only because we had just passed through our seven lean years, cooking in earthen vessels, eating black bread on holidays and wearing cotton; it was chiefly because these wooden chairs and tin pans were American chairs and pans that they shone glorious in our eyes. And if there was anything lacking for comfort or decoration we expected it to be presently supplied—at least, we children did. Perhaps my mother alone, of us newcomers, appreciated the shabbiness of the little apartment, and realized that for her there was as yet no laying down of the burden of poverty.

Our initiation into American ways began with the first step on the new soil. My father found occasion to instruct or correct us even on the way from the pier to Wall Street, which journey we made crowded together in a rickety cab. He told us not to lean out of the windows, not to point, and explained the word "greenhorn." We did not want to be "greenhorns," and gave the strictest attention to my father's instructions.

(1912)

From

THE RISE OF DAVID LEVINSKY
by Abraham Cahan

Ten minutes' walk brought me to the heart of the Jewish East Side. The streets swarmed with Yiddish-speaking immigrants. The sign-boards were in English and Yiddish, some of them in Russian. The scurry and hustle of the people were not merely overwhelmingly greater, both in volume and intensity, than in my native town. It was of another sort. The swing and step of the pedestrians, the voices and manner of the street peddlers, and a hundred and one other things seemed to testify to far more self-confidence and energy, to larger ambitions and wider scopes, than did the appearance of the crowds in my birthplace.

The great thing was that these people were better dressed than the inhabitants of my town. The poorest-looking man wore a hat (instead of a cap), a stiff collar and a necktie, and the poorest woman wore a hat or a bonnet.

The appearance of a newly arrived immigrant was still a novel spectacle on the East Side. Many of the passers-by paused to look at me with wistful smiles of curiosity.

"There goes a green one!" some of them exclaimed.

The sight of me obviously evoked reminiscences in them of the days when they had been "green ones" like myself. It was a second birth that they were witnessing, an experience which they had once gone through themselves and which was one of the greatest events in their lives.

"Green one" or "greenhorn" is one of the many English words and phrases which my mother-tongue has appropriated in England and America. Thanks to the many millions of letters that pass annually between the Jews of Russia and their relatives in the United States, a number of these words have by now come to be generally known among our people at home as well as here. In the eighties, however, one who had not visited any English-speaking country was utterly unfamiliar with them. And so I had never heard of "green one" before. Still, "green," in the sense of color, is Yiddish as well as English, so I understood the phrase at once, and as a contemptuous quizzical appellation for a newly arrived, inexperienced immigrant it stung me cruelly. As I went along I heard it again and again. Some of the passers-by would call me "greenhorn" in a tone of blighting gaiety, but these were an exception. For the most part it was "green one" and in a spirit of sympathetic interest. It hurt me, all the same. Even those glances that offered me a cordial welcome and good wishes had something self-complacent and condescending in them. "Poor fellow! he is a green one," these people seemed to say. "We are not, of course. We are Americanized."

For my first meal in the New World I bought a three-cent wedge of coarse rye bread, off a huge round loaf, on a stand on Essex Street. I was too strict in my religious observances to eat it without first performing ablutions and offering a brief prayer. So I approached a bewigged old woman who stood in the doorway of a small grocery-store to let me wash my hands and eat my meal in her place. She looked old-fashioned enough, yet when she heard my request she said, with a laugh:

"You're a green one, I see."

"Suppose I am," I resented. "Do the yellow ones or black ones all eat without washing? Can't a fellow be a good Jew in America?"

"Yes, of course he can, but—well, wait till you see for yourself."

However, she asked me to come in, gave me some water and an old apron to serve me for a towel, and when I was ready to eat my bread she placed a glass of milk before me, explaining that she was not going to charge me for it.

"In America people are not foolish enough to be content with dry bread," she said, sententiously.

While I ate she questioned me about my antecedents. I remember how she impressed me as a strong, clever woman of few words as long as she catechised me, and how disappointed I was when she began to talk of herself. The astute, knowing mien gradually faded out of her face and I had before me a gushing, boastful old bore.

My intention was to take a long stroll, as much in the hope of coming upon some windfall as for the purpose of taking a look at the great American city. Many of the letters that came from the United States to my birthplace before I sailed had contained a warning not to imagine that America was a "land of gold" and that treasure might be had in the streets of New York for the picking. But these warnings only had the effect of lending vividness to my image of an American street as a thoroughfare strewn with nuggets of the precious metal. Symbolically speaking, this was the idea one had of the "land of Columbus." It was a continuation of the widespread effect produced by stories of Cortes and Pizarro in the sixteenth century, confirmed by the successes of some Russian emigrants of my time.

I asked the grocery-woman to let me leave my bundle with her, and, after considerable hesitation, she allowed me to put it among some empty barrels in her cellar.

I went wandering over the Ghetto. Instead of stumbling upon nuggets of gold, I found signs of poverty. In one place I came across a poor family who—as I learned upon inquiry—had been dispossessed for non-payment of rent. A mother and her two little boys were watching their pile of furniture and other household goods on the sidewalk while the passers-by were dropping coins into a saucer placed on one of the chairs to enable the family to move into new quarters.

What puzzled me was the nature of the furniture. For in my birthplace chairs and a couch like those I now saw on the sidewalk would be a sign of prosperity. But then anything was to be expected of a country where the poorest devil wore a hat and a starched collar.

I walked on.

The exclamation "A green one" or "A greenhorn" continued. If I did not hear it, I saw it in the eyes of the people who passed me.

(1917)

From

THE AMERICANIZATION OF EDWARD BOK
by Edward Bok

The leviathan of the Atlantic Ocean, in 1870, was *The Queen,* and when she was warped into her dock on September 20 of that year, she discharged, among her passengers, a family of four from the Netherlands who were to make an experiment of Americanization.

The father, a man bearing one of the most respected names in the Netherlands, had acquired wealth and position for himself; unwise investments, however, had swept away his fortune, and in preference to a new start in his own land, he had decided to make the new beginning in the United States, where a favorite brother-in-law had gone several years before. But that, never a simple matter for a man who has reached forty-two, is particularly difficult for a foreigner in a strange land. This fact he and his wife were to find out. The wife, also carefully reared, had been accustomed to a scale of living which she had now to abandon. Her Americanization experiment was to compel her, for the first time in her life, to become a housekeeper without domestic help. There were two boys: the elder, William, was eight and a half years of age; the younger, in nineteen days from his landing-date, was to celebrate his seventh birthday.

This younger boy was Edward William Bok. He had, according to the Dutch custom, two other names, but he had decided to leave those in the Netherlands. And the American public was, in later years, to omit for him the "William."

Edward's first six days in the United States were spent in New York, and then he was taken to Brooklyn, where he was destined to live for nearly twenty years.

Thanks to the linguistic sense inherent in the Dutch, and to an educational system that compels the study of languages, English was already familiar to the father and mother. But to the two sons, who had barely learned the beginnings of their native tongue, the English language was as a closed book. It seemed a cruel decision of the father to put his two boys into a public school in Brooklyn, but he argued that if they were to become Americans, the sooner they became part of the life of the country and learned its language for themselves, the better. And so, without the ability to make known the slightest want or to understand a single word, the morning after their removal to Brooklyn, the two boys were taken by their father to a public school.

The American public-school teacher was perhaps even less well equipped in those days than she is to-day to meet the needs of two Dutch boys who could not understand a word she said, and who could only wonder what it was all about. The brothers did not even have the comfort of each other's company, for, graded by age, they were placed in separate classes.

Nor was the American boy of 1870 a whit less cruel than is the American boy of 1920; and he was none the less loath to show that cruelty. This trait was evident at the first recess of the first day at school. At the dismissal, the brothers naturally sought each other, only to find themselves surrounded by a group of tormentors who were delighted to have such promising objects for their fun. And of this opportunity they made the most. There was no form of petty cruelty boys' minds could devise that was not inflicted upon the two helpless strangers. Edward seemed to look particularly inviting, and nicknaming him "Dutchy" they devoted themselves at each noon recess and after school to inflicting their cruelties upon him.

Louis XIV may have been right when he said that "every new language requires a new soul," but Edward Bok knew that while spoken languages might differ, there is one language understood by boys the world over. And with this language Edward decided to do some experimenting. After a few days at school, he cast his eyes over the group of his tormentors, picked out one who seemed to him the ringleader, and before the boy was aware of what had happened, Edward Bok was in the full swing of his first real experiment with Americanization. Of course the American boy retaliated. But the boy from the Netherlands had not been born and brought up in the muscle-building air of the Dutch dikes for nothing, and after a few moments he found himself looking down on his tormentor and into the eyes of a crowd of very respectful boys and giggling girls who readily made a passageway for his brother and himself when they indicated a desire to leave the schoolyard and go home.

Edward now felt that his Americanization had begun; but, always believing that a thing begun must be carried to a finish, he took, or gave—it depends upon the point of view—two or three more lessons in this particular phase of Americanization before he convinced these American schoolboys that it might be best for them to call a halt upon further excursions in torment.

(1920)

From

THE SOUL OF AN IMMIGRANT
by Constantine M. Panunzio

So we went out to hunt our first job in America. For several mornings Louis and I went to North Square, where there were generally a large number of men loitering in groups discussing all kinds of subjects, particularly the labor market. One morning we were standing in front of one of those infernal institutions which in America are permitted to bear the name of "immigrant banks," when we saw a fat man coming toward us. "Buon giorno, padrone," said one of the men. "Padrone?" said I to myself. Now the word "padrone" in Italy is applied to a proprietor, generally a respectable man, at least one whose dress and appearance distinguish him as a man of means. This man not only showed no signs of good breeding in his face, but he was unshaven and dirty and his clothes were shabby. I could not quite understand how he could be called "padrone." However, I said nothing, first because I wanted to get back home, and second because I wanted to be polite when I was in *American* society!

The "padrone" came up to our group and began to wax eloquent and to gesticulate (both in Sicilian dialect) about the advantages of a certain job. I remember very clearly the points which he emphasized: "It is not very far, only twelve miles from Boston. For a few cents you can come back any time you wish, to see 'i parenti e gli amici,' your relatives and friends. The company has a 'shantee' in which you can sleep, and a 'storo' where you can buy your 'grosserie' all very cheap. 'Buona paga'," he continued "(Good pay), $1.25 per day, and you only have to pay me fifty cents a week for having gotten you this 'gooda jobba.' I only do it to help you and because you are my countrymen. If you come back here at six o'clock to-night with your bundles, I myself will take you out."

The magnanimity of this man impressed Louis and me very profoundly; we looked at each other and said, "Wonderful!" We decided we would go; so at the appointed hour we returned to the very spot. About twenty men finally gathered there and we were led to North Station. There we took a train to some suburban place, the name of which I have never been able to learn. On reaching our destination we were taken to the "shantee" where we were introduced to two long open bunks filled with straw. These were to be our beds. The "storo" of which we had been told was at one end of the shanty. The next morning we were taken out to work. It was a sultry autumn day. The "peek" seemed to grow heavier at every stroke and the "shuvle" wider and larger in its capacity to hold the gravel. The second day was no better than the first, and the third was worse than the second. The work was heavy and monotonous to Louis and myself especially, who had never been "contadini" like the rest. The "padrone" whose magnanimity had so stirred us was little better than a brute. We began to do some simple figuring and discovered that when we had paid for our groceries at the "storo," for the privilege of sleeping in the shanty, and the fifty cents to the "padrone" for having been so condescending as to employ us, we would have nothing left but sore arms and backs. So on the afternoon of the third day Louis and I held a solemn conclave and decided to part company with "peek and shuvle,"—for ever. We left, without receiving a cent of pay, of course.

Going across country on foot we came to a small manufacturing village. We decided to try our luck at the factory, which proved to be a woolen mill, and found employment. Our work was sorting old rags and carrying them in wheelbarrows into a hot oven, in which the air was almost suffocating. Every time a person went in it he was obliged to run out as quickly as possible, for the heat was unbearable. Unfortunately for us, the crew was composed almost entirely of Russians, who hated us from the first day, and called us "dagoes." I had never heard the word before; I asked Louis if he knew its meaning, but he did not. In going in and out of the oven the Russians would crowd against us and make it hard for us to pass. One morning as I was coming out, four of the men hedged me in. I thought I would suffocate. I finally succeeded in pushing out, my hand having been cut in the rush of the wheelbarrows.

The superintendent of the factory had observed the whole incident. He was a very kindly man. From his light complexion I think he was a Swede. He came to my rescue, reprimanded the Russians, and led me to his office, where he bandaged my hand. Then he called Louis and explained the situation to us. The Russians looked upon us as intruders and were determined not to work side by side with "the foreigners," but to drive them out of the factory. Therefore, much as he regretted it, the superintendent was obliged to ask us to leave, since there were only two of us, as against the large number of Russians who made up his unskilled crew.

So we left. My bandaged hand hurt me, but my heart hurt more. This kind of work was hard and humiliating enough, but what went deeper than all else was the first realization that because of race I was being put on the road. And often since that day have I felt the cutting thrusts of race prejudice. They have been dealt by older immigrants, who are known as "Americans," as well as by more recent comers. All have been equally heart-rending and head-bending. I hold no grudge against any one; I realize that it is one of the attendant circumstances of our present nationalistic attitude the world over, and yet it is none the less saddening to the human heart. I have seen prejudice, like an evil shadow, everywhere. It lurks at every corner, on every street and in every mart. I have seen it in the tram and on the train; I have felt its dreaded power in school and college, in clubs and churches. It is an ever-present evil spirit, felt though unseen, wounding hearts, cutting souls. It passes on its poison like a serpent from generation to generation, and he who would see the fusion of the various elements into a truly American type must ever take into cognizance its presence in the hearts of some human beings.

We had to hunt another job. We returned to Boston still penniless and to the good graces of the "padrona" of the filthy boarding-house. Louis now spent a penny for an Italian newspaper and looked over the "want ads." He saw what seemed to be a good prospect for a job and we decided to apply for it. If you walk down lower Washington Street in Boston, toward North Station, facing the Italian colony, near Hanover Street you can see, even now, a large sign, "Stobhom Employment Agency." It is a notorious institution, the function of which is to catch men and send them to a company in Bangor, from which place they are sent to the various camps in the woods of Maine.

We called upon said "honorable" agency and were told that they could supply us wih work. "It is out in the country, in the woods of Maine. Wages $30 per month, board and room. Good, healthy job." It sounded too good to let go, so we accepted the offer. We were told to report that night at seven o'clock and we would be directed to our work. These night meetings seem to be quite popular with such agencies! Now, I knew what the country was like, but I had no idea what "woods" meant, and with the best of Louis' wretched Italian, I couldn't quite get it through my head. Moreover, Maine might be anywhere from North Boston to California for all I knew. However, we decided to try it. At $30 per month I would only need to work two months at most; then back home for me!

(1934)

From

EVERY OTHER THURSDAY
by Edna Ferber

Helmi Seppala was being slowly digested in the maw of New York. Her passage money had been sent her by her brother, Abel Seppala. She had sailed from Åbo. New York reached, she had been turned back at Ellis Island. Her country's quota was already filled. The thing had been overwhelming. Months passed. Again Abel sent money, against the protests of his wife, Anni. This time Helmi bribed the steward on the ship, and sailed as one of the stewardesses. One hundred and fifty dollars that had cost. How sick she had been! She was racked now at the thought of it. The boat reached New York. Unforeseen red tape bound Helmi to the ship. The stewardesses were not allowed to land. Frantic, she managed to get word to Abel.

The boat remained five days in New York. On the day it was due to return to Finland, Abel and Anni came on board, ostensibly to bid farewell to a Finnish friend who was going to his home country. Concealed, they carried on board with them American-made clothes—a dress, a coat, shoes, a hat, powder, rouge, eyeglasses. These had been smuggled to Helmi. Feverishly she had shed her uniform, had put on the American clothes, the rouge, the powder, the eyeglasses. When the call had come for visitors to go ashore, Helmi, with Abel and Anni, had passed down the gangplank under the very eyes of the chief steward himself—to the dock, to the street, into the amazing spring sunshine of a New York May morning. Spurned as an alien by her stepmotherland, she had disguised herself as a native daughter and achieved a home that way.

At once she had gone to work. At once she had gone to school. Anni had not been very cordial to this sister of her husband. But she had grudgingly helped the girl, nevertheless. She had got her a "place." The wage was small, for Helmi knew no English and was ignorant of American ways, of New York household usages. But from the first, part of that infinitesimal wage went to pay back the passage money loaned her by Abel and Anni. And from the first she had gone to night school, three nights a week. Three nights a week, from eight until ten, after her dinner dishes were washed, she attended the night-school class, sitting hunched over a scarred school desk used by fourth-grade children in the daytime. It was a class in English for both sexes.

Most of the women were servant girls like herself—Swedish, Finnish, Czech, Latvian, Polish, Hungarian. She had the look of the old country. A big-boned girl, with broad shoulders and great capable hands. She had worn her hair pulled away from her forehead and temples, held with side combs, and wound at the back in a bun of neat, slippery braids. In her ears she wore little gold hoops. Her hair was straw-colored, with no glint of gold in it; her eyes were blue, but not a deep blue. She was not pretty, but there had been about her a certain freshness of coloring and expression. Her hair clung in little damp tendrils at the back of her neck. There was great breadth between her cheekbones, her shoulders, her hipbones. Her legs were sturdy, slim, and quick. She listened earnestly. They read out of a child's reader. The lesson was, perhaps, a nature study.

"What is a frog, Miss Seppala?"

Miss Seppala would look startled, terrified, and uncomprehending, all at once.

Again, articulating painfully with tongue, teeth, palate: "What-is-a-frog, Miss Seppala?"

Much gabbling and hissing from those all about her. Suddenly a great light envelops Miss Seppala. She bounces up.

"A frock iss animal wiss legs iss jumping all the time and iss green." Triumph!

The lesson went on to say, "Dragonflies are called darning needles." Miss Speiser, the good-natured, spectacled teacher, spoke Upper West Side New York English. "Aw dawhning needles hawmful?" she inquired. The result was that Helmi's English accent turned out to be a mixture of early Finnish and late Bronx most mystifying to the hearer. Still it had served.

And now, a year later, her hair was bobbed, and her clothes were American, and she said, "I'll tell the vorld," and got twenty dollars each week at the Mawsons'. She had paid back her passage money down to the last cent, so now Anni, in one of her tempers, could never again call her a dirty Lapp—that insult of insults to the Finn or Swede. She had learned with amazing swiftness to prepare American dishes, being a naturally gifted cook. She knew how to serve from the left, to keep the water glasses filled, not to remove the service plates until the dinner plates were at hand, to keep thumb marks off glass salad dishes, to mix a pretty good Martini cocktail. She was, in short, an excellent middle-class American servant—spunky, independent, capable, unfriendly.

It was a long trip from West Eighty-sixth Street to Finntown, in Brooklyn, where Abel and Anni lived. Helmi begrudged the time this afternoon, but she went out of a sense of duty and custom and a certain tribal loyalty. Anni's house was a neat two-story brick, new, in West Forty-fourth Street, Brooklyn. The neighborhood was almost solidly Finnish. The houses were well kept, prosperous-looking, owned by Finn carpenters, mechanics, skilled workmen, whose wage was twelve, fourteen, sixteen dollars a day. One of Anni's boys, Otto, aged four, was playing outside in the bit of yard. He eyed his aunt coolly, accepted a small sack of hard candies that she presented to him, followed her into the house, which she entered at the rear.

Anni was busy at her housework. Anni was always busy at her housework. Anni was twenty-seven and looked thirty-five. Between the two women no love was lost, but today their manner toward each other was indefinably changed. Helmi was no longer the debtor. Helmi was an independent and free woman, earning her twenty a week. Anni was a married woman bound, tied, and harried by a hundred household tasks and trials. The two talked in their native tongue.

"Well, how goes it?"

"Always the same. You are lucky. You have your day off, you can run out and have a good time."

"She wanted me to stay home today and go tomorrow instead. I soon showed her and that daughter of hers."

They went into that in detail. Their pale-blue eyes were triumphant.

"You are early today. Did you eat?"

"No. Coffee only."

"I'll fix you some *kaalikääreitä* left over from the children's lunch."

Helmi cast a glance of suspicion at her suddenly suave sister-in-law, but she pulled a chair up to the kitchen table and ate the savory stuffed cabbage with a good appetite. She had had no Finnish food for almost two weeks. It was good.

Well, she must be going. Going? Already? Where was she running? Helmi supped up the last of the gravy on her plate and rose. Oh, she had much to do! "Well, now you are so independent I suppose you will spend all your money." "Yes, and suppose I do? What then?" "Nothing, only Abel is so close with his money. I wish I had a dollar or two of my own to spend. I need so many things." Helmi gave her three dollars, grudgingly. She would do this again and again during the year. She was wild to be gone. She went into the bedroom to look at the baby; powdered her nose; drank a final and hasty cup of coffee, and was off. Anni watched her go, her eyes hard.

A long, long ride this time back to New York. Grand Central. Change. The East Side subway. She was spewed up with the crowd at One Hundred and Twenty-fifth Street; plunged vigorously into its colorful, cheerful hurly-burly. A hundred noises attracted her. A hundred sights lured her. But she knew what she wanted to do. She made straight for the shop where Lempi Parta had bought her dress. Bulging glittering plate-glass windows brilliant with blues and pinks and reds and gold.

Helmi entered. The place was full of girls like herself, with bobbed hair and flat faces and broad shoulders and pale-blue eyes. Upper East Side Finland was buying its Easter finery. A woman came forward—an enormous woman with an incredible bust and a measureless waist and bead trimming and carrot-colored hair. And what can I do for you, Miss? Helmi made known her wants. The woman emitted a vocal sound: a squawk.

"Miss S.! Oh, Miss S.! Step this way. . . . The young lady here wants you should show her something in a blue crepe."

You did not pay for it all at once, of course. You paid in part, and they took your name and address and the name of the people you worked for. (Helmi used to be most demanding about the accent over the *a*'s in Seppala, but she was no longer.) But they obligingly let you take the whole ravishing outfit: blue dress; blue coat lined with sand crepe and trimmed with embroidery; blue silk hat; silk stockings, very sheer; high-heeled slippers. She hung the boxes and bundles about herself, somehow, joyously. Miss S. was most gracious.

Into the five-and-ten-cent store. A mass of people surged up and down the aisles. They buffeted and banged Helmi's boxes, but she clung to them rigidly. A handkerchief, edged with blue lace. A small flask of perfume. A pocket comb that cunningly folded up on itself. An exhausting business, this shopping. More tiring than a day's housework. She stopped at an unspeakable counter and ordered and devoured a sandwich of wieners with mustard (10¢) and a glass of root beer (5¢). Thus refreshed, she fought her way out to the street.

It was midafternoon. She walked placidly up One Hundred and Twenty-fifth Street, enjoying the sights and sounds. Her strong arms made nothing of their burden. Music blared forth from the open door of a radio shop. She stopped to listen, entranced. Her feet could scarcely resist the rhythm. She wandered on, crossed the street. "Heh! Watch it!" yelled a tough taxi driver, just skimming her toes. He grinned back at her. She glared after him, gained the curb.

A slim, slick, dark young fellow leaning limply against the corner cigar-store window spoke to her, his cigarette waggling between his lips.

"Watch your step, Swensky."

"Shod op!" retorted Helmi, haughtily.

An open-faced orange-drink bar offered peppermint taffy in ten-cent sacks. Helmi bought a sack and popped one of the sticky confections between her strong yellow teeth. A fake auction, conducted by a swarthy and Oriental-looking auctioneer, held her briefly. He was auctioning a leprous and swollen Chinese vase. A dollar! A dollar! Who offers a dollar? All right. Who says fifty cents! Twenty-five! Step inside. Come inside, lady, won't you? Don't stand like that in the door. She knew better than that; was on her way. Yet the vase would have looked lovely in a parlor. Still, she had no parlor.

Her pale eyes grew dreamy. She walked more quickly now. When she approached the Finnish Progressive Society building in One Hundred and Twenty-sixth Street there was the usual line of surprisingly important-looking cars parked outside. The portion of New York's Finnish chauffeurdom which had Thursday afternoon to itself was inside playing pool, eating in the building's restaurant, or boxing or wrestling in the big gymnasium. The most magnificent car of them all was not there. Helmi knew it would not be. Vaino was free on Thursday nights at ten. Her boxes and bundles in hand, Helmi passed swiftly through the little groups that stood about in the hallway. A flood of Finnish rose to her ears, engulfed her. She drew a long breath. Through the open doorway of the restaurant at the rear. The tables were half filled. Girls eating together. Men, with their hats on, eating together. She ordered a cup of coffee and a plate of Finnish bread—hardtack—*näkki leipä*—with its delicious pungent caraway. This she ate and drank quickly with a relish. The real joy of the day lay still ahead of her.

Into the hallway again and down a short flight of steps to the basement. Through the poolroom, murky with smoke, every table surrounded by pliant, plastic figures intent on the game. The men paid no attention to her, nor she to them. Through the door at the far end of the room. A little office. Down a flight of steps. The steam bath, beloved of every Finn.

All her life Helmi had had her steam bath not only weekly, but often two or three times a week. On the farm in Finland the bathhouse had been built before the farmhouse itself. You used the bathhouse not only for purposes of cleanliness, but for healing: in illness, when depressed. The Finnish women, in the first throes of childbirth, repaired to the soothing, steam-laden atmosphere of the bathhouse. The sick were carried there. In its shelves and on its platforms you lay dreamily for hours, your skin shining and slippery with water. The steam bath was not only an ablution; it was a ceremony, a rite.

On Tuesdays and Thursdays the Finnish Society's steam baths were used only by women. The bath women, huge, blond, genial, met her, took her fifty cents, gave her a locker. Helmi opened her precious boxes and hung her finery away, carefully, lovingly. The room was full of naked girls. They were as lacking in self-consciousness as so many babies. They crowded round her—her friend Lempi Parta, and, too, Hilja Karbin, Saara Johnson, Matti Eskolin, Aili Juhola.

"Oh, Helmi! How beautiful! How much did you pay! The boys will dance with you tonight, all right!" they cried in Finnish.

She disrobed swiftly, and stood a moment in the moist warmth of that outer room. Her body was strong and astonishingly graceful, now rid of its cheap and bungling clothes. Her waist tapered slim and flexible below the breadth of the shoulders. She walked well. Now she went into the steam room. The hot breath of the place met her. She lifted her face to it, enchanted. She loved it. The air was thick, heavy with steam from the hot water that dropped endlessly down on to the hot steam pipes below, sending up a misty cloud. From out of this veil a half-dozen indolent heads were lifted from bunks that lined the walls. On each bunk lay an undraped figure.

Helmi sat a moment on the edge of a bunk. "Hello. Hello, Elli! How goes it, Mari? Oo, this is good!"

She reclined upon the bunk, gratefully, yieldingly. Every nerve, every fiber, every muscle of her being relaxed in the moist heat. This stolid Finn servant girl became a graceful plastic figure in repose, a living Greek statue. The mist enveloped her. Her eyes closed. So she lay for fifteen minutes, twenty, a half-hour. Out, then, with Lempi and a half-dozen others, into the cold green waters of the big pool, stopping first for a moment under a shower in the room adjoining the steam bath.

One after another they stood at the pool's edge, graceful, fearless, unaffected. This bath, to them, was a sacred institution. It was an important and necessary part of their lives. They dropped then, swiftly, beautifully, flashingly, into the pool's green depths. They swam like mermaids. They had learned to swim in the icy waters of the Finland lakes. Their voices were high and clear and eager, like the voices of children at play. They were relaxed, gay, happy, "Oo, look! Look at me!" they called to each other in Finnish. "Can you do this?"

Back, dripping, into the steam room again. Another half-hour. The shower again. The pool again. Helmi gave herself over to the luxury of a massage at the expert hands of the masseuse. The strong electric human fingers kneaded her flesh, spanked her smartly, anointed her with oils. She felt blissful, alive, newborn. The Mawson kitchen did not exist. Zhoolie Mawson was a bad dream. Mrs. Mawson did not matter—never had mattered. Vaino. Vaino only.

She was so long in donning the beautiful new blue finery that Lempi and the rest became impatient. But at last it was finished. She surveyed herself radiantly. The flat Finnish face glowed back at her from the mirror. Helmi could never be pretty. But she approached it as nearly now as she ever would.

She would not curl her hair now. That she would do after she had had her supper. She was ravenously hungry.

They would not eat at the building restaurant. They were tired of it. They would go to Mokki's, on Madison, just off One Hundred and Twenty-fifth. A real Finnish meal. Here they sat at a table for four and talked and laughed in subdued tones, as does your proper Finnish girl. And they ate! Mrs. Mawson would have opened her eyes. They ate first *marja soppa*, which is an incredible soup of cranberries and cornstarch and sugar. They had *mämmi* and cream. They had salt herrings with potatoes. They had *riisi puuro*, which is, after all, little more than rice pudding, but flavored in the Finnish manner. They drank great scalding cups of coffee. It was superb to see them eat.

It was nearly eight. Helmi must still curl her hair, carefully. This you did in the women's room at the Finnish Society's building. She scanned the line of motors at the curb for the great car—no, it was not there. That was as it should be. The hair-curling business took a half-hour. The room was full of girls changing their shoes; changing their stockings; changing their dresses; combing their hair, curling it; washing.

Helmi and Lempi were going to the play that was to be given in the theater two flights up. Another fifty cents. Helmi did not begrudge it. She loved to dance, but she would wait. She would be fresh for ten o'clock. At ten, though the play would not be finished, she would leave for the dance upstairs. She shut her ears determinedly to the music that could faintly be heard when the door opened to admit late-comers. The play was presented by members of the Finnish Society's theatrical group, made up of girls like Helmi and boys like Vaino. Helmi watched it absorbedly. It was, the program told you in Finnish, *The Second Mrs. Tanqueray*. Helmi and Lempi found it fascinating and true and convincing.

Ten o'clock. They vanished. They deserted Thalia for Terpsichore. They spent another ten minutes before the dressing-room mirrors. The dance hall was crowded. Rows of young men, stolid of face, slim, appraising, stood near the door and grouped at the end of the room, partnerless, watching the dancers. Straight as a shot Helmi's eyes found him. How beautiful he was in his blue suit and his shiny tan shoes! His hair shone like his shoes. His cold blue eyes met hers. Her expression did not change. His expression did not change. Yet she knew he had marked her blue dress, and her sheer silk stockings, and her new, shining slippers.

Wordlessly she and Lempi began to dance together. Lempi took the man's part. She was very strong and expert. She whirled Helmi around and around in the waltz so that her blue skirt billowed out, and one saw her straight, sturdy, slim legs to the knees. Her skirt swished against the line of stolid-faced boys as she whirled past; swished against Vaino's dear blue-serge legs. She did not look at him, yet she saw his every feature. He did not look at her. He saw the dress, the stockings, the slippers, the knees. True Finns.

The waltz was over. Soberly and decorously Helmi and Lempi sought chairs against the wall. They conversed in low tones. Helmi did not look at him. Five minutes. The band struck up again. The polka. He stood there a moment. All about were stolid young men advancing stolidly in search of their equally stolid partners. Helmi's heart sank. She looked away. He came toward her. She looked away. He stood before her. He looked at her. She rose. Wordlessly they danced. One, two, three, and a one, two, three, and turn, and turn, and turn, and turn. She danced very well. His expression did not change. Her expression did not change. She was perfectly, blissfully happy.

At twelve it was over. At twelve-fifteen she had deposited her boxes and bundles—the everyday clothes of Cinderella—in the back of the huge, proud car that had an engine like a locomotive. She was seated in the great proud car beside Vaino. She was driven home. She was properly kissed. She would see him Thursday. Not Thursday, but *Thursday*. He understood. Every Other Thursday.

The day was over. She let herself into the Mawson apartment, almost (but not quite) noiselessly. Mrs. Mawson, sharp-eared, heard her. Zhoolie, herself just returned and not so unhappy as she had been sixteen hours earlier, but still resentful, heard her. Helmi entered her own untidy little room, quickly shut the window which Mrs. Mawson had opened, took off the blue dress, kicked off the bright new slippers, peeled the silk stockings (a hole in each toe), flung her underwear to the winds, dived into the coarse cotton nightgown, and tumbled into her lumpy bed with a weary, satisfied, rapturous grunt.

Zhoolie, in her green enamel bed, thought bitterly: Stupid lump! Went and sat at her sister's or whatever it is, all day, swigging coffee. It isn't as if she had had anything to do, really. She didn't do a thing. Not a thing! And I've given her I don't know how many pairs of my old silk stockings.

Mrs. Mawson, in her walnut bed, thought: They're all alike.

Mr. James G. Mawson slept.

(1926)

From

GIANTS IN THE EARTH
by O. E. Rölvaag

Beret had now formed the habit of constantly watching the prairie; out in the open, she would fix her eyes on one point of the sky line—and then, before she knew it, her gaze would have swung around the whole compass; but it was ever, ever the same. . . . Life it held not; a magic ring lay on the horizon, extending upward into the sky; within this circle no living form could enter; it was like the chain inclosing the king's garden, that prevented it from bearing fruit. . . . How could human beings continue to live here while that magic ring encompassed them? And those who were strong enough to break through were only being enticed still farther to their destruction! . . .

They had been here four months now; to her it seemed like so many generations; in all this time they had seen no strangers except the Indians—nor would they be likely to see any others. . . . Almost imperceptibly, her terror because of the stakes which her husband had burned had faded away and disappeared. . . . They had probably belonged to the Indians, so it did not matter; he had become fast friends with them. . . .

People had never dwelt here, people would never come; never could they find home in this vast, wind-swept void. . . . Yes, *they* were the only ones who had been bewitched into straying out here! . . . Thus it was with the erring sons of men; they were lost before they knew it; they went astray without being aware; only others could see them as they were. Some were saved, and returned from their wanderings, changed into different people; others never came back. . . . God pity them: others never came back! . . .

At these times, a hopeless depression would take hold of her; she would look around at the circle of the sky line; although it lay so far distant, it seemed threatening to draw in and choke her. . . .

. . . So she grew more taciturn, given to brooding thoughts.

But then the unthinkable took place: some one from outside broke through the magic circle. . . .

It happened one evening. Ole had ridden the pony west to the swamps; on the way home he noticed a large white speck moving along through the haze on the eastern horizon. It did not seem so very far away; as he watched it came creeping closer; the boy was so startled that he could hear the beating of his own heart; he had to investigate this thing. The pony was fleet-footed; he had plenty of time to make a turn to the eastward; he rode directly toward the speck. When he had satisfied himself that west-movers were coming—the wagons indicated that—he turned toward home and urged the pony till his body lay flat to the ground. On the way in he stopped at Tönseten's with the news, then at Hans Olsa's; hastening on to his own house, he shouted loudly for them to come out and look . . . come out in a hurry!

. . . What a strange feeling it gave them! . . . Two horses in front of a wagon; the wagon covered, just like their own! . . . And like their own, it came slowly creeping out of the eastern haze; like them, these folks were steering for Sunset Land. . . . Alas! thought Beret, some one else has been led astray!

The wagon held on toward Tönseten's; it reached his place and halted. The incident was so unusual and startling that all in the little settlement forgot their good manners and rushed pell-mell over to Tönseten's. Even Beret could not keep away; she put on a clean apron, took And-Ongen by the hand, and joined the others. . . . The whole colony, young and old, were gathered there when she arrived—everyone except Per Hansa. . . . He came up silently at last, carrying a heavy stick.

The company consisted of four men; they were from Iowa. . . . No, they didn't intend to stop here; they were bound for a place about seventy miles to the southwest; the land was nearly all taken up around here, they had been told. . . . Tönseten and the Solum boys were conversing with them in English; Hans Olsa, together with the women and children, stood respectfully listening; as for Per Hansa, he was all eyes and ears, scrutinizing the four visitors from head to foot, trying to make out what they were saying. . . . His grip on the stick relaxed; hadn't he understood that they were going seventy miles farther? . . .

At last he grew impatient, because he was unable to follow the conversation as well as he wished; he grasped Tönseten by the arm and pinched it so hard that he turned around angrily; but the next second he was talking again.

"What sort of people are they?"

"Germans. . . . Don't bother me now!"

"You must tell them not to stop. . . . We want only *Norwegians* here, you know!"

But Tönseten had no time now to waste words on Per Hansa; that could be attended to in due season; he was deep in a long discussion with the strangers, all about the prospects for the future out here.

These four unexpected evening arrivals stayed with them overnight, and went on their way the next morning; the Spring Creek settlers had never seen them before; they would perhaps never see them again; but they all felt that this was the greatest event which had yet happened in the settlement. . . . Seventy miles farther into the evening glow these fellows were going—seventy long miles! Then this place would no longer be life's last outpost! . . . Folks were coming, were passing on . . . folks who intended to build homes! . . .

. . . A living bulwark was springing up between them and the endless desolation! . . .

Before the Germans left in the morning they came to examine Per Hansa's house; Tönseten had told them of one of his neighbours who had built a dwelling and stable under one roof; they thought it would be well worth the trouble to go and look at a structure of that kind; they themselves were just beginning, and needed ideas. While they were there Per Hansa got a chance to sell them some potatoes and vegetables, to the amount of two dollars and seventy-five cents; this was the first produce to be sold out of the settlement on Spring Creek. . . . Tönseten didn't take it kindly at all; he could have done as much himself: but who would ever have thought of such a thing? . . . He certainly watches his chances, that fellow Per Hansa!

*　　*　　*　　*　　*

When he got home the boys were sitting up in bed, undressed and waiting for him; Beret stood by the stove, roasting a substitute for coffee which she made from potatoes; the room was filled with smoke and the door stood open. She looked at him in the faint glimmer from the lamp; his face bore nothing but signs of good, she saw; then no danger hung over them! Perhaps a few more settlers would arrive as the years passed. . . . The boys were asking questions both together in a steady stream; now and then she quietly slipped in a question of her own; but the flood of talk from the bed was so torrential that she could scarcely be heard. The father had to go over and give them a box or two on the ears, to quiet them down; but it turned into skylarking instead of chastising, with screams of laughter and a new flood of questions; they had forgotten their anger at not being allowed to go with him! . . . The wife asked, and the boys asked over and over again: what *nationality* the newcomers belonged to, how many they were, and whether they were going to settle here; how many horses they had, how many cattle; whether they had any women; what they had brought in their wagons; if they had bargained for many potatoes; and the like. It seemed as if their curiosity could never be satisfied. . . . But the father was in such a good humour that he had a bantering answer for everything, no matter what silly questions they asked; he entered wholeheartedly into the hilarity of the boys, till he too was talking only nonsense. . . . These folks were all Irish, he explained; their women were terrible trolls, with noses as long as rake handles. . . . Settle here? Not they! No, they were going on to the end of the world, and a long way farther. They were much, much uglier than the Indians, and spoke so terribly fast that it sounded like *this*. . . . He hardly thought there would be a chance to sell any potatoes; troll women ate the flesh of Christian men, instead of potatoes—didn't they know that? Just the same, he was going to take a couple of sacks along to-morrow, to see whether he couldn't tempt them away from their regular fare.

(1927)

BURYING GROUND BY THE TIES
by Archibald MacLeish

Ayee! Ai! This is heavy earth on our shoulders:
There were none of us born to be buried in this earth:
Niggers we were Portuguese Magyars Pollacks:

We were born to another look of the sky certainly:
Now we lie here in the river pastures:
We lie in the mowings under the thick turf:

We hear the earth and the all day rasp of the grasshoppers:
It was we laid the steel on this land from ocean to ocean:
It was we (if you know) put the U. P. through the passes

Bringing her down into Laramie full load
Eighteen mile on the granite anticlinal
Forty-three foot to the mile and the grade holding:

It was we did it: hunkies of our kind:
It was we dug the caved-in holes for the cold water:
It was we built the gulley spurs and the freight sidings:

Who would do it but we and the Irishmen bossing us:
It was all foreign-born men there were in this country:
It was Scotsmen Englishmen Chinese Squareheads Austrians. . . .

Ayee! but there's weight to the earth under it:
Not for this did we come out—to be lying here
Nameless under the ties in the clay cuts:

But there's nothing good in the world that the rich won't buy it:
Everything sticks to the grease of a gold note—
Even a continent—even a new sky!

Do not pity us much for the strange grass over us:
We laid the steel to the stone stock of these mountains:
The place of our graves is marked by the telegraph poles!

It was not to lie in the bottoms we came out
And the trains going over us here in the dry hollows. . . .

(1933)

From

THE BENEFITS OF AMERICAN LIFE
by James T. Farrell

Ye orphan sons of Greece,
Scattered hither and beyond,
Persecuted and forlorn,
And by all nations beshun.
From a Greek poem
translated by Paul Javaras

Takiss Fillios was a strong shepherd boy whose home land was located just at the hollow valley of two mountains in Arcadia, Greece, in the central section of the Peloponnesus. He grew up on goat's milk and on pitch black bread whose cinders were not separated so as to produce more bread per pound. His hard-working mother sold a piece of land, which produced enough wheat to pull the family through the whole year, in order to pay his steerage fare to America. For in America the streets were paved with gold; the buildings were taller than mountains; the women all dressed like princesses and the men had their pockets lined with money; every boy had a bicycle; and every man and woman owned an automobile. At the age of thirteen, Takiss, large for his age, arrived in a paradise known as Chicago.

He was met at the railroad station, a scared and bewildered boy, by a relative who took him to a home on South Halsted Street. With voluble benef-icence, the relative immediately employed Takiss, offering him a salary of fif-teen dollars a month and the privilege of sleeping on marble slabs in his candy kitchen. He told Takiss that all successful Greek men started that way, and he showed the boy Greek newspapers with pictures of stern, mustachioed Greek restaurant owners and candy-store proprietors who recounted the story of their rise to fame and offered themselves as favorable candidates for marriage. And as a final word of advice, the relative told Takiss that his mother was getting old now, and that he should send her some of his wages to help her out.

Takiss quickly discovered what it meant to live in paradise. It meant working from six in the morning until six in the evening, and until even later on weekends. It meant sweeping out the store, washing dishes and windows, polishing, arranging, mopping, running errands. It meant attending night school to learn English when he could scarcely keep his eyes open and where he was frequently laughed at for his blundering efforts. It meant walking along, living in the midst of dirty streets where coal dust, soot, smoke, and the poisonous fumes of automobiles choked his nostrils and made him cough. It meant lone-some memories. For a long period, Takiss was a lonely boy remembering his homeland and his Grecian mountain, remembering the long, slow days with the sheep, remembering the games he had played with other boys, remembering the smile and kiss of his old mother, remembering always.

And he was afraid of America, and of that tremendous paradise known as Chicago. He worked doggedly day after day, earning his fifteen dollars a month, catching a cough from sleeping on marble slabs. He worked doggedly, and from his wages he saved a pittance which he deposited in an immigrant's savings bank. But he looked ahead to the day when he would be famous, with his picture in the Greek newspapers, a pride and an honor to his native Greece and to the great tradition of the great Socrates about whom his relative so fre-quently boasted. He dreamed of the time when he would become like Ameri-cans, talk like them, wear their clothes, ride in automobiles just as they did, walk along the streets with pretty American girls.

In time, Takiss learned things. He learned American words, but never how to speak them like an American. He learned that he was considered a dirty Greek greenhorn, and that many Americans would have been just as pleased if he and many of his countrymen had never come to their land. And he learned that American girls laughed sardonically at a young Greek greenhorn. Also, he learned of a place owned by a cousin of his, where for a little money he could go and find American girls who did not laugh at a Greek greenhorn, at least for five or ten minutes. He learned how to buy American clothes on installments, to wear a purple silk shirt, purple socks, and an orange tie. And he learned, also, that in the store he could put some of the money received for sales into his pocket instead of into the cash register.

Eventually, the cousin employing him discharged him in anger, branding him a crook, a robber, a traitor. In the heated quarrel, Takiss asked him why, if he wanted honesty, he paid only six dollars a week wages, when he made so much money himself selling bad products and got his picture in the Greek newspapers as a successful pioneer in America.

Takiss was employed by other of his countrymen, in fruit stores, soda parlors, at hot-dog stands, and in restaurants. He acquired additional American knowledge, and more American words. And sometimes when he was dressed up, wearing his purple silk shirt with socks to match, and the orange tie, he would walk in the parks or along Halsted Street, seeing American girls, wishing that he had one of his own, a blonde girl with a beautiful pink-white complexion.

Time slid from under Takiss, and he was a young man in his early twenties, with his first citizenship papers. He had worked like a dog, and he was still slaving at the same jobs, performing the same tasks and chores as he had always done since he had come to America. He earned eight dollars a week and was busy twelve hours a day in a candy store. He cleaned and he mopped; he scrubbed; he polished; he washed; he waited on trade. And often when he was alone in the store he pocketed money from the cash register. Every week he deposited money in the bank, and almost nightly he looked in his bank book, proud of his savings, thinking of how he was going to achieve fame in America. But he was never able to save money, because he was always quitting or losing jobs and having to use savings to support himself between jobs, as well as to send money to his mother.

And he learned another thing . . . he learned how to dance like Americans. A Greek-American friend told him of a dancing school called a taxi-dance hall on West Madison Street, and showed him an advertisement from the Greek-American owner, Professor Christopolos, who stated in the ad that anyone could be as graceful as he if they learned dancing from his beautiful girls at only ten cents a dance. He paid a dollar and was given ten tickets and entered the dimly lighted dancing school of Professor Christopolos on the fourth floor of a dingy and decrepit building. Each ticket was good for one dance which lasted from a minute to a minute and a half. Any girl in the place would dance with him, because she received five cents for each dance. Takiss' tickets were quickly used up, and he bought more. It did not matter if he danced woodenly and clumsily, and the girls acted delighted to teach him. He went to this taxi-dance hall regularly, spending three, four, and five dollars every visit, and once in a while a girl would ask him if he wanted to take her home, and for a few more dollars he could get other favors, too. After he started going to the taxi-dance hall regularly he was able to save less money, and he sent little to his mother.

Takiss then spent some of his savings for a suit with bell-bottom trousers. He cultivated a mustache and long side-burns, greased his hair and parted it in the middle with meticulous attention. He began to look like a sheik, and listened to pick up all the words which the American-born sheiks used. He went to public dance halls where there was only an admission fee and longer dances. At these places, there were always swarms of girls, pretty American girls, some of them tall and beautiful blondes with milky skins and red lips like cherries. He would ask them to dance. Often they would dance with him, once. He would talk, and they would catch his accent, and when he asked them for a second dance they would thank him with great regret and exclaim that all their other dances were taken. So he would quickly be driven to dancing with the homely and ugly girls who were called wall-flowers. And then he would go back to Professor Christopolos' dancing school, where all the girls would dance with him for ten cents a dance.

One day, Takiss was twenty-five. His native Grecian mountains seemed to have receded in time and he saw them only in painful mists of memory, recalling their details and contours with lessening concreteness. Greece to him was a memory. He had been in America for twelve years, and he was working ten hours a day in a hot-dog stand for ten dollars a week, and able to graft from three to five dollars a week extra. He wanted to make money and to become famous like some of his Americanized countrymen. And when he was a rich man with a hot-dog stand or a restaurant of his own, he would return to Greece with an American wife and act like a millionaire. And he had thirty-five dollars in the bank as a start toward these riches. He wanted to get more money, but not by running a brothel as his fourth cousin George did, and not bootlegging as did George's friend, Mike. He remembered the things his mother, now dead, had told him, and he wanted to make his money and his fame in a way that his mother would have approved of. And then he would have his picture in a Greek-American newspaper.

(1935)

THE FIRST DAY
by George and Helen Papashvily

At five in the morning the engines stopped, and after thirty-seven days the boat was quiet.

We were in America.

I got up and stepped over the other men and looked out the porthole. Water and fog. We were anchoring off an island. I dressed and went on deck.

Now began my troubles. What to do? This was a Greek boat and I was steerage, so of course by the time we were half-way out I had spent all my landing money for extra food.

Hassan, the Turk, one of the six who slept in the cabin with me, came up the ladder.

"I told you so," he said as soon as he saw me. "Now we are in America and you have no money to land. They send you home. No money, no going ashore. What a disgrace. In your position, frankly, I would kill myself."

Hassan had been satisfied to starve on black olives and salt cheese all the way from Gibraltar, and he begrudged every skewer of lamb I bribed away from the first-cabin steward.

We went down the gangplank into the big room. Passengers with pictures in their hands was rushing around to match them to a relative. Before their tables the inspectors was busy with long lines of people.

The visitors' door opened and a fellow with a big pile of caps, striped blue and white cotton caps with visors and a top button, came in. He went first to an old man with a karakul hat near the window, then to a Cossack in the line. At last he came to me.

"Look," he said in Russian, "look at your hat. You want to be a greenhorn all your life? A karakul hat! Do you expect to see anybody in the U.S.A. still with a fur hat? The customs inspector, the doctor, the captain—are they wearing fur hats? Certainly not."

I didn't say anything.

"Look," he said. "I'm sorry for you. I was a greenhorn once myself. I wouldn't want to see anybody make my mistakes. Look, I have caps. See, from such rich striped material. Like wears railroad engineers, and house painters, and coal miners." He spun one around on his finger. "Don't be afraid. It's a cap in real American style. With this cap on your head, they couldn't tell you from a citizen. I'm positively guaranteeing. And I'm trading you this cap even for your old karakul hat. Trading even. You don't have to give me one penny."

Now it is true I bought my karakul *coudie* new for the trip. It was a fine skin, a silver lamb, and in Georgia it would have lasted me a lifetime. Still—

"I'll tell you," the cap man said. "So you can remember all your life you made money the first hour you were in America, I give you a cap and a dollar besides. Done?"

I took off my *coudie* and put on his cap. It was small and sat well up on my head, but then in America one dressed like an American and it is a satisfaction always to be in the best style. So I got my first dollar.

Ysaacs, a Syrian, sat on the bench and smoked brown paper cigarettes and watched all through the bargain. He was from our cabin, too, and he knew I was worried about the money to show the examiners. But now, as soon as the cap man went on to the next customer, Ysaacs explained a way to get me by the examiners—a good way.

Such a very good way, in fact, that when the inspector looked over my passport and entry permit I was ready.

"Do you have friends meeting you?" he asked me. "Do you have money to support yourself?"

I pulled out a round fat roll of green American money—tens, twenties— a nice thick pile with a rubber band around.

"O.K." he said. "Go ahead." He stamped my papers.

I got my baggage and took the money roll back again to Ysaac's friend, Arapouleopolus, the money lender, so he could rent it over again to another man. One dollar was all he charged to use it for each landing. Really a bargain.

On the outer platform I met Zurabeg, an Ossetian, who had been down in steerage, too. But Zurabeg was no greenhorn coming for the first time. Zurabeg was an American citizen with papers to prove it, and a friend of Gospadin Buffalo Bill besides. This Zurabeg came first to America twenty years before as a trick show rider, and later he was boss cook on the road with the Gospadin Buffalo Bill. Every few years, Zurabeg, whenever he saved enough money, went home to find a wife—but so far with no luck.

"Can't land?" he asked me.

"No, I can land," I said, "but I have no money to pay the little boat to carry me to shore." A small boat went chuffing back and forth taking off the discharged passengers. "I try to make up my mind to swim, but if I swim how will I carry my baggage? It would need two trips at least."

"Listen, donkey-head," Zurabeg said, "this is America. The carrying boat is free. It belongs to my government. They take us for nothing. Come on."

So we got to the shore.

And there—the streets, the people, the noise! The faces flashing by—and by again. The screams and chatter and cries. But most of all the motion, back and forth, back and forth, pressing deeper and deeper on my eyeballs.

We walked a few blocks through this before I remembered my landing cards and passport and visas. I took them out and tore them into little pieces and threw them all in an ash can. "They can't prove I'm not a citizen, now," I said. "What we do next?"

"We get jobs," Zurabeg told me. "I show you."

We went to an employment agency. Conveniently, the man spoke Russian. He gave Zurabeg a ticket right away to start in a Russian restaurant as first cook.

"Now, my friend? What can you do?" he asked me.

"I," I said, "am a worker in decorative leathers, particularly specializing in the ornamenting of crop handles according to the traditional designs."

"My God!" the man said. "This is the U.S.A. No horses. Automobiles. What else can you do?"

Fortunately my father was a man of great foresight and I have two trades. His idea was that in the days when a man starves with one, by the other he may eat.

"I am also," I said, "a swordmaker. Short blades or long; daggers with or without chasing; hunting knives, plain or ornamented; tempering, fitting, pointing—" I took my certificate of successful completion of apprenticeship out of my *chemidon.*

"My God! A crop maker—a sword pointer. You better take him along for a dishwasher," he said to Zurabeg. "They can always use another dishwasher."

We went down into the earth and flew through tunnels in a train. It was like the caves under the Kazbeck where the giant bats sleep, and it smelled even worse.

The restaurant was on a side street and the lady-owner, the *hasaika,* spoke kindly. "I remember you from the tearoom," she said to Zurabeg. "I congratulate myself on getting you. You are excellent on the *piroshkis,* isn't it?"

"On everything, madame," Zurabeg said grandly. "On everything. Buffalo Bill, an old friend of mine, has eaten thirty of my *piroshkis* at a meal. My friend—" he waved toward me—"will be a dishwasher."

I made a bow.

The kitchen was small and hot and fat—like inside of a pig's stomach. Zurabeg unpacked his knives, put on his cap, and, at home at once, started to dice celery.

"You can wash these," the *hasaika* said to me. "At four we have party."

It was a trayful of glasses. And such glasses—thin bubbles that would hardly hold a sip—set on stems. The first one snapped in my hand, the second dissolved, the third to tenth I got washed, the eleventh was already cracked, the twelfth rang once on the pan edge and was silent.

Perhaps I might be there yet, but just as I carried the first trayful to the service slot, the restaurant cat ran between my feet.

When I got all the glass swept up, I told Zurabeg, "Now, we have to eat. It's noon. I watch the customers eat. It makes me hungry. Prepare a *shashlik* and some cucumbers, and we enjoy our first meal for good luck in the New World."

"This is a restaurant," Zurabeg said, "not a *duquani* on the side of the

Georgian road where the proprietor and the house eat with the guests together at one table. This is a restaurant with very strict organization. We get to eat when the customers go, and you get what the customers leave. Try again with the glasses and remember my reputation. Please."

I found a quart of sour cream and went into the back alley and ate that and some bread and a jar of caviar which was very salty—packed for export, no doubt.

The *hasaika* found me. I stood up. "Please," she said, "please go on. Eat sour cream. But after, could you go away? Far away? With no hard feelings. The glasses—the caviar—it's expensive for me—and at the same time I don't want to make your friend mad. I need a good cook. If you could just go away? Quietly? Just disappear, so to speak? I give you five dollars."

"I didn't do anything," I said, "so you don't have to pay me. All in all, a restaurant probably isn't my fate. You can tell Zurabeg afterward."

She brought my cap and a paper bag. I went down through the alley and into the street. I walked. I walked until my feet took fire in my shoes and my neck ached from looking. I walked for hours. I couldn't even be sure it was the same day. I tried some English on a few men that passed. "What watch?" I said. But they pushed by me so I knew I had it wrong. I tried another man. "How many clock?" He showed me on his wrist. Four-thirty.

A wonderful place. Rapidly, if one applies oneself, one speaks the English.

I came to a park and went in and found a place under a tree and took off my shoes and lay down. I looked in the bag the *hasaika* gave me. A sandwich from bologna and a nickel—to begin in America with.

What to do? While I decided, I slept.

A policeman was waking me up. He spoke. I shook my head I can't understand. Then with hands, and legs, rolling his eyes, turning his head, with motions, with gestures (really he was as good as marionettes I saw once in Tiflis), he showed me that to lie on the grass is forbidden. But one is welcome to the seats instead. All free seats in this park. No charge for anybody. What a country!

But I was puzzled. There were iron arm rests every two feet along the benches. How could I distribute myself under them? I tried one leg. Then the other. But when I was under, how could I turn around? Then, whatever way I got in, my chin was always caught by the hoop. While I thought this over, I walked and bought peanuts for my nickel and fed the squirrels.

Lights began to come on in the towers around the park. It was almost dark. I found a sandy patch under a rock on a little bluff above the drive. I cut a *shashlik* stick and built a fire of twigs and broiled my bologna over it and ate the bread. It lasted very short. Then I rolled up my coat for a pillow like the days during the war and went to sleep.

I was tired from America and I slept some hours. It must have been almost midnight when the light flashed in my face. I sat up. It was from the head lamp of a touring car choking along on the road below me. While I watched, the engine coughed and died. A man got out. For more than an hour he knocked with tools and opened the hood and closed it again.

Then I slid down the bank. In the war there were airplanes, and of course cars are much the same except, naturally, for the wings. I showed him with my hands and feet and head, like the policeman: "Give me the tools and let me try." He handed them over and sat down on the bench.

I checked the spark plugs and the distributor, the timer and the coils. I looked at the feed line, at the ignition, at the gas. In between, I cranked. I cranked until I cranked my heart out onto the ground. Still the car wouldn't move.

I got mad. I cursed it. I cursed it for a son of a mountain devi. I cursed it for the carriage of the diavels in the cave. I cursed it by the black-horned goat, and when I finished all I knew in Georgian I said it again in Russian to pick up the loose ends. Then I kicked the radiator as hard as I could. The car was an old Model T, and it started with a snort that shook the chassis like an aspen.

The man came running up. He was laughing and he shook my hand and talked at me and asked questions. But the policeman's method didn't work. Signs weren't enough. I remembered my dictionary—English-Russian, Russian-English—it went both ways. I took it from my blouse pocket and showed the man. Holding it under the headlights, he thumbed through.

"Work?" he found in English.

I looked at the Russian word beside it and shook my head.

"Home?" he turned to that.

"No," again.

I took the dictionary. "Boat. Today."

"Come home—" he showed me the words—"with me—" he pointed to himself. "Eat. Sleep. Job." It took him quite a time between words. "Job. Tomorrow."

"Automobiles?" I said. We have the same word in Georgian.

"Automobiles!" He was pleased we found one word together.

We got in his car, and he took me through miles and miles of streets with houses on both sides of every one of them until we came to his own. We went in and we ate and we drank and ate and drank again. For that, fortunately, you need no words.

Then his wife showed me a room and I went to bed. As I fell asleep, I thought to myself: "Well, now, I have lived one whole day in America and— just like they say—America is a country where anything, anything at all can happen."

And in twenty years—about this—I never changed my mind.

(1943)

From

GOLD IN THE STREETS
by Mary Vardoulakis

As they went down the hill in the early morning, George noticed that the trees were laden with buds ready to open. Of course, it's April, he thought, remembering the fields of lentil, wheat and flatbeans now all green in Crete. He sighed for having left Anidros before he could enjoy the fruits of the long hard plowing he had done the last winter. Ah, well, he consoled himself the next minute, he would be home to see the next growing season and reap the next harvest. Indeed, with good fortune he might be home in Crete to do the autumn plowing itself. Drakos had sworn that nothing was easier than making a small fortune in America and taking a boat back.

A rooster crowed familiarly in one of the cluttered yards. George smiled and looked at Petro. He was amused by two healthy pigs which were rooting in the soft ground near their pen. The sight of the animals gave him a peculiar pleasure.

"Who lives here in all these houses?" he asked Bakos. "Greeks?"

"Very few Greeks as yet," answered Bakos gravely. "We're just coming to America, don't forget. Of the Greeks who've come to Chicopee, however, most live up here. A handful or so."

"Do they own these houses?"

"Bah! How could they? The *Polonezi* were here first, and they've bought up some land here. They're settling down, and work in hordes at the mill. The more we come, the less they like us. There are troubles already, you'll see."

"Why?"

Just then a woman and a stocky blond man came out of the house which the group was passing. The woman's face hardened as she recognized the Greeks. She nudged her husband. Then, hands on her hips, she threw her head back and shouted in a taunting voice, "Boots, boots!" She pointed first at Petro, then at George, finally at the others, laughed dryly, then elbowed her husband into joining her taunts.

"Let her be," advised Bakos anxiously, urging his friends down the path. "Don't look back. There mustn't be trouble, for we want a good name for ourselves among the Americans, who are fine people. Let her be."

"But why?" George asked. "What does this mean?"

Bakos did not answer, and George carried the picture of the woman's stormy face with him as he followed the others down the hill. His heart became heavy. Who were these *Polonezi* about whom Bakos was giving warning? Drakos had not mentioned them. Had he and his friends been duped? Had Drakos lied? George asked himself.

His suspicions grew as Bakos laughed at the suggestion that anyone would be waiting for the Cretans at the mill. "Who knows you from the devil?" he laughed.

"I meant all of us. Drakos said they wanted us to work here, and they would know we're coming—"

"*Kale mou,* my good friend, when that man told you to come here and you agreed, he finished with you. Forget him."

"Is that right?"

"*Ne.* Don't worry. There are plenty of jobs. And I'll take you myself—" He took out his large gold watch and flipped the case open. "What? By the saints, I'm late, *pedia.* I must get in on time," he said anxiously. "No, I can't take you to the boss now. Go there," he instructed them, pointing to a door across the yard. "Just go in. They're people like us. Say 'job,' that's all."

He turned hurriedly, leaving Meliotes and the Cretans anxious and nervous.

Workers had been hurrying in through the gate all this time. As the hour approached seven, a large group of Poles was coming over the bridge, racing to beat the factory whistle. Before they were through the gate the whistle pierced the air. Panic-stricken, the Poles dashed ahead, pushing Michali and John Meliotes roughly aside. One Pole was cruder than his fellows. He recognized the men in his way to be Greeks. Confident that he would find refuge within the mill in a minute, and eager to vent his feelings, he loosed a storm of abuse, threatening the Greeks with clenched fists. Immediately others copied his language. "Boots, Boots!" and "Greek, Greek!" were their cries, and they filled and echoed through the yard.

"What can the bastards mean?" asked Petro, finding it hard to control his voice. "They're calling us something. These must be the *Polonezi* your uncle told us about," he told Meliotes. "*Vre,* they'll kill us if this continues—"

"You're right, *vre* Petro," cried George, pulling Michali toward him. "Shall we go after them?"

The whistle cut through the air again. Its terrible shriek continued for two long seconds, until the windows of the buildings shook. George dropped his hands to his side with a gesture of futility. When the whistle stopped, it seemed pointless to follow the Poles into the mill, where they had now found protection. If they were to go in at all, it was for work, George thought, trying to be calm.

"Look up there, at the windows," Michali shouted. "See their faces." Quick as a flash he bent over, escaping a wrench thrown into the yard from the second floor. "Bastards," he swore, copying George and Petro.

"A fine way to begin work in America!" said Petro, his face full of wrath.

"Where is that ungodly Drakos, with his smooth tongue? How are we going to work?" The world, despite the April sunlight, seemed black.

"Aren't we going in?" asked Michali, shocked. "What?"

"I think we'd better wait for my uncle," suggested John Meliotes thoughtfully. "Maybe they'll mass together and—" He shook his head and looked gravely at George.

"Maybe they're *anthropofayi*," Michali said dryly. He had changed his mind about going into the mill. He looked to his elders.

"Why do they hate us?" George asked no one in particular. He was puzzled, as well as angry. "Is it our clothes? People laughed at us at the station, I know, but—"

Meliotes remembered his uncle's caution.

"We must buy American clothes as soon as we can," he told them.

"*Kala*," George cried, "but what's wrong with these? Should that be our first worry, eh? *Alimono!*" His heart sank.

"Let's go," urged Meliotes. "Maybe they're afraid of us—to have us work with them, I mean. If we go in, maybe they will have less work to do. Who knows?"

"Come," said George suddenly, turning in disgust. "We won't wait for your uncle, Meliotes. We'll walk a while." He wanted to be where he could think clearly about this happening.

"What about work?" Meliotes asked, walking with George toward the gates. "You're not going home?" He looked puzzled and surprised.

George nodded. "We'll come back later, when we won't be in the way. Or perhaps tomorrow early. I don't know—"

Petro was impatient too. He had lost heart after the unexpected rebuff and wanted to talk with George and Michali.

"That's crazy," Meliotes said, "if I may say so."

"No," George answered firmly. He looked to Petro for confirmation. "Back home in Crete we have a superstition: when a man starts to hunt in the morning and the first shots go wrong, he knows he won't catch even a sparrow. It's true. *Yia sou*, we'll see you tonight at the house.

"But where are you going?" Meliotes asked.

"We'll walk and look around a bit," George said, shrugging.

They waved good-by to Meliotes, who sat on the ground outside the gates, and lit a cigarette. He wished he could follow the Cretans, an adventuresome crew. But he felt obliged to wait for his uncle Bakos. Like a father, Bakos had sent him his passage to America and had taken him into his house. *Ne*, he thought, he would wait for his uncle to come out at lunchtime, or else go home and tell his aunt. "Good luck, Cretans," he shouted. "You'll be all right."

(1945)

AMERICANIZATION
Into the Mainstream

All racial and social elements in our population who live here long enough become acculturated, Americanized in the truest sense of the word, eventually.

> Melville J. Herskovits
> The Negro's Americanism

Stanley. I am not a Polack. People from Poland are Poles, not Polacks. But what I am is a one hundred percent American, born and raised in the greatest country on earth and proud as hell of it, so don't ever call me a Polack.

> Tennessee Williams
> *A Streetcar Named Desire*

Your father's a Pollack, your mother's a Swede
But you were born here, that's all that you need.
You're an American.

> Stephen Sondheim
> *West Side Story*

THE MARCH OF PROGRESS
by Charles W. Chesnutt

The colored people of Patesville had at length gained the object they had for a long time been seeking—the appointment of a committee of themselves to manage the colored schools of the town. They had argued, with some show of reason, that they were most interested in the education of their own children, and in a position to know, better than any committee of white men could, what was best for their children's needs. The appointments had been made by the county commissioners during the latter part of the summer, and a week later a meeting was called for the purpose of electing a teacher to take charge of the grammar school at the beginning of the fall term.

The committee consisted of Frank Gillespie, or "Glaspy," a barber, who took an active part in local politics; Bob Cotten, a blacksmith, who owned several houses and was looked upon as a substantial citizen; and Abe Johnson, commonly called "Ole Abe" or "Uncle Abe," who had a large family, and drove a dray, and did odd jobs of hauling; he was also a class-leader in the Methodist church. The committee had been chosen from among a number of candidates—Gillespie on account of his political standing, Cotten as representing the solid element of the colored population, and Old Abe, with democratic impartiality, as likely to satisfy the humbler class of a humble people. While the choice had not pleased everybody—for instance, some of the other applicants—it was acquiesced in with general satisfaction. The first meeting of the new committee was of great public interest, partly by reason of its novelty, but chiefly because there were two candidates for the position of teacher of the grammar school.

The former teacher, Miss Henrietta Noble, had applied for the school. She had taught the colored children of Patesville for fifteen years. When the Freedmen's Bureau, after the military occupation of North Carolina, had called for volunteers to teach the children of the freedmen, Henrietta Noble had offered her services. Brought up in a New England household by parents who taught her to fear God and love her fellow men, she had seen her father's body brought home from a Southern battlefield and laid to rest in the village cemetery; and a short six months later she had buried her mother by his side. Henrietta had no brothers or sisters, and her nearest relatives were cousins living in the far West. The only human being in whom she felt any special personal interest was a certain captain in her father's regiment, who had paid her some attention. She had loved this man deeply, in a maidenly, modest way; but he had gone away without speaking, and had not since written. He had escaped the fate of many others, and at the close of the war was alive and well, stationed in some Southern garrison.

When her mother died, Henrietta had found herself possessed only of the house where she lived and the furniture it contained, neither being of much value, and she was thrown upon her own resources for a livelihood. She had a fair education and had read many good books. It was not easy to find employment such as she desired. She wrote to her Western cousins, and they advised her to come to them, as they thought they could do something for her if she were there. She had almost decided to accept their offer, when the demand arose for teachers in the South. Whether impelled by some strain of adventurous blood from a Pilgrim ancestry, or by a sensitive pride that shrank from dependence, or by some dim and unacknowledged hope that she might sometime, somewhere, somehow meet Captain Carey—whether from one of these motives or a combination of them all, joined to something of the missionary spirit, she decided to go South, and wrote to her cousins declining their friendly offer.

She had come to Patesville when the children were mostly a mob of dirty little beggars. She had distributed among them the cast-off clothing that came from their friends in the North; she had taught them to wash their faces and to comb their hair; and patiently, year after year, she had labored to instruct them in the rudiments of learning and the first principles of religion and morality. And she had not wrought in vain. Other agencies, it is true, had in time cooperated with her efforts, but anyone who had watched the current of events must have been compelled to admit that the very fair progress of the colored people of Patesville in the fifteen years following emancipation had been due chiefly to the unselfish labors of Henrietta Noble, and that her nature did not belie her name.

Fifteen years is a long time. Miss Noble had never met Captain Carey; and when she learned later that he had married a Southern girl in the neighborhood of his post, she had shed her tears in secret and banished his image from her heart. She had lived a lonely life. The white people of the town, though they learned in time to respect her and to value her work, had never recognized her existence by more than the mere external courtesy shown by any community to one who lives in the midst of it. The situation was at first, of course, so strained that she did not expect sympathy from the white people; and later, when time had smoothed over some of the asperities of war, her work had so engaged her that she had not had time to pine over her social exclusion. Once or twice nature had asserted itself, and she had longed for her own kind, and had visited her New England home. But her circle of friends was broken up, and she did not find much pleasure in boarding-house life; and on her last visit to the North but one, she had felt so lonely that she had longed for the dark faces of her pupils, and had welcomed with pleasure the hour when her task should be resumed.

But for several reasons the school at Patesville was of more importance to Miss Noble at this particular time than it ever had been before. During the last few years her health had not been good. An affection of the heart similar to that from which her mother had died, while not interfering perceptibly with her work, had grown from bad to worse, aggravated by close application to her duties, until it had caused her grave alarm. She did not have perfect confidence in the skill of the Patesville physicians, and to obtain the best medical advice had gone to New York during the summer, remaining there a month under the treatment of an eminent specialist. This, of course, had been expensive and had absorbed the savings of years from a small salary; and when the time came for her to return to Patesville, she was reduced, after paying her traveling expenses, to her last ten-dollar note.

"It is very fortunate," the great man had said at her last visit, "that circumstances permit you to live in the South, for I am afraid you could not endure a Northern winter. You are getting along very well now, and if you will take care of yourself and avoid excitement, you will be better." He said to himself as she went away: "It's only a matter of time, but that is true about us all; and a wise physician does as much good by what he withholds as by what he tells."

Miss Noble had not anticipated any trouble about the school. When she went away, the same committee of white men was in charge that had controlled the school since it had become part of the public-school system of the State on the withdrawal of support from the Freedmen's Bureau. While there had been no formal engagement made for the next year, when she had last seen the chairman before she went away, he had remarked that she was looking rather fagged out, had bidden her good-by, and had hoped to see her much improved when she returned. She had left her house in the care of the colored woman who lived with her and did her housework, assuming, of course, that she would take up her work again in the autumn.

She was much surprised at first, and later alarmed, to find a rival for her position as teacher of the grammar school. Many of her friends and pupils had called on her since her return, and she had met a number of the people at the colored Methodist church, where she taught in the Sunday school. She had many friends and supporters, but she soon found out that her opponent had considerable strength. There had been a time when she would have withdrawn and left him a clear field, but at the present moment it was almost a matter of life and death to her—certainly the matter of earning a living—to secure the appointment.

The other candidate was a young man who in former years had been one of Miss Noble's brightest pupils. When he had finished his course in the grammar school, his parents, with considerable sacrifice, had sent him to a college for colored youth. He had studied diligently, had worked industriously during his vacations, sometimes at manual labor, sometimes teaching a country school, and in due time had been graduated from his college with honors. He had come home at the end of his school life, and was very naturally seeking the employment for which he had fitted himself. He was a "bright" mulatto, with straight hair, an intelligent face, and a well-set figure. He had acquired some of the marks of culture, wore a frock-coat and a high collar, parted his hair in the middle, and showed by his manner that he thought a good deal of himself. He was the popular candidate among the progressive element of his people, and rather confidently expected the appointment.

The meeting of the committee was held in the Methodist church, where, in fact, the grammar school was taught, for want of a separate schoolhouse. After the preliminary steps to effect an organization, Mr. Gillespie, who had been elected chairman, took the floor.

"The principal business to be brought befo' the meet'n' this evenin'," he said, "is the selection of a teacher for our grammar school for the ensuin' year. Two candidates have filed applications, which, if there is no objections, I will read to the committee. The first is from Miss Noble, who has been the teacher ever since the grammar school was started."

He then read Miss Noble's letter, in which she called attention to her long years of service, to her need of the position, and to her affection for the pupils, and made formal application for the school for the next year. She did not, from motives of self-respect, make known the extremity of her need; nor did she mention the condition of her health, as it might have been used as an argument against her retention.

Mr. Gillespie then read the application of the other candidate, Andrew J. Williams. Mr. Williams set out in detail his qualifications for the position: his degree from Riddle University; his familiarity with the dead and living languages and the higher mathematics; his views of discipline; and a peroration in which he expressed the desire to devote himself to the elevation of his race and assist the march of progress through the medium of the Patesville grammar school. The letter was well written in a bold, round hand, with many flourishes, and looked very aggressive and overbearing as it lay on the table by the side of the sheet of small notepaper in Miss Noble's faint and somewhat cramped handwriting.

"You have heard the readin' of the application," said the chairman. "Gentlemen, what is yo' pleasure?"

There being no immediate response, the chairman continued:

"As this is a matter of consid'able importance, involvin' not only the welfare of our schools, but the progress of our race, an' as our action is liable to be criticized, whatever we decide, perhaps we had better discuss the subjec' befo' we act. If nobody else has anythin' to obse've, I will make a few remarks."

Mr. Gillespie cleared his throat, and, assuming an oratorical attitude, proceeded:

"The time has come in the history of our people when we should stand together. In this age of organization the march of progress requires that we help ourselves, or be left forever behind. Ever since the war we have been sendin' our child'n to school an' educatin' 'em; an' now the time has come when they are leavin' the schools an' colleges, an' are ready to go to work. An' what are they goin' to do? The white people won't hire 'em as clerks in their sto's an' factories an' mills, an' we have no sto's or factories or mills of our own. They can't be lawyers or doctors yet, because we haven't got the money to send 'em to medical colleges an' law schools. We can't elect many of 'em to office for various reasons. There's just two things they can find to do—to preach in our own pulpits, an' teach in our own schools. If it wasn't for that, they'd have to go on forever waitin' on white folks, like their fo'fathers have done, because they couldn't help it. If we expect our race to progress, we must educate our young men an' women. If we want to encourage 'em to get education, we must find 'em employment when they are educated. We have now an opportunity to do this in the case of our young friend an' fellow-citizen, Mr. Williams, whose eloquent an' fine-lookin' letter ought to make us feel proud of him an' of our race.

"Of co'se there are two sides to the question. We have got to consider the claims of Miss Noble. She has been with us a long time an' has done much good for our people, an' we'll never forget her work an' frien'ship. But, after all, she has been paid for it; she has got her salary regularly an' for a long time, an' she has probably saved somethin', for we all know she hasn't lived high; an', for all we know, she may have had somethin' left her by her parents. An' then again, she's white, an' has got her own people to look after her; they've got all the money an' all the offices an' all the everythin'—all that they've made an' all that we've made for fo' hundred years—an' they sho'ly would look out for her. If she don't get this school, there's probably a dozen others she can get at the North. An' another thing: she is gettin' rather feeble, an' it 'pears to me she's hardly able to stand teachin' so many child'n, an' a long rest might be the best thing in the world for her.

"Now, gentlemen, that's the situation. Shall we keep Miss Noble, or shall we stand by our own people? It seems to me there can hardly be but one answer. Self-preservation is the first law of nature. Are there any other remarks?"

Old Abe was moving restlessly in his seat. He did not say anything, however, and the chairman turned to the other member.

"Brother Cotten, what is yo' opinion of the question befo' the board?"

Mr. Cotten rose with the slowness and dignity becoming a substantial citizen, and observed:

"I think the remarks of the chairman have great weight. We all have nothin' but kind feelin's fer Miss Noble, an' I came here tonight somewhat undecided how to vote on this question. But after listenin' to the just an' forcible arguments of Brother Glaspy, it 'pears to me that, after all, the question befo' us is not a matter of feelin', but of business. As a businessman, I am inclined to think Brother Glaspy is right. If we don't help ourselves when we get a chance, who is goin' to help us?''

"That bein' the case," said the chairman, "shall we proceed to a vote? All who favor the election of Brother Williams—"

At this point Old Abe, with much preliminary shuffling, stood up in his place and interrupted the speaker.

"Mr. Chuhman," he said, "I s'pose I has a right ter speak in dis meet'n'? I *s'pose* I is a member er dis committee?''

"Certainly, Brother Johnson, certainly; we shall be glad to hear from you."

"I s'pose I's got a right ter speak my min', ef I is po' an' black, an' don' weah as good clo's as some other members er de committee?''

"Most assuredly, Brother Johnson," answered the chairman, with a barber's suavity, "you have as much right to be heard as anyone else. There was no intention of cuttin' you off.''

"I s'pose," continued Abe, "dat a man wid fo'teen child'n kin be 'lowed ter hab somethin' ter say 'bout de schools er dis town?''

"I am sorry, Brother Johnson, that you should feel slighted, but there was no intention to igno' yo' rights. The committee will be please' to have you ventilate yo' views.''

"Ef it's all be'n an' done reco'nized an' 'cided dat I's got de right ter be heared in dis meet'n', I'll say w'at I has ter say, an' it won't take me long ter say it. Ef I should try ter tell all de things dat Miss Noble has done fer de niggers er dis town, it'd take me till termorrow mawnin'. Fer fifteen long yeahs I has watched her incomin's an' her outgoin's. Her daddy was a Yankee kunnel, who died fightin' fer ou' freedom. She come heah when we—yas, Mr. Chuhman, when you an' Br'er Cotten—was jes' sot free an' when none er us didn' have a rag ter ou' backs. She come heah, an' she tuk yo' child'n an' my child'n, an' she teached 'em sense an' manners an' religion and book-l'arnin'. When she come heah we didn' hab no chu'ch. Who writ up No'th an' got a preacher sent to us, an' de fun's ter buil' dis same chu'ch-house we're settin' in ternight? Who got de money f'm de Bureau to s'port de school? An' when dat was stop', who got de money f'm de Peabody Fun'? Talk about Miss Noble gittin' a sal'ry! Who paid dat sal'ry up ter five years ago? Not one dollah of it come outer ou' pockets!

"An' den, w'at did she git fer de yuther things she done? Who paid her fer teachin' de Sunday school? Who paid her fer de gals she kep' f'm throwin' deyse'ves away? Who paid fer de boys she kep' outer jail? I had a son dat seemed to hab made up his min' ter go straight ter hell. I made him go ter Sunday school, an' somethin' dat woman said teched his heart, an' he behaved hisse'f, an' I ain' got no reason fer ter be 'shame' er 'im. An' I can 'member, Br'er Cotten, when you didn' own fo' houses an' a fahm. An' when yo' fus' wife was sick, who sot by her bedside an' read de Good Book ter 'er, w'en dey wuzn' nobody else knowed how ter read it, an' comforted her on her way across de col', dahk ribber? An' dat ain' all I kin 'member, Mr. Chuhman!

When yo' gal Fanny was a baby, an' sick, an' nobody knowed what was de matter wid 'er, who sent fer a doctor, an' paid 'im fer comin', an' who he'ped nuss dat chile, an' tol' yo' wife w'at ter do, an' save' dat chile's life, jes' as sho' as de Lawd has save' my soul?

"An' now, aftuh fifteen yeahs o' slavin' fer us, who ain' got no claim on her, aftuh fifteen yeahs dat she has libbed 'mongs' us an' made herse'f one of us, an' endoyed havin' her own people look down on her, aftuh she has growed ole an' gray wukkin' fer us an' our child'n, we talk erbout turnin' 'er out like a' ole hoss ter die! It 'pears ter me some folks has po' mem'ries! Whar would we 'a' be'n ef her folks at de No'th hadn' 'membered us no bettuh? An' we hadn' done nothin', neither, fer dem to 'member us fer. De man dat kin fergit w'at Miss Noble has done fer dis town is unworthy de name er nigger! He oughter die an' make room fer some 'spectable dog!

"Br'er Glaspy says we got a' educated young man, an' we mus' gib him sump'n' ter do. Let him wait; ef I reads de signs right he won't hab ter wait long fer dis job. Let him teach in de primary schools, er in de country; an' ef he can't do dat, let 'im work awhile. It don't hahm a' educated man ter work a little; his fo'fathers has worked fer hund'eds of years, an' we's worked, an' we're heah yet, an' we're free, an' we's gettin' ou' own houses an' lots an' hosses an' cows—an' ou' educated young men. But don't let de fus' thing we do as a committee be somethin' we ought ter be 'shamed of as long as we lib. I votes for Miss Noble, fus', las', an' all de time!"

When Old Abe sat down the chairman's face bore a troubled look. He remembered how his baby girl, the first of his children that he could really call his own, that no master could hold a prior claim upon, lay dying in the arms of his distracted young wife, and how the thin, homely, and short-sighted white teacher had come like an angel into his cabin, and had brought back the little one from the verge of the grave. The child was a young woman now, and Gillespie had well-founded hopes of securing the superior young Williams for a son-in-law; and he realized with something of shame that this later ambition had so dazzled his eyes for a moment as to obscure the memory of earlier days.

Mr. Cotten, too, had not been unmoved, and there were tears in his eyes as he recalled how his first wife, Nancy, who had borne with him the privations of slavery, had passed away, with the teacher's hand in hers, before she had been able to enjoy the fruits of liberty. For they had loved one another much, and her death had been to them both a hard and bitter thing. And, as Old Abe spoke, he could remember, as distinctly as though they had been spoken but an hour before, the words of comfort that the teacher had whispered to Nancy in her dying hour and to him in his bereavement.

"On consideration, Mr. Chairman," he said, with an effort to hide a suspicious tremor in his voice and to speak with the dignity consistent with his character as a substantial citizen, "I wish to record my vote fer Miss Noble."

"The chair," said Gillespie, yielding gracefully to the majority, and greatly relieved that the responsibility of his candidate's defeat lay elsewhere, "will make the vote unanimous, and will appoint Brother Cotten and Brother Johnson a committee to step round the corner to Miss Noble's and notify her of her election."

The two committeemen put on their hats, and, accompanied by several people who had been waiting at the door to hear the result of the meeting, went around the corner to Miss Noble's house, a distance of a block or two away. The house was lighted, so they knew she had not gone to bed. They went in at the gate, and Cotten knocked at the door.

The colored maid opened it.

"Is Miss Noble home?" said Cotten.

"Yes; come in. She's waitin' ter hear from the committee."

The woman showed them into the parlor. Miss Noble rose from her seat by the table, where she had been reading, and came forward to meet them. They did not for a moment observe, as she took a step toward them, that her footsteps wavered. In her agitation she was scarcely aware of it herself.

"Miss Noble," announced Cotten, "we have come to let you know that you have be'n 'lected teacher of the grammar school for the next year."

"Thank you; oh, thank you so much!" she said. "I am very glad. Mary"— she put her hand to her side suddenly and tottered—"Mary, will you—"

A spasm of pain contracted her face and cut short her speech. She would have fallen had Old Abe not caught her and, with Mary's help, laid her on a couch.

The remedies applied by Mary, and by the physician who was hastily summoned, proved unavailing. The teacher did not regain consciousness.

If it be given to those whose eyes have closed in death to linger regretfully for a while about their earthly tenement, or from some higher vantage-ground to look down upon it, than Henrietta Noble's tolerant spirit must have felt, mingling with its regret, a compensating thrill of pleasure; for not only those for whom she had labored sorrowed for her, but the people of her own race, many of whom, in the blindness of their pride would not admit during her life that she served them also, saw so much clearer now that they took charge of her poor clay, and did it gentle reverence, and laid it tenderly away amid the dust of their own loved and honored dead.

Two weeks after Miss Noble's funeral the other candidate took charge of the grammar school, which went on without any further obstacles to the march of progress.

(1901)

From

THE RISE OF DAVID LEVINSKY
by Abraham Cahan

It was the spring of 1910. The twenty-fifth anniversary of my coming to America was drawing near.

The day of an immigrant's arrival in his new home is like a birthday to him. Indeed, it is more apt to claim his attention and to warm his heart than his real birthday. Some of our immigrants do not even know their birthday. But they all know the day when they came to America. It is Landing Day with red capital letters. This, at any rate, is the case with me. The day upon which I was born often passes without my being aware of it. The day when I landed in Hoboken, on the other hand, never arrives without my being fully conscious of the place it occupies in the calendar of my life. Is it because I do not remember myself coming into the world, while I do remember my arrival in America? However that may be, the advent of that day invariably puts me in a sentimental mood which I never experience on the day of my birth.

It was 1910, then, and the twenty-fifth anniversary of my coming was near at hand. Thoughts of the past filled me with mixed joy and sadness. I was overcome with a desire to celebrate the day. But with whom? Usually this is done by "ship brothers," as East-Siders call fellow-immigrants who arrive here on the same boat. It came back to me that I had such a ship brother, and that it was Gitelson. Poor Gitelson! He was still working at his trade. I had not seen him for years, but I had heard of him from time to time, and I knew that he was employed by a ladies' tailor at custom work somewhere in Brooklyn. (The custom-tailoring shop he had once started for himself had proved a failure.) Also, I knew how to reach a brother-in-law of his. The upshot was that I made an appointment with Gitelson for him to be at my office on the great day at 12 o'clock. I did so without specifying the object of the meeting, but I expected that he would know.

Finally the day arrived. It was a few minutes to 12. I was alone in my private office, all in a fidget, as if the meeting I was expecting were a love-tryst. Reminiscences and reflections were flitting incoherently through my mind. Some of the events of the day which I was about to celebrate loomed up like a ship seen in the distance. My eye swept the expensive furniture of my office. I thought of the way my career had begun. I thought of the Friday evening when I met Gitelson on Grand Street, he an American dandy and I in tatters. The fact that it was upon his advice and with his ten dollars that I had become a cloak-maker stood out as large as life before me. A great feeling of gratitude welled up in me, of gratitude and of pity for my tattered self of those days. Dear, kind Gitelson! Poor fellow! He was still working with his needle. I was seized with a desire to do something for him. I had never paid him those ten dollars. So I was going to do so with "substantial interest" now. "I shall spend a few hundred dollars on him—nay, a few thousand!" I said to myself. "I shall buy him a small business. Let him end his days in comfort. Let him know that his ship brother is like a real brother to him."

It was twenty minutes after 12 and I was still waiting for the telephone to announce him. My suspense became insupportable. "Is he going to disappoint me, the idiot?" I wondered. Presently the telephone trilled. I seized the receiver.

"Mr. Gitelson wishes to see Mr. Levinsky," came the familiar pipe of my switchboard girl. "He says he has an appointment—"

"Let him come in at once," I flashed.

Two minutes later he was in my room. His forelock was still the only bunch of gray hair on his head, but his face was pitifully wizened. He was quite neatly dressed, as trained tailors will be, even when they are poor, and at some distance I might have failed to perceive any change in him. At close range, however, his appearance broke my heart.

"Do you know what sort of a day this is?" I asked, after shaking his hand warmly.

"I should think I did," he answered, sheepishly. "Twenty-five years ago at this time—"

He was at a loss for words.

"Yes, it's twenty-five years, Gitelson," I rejoined. I was going to indulge in reminiscences, to compare memories with him, but changed my mind. I would rather not speak of our Landing Day until we were seated at a dining-table and after we had drunk its toast in champagne.

"Come, let us have lunch together," I said, simply.

I took him to the Waldorf-Astoria, where a table had been reserved for us in a snug corner.

Gitelson was extremely bashful and his embarrassment infected me. He was apparently at a loss to know what to do with the various glasses, knives, forks. It was evident that he had never sat at such a table before. The French waiter, who was silently officious, seemed to be inwardly laughing at both of us. At the bottom of my heart I cow before waiters to this day. Their white shirt-fronts, reticence, and pompous bows make me feel as if they saw through me and ridiculed my ways. They make me feel as if my expensive clothes and ways ill became me.

"Here is good health, Gitelson," I said in plain old Yiddish, as we touched glasses. "Let us drink to the day when we arrived in Castle Garden."

There was something forced, studied, in the way I uttered these words. I was disgusted with my own voice. Gitelson only simpered. He drained his glass, and the champagne, to which he was not accustomed, made him tipsy at once. I tried to talk of our ship, of the cap he had lost, of his timidity when we had found ourselves in Castle Garden, of the policeman whom I asked to direct us. But Gitelson only nodded and grinned and tittered. I realized that I had made a mistake—that I should have taken him to a more modest restaurant. But then the chasm between him and me seemed to be too wide for us to celebrate as ship brothers in any place.

"By the way, Gitelson, I owe you something," I said, producing a ten-dollar bill. "It was with your ten dollars that I learned to be a cloak-operator and entered the cloak trade. Do you remember?" I was going to add something about my desire to help him in some substantial way, but he interrupted me.

"Sure, I do," he said, with inebriate shamefacedness, as he received the money and shoved it into the inside pocket of his vest. "It has brought you good luck, hasn't it? And how about the interest? He, he, he! You've kept it over twenty-three years. The interest must be quite a little. He, he he!"

"Of course I'll pay you the interest, and more, too. You shall get a check."

"Oh, I was only joking."

"But *I* am not joking. You're going to get a check, all right."

He revolted me.

I made out a check for two hundred dollars; tore it and made out one for five hundred.

He flushed, scanned the figure, giggled, hesitated, and finally folded the check and pushed it into his inner vest pocket, thanking me with drunken ardor.

Some time later I was returning to my office, my heart heavy with self-disgust and sadness. In the evening I went home, to the loneliness of my beautiful hotel lodgings. My heart was still heavy with distaste and sadness.

(1917)

From

A CYCLE OF MANHATTAN
by Thyra Samter Winslow

The Rosenheimers arrived in New York on a day in April. New York, flushed with the first touch of Spring, moved on inscrutably, almost suavely unaware. It was the greatest thing that had ever happened to the Rosenheimers, and even in the light of the profound experiences that were to follow it kept its vast grandeur and separateness, its mysterious and benumbing superiority. Viewed later, in half-tearful retrospect, it took on the character of something unearthly, unmatchable and never quite clear—a violent gallimaufry of strange tongues, humiliating questionings, freezing uncertainties, sudden and paralyzing activities.

The Rosenheimers came by way of the Atlantic Ocean, and if anything remained unclouded in their minds it was a sense of that dour and implacable highway's unfriendliness. They thought of it ever after as an intolerable motion, a penetrating and suffocating smell. They saw it through drenched skylights—now and then as a glimpse of blinding blue on brisk, heaving mornings. They remembered the harsh, unintelligible exactions of officials in curious little blue coats. They dreamed for years of endless nights in damp, smothering bunks. They carried off the taste of strange foods, barbarously served. The Rosenheimers came in the steerage.

There were, at that time, seven of them, if you count Mrs. Feinberg. As Mrs. Feinberg had, for a period of eight years—the age of the oldest Rosenheimer child—been called nothing but Grandma by the family and occasionally Grandma Rosenheimer by outsiders, she was practically a Rosenheimer, too. Grandma was Mrs. Rosenheimer's mother, a decent simple, round-shouldered "sheideled," little old woman, to whom life was a ceaseless washing of dishes, making of beds, caring for children and cooking of meals. She ruled them all, unknowing.

The head of the house of Rosenheimer was, fittingly, named Abraham. This had abbreviated itself, even in Lithuania, to a more intimate Abe. Abe Rosenheimer was thirty-three, sallow, thin-cheeked and bearded, with a slightly aquiline nose. He was already growing bald. He was not tall and he stooped. He was a clothing cutter by trade. Since his marriage, nine years before, he had been saving to bring his family over. Only the rapid increase of its numbers had prevented him coming sooner.

Abraham Rosenheimer was rather a silent man and he looked stern. Although he recognized his inferiority in a superior world, he was not without his ambitions. These looked toward a comfortable home, his own chair with a lamp by it, no scrimping about meat at meals and a little money put by. He had heard stories about fortunes that could be made in America and in his youth they had stirred him. Now he was not much swayed by them. He was fond of his family and he wanted them "well taken care of," but in the world that he knew the rich and the poor were separated by an unscalable barrier. Unless incited temporarily to revolution by fiery acquaintances he was content to hope for a simple living, work not too hard or too long, a little leisure, tranquillity.

He had a comfortable faith which included the belief that, if a man does his best, he'll usually be able to make a living for his family. "Health is the big thing," he would say, and "The Lord will provide." Outside of his prayerbook, he did little reading. It never occurred to him that he might be interested in the outside world. He knew of the existence of none of the arts. His home and his work were all he had ever thought about.

Mrs. Rosenheimer, whose first name was Minnie, was thirty-one. She was a younger and prettier reproduction of her mother, plump and placid, with a mouth inclined to petulancy.

There were four Rosenheimer children. Yetta was eight, Isaac six, Carrie three and little Emanuel had just had his first birthday. Yetta and Carrie were called by their own first names, but Isaac, in America, almost immediately gave way to Ike and little Emanuel became Mannie. They were much alike, dark-haired, dark-eyed, restless, shy, wondering.

The Rosenheimers had several acquaintances in New York, people from the little village near Grodno who had preceded them to America. Most of these now lived in the Ghetto that was arising on the East Side of New York, and Rosenheimer had thought that his family would go there, too, so as to be near familiar faces. He had written several months before, to one Abramson, a sort of a distant cousin, who had been in America for twelve years. As Abramson had promised to meet them, he decided to rely on Abramson's judgment in finding a home in the city.

Abramson was at Ellis Island and greeted the family with vehement embraces. He seemed amazingly well dressed and at home. He wore a large watchchain and no less than four rings. He introduced his wife, whom he had married since coming to America, though she, too, had come from the old country. She wore silk and carried a parasol.

"I've got a house all picked out for you," he explained in familiar Yiddish. "It isn't in the Ghetto, where some of our friends live, but it's cheap, with lots of comforts and near where you can get work, too."

Any house would have suited the Rosenheimers. They were pitifully anxious to get settled, to rid themselves of the foundationless feeling which had taken possession of them. With eager docility, Yetta carrying Mannie and each of the others carrying a portion of the bundles of wearing apparel and feather comforts which formed their luggage, they followed Abramson to a surface car and to their new home. In their foreign clothes and with their bundles they felt almost as uncomfortable as they had been on shipboard.

The Rosenheimers' new home was in MacDougal Street. They looked with awe on the exterior and pronounced it wonderful. Such a fine building! Of red brick it was! There were three stories. The first story was a stable, the big open door. Little Isaac had to be pulled past the restless horses in front of it. The whole family stood for a moment, drinking in the wonders, then followed Abramson up the stairs. On the second floor several families lived in what the Rosenheimers thought was palatial grandeur. Even their own home was elegant. It consisted of two rooms—the third floor front. They could hardly be convinced that they were to have all that space. There was a stove in the second room and gas fixtures in both of them—and there was a bathroom, with running water, in the general hall! The Rosenheimers didn't see that the paper was falling from the walls and that, where it had been gone for some years, the plaster was falling, too. Nor that the floor was roughly uneven.

"Won't it be too expensive?" asked Rosenheimer. Abramson chuckled.

Though he himself was but a trimmer by trade, he was pleased with the role of fairy godfather. He liked twirling wonders in the faces of these simple folk. In comparison, he felt himself quite a success, a cosmopolite. Just about Rosenheimer's age, he had small deposits in two savings banks, a three-room apartment, a wife and two American sons, Sam and Morrie. Both were in public school, and both could speak "good English." He patted Rosenheimer on the back jovially.

"You don't need to worry," he said. "A good cutter here in New York don't have to worry. Even a 'greenhorn' makes a living. There's half a dozen places *you* can choose from. I'll tell you about it, and where to go, tomorrow. Now, we'll go over to my house and have something to eat. Then you'll see how you'll be living in a few years. You can borrow some things from us until you get your own. My wife will be glad to go with Mrs. Rosenheimer and show her where to buy."

The Rosenheimers gave signs of satisfaction as they dropped their bundles and sat down on the empty boxes that stood around, or on the floor. This was something like it! Here they had a fine home in a big brick house, a sure chance of Rosenheimer getting a good job, friends to tell them about things— they had already found their place in New York! Grandma, trembling with excitement, took Mannie in her arms and held him up dramatically.

"See, Mannie, see Mannischen—this is fine—this is the way to live!"

*   *   *   *   *

Manning stopped school the year after the family moved into their new home. He had had a year at Harvard and a year or so at art school. Now, at twenty-two, he felt that he was a sculptor. His father was disappointed—Manning had started out a nice boy—it did seem that one of the boys . . .

But Manning shrugged sensitive shoulders at anything as crude as the clothing business, even wholesale. His soul was not in such things. And Mr. Ross had to admit that the position of model was about the only one in the establishment that Manning could have filled. Manning went in, rather heavily, for the arts that the rest of the family had neglected. Of course Dorothea read, but Manning thought she skimmed too lightly over real literature. And Irwin— an impossible, material fellow.

Manning wore his hair a trifle long. He talked knowingly of Byzantine enamels and the School of Troyes. He knew Della Robbia and the Della-Cruscans. There was nothing he didn't know about French ivories. He knew how champlevé enameling differed from other methods . . . there were few mysteries for Manning. His personal contributions to Wanty consisted of fantastic heads, influenced slightly by the French of the Fourteenth Century, in bas-relief—very flat relief, of course.

Manning's friends felt they formed a real part of New York's "new serious Bohemia." They ate in "unexploited" Greenwich Village restaurants, never complaining about the poorly cooked food, sitting for hours at the bare, painted tables, talking eagerly in the dim candle or lamp light. They expressed disgust when "uptowners" discovered their retreats and sometimes moved elsewhere. You could find them every Saturday and Sunday night in parties of from four to ten, at the Brevoort, sometimes with pretty girls who didn't listen to what they were saying, sometimes with homely little "artistic" ones, hung with soiled embroidered smocks, who listened too eagerly, talking of life and art, revolution and undiscovered genius.

There was no question that Manning's father should continue his allowance—there is no money in sincere art these days. Manning knew that even his father must recognize that. Manning spent his summer with the family on Long Island—it was hot in town. But, when one's family is of the bourgeoisie, it does draw one's energy so. In the autumn Manning decided he must have a real studio, some place he could work and expand, going to "the town house" for week-ends. Having one's family uptown was quite all right, of course—but you couldn't expect an artist to live with them.

Mr. Ross agreed to the studio. He was getting accustomed to Dorothea's friends, unbelievers though they were. He found he could not accept the artistic friends that Manning thought so delightful.

Manning found his studio, finally. The rent was terrific, of course, but the building had been rebuilt at great expense and was absolutely desirable in location, construction, everything. He furnished it himself in Italian and Spanish Renaissance things. Rather nice! When it was furnished—though they probably couldn't "get it" he'd let the family see it.

One Sunday, after a family reunion dinner, Manning announced that his studio was done. If the family liked they might all run down that way—a sort of informal reception . . . of course, they probably couldn't understand it all. . . .

It was in the Village, of course, but not "of" it. Did they think the Village was slumming? Uptown people did. But that's where you'd find real thought, people who accomplished things. . . .

"Why, my new studio has real atmosphere"—Manning ran his fingers through his hair as he spoke. "It's in a wonderful old building, magnificent lines and the architect left them all—it's just inside he's remodeled. I've the third floor front, two magnificent rooms, a huge fireplace, some lovely Italian things . . . and the view from the window is so quaint and artistic . . . of course you may not understand it . . . this family . . . it's just a block from Washington Square."

"Why, that's where . . ." began Mrs. Ross.

Irwin silenced her.

"Don't begin old times, Mamma. Most of us haven't as long memories as you," he said.

"Come on, now that we're all here, let's go down," Manning went on, "I want you to see something really artistic. A friend of mine, DuBroil—I think you've met him—did me a stunning name plate in copper, just my name, Manning Cuyler Ross. I'm so glad I took Cuyler for a middle name last year. And there is just the single word, 'masks.' I thought it was—rather good. And I've a stunning bit of tapestry on the south wall. Come on—you've got your cars here, we'd better get started—''

It was a pleasant drive. The three cars drew up, almost at once, in front of Manning's studio, as he, in the front car, pointed it out to them.

They made quite a party as they turned out in front of the building—a prosperous American family—Mr. and Mrs. Lincoln Ross, well-dressed, commanding, in their fifties, which isn't old, these days; MacDougal Adams, plump, pompous; Yvette Ross Adams, in handsome furs and silks; Jack Morton, sleek, black-haired; his always exquisitely gowned wife, Carolyn Ross Morton; Irwin Ross, in a well-fitting cutaway, eyebrows raised inquiringly, chatting alertly; Dorothea Ross, attractive and girlish in rough tan homespun, and Manning Cuyler Ross, their host, pleasantly artistic.

"Here's the place," said Manning. "No elevator, real Bohemia, three flights up, uncarpeted stairs. Come on, Mother."

Mrs. Ross was strangely pale, and on the faces of Yvette and Irwin and MacDougal Adams there were curious shadows. The rest, save for Mr. Ross, were too young to remember. As for him he broke, for the first time in years, into a broad smile. Manning went rattling on.

"This," he proclaimed, "is the way to live! None of your middle-class fripperies. Plain living, high thinking—this is the life!"

They came to the studio at last, and all stood about in silence while Manning explained its charms—the clear light, the plain old woodwork, the lovely view of the square, the remote, old-world atmosphere. In the midst of his oratory Mr. Ross sidled up to Mamma Ross and reached stealthily for her hand.

"Do you remember, Minnie," he whispered, "this room—this old place—those old days—"

"Hush," said Momma Ross, "the children will hear you."

(1923)

From

THE AUTOBIOGRAPHY OF LINCOLN STEFFENS
by Lincoln Steffens

The *Post* printed a murder, a mere mean murder, as news, and there was no news in it; only life. "We" published crime after that, all sorts of sensational stuff. Why not? Nobody noticed it, as crime. I soon found out that by going with the reporters to a fire or the scene of an accident was a way to see the town and the life of the town.

A synagogue that burned down during a service introduced me to the service; I attended another synagogue, asked questions, and realized that it was a bit of the Old Testament repeated after thousands of years, unchanged. And so I described that service and other services. They fascinated me, those old practices, and the picturesque customs and laws of the old orthodox Jews from Russia and Poland. Max, an East Side Jew himself, told me about them; I read up and talked to funny old, fine rabbis about them, and about their conflicts with their Americanized children. The *Post* observed all the holy days of the Ghetto. There were advance notices of their coming, with descriptions of the preparations and explanations of their sacred, ancient, biblical meaning, and then an account of them as I saw these days and nights observed in the homes and the churches of the poor. A queer mixture of comedy, tragedy, orthodoxy, and revelation, they interested our Christian readers. The uptown Jews complained now and then. Mr. Godkin himself required me once to call personally upon a socially prominent Jewish lady who had written to the editor asking why so much space was given to the ridiculous performances of the ignorant, foreign East Side Jews and none to the uptown Hebrews. I told her. I had the satisfaction of telling her about the comparative beauty, significance, and character of the uptown and downtown Jews. I must have talked well, for she threatened and tried to have me fired, as she put it. Fortunately, the editorial writers were under pressure also from prominent Jews to back up their side of a public controversy over the blackballing of a rich Jew by an uptown social club. "We" were fair to the Jews, editorially, but personally irritated. I was not "fired"; I was sent out to interview the proprietor of a hotel which excluded Jews, and he put his case in a very few words.

"I won't have one," he said. "I have had my experience and so learned that if you let one in because he is exceptional and fine, he will bring in others who are not exceptional, etc. By and by they will occupy the whole house, when the Christians leave. And then, when the Christians don't come any more, the Jews quit you to go where the Christians have gone, and there you are with an empty or a second-class house.''

It would have been absurd to discharge me since I at that time was almost a Jew. I had become as infatuated with the Ghetto as eastern boys were with the wild west, and nailed a mazuza on my office door; I went to the synagogue on all the great Jewish holy days; on Yom Kippur I spent the whole twenty-four hours fasting and going from one synagogue to another. The music moved me most, but I knew and could follow with the awful feelings of a Jew the beautiful old ceremonies of the ancient orthodox services. My friends laughed at me; especially the Jews among them scoffed. ''You are more Jewish than us Jews,'' they said, and since I have traveled I realize the absurdity of the American who is more French than the French, more German than the Kaiser. But there were some respecters of my respect. When Israel Zangwill the author of *Tales of the Ghetto,* came from London to visit New York, he heard about me from Jews and asked me to be his guide for a survey of the East Side; and he saw and he went home and wrote *The Melting Pot.*

The tales of the New York Ghetto were heart-breaking comedies of the tragic conflict between the old and the new, the very old and the very new; in many matters, all at once: religion, class, clothes, manners, customs, language, culture. We all know the difference between youth and age, but our experience is between two generations. Among the Russian and other eastern Jewish families in New York it was an abyss of many generations; it was between parents out of the Middle Ages, sometimes out of the Old Testament days hundreds of years B.C., and the children of the streets of New York today. We saw it everywhere all the time. Responding to a reported suicide, we would pass a synagogue where a score or more of boys were sitting hatless in their old clothes, smoking cigarettes on the steps outside, and their fathers, all dressed in black, with their high hats, uncut beards, and temple curls, were going into the synagogues, tearing their hair and rending their garments. The reporters stopped to laugh; and it was comic; the old men, in their thrift, tore the lapels of their coats very carefully, a very little, but they wept tears, real tears. It was a revolution. Their sons were rebels against the law of Moses; they were lost souls, lost to God, the family, and to Israel of old. The police did not understand or sympathize. If there was a fight—and sometimes the fathers did lay hands on their sons, and the tough boys did biff their fathers in the eye; which brought out all the horrified elders of the whole neighborhood and all the sullen youth—when there was a ''riot call,'' the police would rush in and club now the boys, now the parents, and now, in their Irish exasperation, both sides, bloodily and in vain. I used to feel that the blood did not hurt, but the tears did, the weeping and gnashing of teeth of the old Jews who were doomed and knew it. Two, three, thousand years of continuous devotion, courage, and suffering for a cause lost in a generation.

(1931)

From

FIG TREE JOHN
by Edwin Corle

The road was paved in 1921. Traffic between the Imperial Valley towns and the Coachella Valley towns and the markets in, around and about Los Angeles warranted it. From Banning, up in the mountains, the road ran straight down into the desert country, jogged through Indio, skirted Coachella, ignored Mecca, and then ran parallel to the southern shore line of the Salton Sea for a long straight sweep across the desert and finally reached the Imperial Valley towns of Brawley and El Centro.

Traffic and trucking had made this highway necessary. Cotton, alfalfa, lettuce, and melons were brought up from the Imperial country that had once been a sterile sandy desert below sea level. And alfalfa, grapefruit, and the famous Deglet-Noor dates, the first sprays of which had been imported from Morocco, were the chief products of the Coachella country. First the railroad and then the highway opened these valleys to prosperity.

The road passed within a mile of Agocho's home in the clearing, but there was no way to tell that from the highway. Motorists sped by without stopping and only the local people knew that Fig Tree John had a water hole over there somewhere. Fig Tree was seldom seen on the highway. He was not a man to seek publicity. But if you looked carefully, even before the road had been paved, you might see an Indian boy sitting back from the road in the sagebrush, or perhaps get a glimpse of him jogging along on horseback anywhere between Coachella and the lower end of the Salton Sea. In the old days your own dust flew up so much that a fleeting glimpse of him was all you could get. And then the road was often corduroy or sandy or both and there was no time to take your eyes off the tracks ahead of you. But with the pavement, driving was easier and those who passed over the road many times had been sure to see, at some time or other, a young Indian boy who stared at them as long as they were in sight. He was Fig Tree John's son and whenever any one mentioned him they called him Johnny. He was fourteen years old when the paving began and he was fifteen before it was finished. Most people would have said he was older. But fifteen years of brilliant sun, and an active life on foot and horseback across the floor of the desert from the Chocolate Mountains to the Santa Rosas, and simple food and good hours and no dissipation, had given him a physique beyond his years.

But the white civilization so close at hand and so accessible piqued more and more his interest. One day, a year or two before the road was paved, he sat beside an ironwood tree and watched the automobiles. There might be two or three of them in a few minutes. And then an hour might go by with only one car passing in that time. They were interesting things, and thrilling, and he had a great desire to ride in one. Sometimes they were painted in bright colors, but most of them were dark. He liked the bright ones best. But no matter what the color, they all threw a lot of dust and sand into the air and he was sure that riding one of these things must be more fun than riding the most spiritied horse.

That he might ever ride in one of these white man's speed wagons seemed impossible. After the road was paved there were many more of them and he thought about it a great deal and even considered going to one of the nearby date ranches and getting in one of these cars when nobody was looking. But then he wouldn't know what to do to make it run and probably the white men would be angry and might take a shot at him.

The opportunity, however, of riding in a white man's car came about more quickly and simply than he had expected. Agocho thought they were one of the white man's many inventions, all of which made the world more unpleasant to live in, and N'Chai Chidn gave up trying to talk to him about it. It was hard to talk to Agocho about such things anyway because there were no words in Apache to describe the things he wanted to say. And he knew so little English that it was impossible to talk very much in that language. Still, he was learning more. He was old enough to ride anywhere he pleased by himself, and once he had gone into Mecca and stayed there all day in front of the fat man's store listening to the white men and watching everything they did. Nobody molested him, in fact most of the white people paid no heed to him at all, and the round fat man called him "Fig Tree Junior," and "the young sprout," and "the chip off the old block" and other funny names. It must have been all right because the fat man smiled when he did it and nobody seemed to mind his being there. N'Chai Chidn didn't speak to anybody at all, but he listened and watched and learned a lot. He never said anything to Agocho about it because Agocho hated and mistrusted all white men and would have been angry if he thought his son had been in the white man's town all day.

For several days after that Agocho and N'Chai Chidn went hunting together. They went up into the Santa Rosas, across the ridge to what the white men called Clark's dry lake and around through the Borego country and the Vallecito Mountains and back to the Salton Sea by way of Kane Spring. About white men they said nothing and thought nothing, and it wasn't until they were almost home and were crossing the highway that the boy thought of automobiles again. It had been a good trip. They had the carcasses of a mountain lion and two mountain sheep and a burden basket stuffed with piñon. Agocho wanted the boy to be a good hunter. After all, he himself was nearing sixty and not as active as the boy. Together, with Agocho's skill and experience and N'Chai Chidn's youth and vigor they had all the requisites of the hunt.

Two days in camp, and the boy was ready for more activity. Agocho was not. He had plenty to eat and his only concern was to get some corn so that he could make tizwin. The boy knew where there was some corn and he said that he might be able to get it. He wasn't sure. Agocho didn't ask any questions, so the boy saddled up and rode north.

The date ranches now came down to a short distance from the clearing. It was only two miles north to Mack's ranch and one mile straight up the beach to Paul's property that had been set out in dates the year before. These were the nearest ranches, and between them and the clearing the country was still raw desert. Water below the surface of the ground and irrigation was the answer to successful date farming. Agocho's own property had a quantity of alkali soil around it or the white men would have found a means of getting him out before this.

N'Chai Chidn rode west to the highway and then north until he came to the Mack ranch. After his experience in Mecca he had no fear about boldly riding up to a ranch house. He felt that white people were not as dangerous as Agocho had led him to believe.

At the Mack ranch there was a Mexican youth named Jose who was perhaps twenty-one, and who was Mack's hired man and jack of all trades. Jose had seen N'Chai Chidn before, and while they had never spoken, they knew each other by sight. Jose had a wife and baby, and they lived in a little shack near the main house. As the Indian boy rode up he could see Jose moving about near a carpenter shop and tool shed. The water pump was making a chugging noise and Jose was busy beside the carpenter shop. He did not see the boy until he turned around. He started over toward the water pump, a wrench in his hand, and looked up quickly. The Indian sat on his horse and said nothing.

"Hola!" said Jose. "What you want, huh?"

"Hola," said N'Chai Chidn, believing that it was an English word.

Jose went to the water pump, placed the wrench on a nut, and slowly tightened it.

"Sì, you devil," he said. "Old son of a bitch. He go bust when I very busy."

He looked at N'Chai Chidn and grinned. "I know you," he said. "Usted es Juanito Fig Tree. Verdad?"

Juanito Fig Tree grinned back.

"Say, you listen to me," said Jose. "Maybe you like to work some. Maybe you like for to get little job."

Juanito Fig Tree didn't say yes or no.

"You get off caballo and I show you some work, muy pronto," said Jose. "I very busy. Mr. Mack he go Los Angeles and water pump go bust and I try all day to fix him and now very busy. Mucho trabajo y alguno trabajo para usted."

He picked up an ax and pointed to a pile of wood.

"I have too busy time to chop kindling for Mrs. Mack's stove. You chop him up. Sabe usted?"

Not far from the woodpile was Jose's Ford roadster. It was an old model and had seen a lot of service. But in an idle afternoon Jose had painted it a brilliant green. Johnny Fig Tree looked at the woodpile and the ax and the Ford. He understood that Jose wanted him to cut the wood, and he swung himself off his horse, tethered it to the tool shed, and said the single word "work."

"Bueno muchacho," said Jose, taking the ax and chopping a few pieces of the wood. Then, grinning broadly, he handed the ax to the Indian.

"Little pieces. Not too big," said Jose. "Chop it all and I give you something nice. What you want? Que quiere usted, Juanito?"

Johnny was looking at the Ford.

"Nice car," he said.

"Ho, no, no," said Jose. "I no give you the Ford car. Ford car cost plenty dinero. You like him?"

Johnny admired the Ford. He walked over toward it and looked it over carefully without getting too close to it. The Mexican was flattered by this admiration of his property.

"Say, I tell you what," said Jose. "I got to go to the store and buy new washers for that damn water pump. I let you ride to town and buy you a smoke if you cut up all that wood like a good Juanito. Sabe? You, me, we go ride in Ford after you chop woodpile."

He pantomimed steering the Ford and made a buzzing noise with his mouth as if he were spinning the engine.

"You and me in the Ford," he said.

Johnny got the idea. It was exciting. Certainly he was willing to chop a little wood. He took another look at the green roadster and then went to work on the woodpile with a great display of energy. Sticks flew up in the air and chips and splinters went flying in all directions. Jose was a friend and he wanted to make a trade. He wanted that wood chopped into pieces and into pieces it was going. He threw the ax over his shoulder and brought it down with terrific force. Blow after blow he struck, and Jose, satisfied with this exhibition, went back to work in the tool shed.

For something more than half an hour Jose worked in the tool shed. At the end of that time his assistant was still cutting wood, but his pace had slowed down considerably, and the willing grin with which he had started had changed to a look of persistent determination. Sweat was standing out on his forehead and running down his neck. He gritted his teeth and swung the ax again. Jose was pleased to see so much wood cut. Probably he wouldn't have to cut any to-morrow.

"Bueno muchacho," he said. "Bastante."

Johnny looked up. He had done enough and he had decided that for himself. He swung the ax over his head and hurled it twenty feet away.

"Ee-yah," he said, breathing deeply.

"Careful that ax," said Jose. "I got to use him again. Now we go to town. Say, you work good."

Jose stepped into the Ford and beckoned to Johnny to get in beside him. Johnny did so, looking at everything with great interest, while Jose stepped on the starter, pulled the choke, and the engine opened up in a series of loud explosions.

"Gettin' warmed up," said Jose, cheerfully. "Damn good Ford car."

He backed it around in a half circle, threw in the clutch, and they were off with a jerk that snapped Johnny's head back. Jose's idea of driving was to grip the steering wheel tightly and step on the gas. He maintained the same speed whether the road was rough or smooth. They bounced along the ranch road, hit the highway with a thud and rattle and then clattered along on the hard surface at thirty miles an hour.

"Paid fifty dollars for this Ford car," Jose said, raising his voice above the rattle of the engine, "and paid thirty more dollars gettin' it all nice. Damn nice now."

Johnny didn't say anything. He was thrilled beyond his limited vocabulary. Never had the world raced past him like this. Never had a horse been as smooth under him as Jose's Ford car. He sat straight in the seat and let the wind blow on him. It was an exciting and delightful experience.

About a mile from Mecca an element of danger appeared, and for a moment Johnny was frightened. Another car was coming toward them from the opposite direction. That strip of highway wasn't very wide and Jose didn't seem to see the oncoming car. At least he paid no attention to it whatever. And just as Johnny had almost decided to leap out of the Ford the approaching car whisked by in the flash of an instant so close that the two drivers could have leaned out and touched hands as they passed. Johnny looked back at the other car rapidly disappearing in the rear and then he looked at Jose. But Jose seemed to take it all as a matter of course and nothing at all unusual or worth mentioning.

Presently they banged across the railroad tracks and came to a stop before Petterman's store. Jose climbed out of the car and went into the store. Johnny didn't move. He was proud to sit in a white man's Ford and calmly wait to be driven back to the Mack ranch. He felt very important and he admired Jose who was able to come and go at will in so handsome a vehicle. He hoped that the white people in the town might see him and think that the car was his. He wished that he were as smart as Jose and able to own a fine car.

In a few minutes Jose came out of the store. Mr. Petterman wasn't in sight and Johnny was sorry because he wanted Mr. Petterman to see him in the car. Jose had a paper bag with some washers in it and two packs of cigarettes. He gave one pack to Johnny and tore off the top of his own pack. Then he struck a match and lit a cigarette for himself, and gave the packet of matches to Johnny.

Again Jose spun the car around in reverse and again they started off with a jolt. Johnny knew what to do with the cigarettes for he had seen white men use them before. He had a difficult time lighting a cigarette in the moving car, and several times the matches burnt his fingers. Finally he succeeded, but as he did so the Ford was banging over the railroad tracks and Johnny bit off the end of the cigarette. The tobacco flakes got in his mouth and the wind made the cigarette burn up one side. It was not as pleasant a sensation as he expected and he looked at Jose who kept his cigarette going nicely and hanging loosely between his lips. Johnny took a couple of long puffs and swallowed some pieces of loose tobacco and found bits of paper on his tongue. He became disgusted and threw the thing away. Then he looked back to see where it landed, but the Ford was spinning along so rapidly that his eyes could not follow it. He enjoyed every bit of the ride back to the ranch house, and this time, when an oncoming car sped past them, he was not afraid of a collision.

Jose swung the car off the highway, bumped and rattled across the sandy road, and came to a stop right beside the tool shed where Johnny's horse watched them arrive with signs of alarm.

For the rest of the afternoon Jose was busy about the ranch. He turned the water into the date palms, and slowly it made its way along the shallow ditches and furrows until it had flooded most of the grove. He returned to the tool shed and did several mysterious things with tools that Johnny had never seen before. He went to the corral and fed and watered the stock. He was a very active Mexican boy and Johnny was greatly impressed with his many duties and the ease and importance with which he carried them off. He had come to admire Jose very much.

Toward sunset he untied his horse and rode back to the clearing. It had been one of the most interesting days of his life.

*   *   *   *   *

One day . . . when he was starting out alone for the Santa Rosas, he changed his course and rode north along the highway. Several cars passed him and one of the drivers waved to him.

At the entrance of the Mack ranch he turned in. It would be nice to see that Jose again and have another look at that Ford car. Jose was sitting in the shade doing nothing. His wife was washing some clothes near their little shack and the baby was crawling around on the ground.

"Hallo, Juanito," said Jose.

Juanito smiled and dismounted.

"No work to-day," said Jose. "Plenty time."

Johnny said nothing.

"Say, you didn't think I give you that ax last week for workin' here, did you?"

"No," said Johnny.

"I can't find that damn ax no place. Beat hell where he go to."

"Sure," said Johnny. He stood beside his horse and looked at Jose.

Jose lay almost flat on his back with his knees raised and his hat well down over his eyes. He felt lazy and comfortable and happy. He had nothing to do for half an hour until Mr. Mack called him and then they would go to work at pollenizing the dates. He carried on a desultory conversation with Johnny and he thought that Johnny wasn't very bright.

"Cuantos años?" he finally asked, and when Johnny said nothing he asked in English, "How old are you?"

Johnny didn't know what to answer. He was sixteen but he didn't know it.

"You're kinda dumb," Jose said. "Didn't you go to school?"

"No," said Johnny.

"Don't you know nothing?" Jose asked.

"No," said Johnny.

"If I was you I'd go to school and learn something. Reading and writing. Everybody has to read and write. Why don't you go to school and learn something, huh?"

"No sabe," said Johnny.

Jose laughed. He rolled over on one side and rested his head on his arm and elbow. He chuckled at Johnny, and presently he spat, and then spoke some more.

"You're never gonna get no place," he said. "You're never gonna get any money, or any wife, or any Ford car. I went to school and now I got a job and wife and a Ford car. I speak English just like American and I'm the best dancer in the valley. You don't know nothing."

Johnny didn't understand all of this but he understood the reproach and the criticism. He felt that Jose was a superior person and he envied him.

"You don't know the first lesson they say in school," said Jose. "Who was the father of your country? Can you tell me who was the father of your country?"

"No," said Johnny.

"Everybody knows that," Jose said. "I know it. My wife knows it. Mr. Mack knows it. Everybody in the valley knows who was the father of your country. Everybody except you."

"Who," said Johnny.

Jose laughed again.

"George Washington," he said, and sat up. "George Washington. You don't know it. George Washington."

"George Washington," said Johnny.

Then Jose rolled on the ground in glee, but Johnny failed to see anything funny in the strange words "George Washington." He didn't like to be laughed at. This place wasn't amusing him at all. He swung himself onto his horse and rode away. Jose called something after him but he couldn't hear what it was. He went back to the highway and rode on north.

Instead of crossing the railroad tracks and going into Mecca he rode further north than he had ever been before, and a few miles brought him to Coachella. He was surprised to find this town larger than Mecca. It was almost in the center of the valley and the main highway intersected its one main street which ran for a quarter of a mile from the highway to the railroad. Where Mecca had ten or a dozen buildings, Coachella had four or five blocks of houses and stores. Johnny thought it very impressive, and if he hadn't seen Mecca and white men before this he would not have ridden into Coachella.

There were a number of people in the main street and a dozen automobiles standing around the store buildings. There were white men and there were darker men who were Mexicans like Jose, but nevertheless white men, and there were one or two men who were darker still and different from the white men in many ways; and while he recognized the superficial differences of the darker men he didn't know that they were Indians like himself and that they were Cahuillas from the San Jacinto Mountains. Indians or not, they were strangers to him, and he classified all of the people he saw under the grouping of white men.

He saw a store that was something like the fat man's in Mecca and he rode up to it and dismounted. It had a window full of clothing and canned goods and saddles and rifles and revolvers. It was very interesting to look at, and when he tired of that he sat down on the curb beside his horse and watched everything that went on in the main street and listened to everything that was said by the people who passed within earshot. Sometimes people stopped in front of the store and talked and when they did he found he could understand a lot of the words if they didn't talk too fast.

He tried to think of the significance of Jose's words to him, and he understood that all of these people were saying and doing a lot of things that he knew nothing about. Jose had been right. He didn't know very much. He had never been to a place called school. Without a doubt every one of these people knew that the father of the country was George Washington. But now he knew that, too, and if he kept his ears open he would probably learn everything that they knew. Yet his own father thought that these people were all wrong and shouldn't be listened to, and his father knew everything. Perhaps he ought to ride home and forget this. But no, he was here, and he might just as well sit here for a while. If this weren't right he could forget it later.

For the rest of the day he sat on the curb in Coachella and let the white civilization explain itself to him in whatever way it could. Late in the afternoon he got up and mounted the horse and rode out of town. It was a day of wonder—a curious world indeed. He decided to try to talk to his father about it again and to see if his father couldn't give him a better idea of just what it all meant.

There was no use. Agocho was sullen and angry because he had gone to Coachella. He couldn't understand why the boy had any curiosity about it at all. He hoped he would outgrow it. He told him that white men would ruin his life and make a slave out of him. He didn't want that, did he? No. Then leave the white men alone.

The boy wanted to know what was meant by school. Agocho had an idea of the meaning even though he had never been in a school. There had been a government school in the White River Reservation and he knew that the young Apaches went there and learned a lot of useless things.

To the boy there was something unconvincing about Agocho's adamant remarks. That white world was there and it didn't care whether you came to it or not. But Agocho's world was here and it insisted that you belonged to it. He wondered how wise Agocho would be in the white world. He wondered for the first time in his life if his father were really the greatest man on earth, which he had always supposed him to be. For the first time he questioned it. And in questioning it a test occurred to him. Even while Agocho was talking the boy interrupted him in English.

"Who is the father of your country?" he asked.

Agocho stopped speaking. N'Chai Chidn was learning a lot of white talk. He must find a way to stop it.

The boy was waiting intensely. That question meant a great deal. Everybody in the white world knew the answer. It was the first thing they learned. If Agocho knew it too, then he was wise, completely wise, not only in the white world but in his own world. If he could give the answer to that he must be right about everything.

Agocho looked at him.

"Who is the father of your country?" the boy asked again.

Agocho didn't know what he meant. The question had no meaning. Mangus Colorado and Geronimo had been the greatest warriors. And the Goddess, Ste-na-tlih-a, had conceived two Gods, one by the sun and one by the sea. There was no father unless it be those two powers.

He looked at the boy and said in Apache, "The fire and the water."

The intensity left the boy's face. The answer was a disappointment. An idol had crashed and he felt sorry.

"Nope," he said, in newly acquired English, "George Washington."

(1935)

From

THE SURROUNDED
by D'Arcy McNickle

In the old days the Salish people held a great dance in midsummer, just as the sun reached its highest point. They would come together from all parts of the country; all branches of the nation would be there; their tents would be scattered over miles of prairie land. At night their camp fires would be like a host of stars fallen out of heaven. This dance was the expression of their exultation at being alive, it sang of their pride, their conquests, their joys. For them the sun at its height was the most favored time of the year, as they were the most favored children of "Grandfather Sun." In this dance only the toughest and longest enduring took part, because it was a supreme test of strength; they danced until exhaustion struck them down and no one wanted to be the first to drop. It was shameful not to last long enough to express what was felt.

Such a dance could not be tolerated in later years. Its barbarous demands on strength offended those who came to manage the affairs of the Indians in their own homes. There was nothing wrong with the dance in itself but it ought to be kept within reasonable limits. If the Indians wished to express their joy for, say, ten hours a day and then rest, like a factory or office worker, that would be all right. They could go on dancing for as many days as they liked on that arrangement, only they ought not to lose too much time at it. It was probably a fair arrangement because, though the dance was curtailed, so was the exultation it expressed. They decided to dance while they could. Some dances had been stopped completely.

There was the scalp dance of long ago. That of course had to be stopped at once. Maybe it wasn't a beautiful dance but it had its purpose. It took place after a battle, if there were any enemy trophies to celebrate over. It was like a "grand review" without the finer points. The dance wasn't held immediately upon the return of the warriors because those who had returned with scalps had to have a few days to talk about what they had done and point to the scalps they had taken. The scalps were hung up for display like captured flags, then after a few days when they began to "break down" they were thrown into the dust and the dance began. This dance was performed by the women. They simply stamped upon the scalps and uttered insulting language. It was a dance of vengeance and of exultation over the prowess of the men. A dance like that had to be stopped.

Another of the old-time dances which had offended the Indians' guardians was the marriage dance, which in its way was a pleasant performance. The young people used to enjoy it and the old wiseheads would look on and reflect pleasantly on how they had enjoyed it in their time. In this dance the young unmarried women formed a circle about the drummers; they linked their arms together and sidestepped round and round, and they kept up a certain song. If a young man wanted one of those girls he went with one or two friends, for encouragement perhaps, and broke through the chain. Within the circle, he waited for his choice to come opposite him, then he stepped forward and placed a small stick on her shoulder, and then it was up to the girl. If she did not want him she made a face, shrugged her shoulder and let the stick fall off. At that everybody laughed and the suitor would run off and perhaps would not be seen for quite a while. If she accepted him, she bent her head sideways until her cheek rested on the stick and held it in place. Then he would take her by the hand and they would go to his lodge, if he was old enough to have one of his own;

or they simply went to the brush. A dance like that didn't hurt anybody but they had to give it up.

This dance which was being held on the Fourth of July was a survival of the old midsummer dance. It was no longer an endurance test and there was not much exultation expressed by it, but the Indians enjoyed it because it brought many of them together and for a while they could forget how bad it was at home.

Before life changed for the Salish people they would not have begun a ceremony like the midsummer dance without first having met and cleansed themselves. All old scores would have been settled, the pipe would have been smoked between men who had quarreled, and restitution would have been made of any damages which had been inflicted upon another. And finally the lash would have been laid on anyone who was guilty of wrongdoing. (No one could now remember exactly what was punishable with the lash in those days, because after the Fathers came many new "crimes" were added, such as creating a disturbance at church or prayers.) The "whip covered the fault."

Whipping, like the scalp and marriage dance, was now a thing of the past. At first the practice was denounced because it was reported that the Jesuits had introduced it among the innocent Indians. When that story was proved false, the practice was still denounced, and finally abolished, as being too barbarous. The guardians might not always know why they objected to a native custom, but if they objected it didn't make much difference what the reason was.

(1936)

MR. K★A★P★L★A★N, THE COMPARATIVE, AND THE SUPERLATIVE
by Leonard Q. Ross

For two weeks Mr. Parkhill had been delaying the inescapable: Mr. Kaplan, like the other students in the beginners' grade of the American Night Preparatory School for Adults, would have to present a composition for class analysis. All the students had had their turn writing the assignment on the board, a composition of óne hundred words, entitled "My Job." Now only Mr. Kaplan's rendition remained.

It would be more accurate to say Mr. K★A★P★L★A★N's rendition of the assignment remained, for even in thinking of that distinguished student, Mr. Parkhill saw the image of his unmistakable signature, in all its red-blue-green glory. The multicolored characters were more than a trademark; they were an assertion of individuality, a symbol of singularity, a proud expression of Mr. Kaplan's Inner Self. To Mr. Parkhill, the signature took on added meaning because it was associated with the man who had said his youthful ambition had been to become "a physician and sergeant," the Titan who had declined the verb "to fail": "fail, failed, bankropt."

One night, after the two weeks' procrastination, Mr. Parkhill decided to face the worst. "Mr. Kaplan, I think it's your turn to—er—write your composition on the board."

Mr. Kaplan's great, buoyant smile grew more great and more buoyant. "My!" he exclaimed. He rose, looked around at the class proudly as if surveying the blessed who were to witness a linguistic *tour de force,* stumbled over Mrs. Moskowitz's feet with a polite "Vould you be so kindly?" and took his place at the blackboard. There he rejected several pieces of chalk critically, nodded to Mr. Parkhill—it was a nod of distinct reassurance—and then printed in firm letters:

My Job A Cotter In Dress Faktory
Comp. by
H★Y★

"You need not write your name on the board," interrupted Mr. Parkhill quickly. "Er—to save time . . ."

Mr. Kaplan's face expressed astonishment. "Podden me, Mr. Pockheel. But de name is by me *pot* of mine composition."

"Your name is *part* of the composition?" asked Mr. Parkhill in an anxious tone.

"Yas*sir!*" said Mr. Kaplan with dignity. He printed the rest of H★Y★M★A★N K★A★P★L★A★N for all to see and admire. You could tell it was a disappointment for him not to have colored chalk for this performance. In pale white the elegance of his work was dissipated. The name, indeed, seemed unreal, the letters stark, anemic, almost denuded.

His brow wrinkled and perspiring, Mr. Kaplan wrote the saga of A Cotter In Dress Faktory on the board, with much scratching of the chalk and an undertone of sound. Mr. Kaplan repeated each word to himself softly, as if trying to give to its spelling some of the flavor and originality of his pronunciation. The smile on the face of Mr. Kaplan had taken on something beatific and imperishable: it was his first experience at the blackboard; it was his moment of glory. He seemed to be writing more slowly than necessary as if to prolong the ecstasy of his Hour. When he had finished he said "Hau Kay" with distinct regret in his voice, and sat down. Mr. Parkhill observed the composition in all its strange beauty:

My Job A Cotter In Dress Faktory
Comp. by
H★Y★M★A★N K★A★P★L★A★N

Shakespere is saying what fulls man is and I am feeling just the same way when I am thinking about mine job a cotter in Dress Faktory on 38 st. by 7 av. For why should we slafing in dark place by laktric lights and all kinds hot for $30 or maybe $36 with overtime, for Boss who is fat and driving in fency automobil? I ask! Because we are the deprassed workers of world. And are being exployted. By Bosses. In mine shop is no difference. Oh how bad is laktric light, oh how is all kinds hot. And when I am telling Foreman should be better conditions he hollers, Kaplan you redical!!

At this point a glazed look came into Mr. Parkhill's eyes, but he read on.

So I keep still and work by bad light and always hot. But somday will the workers making Bosses work! And then Kaplan will give to them bad laktric and positively no windows for the air should come in! So they can know what it means to slafe! Kaplan will make Foreman a cotter like he is. And give the most bad dezigns to cot out. Justice.
    Mine job is cotting Dress dezigns.
T-H-E E-N-D

Mr. Parkhill read the amazing document over again. His eyes, glazed but a moment before, were haunted now. It was true: spelling, diction, sentence structure, punctuation, capitalization, the use of the present perfect for the present—all true.

"Is planty mistakes, I s'pose," suggested Mr. Kaplan modestly.

"Y-yes . . . yes, there are many mistakes."

"Dat's because I'm tryink to give *dip ideas*," said Mr. Kaplan with the sigh of those who storm heaven.

Mr. Parkhill girded his mental loins. "Mr. Kaplan—er—your composition doesn't really meet the assignment. You haven't described your *job*, what you *do*, what work is."

"Vell, it's not soch a interastink jop," said Mr. Kaplan.

"Your composition is not a simple exposition. It's more of a—well, an *essay* on your *attitude.*"

"Oh, fine!" cried Mr. Kaplan with enthusiasm.

"No, no," said Mr. Parkhill hastily. "The assignment was *meant* to be a composition. You see, we must begin with simple exercises before we try—er—more philosophical essays."

Mr. Kaplan nodded with resignation. "So naxt time should be no ideas, like abot Shaksbeer? Should be only *fects?*"

"Y-yes. No ideas, only—er—facts."

You could see by Mr. Kaplan's martyred smile that his wings, like those of an eagle, were being clipped.

"And Mr. Kaplan—er—why do you use 'Kaplan' in the body of your composition? Why don't you say *'I* will make the foreman a cutter' instead of *'Kaplan* will make the foreman a cutter'?"

Mr. Kaplan's response was instantaneous. "I'm so glad you eskink me dis! Ha! I'm usink 'Keplen' in de composition for plain and tsimple rizzon:

becawss I didn't vant de reader should tink I am *prajudiced* against de foreman, so I said it more like abot a strenger: *'Keplen* vill make de foreman a cotter!' "

In the face of this subtle passion for objectivity, Mr. Parkhill was silent. He called for corrections. A forest of hands went up. Miss Mitnick pointed out errors in spelling, the use of capital letters, punctuation; Mr. Norman Bloom corrected several more words, rearranged sentences, and said, "Woikers is exployted with an *'i,'* not *'y'* as Kaplan makes"; Miss Caravello changed "fulls" to "fools," and declared herself uncertain as to the validity of the word "Justice" standing by itself in "da smalla da sentence"; Mr. Sam Pinsky said he was sure Mr. Kaplan meant *"opprassed* voikers of de voild, not *deprassed,* aldough dey are deprassed *too,"* to which Mr. Kaplan replied, "So ve bote got right, no? Don' *chenge* 'deprassed,' only *add* 'opprassed.' "

Then Mr. Parkhill went ahead with his own corrections, changing tenses, substituting prepositions, adding the definite article. Through the whole barrage Mr. Kaplan kept shaking his head, murmuring "Mine gootness!" each time a correction was made. But he smiled all the while. He seemed to be proud of the very number of errors he had made; of the labor to which the class was being forced in his service; of the fact that his *ideas,* his creation, could survive so concerted an onslaught. And as the composition took more respectable form, Mr. Kaplan's smile grew more expansive.

"Now, class," said Mr. Parkhill, "I want to spend a few minutes explaining something about adjectives. Mr. Kaplan uses the phrase—er—'most bad.' That's wrong. There is a word for 'most bad.' It is what we call the superlative form of 'bad.' " Mr. Parkhill explained the use of the positive, comparative, and superlative forms of the adjective. " 'Tall, taller, tallest.' 'Rich, richer, richest.' Is that clear? Well then, let us try a few others."

The class took up the game with enthusiasm. Miss Mitnick submitted "dark, darker, darkest"; Mr. Scymzak, "fat, fatter, fattest."

"But there are certain exceptions to this general form," Mr. Parkhill went on. The class, which had long ago learned to respect that gamin, The Exception to the Rule, nodded solemnly. "For instance, we don't say 'good, gooder, goodest,' do we?"

"No, sir!" cried Mr. Kaplan impetuously. " 'Good, gooder, good*est?'* Ha! It's to leff!"

"We say that X, for example, is good. Y, however, is—?" Mr. Parkhill arched an eyebrow interrogatively.

"Batter!" said Mr. Kaplan.

"Right! And Z is—?"

"High-cless!"

Mr. Parkhill's eyebrow dropped. "No," he said sadly.

"Not high-cless?" asked Mr. Kaplan incredulously. For him there was no word more superlative.

"No, Mr. Kaplan, the word is 'best.' And the word 'bad,' of which you

tried to use the superlative form . . . It isn't *bad, badder, baddest.'* It's 'bad'
. . . and what's the comparative? Anyone?''

"Worse,'' volunteered Mr. Bloom.

"Correct! And the superlative? Z is the—?''

" 'Worse' also?'' asked Mr. Bloom hesitantly. It was evident he had never
distinguished the fine difference in sound between the comparative and superlative forms of "bad.''

"No, Mr. Bloom. It's not the *same* word, although it—er—sounds a good
deal like it. Anyone? Come, come. It isn't hard. X is *bad,* Y is *worse,* and Z
is the—?''

An embarrassed silence fell upon the class, which, apparently, had been
using "worse'' for both the comparative and superlative all along. Miss Mitnick blushed and played with her pencil. Mr. Bloom shrugged, conscious that
he had given his all. Mr. Kaplan stared at the board, his mouth open, a desperate concentration in his eye.

"Bad—worse. What is the word you use when you mean 'most bad'?''

"Aha!'' cried Mr. Kaplan suddenly. When Mr. Kaplan cried "Aha!'' it
signified that a great light had fallen on him. "I know! De exect void! So easy!
Ach! I should know dat ven I was wridink! *Bad—voise—*''

"Yes, Mr. Kaplan!'' Mr. Parkhill was definitely excited.

"Rotten!''

Mr. Parkhill's eyes glazed once more, unmistakably. He shook his
head dolorously, as if he had suffered a personal hurt. And as he wrote
"w-o-r-s-t'' on the blackboard there ran through his head, like a sad refrain,
this latest manifestation of Mr. Kaplan's peculiar genius: "bad—worse—rotten; bad—worse . . .''

(1937)

From

CHRIST IN CONCRETE
by Pietro Di Donato

March whistled stinging snow against the brick walls and up the gaunt girders.
Geremio, the foreman, swung his arms about, and gaffed the men on.

Old Nick, the "Lean,'' stood up from over a dust-flying brick pile, and
tapped the side of his nose.

"Master Geremio, the devil himself could not break his tail any harder than we here."

Burly Vincenzo of the walrus moustache, and known as the "Snout-nose," let fall the chute door of the concrete hopper and sang over the Lean's direction: "Mari-Annina's belly and the burning night will make of me once more a milk-mouthed stripling lad . . ."

The Lean loaded his wheelbarrow and spat furiously. "Sons of two-legged dogs . . . despised of even the devil himself! Work! Sure! For America beautiful will eat you and spit your bones into the earth's hole! Work!" And with that his wiry frame pitched the barrow violently over the rough floor.

Snoutnose waved his head to and fro and with mock pathos wailed, "Sing on, oh guitar of mine . . ."

Short, cherry-faced Joe Chiappa, the scaffoldman, paused with hatchet in hand and tenpenny spike sticking out from small dice-like teeth to tell the Lean as he went by, in a voice that all could hear, "Ah, father of countless chicks, the old age is a carrion!"

Geremio chuckled and called to him: "Hey, little Joe, who are you to talk? You and big-titted Cola can't even hatch an egg, whereas the Lean has just to turn the doorknob of his bedroom and old Philomena becomes a balloon!"

Coarse throats tickled and mouths opened wide in laughter.

Mike, the "Barrel-mouth," pretended he was talking to himself and yelled out in his best English . . . he was always speaking English while the rest carried on in their native Italian: "I don't know myself, but somebodys whose gotta bigga buncha keeds and he alla times talka from somebody's elsa!"

Geremio knew it was meant for him and he laughed. "On the tomb of Saint Pimplelegs, this little boy my wife is giving me next week shall be the last! Eight hungry Christians to feed is enough for any man."

Joe Chiappa nodded to the rest. "Sure, Master Geremio had a telephone call from the next bambino. Yes, it told him it had a little bell there instead of a rosebush . . . It even told him its name!"

"Laugh, laugh all of you," returned Geremio, "but I tell you that all my kids must be boys so that they some day will be big American builders. And then I'll help them to put the gold away in the basements for safe keeping!"

A great din of riveting shattered the talk among the fast-moving men. Geremio added a handful of "Honest" tobacco to his corncob, puffed strongly, and cupped his hands around the bowl for a bit of warmth. The chill day caused him to shiver, and he thought to himself, "Yes, the day is cold, cold . . . but who am I to complain when the good Christ himself was crucified?

"Pushing the job is all right (when has it been otherwise in my life?) but this job frightens me. I feel the building wants to tell me something; just as one Christian to another. I don't like this. Mr. Murdin tells me, 'Push it up!' That's all he knows. I keep telling him that the underpinnings should be doubled and the old material removed from the floors, but he keeps the inspector drunk and

. . . 'Hey, Ashes-ass! Get away from under that pilaster! Don't pull the old work. Push it way from you or you'll have a nice present for Easter if the wall falls on you!' . . . Well, with the help of God I'll see this job through. It's not my first, nor the . . . 'Hey, Patsy number two! Put more cement in that concrete; we're putting up a building, not an Easter cake!' "

Patsy hurled his shovel to the floor and gesticulated madly. "The padrone Murdin-sa tells me, 'Too much! Lil' bit is plenty!' And you tell me I'm stingy! The rotten building can fall after I leave!"

Six floors below, the contractor called: "Hey Geremio! Is your gang of dagos dead?"

Geremio cautioned to the men: "On your toes, boys. If he writes out slips, someone won't have big eels on the Easter table."

The Lean cursed that "the padrone could take the job and shove it . . . !"

Curly-headed Sandino, the roguish, pigeon-toed scaffoldman, spat a clod of tobacco-juice and hummed to his own music.

"Yes, certainly yes to your face, master padrone . . . and behind, this to you and all your kind!"

The day, like all days, came to an end. Calloused and bruised bodies sighed, and numb legs shuffled towards shabby railroad flats. . . .

"Ah, *bella casa mio*. Where my little freshlets of blood, and my good woman await me. Home where my broken back will not ache so. Home where midst the monkey chatter of my piccolinos I will float off to blessed slumber with my feet on the chair and the head on the wife's soft full breast."

These great child-hearted ones leave each other without words or ceremony, and as they ride and walk home, a great pride swells the breast. . . .

"Blessings to Thee, oh Jesus. I have fought winds and cold. Hand to hand I have locked dumb stones in place and the great building rises. I have earned a bit of bread for me and mine."

The mad day's brutal conflict is forgiven, and strained limbs prostrate themselves so that swollen veins can send the yearning blood coursing and pulsating deliciously as though the body mountained leaping streams.

The job alone remained behind . . . and yet, they too, having left the bigger part of their lives with it. The cold ghastly beast, the Job, stood stark, the eerie March wind wrapping it in sharp shadows of falling dusk.

That night was a crowning point in the life of Geremio. He bought a house! Twenty years he had helped to mould the New World. And now he was to have a house of his own! What mattered that it was no more than a wooden shack? It was his own!

He had proudly signed his name and helped Annunziata to make her X on the wonderful contract that proved them owners. And she was happy to think that her next child, soon to come, would be born under their own rooftree. She heard the church chimes, and cried to the children: "Children, to bed! It is near midnight. And remember, shut-mouth to the *paesanos!* Or they will send the evil eye to our new home even before we put foot."

The children scampered off to the icy yellow bedroom where three slept in one bed and three in the other. Coltishly and friskily they kicked about under the covers; their black iron-cotton stockings not removed . . . what! and freeze the peanut-little toes?

Said Annunziata, "The children are so happy, Geremio; let them be, for even I would a Tarantella dance." And with that she turned blushing. He wanted to take her on her word. She patted his hands, kissed them, and whispered, "Our children will dance for us . . . in the American style some day."

Geremio cleared his throat and wanted to sing. "Yes, with joy I could sing in a richer feeling than the great Caruso." He babbled little old country couplets and circled the room until the tenant below tapped the ceiling.

Annunziata whispered: "Geremio, to bed and rest. Tomorrow is a day for great things . . . and the day on which our Lord died for us."

The children were now hard asleep. Heads under the cover, over . . . moist noses whistling, and little damp legs entwined.

In bed Geremio and Annunziata clung closely to each other. They mumbled figures and dates until fatigue stilled their thoughts. And with chubby Johnnie clutching fast his bottle and warmed between them . . . life breathed heavily, and dreams entertained in far, far worlds, the nation-builder's brood.

But Geremio and Annunziata remained for a while staring into darkness, silently.

"Geremio?"

"Yes?"

"This job you are now working. . . ."

"So?"

"You used always to tell about what happened on the jobs . . . who was jealous, and who praised. . . ."

"You should know by now that all work is the same. . . ."

"Geremio the month you have been on this job, you have not spoken a word about the work . . . And I have felt that I am walking in a dream. Is the work dangerous? Why don't you answer . . . ?"

Job loomed up damp, shivery grey. Its giant members waiting.

Builders quietly donned their coarse robes, and waited.

Geremio's whistle rolled back into his pocket and the symphony of struggle began.

Trowel rang through brick and slashed mortar rivets were machine-gunned fast with angry grind Patsy number one check Patsy number two check the Lean three check Vincenzo four steel bellowed back at hammer donkey engines coughed purple Ashes-ass Pietro fifteen chisel point intoned stone thin steel whirred and wailed through wood liquid stone flowed with dull rasp through iron veins and hoist screamed through space Carmine the Fat twenty-four and Giacomo Sangini check . . . The multitudinous voices of a civilization rose from the surroundings and welded with the efforts of the Job.

To the intent ear, Nation was voicing her growing pains, but, hands that create are attached to warm hearts and not to calculating minds. The Lean as he fought his burden on looked forward to only one goal, the end. The barrow he pushed, he did not love. The stones that brutalized his palms, he did not love. The great God Job, he did not love. He felt a searing bitterness and a fathomless consternation at the queer consciousness that inflicted the ever mounting weight of structure that he HAD TO! HAD TO! raise above his shoulders! When, when and where would the last stone be? Never . . . did he bear his toil with the rhythm of song! Never . . . did his gasping heart knead the heavy mortar with lifting melody! A voice within him spoke a wordless language.

The language of worn oppression and the despair of realizing that his life had been left on brick piles. And always, there had been hunger and her bastard, the fear of hunger.

Murdin bore down upon Geremio from behind and shouted:

"Goddamnit, Geremio, if you're givin' the men two hours off today with pay, why the hell are they draggin' their tails? And why don't you turn that skinny old Nick loose, and put a young wop in his place?"

"Now, listen-a to me. Mister Murdin——"

"Don't give me that! And bear in mind that there are plenty of good barefoot men in the streets who'll jump for a day's pay!"

"Padrone—padrone, the underpinning gotta be made safe and——"

"Lissenyawopbastard! If you don't like it, you know what you can do!"

(1939)

From

MY COUSIN DIKRAN, THE ORATOR
by William Saroyan

Twenty years ago, in the San Joaquin Valley, the Armenians used to regard oratory as the greatest, the noblest, the most important, one might say the *only*, art. About ninety-two per cent of the vineyardists around Fresno, by actual count, believed that any man who could make a speech was a cultured man. This was so, I imagine after all these years, because the vineyardists themselves were so ineffective at speechmaking, so self-conscious about it, so embarrassed, and so profoundly impressed by public speakers who could get up on a platform, adjust spectacles on their noses, look at their pocket watches, cough politely, and, beginning quietly, lift their voices to a roar that shook the farmers to the roots and made them know the speaker was educated.

What language! What energy! What wisdom! What magnificent roaring! the farmers said to themselves.

The farmers, assembled in the basement of one or another of the three churches, or in the Civic Auditorium, trembled with awe, wiped the tears from their eyes, blew their noses, and, momentarily overcome, donated as much money as they could afford. On some occasions, such as when money was being raised for some especially intimate cause, the farmers, in donating money, would stand up in the auditorium and cry out, Mgerdich Kasabian, his wife Araxie, his three sons, Gourken, Sirak, and Toumas—fifty cents! and sit down amid thunderous applause, not so much for the sum of money donated as for the magnificent manner of speaking, and the excellent and dramatic pronunciation of the fine old-country names: Mgerdich, Araxie, Gourken, Sirak, Toumas.

In this matter of speaking and donating money, the farmers competed with one another. If a farmer did not get up and publicly make his announcement like a man—well, then, the poor fellow! Neither money nor the heart to get up fearlessly and throw away the trembling in his soul! Because of this competition, a farmer unable to donate money (but with every impulse in the world to help the cause), would sit nervously in shame year after year, and then finally, with the arrival of better days, leap to his feet, look about the auditorium furiously, and shout, Gone are the days of poverty for this tribe from the lovely city of Dikranagert—the five Pampalonian brothers—twenty-five cents! and go home with his head high, and his heart higher. Poor? In the old days, yes. But no more. (And the five enormous men would look at one another with family pride, and push their sons before them—with affection, of course; that strange Near-Eastern, Oriental affection that came from delight in no longer being humiliated in the eyes of one's countrymen.)

No farmer was prouder, however, than when his son, at school, at church, at a picnic, or anywhere, got up and made a speech.

The boy! the farmer would shout at his eighty-eight-year-old father. Listen to him! It's Vahan, my son, *your* grandson—eleven years old. He's talking about Europe.

The grandfather would shake his head and wonder what it was all about, a boy of eleven so serious and so well-informed, talking about Europe. The old man scarcely would know where Europe was, although he would know he had visited Havre, in France, on his way to America. Perhaps Havre—perhaps that was it. *Yevroba.* Europe. But what in the world could be the matter with Havre suddenly—to make the boy so tense and excited? Ahkh, the old man would groan, it is all beyond me. I don't remember. It was a pleasant city on the sea, with ships.

The women would be overjoyed and full of amazement at themselves, the mothers. They would look about at one another, nodding, shaking their heads, and after ten minutes of the boy's talking in English, which they couldn't understand, they would burst into sweet silent tears because it was all so amazing and wonderful—little Berjie, only yesterday a baby who couldn't speak two words of Armenian, let alone English, on a platform, speaking, swinging his arms, pointing a finger, now at the ceiling, now west, now south, now north, and occasionally at his heart.

(1940)

From

THE FREE MAN
by Conrad Richter

His real name was Henry Dellicker, but for fifty years Pennsylvania knew him as Henry Free—or Frey, as he was called in the dialect. Scotch and English settlers along the West Branch boiled his tea. The Welsh and Irish on the North Branch shot his lead into game and man. His flour and iron jolted on the backs of horse trains over the rocky paths of the Alleghenies and down to the Ohio shore, but his Pennsylvania Dutch neighbors knew him best, for they dealt and joked with him over his counters summer and winter, rain in and snow out, from one year's end to another.

Not too far from Reading town and not too far from what had once been Harris's Ferry, his solid little empire of limestone buildings stood, deep as Berks County barns. They only had to stand there, for the canal and the turnpike came up to their doors. The gentry in the towns called his place Walnut Mills from all the fan-leaved trees he had left standing among the grey-white walls. But you wouldn't catch such a fancy name in Pennsylvania Dutch mouths. Frey's Mills or Free's Store was good enough for them.

Henry Free himself simply called it The Store or The Mills. He could talk Pennsylvania Dutch to a farmer or the King's English to a gentleman from town. Once when the district had sent him to Congress, the gentleman from Virginia had attacked him for denouncing Henry Clay's betrayal of Jackson. The Virginian had quoted from the Classics, each time adding "from the Latin" or "from the Greek." When he was through, Henry Free rose. He said that Latin and Greek and other dead languages he did not know, but he would quote from a living language. Then he launched into a rebuttal, pausing from time to time for strange, humorous-sounding phrases, after which he would add impressively, "from the Pennsylvania Dutch." Never had he heard Congress laugh so much, and when he had finished, the gentleman from Virginia had shaken his hand and become his friend.

Henry Free wore the same kind of clothes now that he wore then. He was a tall, spare man with snow white mane against the red of his cheeks and black of his hat. His stone house stood against the hill. When his English wife lived, he had had a fine office upstairs but the last years found him doing business in the basement over the long kitchen table, which at meal time sometimes seated ten or twenty people. Here at the head, he sat in state within close reach of his desk which was reputed through the countryside to be stuffed with money. The carpetless floor was scrubbed every Saturday. The Longplate stove stood a little way out of the huge black fireplace and handy to one side was the little washstand with the tin basin that Catrina, his housekeeper, jumped to fill with warm water when she heard him getting up in the morning or coming in from his rounds of the place. He had to make those rounds when he could, for a stream of men found their way to this kitchen, to buy and sell, to pay and be paid, to borrow, to settle or put off, and incidentally to have the customary drink of applejack and to stay for the ensuing dinner or supper.

Today when his nephew and the city lawyer found him, he looked like an old Quaker, as he sat at his place at the table with his broad-brimmed hat on, writing in one of his leather-bound books.

After a while he looked up.

"Oh, it's you," he said.

"Uncle Henner, you know Lawyer Hartranft from Reading," his nephew reminded him.

At the notice of a lawyer present, a gleam came into the old gentleman's eyes.

"How are you," he greeted. "Now what's dead around the country?"

But he waved them hospitably to a long plank settee painted with doves and tulips, where governors and a president had sat before them. Then he scraped back the legs of his hickory armchair with its worn red cushion. But he did not lay down his quill.

"Uncle Henner," his nephew began, bending forward, "do you know how old you are today?"

Henry Free looked at them. Now what were they after, he wondered.

"Every year I don't get any younger," he admitted reluctantly.

"There aren't many Revolutionary soldiers left any more," the lawyer from Reading said.

"Not on top the ground anyways," Henry agreed drily.

It grew silent. The nephew leaned forward again.

"Lawyer Hartranft here writes the history of Reading people for the paper. He writes their epitaphs too. If you would tell him a little now, he would have it right later on, especially that part how your name got different."

"I understand your name used to be Dellicker, Captain Free?" the lawyer said.

The old gentleman sat quietly in his chair. He glanced at his nephew.

"You could tell him once. I told you plenty already."

"Yes, but when you're little, Uncle Henner, it goes in one ear and out the other. Besides, he wants you to start in the old country."

"Start back in the old country?" the old man echoed.

"If you can remember."

"Oh, my mind's as good as yours yet!" Henry Free told him.

He turned his chair and looked out through the kitchen window. He could see his store, the forge shop and grist mill by the race. His tanyard and still-house under the spring he could not see, but he could hear the orphan boys playing around the solid stone schoolhome he had built and now kept for them on the hill. He had been one like that himself once, soon after they got on the water. He was a Pennsylvanian now, an American this long time. And yet they wanted him to talk about the old country.

"These things don't come out by themselves, mind!" he told his nephew. "They're like potatoes. You got to dig them out a little first."

He twisted around now and closed his book on the quill. One hand picked up his clay pipe and he began filling it thoughtfully from his open pouch, not offering any to the others. Usually he took a coal from the open plate stove, but today that would be too quick. He took out his tinder box and struck the small steel rod on the rifle flint he kept screwed fast to the lid. He struck slowly and methodically. He would rather it wouldn't make a fire for a little. After a while a brighter spark flew and the dry cotton and inner bark flared in flame. He held the box so he could draw on his pipe. Then he blew it out and puffed awhile with a sharp sucking sound that you could hear over the kitchen.

"I don't think any more about the old country," he said after a while. "It didn't go so good over there."

"Can you remember anything of the trip over?" the Reading lawyer asked, leaning forward, pencil and paper in hand.

That twinkle which as a young man must have been the very look of the devil came again into his eye.

"Yes," the old man said gravely. "I remember we went down the Rhine on a Monday and got to Philadelphia on a Friday."

"Didn't something happen on the way over?" his nephew prompted.

"Yes," the old man said gravely. "A good many died."

The kitchen door opened and a rusty-bearded farmer in a tattered blue overcoat looked hesitantly in.

"Come in, Balser," the old man said. "I guess you smell your money. Catrina, pour Balser his glass. Lawyer Hartranft, you must excuse me a few minutes."

It took only ten minutes to send the farmer away with his money for the two wagon loads of distillery apples. But it was much later in the afternoon when his nephew and the lawyer left.

The days were getting shorter now, the old man thought. In the house it looked half dark already. He sat silent, hunched up in his armchair, and it seemed that in the smell of the applejack still in the kitchen he could smell the tang of salt water and that in the dusk floating through the room he could see the brig sailing through the gray mist of that early Colonial sea. A faint foggy wetness touched his cheek and he was a yellow-haired Rhine boy again with the spread of groaning canvas over his head, and under him the deck rising and falling on its way to the new land.

(1943)

From

FATHER AND
GLORIOUS DESCENDANT
by Pardee Lowe

While Father himself had never been religious, he, like Mother, had never hesitated to encourage us to attend Western churches and Sunday school. My religious affiliations, however, were determined primarily by neighborhood playmates, and we switched religious allegiances as frequently as we found new friends. Before I graduated from grammar school it was quite common for either my sister or me to take him to church for some special service such as Easter or Christmas.

I remember the first occasion I ever took Father to a small Christian church. It was before automobiles were common. The church was not far off and Father and I walked to it. I have forgotten the name, but it was of the Holy Roller type, and its members were filled to overflowing with evangelical enthusiasm.

After the Sunday services were over he questioned us. He said he was very pleased to see us partake in the program, waving palms and praising the Lord. He told me that he liked the frequent references to "The Heavenly Father." Those he could appreciate. However, the emotional outbursts of certain of the members of the congregation nonplused him. It seemed to him that they were possessed. And he wasn't sure, he said, that they weren't possessed by the devil. Father said he preferred tears and less bellowings. He didn't favor their jumpings up and down either. If that was dancing, Father added, he had never seen anything like it, and if it was religion, he'd rather keep both feet on solid ground.

I became somewhat distraught because this was the first time Father had accompanied us to church. I wanted him to feel at home so he would go with us more often. It was well that soon after my playmates changed, and I decided to go to another church, for it's doubtful whether Father could have endured a repetition of such an outpouring of tears and wailing. The sect, even I agreed, was too emotional.

The next church I went to belonged to the Presbyterians. It was situated a little out of our neighborhood on Federal Street, in a run-down residential district which had once been primarily Anglo-Saxon, but had changed. Around it had crowded successive groups of new immigrants, mostly Catholics: Irish, Germans, Scandinavians, Italians, Portuguese, Spanish, and Mexicans. They were not interested. Their cosmopolitan children never bothered to attend our Sunday school, although its fellowship and hospitality were never denied them. This church could no longer support itself, and constantly required the help of the Home Mission Board. Because it was the second oldest Presbyterian church in the community, the remaining members, weak though they were in number, declined to desert their old house of worship.

I was no minister's son, but for the next twenty years I was to grow up in that church, to pass through as full a religious experience as any child of a preacher's family could desire. At first I attended only the Sunday-school socials and picnics. When I entered East Belleville High, I taught a small Sunday-school class of boys, all about five years old. Four years later I was promoted to assisting the Sunday-school superintendent, and helping out in the daily Vacation Bible School.

As I look back, it does not seem to me that these children learned very much in the way of religion from me. What they did acquire, I hope, was a more human and sensible approach towards interracial and social relationships, and, perhaps, a smattering of Christian ethics, heavily modified by Father's pragmatic Confucianism.

At this time, because of the differences between Father and myself, it seemed that practically all my spare time was spent in the church. I found it congenial and friendly, and also a spot in which to exercise all my American proclivities. After school I did not hesitate to go there to assist the superintendent. In the evenings, twice a week, I ran a gymnasium class for the boys of the neighborhood, following a somewhat modified Y.M.C.A. program. Saturday evenings were usually spent at church socials, or in helping the superintendent prepare for the Sabbath services.

But of all days, Sunday was the most engrossing. At nine in the morning we would rush to the church. At nine-thirty we would prepare for our Sunday-school lesson. At ten sharp, the children would come trooping in, and our work would begin. At eleven it was our custom to attend the church services. Since the congregation was small, the superintendent and the pastor always considered it necessary to augment the audience with as many of the young folks as possible. At one, after the service, it was quite customary for me to join one of the youths of an American family at their noonday meal.

The only free period was in the afternoon, because beginning at five o'clock the activities of the morning were repeated. I returned once again to the church and participated in Christian Endeavor meetings, and in the evening service. Likely as not, I would lend a lusty but somewhat quavering voice to the choir, or, perhaps, pump by hand the wheezing church organ. Always, the day ended for me as it had begun: in an overwhelming aura of religious fervor.

Father was always astounded at this tremendous religious activity of mine. He was not against it, nor did he seem to be wholeheartedly for it. It perplexed him to see me spend hour after hour, and day after day, in doing something which he did not quite understand, except that it kept me out of mischief. He confided often to our kinsmen: "I don't see why Glorious Descendant shows such a religious bent. In my own life, I never found much need of the Church!"

In those days, Father didn't believe much in religion. Occasionally a queer-looking Barbarian zealot would drop at Sun Loy a religious tract all about hell and damnation. Father wasn't disturbed in the least, but consigned these tracts to the oblivion of the wastepaper basket. Fire-breathing evangelism had no appeal to him.

Nor did Father pay much attention to the Salvation Army which paraded through Chinatown each night at eight with waving banners and blaring bugles, exhorting the heathen to be saved. Father and his friends called the Army the "Boom-Boom Society" because they made such a racket with their bass drums. I would stand on the street corner and admire the enthusiasm of the ten Salvationists in their blue-and-red uniforms. Occasionally there would be a Chinese convert, who would preach salvation and sin to the listeners, who, strangely enough, were usually American tourists or beachcombers from the adjoining Barbary Coast. Few Chinese paid much attention to them. Although the Chinese children loved to look on goggle-eyed at the service, their elders didn't find the Christian life attractive. And when the Army marched away with soaring tambourines and plunging bass-drum sticks, few Chinese followed them. This did not deter the Army. It never failed to appear at the appointed hour each night. To their everlasting credit, they kept their rendezvous with God, but the Chinese, as far as I could see, were decidedly timid about meeting their Maker. When I asked Father the reason, he replied: "Our stomachs are empty. We are too busy trying to fill them. We cannot afford to worry about the holiness of our souls."

The Chinese did not find the Christian life attractive. They disliked, for instance, the martial trappings of the Salvationists, and the fervor of their followers seemed immoderate and not harmonious with the Chinese tradition of Confucian moderation. Worst of all, the barren ugliness of Protestant missions offered no spiritual uplift. Accustomed to the flamboyant decorations of Chinese temples, they were not intrigued by what they saw in the Protestant missions. The Catholic churches with their lovely altars, flaming candles and gleaming statuary appealed more, but up to the end of World War I most of its Irish and Italian members were too thoroughly identified with anti-Chinese exclusion to impress Chinatown. Hence, the Chinese did not join. After the 1918 armistice it was a different story. As anti-Chinese discrimination disappeared, the Paulist Fathers redoubled their missionary zeal among the poorer Chinese families.

Slowly but surely they labored, until today the Catholic Church is represented by the largest single religious group in the Chinese community. Rome fully appreciated the bountiful harvests to be found in Chinatown.

(1943)

From

MAMA'S BANK ACCOUNT
by Kathryn Forbes

In those days, if anyone had asked Mama unexpectedly, "What nationality are you?" I believe she would have answered without hesitation, "I am a San Franciscan."

Then quickly, lest you tease her, she would add, "I mean Norvegian. American citizen."

But her first statement would be the true one.

Because from the moment she was to step off the ferryboat, confused and lonely in a strange land, San Francisco was to become suddenly and uniquely her own.

"Is like Norvay," the Aunts said Mama had declared.

And straightway she'd taken the city to her heart.

Mama learned so many things about San Francisco. She could tell you how to get to Telegraph Hill; what time the boats came in at Fisherman's Wharf; the names of the young boys who tended the steaming crab kettles along Bay Street; and where to find the blue and yellow lupins at Land's End.

The cable cars were an endless delight, and Mama's idea of a perfect Sunday afternoon was for Papa to take us riding on them from one transfer point to another.

Papa would tell of the time Mama took out her citizenship papers and astounded the solemn court by suddenly reciting the names of the streets. "Turk, Eddy, Ellis, O'Farrell," Mama had said proudly, "Geary, Post, Sutter, Bush, and Pine."

Papa said the clerk had quite a time making Mama understand that such knowledge was not necessary for citizenship.

Mama made friends with an Armenian lady who had a store out on Third Street, and gave her her best *lutefisk* recipe. Best of all, though, Mama liked to explore Chinatown. Old Sing Fat and Mama held long conversations over the counters of his Grant Avenue Bazaar. Like as not, she would come home to Castro Street with a tiny bag of lichee nuts or preserved ginger. And if any of us were ill in bed, Mama would go down and get us a small package of those Chinese water flowers that open into amazing beauty when dropped into water.

And if anyone ever asked us where we were born, Mama instructed us, we should say "San Francisco." Didn't copies of our birth certificates, neatly framed and hung on the wall of Papa's and Mama's room, testify to that proud fact?

"After all," Papa used to tease her, "after all, San Francisco isn't the *world*."

But to Mama it was just that. The world.

Papa had been working steadily for a long time now, and for once we had a little money ahead. And Mama had told us that within a few months there would be a new brother or sister.

Then—a Real Estate Salesman got hold of Papa and tried to sell him a chicken ranch across the Bay.

Just a little money down, the salesman said, and Papa could pay off the balance like rent. And just think, he told us, there were also five whole acres of fruit trees.

"Sunshine!" the man said enthusiastically. "No fog."

Mama bridled as if someone had said something against one of her children.

"Fog is good," she declared. "Is healthy."

"But there will be eggs for the little ones," he countered. "And plenty of milk."

"There is a cow?" Papa asked.

Well, no, the salesman admitted, no cow. But there were four fine goats. I saw Mama wrinkle her nose.

Only after Papa said that it would be nice to be your own boss and have a place of your own, instead of being a carpenter—only after we children and Nels had coaxed and pleaded—did Mama reluctantly agree to the move across the Bay.

It was fun at first, helping Papa to prune the trees and to mend the roof of the sagging little house; fun to carry the water from the well and to chop the wood. I remember what a great time Nels had white-washing the chicken coop. Dagmar helped Mama start a little vegetable garden, and Christine and I took turns milking the ever present goats.

But when the cold weather came, our enthusiasm for country life waned rapidly. We children were not used to tumbling sleepily out of bed while it was still dark, eating our breakfast by lamplight, then trudging miles to school.

Nor were we used to a one-room schoolhouse, to playmates who called us "Scandahoovians." Ours had been a more cosmopolitan atmosphere.

"Hicks!" Christine and I retaliated sulkily. "Country hicks!" And knew a deep homesickness.

Dagmar mourned the merry-go-round and the ponies at the park, while Nels spoke often and wistfully of the big city library with its thousands of books.

Christine and I missed the sidewalks. Our beloved roller skates hung idly in the closet, and as we oiled them carefully every Saturday morning, we remembered that once we had been the very best skaters on the block.

Only Mama never complained. But we saw her stand for long moments at the window—looking westward.

Papa worked early and late, but fought a losing battle. We watched the young trees in the orchard, our carefully tended garden, shrivel and blacken with frost. We had not had money enough to provide smudge pots.

The chickens came down with a strange and baffling illness; most of them died and the few surviving hens stopped laying eggs.

Only the goats kept producing. Our pantry shelves were stocked with the brown goat cheese Mama had made.

For the first Christmas in our lives, we children did not get to see the big city stores and the wonderful window displays. And Papa's toolbox was packed away in the closet with our skates.

On New Year's Eve we were allowed to stay up. Mama made "sweet soup" for us, and she and Papa said Skoal! and wished us each a *Godt Nytaar* as they drank their coffee.

At midnight Mama held up her hand. "Listen!" she said.

We couldn't hear anything.

"Bells!" Mama said. "Bells and whistles in San Francisco."

Papa looked worried. "Is too far to hear," he told her gently. "You imagine things."

I thought I saw tears in Mama's eyes, but I must have been mistaken. Mama never cried.

"It is not good," Papa said heavily, "for carpenter to try to be farmer."

"Such talk!" Mama protested. But Papa's shoulders did not straighten. And the next day he went to see the Real Estate Salesman. But the man didn't seem interested in us any more. So then Papa had Nels write out an advertisement for the newspaper. But even that wasn't successful.

We only had one answer, an old couple by the name of Sonderman. They liked the chicken ranch, but as Mr. Sonderman explained, they had their big house on Steiner Street to dispose of first.

"Eleven rooms," Mrs. Sonderman told us, "and since our boys are grown and gone away, Mr. Sonderman and I just rattle around in it."

Of course eleven rooms was too big for us, and never in the world could we get enough money together to put a down payment on it—even counting what Papa had in the chicken ranch.

But Mama never seemed to know when something was hopeless. She made several trips over to the city to see the Steiner Street house and to talk with the Sondermans.

Then Aunt Jenny came over to see us.

"To visit for a while," she said brightly. And we children were much too polite to tell her we knew she'd come to stay with us until after our new baby was born.

Mama made fresh coffee and she and Aunt Jenny and Papa sat down to the kitchen table.

"What is wrong with the children?" Aunt Jenny demanded.

Mama's eyes were worried as she looked at each of us.

"They do not look good?" she asked anxiously.

"Such long faces they have," Aunt Jenny explained.

Mama looked at us again. "I see what you mean," she said slowly. "They have not happiness."

Aunt Jenny told us news of the old neighborhood. We remembered the Andersons? Well, they had moved over to Castro Street.

And Peter Larson, Anna Lundquist's brother, had got the carpenter contract on the new high school, and he had told Aunt Jenny he just wished he had Papa for a carpenter foreman.

Papa held out his earth-stained hands. "Would be good," he sighed, "to hold tools again. To smell the fresh new wood."

Mama stood up suddenly. "I just think," she said. "That Sonderman house—eleven rooms. Jenny, that would make a fine boardinghouse."

Aunt Jenny laughed shortly. "Indeed. And where would you find time—now—to do the work?"

Mama's face reddened. "But after—Papa, the children—all would help. We would work together."

Absolute nonsense, Aunt Jenny declared. Besides, she pointed out, we had only about four rooms of furniture.

"But we could get more, Jenny. With Papa working for Peter Larson."

Aunt Jenny shook her head as if the whole plan was hopeless.

"I think," Mama said stubbornly, "that the Sondermans would be willing to give us three—maybe four—months' rent on the Steiner house for what we have paid on this place. Mrs. Sonderman *likes* chicken farm."

Papa laughed out loud for the first time in months. "And goats," he said. "Old Mr. Sonderman likes goats."

Mama and Papa looked at each other for a long time. Then Papa went down the road to phone. When he came back he nodded his head and said, "Four months' free rent." And he brought his tool chest out of the closet and started sharpening the tools.

"We go," Mama said happily, "we go." And sent Nels for boxes.

"Wait," Aunt Jenny pleaded. "Wait and talk this over. You should think a long time before you make a move like this."

"We go," Mama said again, "we go today." And started taking the dishes off the shelves.

Aunt Jenny choked on her coffee. "Such foolishness! You can't. You must wait until after—"

There was a strange urgency in Mama's voice. "We go *today*. The house is vacant. The Sondermans moved their things over to their married son's last week.''

"And what of all your hard work here?" Aunt Jenny demanded. "What have you got out of it?"

"Four months' free rent in a big house in San Francisco," Mama said. "And goat cheese." She pointed to the pantry shelves. *"Lots* of goat cheese." And Mama was smiling.

Late that afternoon, when Papa had brought the last box into what had been the Sondermans' house and was now ours, Mama told Nels he could go to the library, and she sent us children out to play.

Eagerly and joyously we skated up and down the block, exploring the new neighborhood, making plans for the next day.

When it grew dark, we went home for dinner and found that all the Aunts were there. It was Aunt Jenny, however, who told us the news. She looked as if someone had played a trick on her.

"You have a new baby sister," she told us grimly, and took us down the hall to the room that was now Papa's and Mama's.

Mama smiled reassuringly at us as we tiptoed in. She lifted the blanket from the tiny bundle on her arm. "Her name is Kaaren," she said.

Papa turned to beam at us and we saw that he was hanging our framed birth certificates in a neat row against the wall. He took a tack out of his mouth.

Aunt Sigrid came in with soup for Mama. "Say," she said, "isn't it funny how all your children are born in San Francisco?"

"Funny?" Aunt Jenny demanded crossly. *"Funny?"*

"Is good," Mama said happily, "is good."

(1943)

From

BOSTON ADVENTURE
by Jean Stafford

To my mother, my father's desertion was like an eternally renewing spring from which she hourly drew accusations and complaints, and she shared her poisoned, enervating drink with anyone who would partake. Her companions in misery were poor neighbor women who, alternately pitying and envying, welcomed our misfortune as a distraction from their own worries. Mrs. Kadish, a thin, pinched, crotchety woman, the wife of a ferryboat engineer and the mother of six famished children, often came to call. She sat prissily erect, her hands folded tightly in her lap, nodding her long, hard head which was topped by a coil of graying hair. When she was not speaking, she pursed her lips in permanent displeasure, and when she did speak, it was in a high, nasal key, not loud, but like a distant scream.

As I came in one afternoon, she was saying, "I was on my feet at five A.M. this morning and I'm telling you, I've been on the go ever since. It's pick up! Wash up! Sew up! Rinse out! till a person could drop down senseless. You was saying, Mrs. Marburg, that it's hard if the man goes off and leaves the woman, but to my mind it's six of one and half a dozen of the other. If you don't have a grown man around, you don't have to cook so much and do up all them work shirts. Kadish could leave tomorrow and I wouldn't hardly notice only for the little dab of money he brings in."

"He hasn't left you yet, sweetheart," said my mother. "It's not the money. It's the *shame*. My God! You'd think this here wasn't his child not born yet and he went off to punish me. I know *you* don't think so, Mrs. Kadish, darling, nor Mrs. Henderson nor two or three other Chichester ladies, but what about the *other* people?"

Mrs. Kadish did not regard it a likely suspicion though it interested her. "You mean maybe they think you you-know? Oh, no, I don't *think* so. Why, Mrs. Marburg, nobody would say you was that type lady."

My mother began on a new tack: "Well, then, maybe they say *he* was the bad one and went off with one of those women from Marblehead, and maybe that's true, Mrs. Kadish, who knows? I'm no fool and I used to see them last summer wobbling down the beach by the gentlemen's house in dresses no longer than your camisole." The "gentlemen" were the Coast Guards, so known because one of them, five years before, had gone to Harvard.

"You're not telling me news," returned her friend. "But I wouldn't think that a family man like Mr. Marburg would take up with that type."

"Whatever people say—if they blame it on drink or on the other thing or something else besides—it's all a shame. But what can you do with Hermann Marburg? He is a *German*, dear."

Her voice fell upon the word "German" in such a way that the emphasis was ambiguous: either a German was infamous beyond pardon or pitiable beyond hope. Mrs. Kadish, after this statement, perused my face for a time. "German," she intoned. "And you, Mrs. Marburg, what was you saying was your nationality?"

"I am a Russian," said my mother without pride and without deprecation but with a kind of finality which set "Russian" distinctly apart from "German" as though it was perhaps not ultimately the best thing to be but was at least comprehensible. I could have corrected her: Russians, to the children at school, were utterly improbable though all that was known about them was that they had ludicrous names. A favorite sport was to tease me by saying: "Hisky, Sonivitch, have you got your geographysky home-worskivitch?" In a way, I was flattered by this, for it had replaced Pig-Latin and was known as Sonie-Latin. On the other hand, Germans were perfectly credible and, because of their reputation for cutting off the hands of sleeping children and of being sired by Kaiser Bill, they enjoyed a certain prestige. Sometimes, the three or four of us in the lower grades who knew a little German were bribed to sing, in a secret place, *"Stille Nacht, Heilige Nacht"* and the eyes of our audience grew more enraptured with each evil word.

"Rooshun," brooded Mrs. Kadish in her piercing voice. "So your kid is half Rooshun and half German—half Hun, as they say. Well, mine are bad enough: half Jew and half American. But not so bad as that." I felt a rush of shame which my distaste for her smelly children did not intercept. "But I don't doubt," she added in the same shrill note of lamentation, "but what she's a bright little slip."

"Bright!" cried my mother. "She's full of brains as big as an apple, that little thing is. And helpful, my God! Well, she's everything in the world you could want, Mrs. Kadish. Come here, Sonia girl, let me show Mrs. K. how long your eyelashes are," and she gathered me to her, pulling my hair as she held up my head for our neighbor's admiration.

"Tchk, tchk," said Mrs. Kadish. "She'll be pretty. She won't have no trouble getting herself a man, you know what I mean?"

"There's where you're wrong," replied my mother. "Not but she couldn't have any man in the world for the asking even now and only twelve going on thirteen, but what kind of a mother would I be to let an angel like her be treated the way my poor self has been?"

"You wait and see," warned Mrs. Kadish. "The time will come and whoosh! she's gone. But I wouldn't be thinking so far ahead, Mrs. Marburg. I must say I don't agree with you that she could get a man right now at her time of life. To my way of thinking she looks poorly. My Nathan might take her, along about sixteen or seventeen."

My mother gave a foolish laugh. "Your Nathan! Well, pardon *me*, Mrs. Kadish, but no thank you. I don't mean anything by that only I couldn't do without her." She pressed my head into her breast until I could scarcely breathe, but I had the strength to pull away from her and turn aside, my cheeks blazing. I did not know, indeed, what she would do without me, but I knew well enough what I would do without her. Right now, I thought bitterly, I would be *playing* with Betty Brunson instead of being on my way to her house to *work*. I murmured that I must go, that I would be late, for the sun was already going down.

"Poor baby," said my mother, stroking my hand. "She is her mother's staff of life."

"Would you mind telling me, Sonie," said Mrs. Kadish with a wily leer, "just what them Brunsons pay you?"

I told her they gave me three dollars a week. "Well, I'll be!" she exclaimed. "They're real free, ain't they? If you ask me, that's pure charity or pure show-off, I don't know which. Three dollars! And pretty soft, I expect?"

"Soft!" burst out my mother. "Soft! She slaves herself to the bone!"

Mrs. Kadish's curiosity was not satisfied. "You live high on three dollars a week now, and I'm not saying that isn't dandy, I'd just like to know how you do it. Now, me, I have close to ten a week and I can't hardly make both ends meet."

"We have a golden egg," said my mother proudly. "But we don't touch it only now and then."

"A golden egg?" queried the neighbor. "How's that?"

I was infuriated with my mother. She was talking about our "nest" egg as Miss Pickens had called it, the fifty dollars her friend had paid us for my father's skis, poles, boots, and leather shorts. I had wanted to keep our wealth a secret for I was sure it would be stolen as we had no good hiding place for it. Miss Pickens had advised me to take it to the bank in Marblehead, but I was afraid to go so far alone with that much money on my person, and we had put it between the leaves of my father's Bible, so close to Mrs. Kadish at this very moment that she could stretch out her hand without moving from her chair and take it all.

"You know the teacher, Miss Pickens?" whispered my mother. Her friend nodded, leaning forward. "She brought a man here and he bought all Hermann's trash for fifty dollars."

"No!" Mrs. Kadish's lips curled into a smile of disbelief. "May I inquire what this here trash was?"

I said, quoting the purchaser, a sickly young man who had resembled Miss Pickens and who had scarcely been able to contain himself at the sight of my father's belongings, "Four pairs of Bavarian skis and poles covered with plaited leather and four pairs of genuine Salzburg *Lederhosen* and galluses to match."

"Galluses?"

"I don't know the English word," I said.

The woman looked at me with respect. "Nathan knows some foreign words, too. Fifty dollars. I'm glad for you, I surely am. No telling what will happen. Sonie might get appendicitis and have to have them out. That fifty dollars would come in handy." She rose to leave and my mother extended her hand, fingers pointing downward as though she expected it to be kissed. "You come again, sweetheart, I'm always here in the afternoon."

"Some pregnant women crave dill pickles," said Mrs. Kadish. "I'll bring along four or five when I come next time. I was always crazy for them myself."

When she had gone I put out my mother's supper for her: a plate of cole slaw, a loaf of rye bread, a dish of Liederkranz, and a casserole of beans that had been heating. She looked with displeasure on the meal. "If only I could have one small cucumber in a dish of sour cream, I wouldn't ask for anything else in the world." We had been through the cucumber argument many times before.

"Oh, Mamma!" I cried. "You *know* they don't have them at this time of year."

But, as always before, she either did not hear or did not believe me. "A cucumber is a little thing to ask. If I could have just *one,* just a small withered one in just a little bit of sour cream, ah, ah, I could bear all the rest!"

She did not move from her chair beside the stove, and knowing that she would only eat when the notion struck her, I went out. But I did not go at once in the direction of the Brunsons' house where I had long since been due. Instead, I ran across to the Kadishes' house where a light was burning. Through the uncurtained window, I could see the children gathered about a round table in the kitchen, each of the six intent upon some project, piling up matches or painting with water colors or cleaning a comb, but not too absorbed to chatter now and then and to dart their black eyes about the table with a controlled ferocity as though they all hated one another but knew that they must stick together. All of them came from the same mold: the same crisp black hair glittered under the lamplight; their faces wore sharp, shrewd expressions, the upper half seeming to be drawn down by the weight of the nose, loosening then below the nostrils into soft lips and little chins.

Nathan, the oldest, a boy of fourteen, sat near the window reading, and as the lamp was directly shining upon him, brightly illuminating his face, I was able to study the birthmark on his cheek. It was probably because of this shocking purple disfigurement that he was so ill-tempered and also so precocious. He was as sensitive as if his mark were a raw sore, continually being rubbed against or hit. It extended from the cheekbone, over the eyelid and the low forehead, to the hairline, appearing the more brilliant because of the dead pallor it interrupted. His lips were pouted in profound misanthropy and he seemed, for all his concentration, to detest his book, for his forehead was drawn into a scowl and his erect body wore an air of unwillingness. I knew by hearsay as well as by the ever meditative look upon his face and by the constant presence of a book under his arm that he was learned. He did not read *The Boy Scouts in Arizona* or the *Motor Boat Boys,* but instead, lives of Napoleon and histories of Rome and the Waverley novels. He had greatly admired my father, and often on Sunday afternoon had come to the door, inviting him to take a walk. My father never refused him, and it was on these expeditions round Chichester that Nathan had learned the foreign words of which his mother was so proud. Tonight it was *Quo Vadis* that he had propped up against a sugar bowl.

I respected his scholarship, but in my lassitude felt no urge to emulate him. I sometimes wished that we were friends so that I might absorb his culture through our association. But I did nothing to make myself commendable to him, nor could I have, for he was a formidable critic of everyone and especially of girls. A foolish girl of his age had once cried out in derision, "Cranberry Kadish is my ideal of a perfect man, like fun!" "Her ideal," said Nathan with a contempt that far surpassed hers, "I suppose she means Platonic ideal because I wouldn't touch her with a ten-foot pole." The girl blushed and said, "You know what I *meant*. I meant 'idea.' " But her correction was too late and as she fretted over the failure of her arrow to kill, he regarded her with a triumphant sneer that twitched at his birthmark.

Tonight, made thoughtful by my mother's conversation with his mother, and, restless in my trap, I wished more than ever that Nathan were my "best friend" and that we took walks together in the evening, confiding in one another our sorrows and our ambitions. The desire for his companionship was tantamount to a betrayal of my mother who for so many years and so diligently had schooled me in the treacheries of men, although I believed she assumed that I would marry in spite of her warnings, would profit by none of her precepts, but by my experience would confirm what she had told me. And I, although it was my intention to remain unmarried (more in imitation of Miss Pride than to escape the pitfalls my mother had described to me), had a quite reasonable curiosity to know what were the manifestations of a man's descent from Satan. The marred Jewish boy, at his sullen labors, roused in me a strange new ravening and I all but tapped on the window glass as a sign that he was to come out to speak to me. As quickly, the impulse waned and I turned to go. But as I did so, I resolved hereafter to come each night about this time and take up my brief, secret vigil. I was light-headed as I went on my way and I felt a little sick. Each time his image returned to my mind, my throat thickened and my footsteps faltered.

(1944)

PAPA, MAMA AND ECONOMICS
by George Panetta

Papa couldn't read and write when he came off the boat, but in those days it was just as it is now in America, and the first thing Papa did was go in business. He opened a big dress factory on Lafayette Street and began making money like an Irishman. It even looked as if he was smarter than the Irishmen, because although they were making money, too, they were always breaking their heads or falling off scaffolds and forgetting to come out of a hole before the backfill. Besides, there was more dignity to what Papa was doing, and once in a while he wore a clean shirt.

But as Papa made the money, Mama spent it by having one of us every year, and by lending Clara to Uncle George in Italy so that after that Mamma could make three trips to Italy to see if she couldn't get Clara back. Papa couldn't get over all the money he was making, and for years he had Mama write letters to everybody in Italy, telling them to come quick because the gold was in the streets. And in 1926, when Papa was ruined, he was glad he had Mama write the letters, because from 1927 to 1931 he was able to live on what he borrowed from fifty or sixty of his friends that came over. After that they all came bothering Papa with sad stories; they didn't mind so much that he had brought them to this country in the first place, but please as a favor give them back some of the money they lent him so that they could go back to Italy.

That was in 1930, when everybody except Hoover wanted to go and die somewhere.

But up to 1926 Papa made money as if he were born here, and he could afford to have the seven of us—and almost anything else. In the summer we would go to the country, in South Beach, Staten Island. All the years before 1926 we lived in that big apartment on Kenmare Street where we had four rooms and a toilet of our own. We had three beds and didn't have to sleep mixed. The boys slept in the bedroom which faced Mulberry Street, Aly near the wall because he was the youngest. The girls slept in the living-room, and when Grandpa took Clara on that loan to Uncle George, Grandma came over because there was plenty of room. There was even room on the kitchen floor for uncles that were always coming off the boat.

While Papa made the money he spent it, and if he had made it long enough all of us would be big people today. At supper every night Papa used to call on each of us to recite what we were going to be when we grew up; it was what Papa was giving us for the future and he liked to hear it over and over again. I was going to be a doctor. I had a big chest and could make a long noise with my mouth, so Papa thought I should be a doctor. Viola was going to be a great music teacher because one week Papa was making so much money that he happened to buy a piano. Nothing ever came out of it except La Donna Mobile one finger by Papa himself, and later, when Papa was ruined, Jenny began playing it by ear. Jenny had become a pianist, but when she was sitting at the supper table with us she was going to be a kindergarten teacher. Peter, PJ, was going to be a doctor too and, because he was older, it looked as if he would beat me to it, but I kept making those long noises and PJ would be a little afraid and wonder if it wasn't better to be a lawyer.

Only little Aly never wanted to be anything. He always had convulsions and Lando was always bopping him on the head and calling him half-cigar, and I suppose poor Aly thought it was better just to try and keep alive. Lando himself was Papa's pride, and when all the wine was drunk Papa would tell everybody to keep quiet and listen to what Lando was going to be. He was going to be an actor because he had blue eyes and nobody thought he was Italian. Mama used to take him to an actors' school on 44th Street every Tuesday and Thursday. Papa paid ten dollars a lesson, and Lando went to the school for nine weeks.

Nobody became anything, although Clara came back from Italy in 1925 with kidney trouble and a bald head.

Still, it wasn't Papa's fault. Up to 1926 he had no idea that the reason a man had children was to support him when he was old. He worked hard. He never saved any money, but look at all the money you could always make in America, and what were you going to do with it all? When he came home at night and had us talk about what we were going to be, it was what he was giving us, and it made him happy.

One day in 1926 the bank sent Papa's check back even though it had the cross on. He couldn't make the payroll to pay the people. It wasn't Papa's fault.

"What happen, Domenick?" Uncle Louie asked him.

"Who know?" said Papa. "Crazy man at bank."

"You sure you got money, Domenick?"

"Louie, shut up you too."

"Fix up with bookkeep, Domenick."

"Fix nothing. The bank send tomorrow."

"Fix up with bookkeep. Make sure."

"Louie, shut up. Go home."

Uncle Louie knew Papa was broke; he was a little smarter than Papa, had learned to shoot pool and had become a citizen when his wife explained the widow's pension they give you in this country. He was even smart enough to get in the Army in the first war, become a cook, and get shot in the behind when his company was retreating. He could figure it all out how Papa was broke, and as he was going home he kept saying it over. . . . The wife three times Italy . . . coupla thousan, another coupla just kids born, and twenn thousan just kids eat, sleep, dress him up like somebody. Summer comes—country— South Beach. Gotta go country? Jeesa, how can have money! And then the doctors, Jeesa! The small one get the convulsion, the fat one falls swamp, the big one puts bean in nose. Gotta call doctors. Say five thousan just call lousa doctor. And the girl gotta go college? That's coupla thousan more. And factory. Fifty dollar bookkeep, make check, telephone, hello, goodbye, fifty dollar. . . .

Uncle Louie kept talking to himself all the way home, and by the time he was home he figured that Papa had spent two hundred thousand dollars since he had come to America.

"Jeesa," Uncle Louie said, "how can have money my brother?"

The next day Papa went to the bank, first thing. "Whatsa matter no money?" he said.

"Your checking account is overdrawn," said the bank. "You owe us a dollar and sixty-two cents. You haven't made a deposit in two months."

"I don't want know deposits," Papa said. "When I get money pay people?"

"You don't understand, Mr. Caparooti."

"I understand all about. I put in put in put in. Now I wants to take out."

The bank looked at Papa as if it were almost human, as if it were sorry for all these human beings who were mad.

"Isa right?" Papa asked, looking back.

"But, Mr. Caparooti, you must check your account."

"Damma who know this account? For twenn years I look book? I see whats all this? No. Whats got to do book? The people want money; they work, no? Can tell go home people, no money? For twenn years Mr. Caparooti no do this thing. Now you talk account account. What's got to do account?"

"I'm sorry, Mr. Caparooti, the check is no good with your account in this condition."

Papa looked at the bank right in the eye and in Italian he told the bank first of all to go to hell, then he said it was no wonder we had bank robbers and that he hoped they would come around that night with sacks and take everything, even the pennies.

Papa smoked out of the bank, back to the factory, and right into the bookkeeper's face.

"Why you no tell me?"

"I told you a dozen times, Mr. Caparooti."

"You tell me? What, you liar now too?"

"Even when I was writing out the check, I told you there was no money."

"You crazy, Antonette? You tell me?"

It wasn't Papa's fault. When he came off the boat, he couldn't read and write, but he opened this factory and got in the habit of making money. Every time he put his cross on the check, they sent the money. Now all of a sudden they didn't send it. And even if the bookkeeper did tell him, it wasn't his fault. Could you believe a thing like that after twenty years? How could it be?

It wasn't Papa's fault. And when Uncle Louie came over one night and talked about putting fire to the factory, that wasn't Papa's fault either.

"Domenick, that's we do," Uncle Louie said.

"But you sure money comes?"

"Sure, Domenick. Sure."

It wasn't Uncle Louie's fault either. How could he know the factory was not insured?

One night Uncle Louie forgot his cigar between forty yards of cloth. He came running home to Papa that the factory was on fire.

Together they stood on the corner of Broome and Lafayette looking at the fire.

After that Papa began sitting around the house waiting for Them to send the check. They didn't send the check right away so Mama started buying everything on credit. It was the beginning of our credit system and the way we got to know everybody. Mama started with the poor grocer on the corner of Mulberry. At first Mama used to go down herself, but after a week the grocer was looking at her as if he were wondering, and Mama decided she had too much cooking and cleaning to do and began sending Aly down. It had to be Aly. It couldn't be Viola because she was going to college and was getting intelligent enough to be ashamed. It couldn't be Clara because she had just come back from Italy with a bald head. And Jenny was twelve and just starting in with the piano and learning to faint any time anybody asked her to do anything. And none of the other boys could go because PJ could fight me and I could fight Lando and Lando could fight Aly. It had to be Aly.

He used to go down every day with four or five of Mama's lists, written on both sides of a paper bag, with a promise on the bottom of each—don't worry, as soon as the check comes Mama will be down. The grocer didn't mind at first, because now that Papa was out of work, we were spending five or six dollars more every day. But after a few weeks he began to shake his head, scratch out items like provolone and salami, and send notes back to Mama. Then Mama would ask Papa when the check was coming.

"Shut up, do you cook," Papa would say.

One day the grocer sent Aly back with nothing, and Mama sent Aly right back with a long letter written by Viola.

The grocer's name was Max, but he spoke Italian, all dialects, and he ate macaroni like the Italians, had as many children, and the only reason he wasn't a Christian was because nobody really wanted to know.

"Who understands this?" he said. "Here, take, take. I should worry."

After all, why should he worry? People owed him, he owed the people. If people bought more retail, he bought more wholesale. If the people had no money for him, he had no money for the other people.

He shrugged and filled the bags up for Aly. "Here, take the salami, too."

Aly came up with the stuff that day smiling for the first time since he had the convulsions. Mama smiled too, and I think if it wasn't for Max giving us all that food and showing Mama how easy it was to get everything for nothing, we would have starved many times all the while Papa was waiting for the check. It taught Mama the economics of small business. We kept eating just as if Papa still had the factory, but at the end of the month the landlord kept coming every day to the door. One day Papa got out of the chair in which he was waiting for the check and answered the door.

"The rent, Mr. Caparooti?"

Papa wanted to kill him. "How long I here?"

"Twenty years," the landlord said.

"How long I pay you?"

"You always pay before."

"Well, whatch you want?"

"This is a new month. I've got taxes to pay."

"Figure out whatch I pay you twenn years."

At thirty-five dollars a month it came to about eight or nine thousand dollars, and it was hard to understand you didn't own the rooms, even if you weren't Papa who had come off the boat without knowing how to read and write.

"Get out my house," Papa said. "Come back I throw you downstairs."

The landlord went down the stairs, walking, and stayed away for two months.

When Mama asked Papa about the check again, he just said "What the hell what's matter with you? Sure check come. Go cook and shut up." Papa was patient and waited another month for it. When it came he was going to Boston to see "what's going be" and Mama was going to get a new bed and Viola was going to get money for college and we were going to find a doctor who could put the hair back on Clara's head. Meanwhile, Mama learned how to get more and more on credit.

A little old man named Blau was beginning to come around every Monday for six petticoats that Mama had bought for the girls. Mama started with Blau in 1926 with a bill of twelve dollars, and in 1936 poor Blau was still coming around and Mama owed him three hundred and sixty-two dollars. Blau disappeared in 1936, and after that Mama got Mr. Klide. The first two dollars Mama spent with Mr. Klide was cash, but now, in 1944, Mama owes him three hundred and forty-eight dollars and thirty-two cents, and she has forgotten all about Blau.

Still, when Papa got the check Mama was going to pay everybody, even Max the grocer, although when the check never came she realized she never had to. But Mama worried a little and one night she got after Papa about the check, and they had one of those fights Grandma used to tell us about. He grabbed Mama by the hair and pulled and if Mama hadn't screamed we would have had another bald head around the house.

The boys and girls all got up, and PJ, who was eighteen and five feet three, asked what was the matter. Papa banged him on the head with one of the pots on the stove. Viola was his favorite then and she pleaded with Papa to stop and he told us all to go to bed before he threw us all out the window. That night he went out to see Uncle Louie.

"When hell come this check?" Papa said.

"Check no come?" Uncle Louie said.

Aunt Angie, Uncle Louie's big wife, was in the kitchen moving around like a giant. They had a big house but if Aunt Angie fell over straight, she would fall on Uncle Louie talking with Papa in the living-room.

"Why no come?" said Uncle Louie. "You send policy, all right?"

"Powicy?" Papa said.

"The policy for fire," said Uncle Louie.

"What the hell this powicy?"

"Isa insurance, Domenick. You no get check without policy."

"Dope, lousa," Papa cried, putting out a hand to strangle Uncle Louie. "You say that when burn factory? I tell you burn? I break you head."

Aunt Angie called "What's this? You put fire to Domenick's shop?"

"Was cigar, Angie," Uncle Louie said. "Cigar in goods. Was accident."

"Was nothing accident," said Papa. "Lousa dope, no you say, Domenick, go head burn factory, no worry? No you say send check?"

"No policy," said Uncle Louie.

"Listen, Angie. This better no fooling. Louie burn factory. I want pay."

Aunt Angie put out her arm and caught Uncle Louie's right ear. She began twisting it and Uncle Louie hollered blue murder. "Was cigar, Angie. I swear Blessed Virgin."

"This true?" she asked, still twisting.

"I swear on God," Uncle Louie cried, kicking his legs from the pain in the ear. "I swear, swear, swear. . . ."

Aunt Angie let go the ear. "Go home, Domenick," she said. "I believe my husband."

Papa left, and Uncle Louie was happy that his wife was convinced he had told the truth about the cigar, but when he began to talk to her she didn't answer him and later, when he turned around, he got a boot in the behind he didn't know what for.

Papa waited for Uncle Louie to pay. He sat around talking to himself about breaking Uncle Louie's head if he didn't come with the money. But Uncle Louie had nothing, only nine children, and they ate like horses.

"He pay," Papa said to himself. "He get money from Angie's father."

Angie's father had worked steady as a pantsmaker, and Papa figured he had a lot of money. When the old man died in 1934, Uncle Louie had to pay for half the funeral.

Once while he was waiting, Papa got up to chase the landlord up the roof, and that scared him for four more months. Mama keeps saying Papa never wanted to work after the fire, but it wasn't Papa's fault. He waited for the fire check and then for Uncle Louie to pay up, and that kept him worried almost all of 1926. Then from 1927 to about 1931, when we began moving all over Brooklyn with the piano, Papa was borrowing from all the friends he had invited to America, and you couldn't expect him to look for work while he had that on his mind all the time. And after 1931, when nobody had money any more, Papa spent most of his time learning to sign his name because he didn't want to take chances with the relief checks the way he did with the factory; and while he was doing this, you couldn't expect him to look for work and make it seem he was putting something over on the Government. And in 1935, when Mama got a new refrigerator on her credit and the Government thought it was the same as money and stopped the relief checks, didn't Papa ask somebody if somebody was building a building somewhere because he was thinking of being a watchman? And wasn't he getting more active, leaving his chair every five or ten minutes, surprising everybody? It wasn't Papa's fault that it happened to be diabetes.

(1944)

From

CANNERY ROW
by John Steinbeck

Lee Chong's grocery, while not a model of neatness, was a miracle of supply. It was small and crowded but within its single room a man could find everything he needed or wanted to live and to be happy—clothes, food, both fresh and canned, liquor, tobacco, fishing equipment, machinery, boats, cordage, caps, pork chops. You could buy at Lee Chong's a pair of slippers, a silk kimono, a quarter pint of whiskey and a cigar. You could work out combinations to fit almost any mood. The one commodity Lee Chong did not keep could be had across the lot at Dora's.

The grocery opened at dawn and did not close until the last wandering vagrant dime had been spent or retired for the night. Not that Lee Chong was avaricious. He wasn't, but if one wanted to spend money, he was available. Lee's position in the community surprised him as much as he could be surprised. Over the course of the years everyone in Cannery Row owed him money. He never pressed his clients, but when the bill became too large, Lee cut off credit. Rather than walk into the town up the hill, the client usually paid or tried to.

Lee was round-faced and courteous. He spoke a stately English without ever using the letter R. When the tong wars were going on in California, it happened now and then that Lee found a price on his head. Then he would go secretly to San Francisco and enter a hospital until the trouble blew over. What he did with his money, no one ever knew. Perhaps he didn't get it. Maybe his wealth was entirely in unpaid bills. But he lived well and he had the respect of all his neighbors. He trusted his clients until further trust became ridiculous. Sometimes he made business errors, but even these he turned to advantage in good will if in no other way. It was that way with the Palace Flophouse and Grill. Anyone but Lee Chong would have considered the transaction a total loss.

Lee Chong's station in the grocery was behind the cigar counter. The cash register was then on his left and the abacus on his right. Inside the glass case were the brown cigars, the cigarettes, the Bull Durham, the Duke's mixture, the Five Brothers, while behind him in racks on the wall were the pints, half pints and quarters of Old Green River, Old Town House, Old Colonel, and the favorite—Old Tennessee, a blended whiskey guaranteed four months old, very cheap and known in the neighborhood as Old Tennis Shoes. Lee Chong did not stand between the whiskey and the customer without reason. Some very practical minds had on occasion tried to divert his attention to another part of the store. Cousins, nephews, sons and daughters-in-law waited on the rest of the store, but Lee never left the cigar counter. The top of the glass was his desk. His fat delicate hands rested on the glass, the fingers moving like small restless sausages. A broad golden wedding ring on the middle finger of his left hand was his only jewelry and with it he silently tapped on the rubber change mat from which the little rubber tits had long been worn. Lee's mouth was full and benevolent and the flash of gold when he smiled was rich and warm. He wore half-glasses and since he looked at everything through them, he had to tilt his head back to see in the distance. Interest and discounts, addition, subtraction he worked out on the abacus with his little restless sausage fingers, and his brown friendly eyes roved over the grocery and his teeth flashed at the customers.

On an evening when he stood in his place on a pad of newspaper to keep his feet warm, he contemplated with humor and sadness a business deal that had been consummated that afternoon and reconsummated later that same afternoon. When you leave the grocery, if you walk catty-cornered across the grass-grown lot, threading your way among the greaty rusty pipes thrown out of the canneries, you will see a path worn in the weeds. Follow it past the cypress tree, across the railroad track, up a chicken walk with cleats, and you will come to a long low building which for a long time was used as a storage place for fish meal. It was just a great big roofed room and it belonged to a worried gentleman named Horace Abbeville. Horace had two wives and six children and over a period of years he had managed through pleading and persuasion to build a grocery debt second to none in Monterey. That afternoon he had come into the grocery and his sensitive tired face had flinched at the shadow of sternness that crossed Lee's face. Lee's fat finger tapped the rubber mat. Horace laid his hands palm up on the cigar counter. "I guess I owe you plenty dough," he said simply.

Lee's teeth flahed up in appreciation of an approach so different from any he had ever heard. He nodded gravely, but he waited for the trick to develop.

Horace wet his lips with his tongue, a good job from corner to corner. "I hate to have my kids with that hanging over them," he said. "Why, I bet you wouldn't let them have a pack of spearmint now."

Lee Chong's face agreed with this conclusion. "Plenty dough," he said.

Horace continued, "You know that place of mine across the track up there where the fish meal is."

Le Chong nodded. It was his fish meal.

Horace said earnestly, "If I was to give you that place—would it clear me up with you?"

Lee Chong tilted his head back and stared at Horace through his half-glasses while his mind flicked among accounts and his right hand moved restlessly to the abacus. He considered the construction which was flimsy and the lot which might be valuable if a cannery ever wanted to expand. "Shu," said Lee Chong.

"Well, get out the accounts and I'll make you a bill of sale on that place." Horace seemed in a hurry.

"No need papers," said Lee. "I make paid-in-full paper."

They finished the deal with dignity and Lee Chong threw in a quarter pint of Old Tennis Shoes. And then Horace Abbeville walking very straight went across the lot and past the cypress tree and across the track and up the chicken walk and into the building that had been his, and he shot himself on a heap of fish meal. And although it has nothing to do with this story, no Abbeville child, no matter who its mother was, knew the lack of a stick of spearmint ever afterward.

But to get back to the evening. Horace was on the trestles with the embalming needles in him, and his two wives were sitting on the steps of his house with their arms about each other (they were good friends until after the funeral, and then they divided up the children and never spoke to each other again). Lee Chong stood in back of the cigar counter and his nice brown eyes were turned inward on a calm and eternal Chinese sorrow. He knew he could not have helped it, but he wished he might have known and perhaps tried to help. It was deeply a part of Lee's kindness and understanding that man's right to kill himself is inviolable, but sometimes a friend can make it unnecessary. Lee had already underwritten the funeral and sent a wash basket of groceries to the stricken families.

Now Lee Chong owned the Abbeville building—a good roof, a good floor, two windows and a door. True it was piled high with fish meal and the smell of it was delicate and penetrating. Lee Chong considered it as a storehouse for groceries, as a kind of warehouse, but he gave that up on second thought. It was too far away and anyone can go in through a window. He was tapping the rubber mat with his gold ring and considering the problem when the door opened and Mack came in. Mack was the elder, leader, mentor, and to a small extent the exploiter of a little group of men who had in common no families, no money, and no ambitions beyond food, drink, and contentment. But whereas most men in their search for contentment destroy themselves and fall wearily short of their targets, Mack and his friends approached contentment casually, quietly, and absorbed it gently. Mack and Hazel, a young man of great strength, Eddie who filled in as a bartender at La Ida, Hughie and Jones who occasionally collected frogs and cats for Western Biological, were currently living in those large rusty pipes in the lot next to Lee Chong's. That is, they lived in the pipes when it was damp but in fine weather they lived in the shadow of the black cypress tree at the top of the lot. The limbs folded down and made a canopy under which a man could lie and look out at the flow and vitality of Cannery Row.

Lee Chong stiffened ever so slightly when Mack came in and his eyes glanced quickly about the store to make sure that Eddie or Hazel or Hughie or Jones had not come in too and drifted away among the groceries.

Mack laid out his cards with a winning honesty. "Lee," he said, "I and Eddie and the rest heard you own the Abbeville place."

Lee Chong nodded and waited.

"I and my friends thought we'd ast you if we could move in there. We'll keep up the property," he added quickly. "Wouldn't let anybody break in or hurt anything. Kids might knock out the windows, you know—" Mack suggested. "Place might burn down if somebody don't keep an eye on it."

Lee tilted his head back and looked into Mack's eyes through the half-glasses and Lee's tapping finger slowed its tempo as he thought deeply. In Mack's eyes there was good will and good fellowship and a desire to make everyone happy. Why then did Lee Chong feel slightly surrounded? Why did his mind pick its way as delicately as a cat through cactus? It had been sweetly done, almost in a spirit of philanthropy. Lee's mind leaped ahead at the possibilities—no, they were probabilities, and his finger tapping slowed still further. He saw himself refusing Mack's request and he saw the broken glass from the windows. Then Mack would offer a second time to watch over and preserve Lee's property—and at the second refusal, Lee could smell the smoke, could see the little flames creeping up the walls. Mack and his friends would try to help to put it out. Lee's finger came to a gentle rest on the change mat. He was beaten. He knew that. There was left to him only the possibility of saving face and Mack was likely to be very generous about that. Lee said, "You like pay lent my place? You like live there same hotel?"

Mack smiled broadly and he was generous. "Say—" he cried. "That's an idear. Sure. How much?"

Lee considered. He knew it didn't matter what he charged. He wasn't going to get it anyway. He might just as well make it a really sturdy face-saving sum. "Fi' dolla' week," said Lee.

Mack played it through to the end. "I'll have to talk to the boys about it," he said dubiously. "Couldn't you make that four dollars a week?"

"Fi' dolla," said Lee firmly.

"Well, I'll see what the boys say," said Mack.

And that was the way it was. Everyone was happy about it. And if it be thought that Lee Chong suffered a total loss, at least his mind did not work that way. The windows were not broken. Fire did not break out, and while no rent was ever paid, if the tenants ever had any money, and quite often they did have, it never occurred to them to spend it any place except at Lee Chong's grocery. What he had was a little group of active and potential customers under wraps. But it went further than that. If a drunk caused trouble in the grocery, if the kids swarmed down from New Monterey intent on plunder, Lee Chong had only to call and his tenants rushed to his aid. One further bond it established—you cannot steal from your benefactor. The saving to Lee Chong in cans of beans and tomatoes and milk and watermelons more than paid the rent. And if there was a sudden and increased leakage among the groceries in New Monterey that was none of Lee Chong's affair.

(1945)

From

THE MOHAWKS IN HIGH STEEL
by Joseph Mitchell

The most footloose Indians in North America are a band of mixed-blood Mohawks whose home, the Caughnawaga Reservation, is on the St. Lawrence River
in Quebec. They are generally called the Caughnawagas. In times past, they
were called the Christian Mohawks or the Praying Mohawks. There are three
thousand of them, at least six hundred and fifty of whom spend more time in
cities and towns all over the United States than they do on the reservation. Some
are as restless as gypsies. It is not unusual for a family to lock up its house,
leave the key with a neighbor, get into an automobile, and go away for years.
There are colonies of Caughnawagas in Brooklyn, Buffalo, and Detroit. The
biggest colony is in Brooklyn, out in the North Gowanus neighborhood. It was
started in the late twenties, there are approximately four hundred men, women,
and children in it, it is growing, and it shows signs of permanence. A few families have bought houses. The pastor of one of the churches in the neighborhood, the Cuyler Presbyterian, has learned the Mohawk dialect of the Iroquois
language and holds a service in it once a month, and the church has elected a
Caughnawaga to its board of deacons. There have been marriages between
Caughnawagas and members of other groups in the neighborhood. The Caughnawaga women once had trouble in finding a brand of corn meal (Quaker White
Enriched and Degerminated) that they like to use in making *ka-na-ta-rok,* or
Indian boiled bread; all the grocery stores in North Gowanus, even the little
Italian ones, now carry it. One saloon, the Nevins Bar & Grill, has become a
Caughnawaga hangout and is referred to in the neighborhood as the Indian Bank;
on weekend nights, two-thirds of its customers are Caughnawagas; to encourage their patronage, it stocks one Montreal ale and two Montreal beers. A say-
ing in the band is that Brooklyn is the downtown of Caughnawaga.

*   *   *   *   *

Sometime in 1915 or 1916, a Caughnawaga bridgeman named John Diabo
came down to New York City and got a job on Hell Gate Bridge. He was a
curiosity and was called Indian Joe; two old foremen still remember him. After
he had worked for some months as bucker-up in an Irish gang, three other
Caughnawagas joined him and they formed a gang of their own. They had worked
together only a few weeks when Diabo stepped off a scaffold and dropped into
the river and was drowned. He was highly skilled and his misstep was freakish;

recently, in trying to explain it, a Caughnawaga said, "It must've been one of those cases, he got in the way of himself." The other Caughnawagas went back to the reservation with his body and did not return. As well as the old men in the band can recollect, no other Caughnawagas worked here until the twenties. In 1926, attracted by the building boom, three or four Caughnawaga gangs came down. The old men say that these gangs worked first on the Fred F. French Building, the Graybar Building, and One Fifth Avenue. In 1928, three more gangs came down. They worked first on the George Washington Bridge. In the thirties, when Rockefeller Center was the biggest steel job in the country, at least seven additional Caughnawaga gangs came down. Upon arriving here, the men in all these gangs enrolled in the Brooklyn local of the high-steel union, the International Association of Bridge, Structural, and Ornamental Iron Workers, American Federation of Labor. Why they enrolled in the Brooklyn instead of the Manhattan local, no one now seems able to remember. The hall of the Brooklyn local is on Atlantic Avenue, in the block between Times Plaza and Third Avenue, and the Caughnawagas got lodgings in furnished-room houses and cheap hotels in the North Gowanus neighborhood, a couple of blocks up Atlantic from the hall. In the early thirties, they began sending for their families and moving into tenements and apartment houses in the same neighborhood. During the war, Caughnawagas continued to come down. Many of these enrolled in the Manhattan local, but all of them settled in North Gowanus.

At present, there are eighty-three Caughnawagas in the Brooklyn local and forty-two in the Manhattan local. Less than a third of them work steadily in the city. The others keep their families in North Gowanus and work here intermittently but spend much of their time in other cities. They roam from coast to coast, usually by automobile, seeking rush jobs that offer unlimited overtime work at double pay; in New York City, the steel-erecting companies use as little overtime as possible. A gang may work in half a dozen widely separated cities in a single year. Occasionally, between jobs, they return to Brooklyn to see their families. Now and then, after long jobs, they pick up their families and go up to the reservation for a vacation; some go up every summer. A few men sometimes take their families along on trips to jobs and send them back to Brooklyn by bus or train. Several foremen who have had years of experience with Caughnawagas believe that they roam because they can't help doing so, it is a passion, and that their search for overtime is only an excuse. A veteran foreman for the American Bridge Company says he has seen Caughnawagas leave jobs that offered all the overtime they could handle. When they are making up their minds to move on, he says, they become erratic. "Everything will be going along fine on a job," he says. "Good working conditions. Plenty of overtime. A nice city. Then the news will come over the grapevine about some big new job opening up somewhere; it might be a thousand miles away. That kind of news always causes a lot of talk, what we call water-bucket talk, but the Indians don't talk; they know what's in each other's mind. For a couple of days, they're tensed up and edgy. They look a little wild in the eyes. They've heard the call. Then, all of a sudden, they turn in their tools, and they're gone. Can't wait another minute. They'll quit at lunchtime, in the middle of the week. They won't even wait for their pay. Some other gang will collect their money and hold it until a postcard comes back telling where to send it." George C. Lane, manager of erections in the New York district for the Bethlehem Steel Company, once said that the movements of a Caughnawaga gang are as impossible to foresee as the movements of a flock of sparrows. "In the summer of 1936," Mr. Lane said, "we finished a job here in the city and the very next day we were starting in on a job exactly three blocks away. I heard one of our foremen trying his best to persuade an Indian gang to go on the new job. They had got word about a job in Hartford and wanted to go up there. The foreman told them the rate of pay was the same; there wouldn't be any more overtime up there than here; their families were here; they'd have travelling expenses; they'd have to root around Hartford for lodgings. Oh, no; it was Hartford or nothing. A year or so later I ran into this gang on a job in Newark, and I asked the heater how they made out in Hartford that time. He said they didn't go to Hartford. 'We went to San Francisco, California,' he said. 'We went out and worked on the Golden Gate Bridge.' "

In New York City, the Caughnawagas work mostly for the big companies—Bethlehem, American Bridge, the Lehigh Structural Steel Company, and the Harris Structural Steel Company. Among the structures in and around the city on which they worked in numbers are the R.C.A. Building, the Cities Service Building, the Empire State Building, the Daily News Building, the Chanin Building, the Bank of the Manhattan Company Building, the City Bank Farmers Trust Building, the George Washington Bridge, the Bayonne Bridge, the Passaic River Bridge, the Triborough Bridge, the Henry Hudson Bridge, the Little Hell Gate Bridge, the Bronx-Whitestone Bridge, the Marine Parkway Bridge, the Pulaski Skyway, the West Side Highway, the Waldorf-Astoria, London Terrace, and Knickerbocker Village.

North Gowanus is an old, sleepy, shabby neighborhood that lies between the head of the Gowanus Canal and the Borough Hall shopping district. There are factories in it, and coal tipples and junk yards, but it is primarily residential, and red-brick tenements and brownstone apartment houses are most numerous. The Caughnawagas all live within ten blocks of each other, in an area bounded by Court Street on the west, Schermerhorn Street on the north, Fourth Avenue on the east, and Warren Street on the south. They live in the best houses on the best blocks. As a rule, Caughnawaga women are good housekeepers and keep their apartments Dutch-clean. Most of them decorate a mantel or a wall with heirlooms brought down from the reservation—a drum, a set of rattles, a mask, a cradleboard. Otherwise, their apartments look much the same as those of their white neighbors. A typical family group consists of husband and wife and a couple of children and a female relative or two. After they get through school on the reservation, many Caughnawaga girls come down to North Gowanus and work in factories. Some work for the Fred Goat Company, a metal-stamping factory in the neighborhood, and some work for the Gem Safety Razor Corporation, whose factory is within walking distance. Quite a few of these girls have married whites; several have broken all ties with the band and the reservation. In the last ten years, Caughnawaga girls have married Filipinos, Germans, Italians, Jews, Norwegians, and Puerto Ricans. Many North Gowanus families often have relatives visiting them for long periods; when there is a new baby in a family, a grandmother or an aunt almost always comes down from the reservation and helps out. Caughnawagas are allowed to cross the border freely. However, each is required to carry a card, to which a photograph is attached, certifying that he or she is a member of the band. These cards are issued by the Indian Affairs Branch; the Caughnawagas refer to them as "passports." More than half of the North Gowanus housewives spend their spare time making souvenirs. They make a lot of them. They specialize in dolls, handbags, and belts, which they ornament with colored beads, using variations of ancient Iroquois designs such as the sky dome, the night sun, the day sun, the fern head, the ever-growing tree, the world turtle, and the council fire. Every fall, a few of the most Indian-looking of the men take vacations from structural steel for a month or so and go out with automobile loads of these souvenirs and sell them on the midways of state, county, and community fairs in New York, Connecticut, New Jersey, and Pennsylvania. The men wear buckskins and feathers on these trips and sleep in canvas tepees pitched on fairgrounds. Occasionally, on midways, to attract attention, they let out self-conscious wahoos and do fragments of the Duel Dance, the Dove Dance, the Falseface Dance, and other old half-forgotten Mohawk dances. The women obtain the raw materials for souvenirs from the Plume Trading & Sales Company, at 155 Lexington Avenue, in Manhattan, a concern that sells beads, deerskin, imitation eagle feathers, and similar merchandise to Indian handicraftsmen all over the United States and Canada. There are approximately fifty children of school age in the colony. Two-thirds go to Public School 47, on Pacific Street, and the others go to parochial schools—St. Paul's, St. Agnes's, and St. Charles Borromeo's. Caughnawaga children read comic books, listen to the radio while doing their homework, sit twice through double features, and play stick ball in vacant lots the same as the other children in the neighborhood; teachers say that they differ from the others mainly in that they are more reserved and polite. They have unusual manual dexterity; by the age of three, most of them are able to tie their shoelaces. The adult Caughnawagas are multilingual; all speak Mohawk, all speak English, and all speak or understand at least a little French. In homes where both parents are Caughnawagas, Mohawk is spoken almost exclusively, and the children pick it up. In homes where the mother is non-Indian and the father is away a good deal, a situation that is becoming more and more frequent, the children sometimes fail to learn the language, and this causes much sadness.

The Caughnawagas are churchgoers. The majority of the Catholics go to St. Paul's Church, at Court and Congress Streets, and the majority of the Protestants go to Cuyler Presbyterian Church, on Pacific Street. Dr. David Munroe Cory, the pastor at Cuyler, is a man of incongruous interests. He is an amateur wrestler; he is vice-president of the Iceberg Athletic Club, a group that swims in the ocean at Coney Island throughout the winter; he once ran for Borough President of Brooklyn on the Socialist ticket; he is an authority on Faustus Socinus, the sixteenth-century Italian religious thinker; he studies languages for pleasure and knows eight, among them Hebrew, Greek, and Gaelic. A few Caughnawagas started turning up at Cuyler Church in the middle thirties, and Dr. Cory decided to learn Mohawk and see if he could attract more of them. He has not achieved fluency in Mohawk, but Caughnawagas say that he speaks it better than other white men, mostly anthropologists and priests, who have studied it. He holds a complete service in Mohawk the first Sunday evening in each month, after the English service, and twenty or thirty Caughnawagas usually attend. Twenty-five have joined the church. Michael Diabo, a retired riveter, was recently elected a deacon. Steven M. Schmidt, an Austrian-American who is married to Mrs. Josephine Skye Schmidt, a Caughnawaga woman, is an elder. Mr. Schmidt works in the compensation-claim department of an insurance company. Under Dr. Cory's guidance, two Caughnawaga women, Mrs. Schmidt and Mrs. Margaret Lahache, translated a group of hymns into Mohawk and compiled a hymnal, *The Caughnawaga Hymnal,* which is used in Cuyler and in the Protestant church on the reservation. Dr. Cory himself translated the Gospel According to Luke into Mohawk. Dr. Cory is quiet and serious, his sermons are free of cant, he has an intuitive understanding of Indian conversational taboos, and he is the only white person who is liked and trusted by the whole colony. Caughnawagas who are not members of his congregation, even some Catholics and longhouse people, go to him for advice.

(1949)

THE DARK
PAST
The Burden
of Bondage

No more auction block for me,
No more, no more,
No more auction block for me,
Many thousand gone.
> Spiritual

It is better to die than to grow up and find that
you are colored.
> Fenton Johnson
> Tired

From

THE REIGN OF LAW
by James Lane Allen

A pair of recalcitrant feet were now heard mounting the stair: the flowers on the pillow closed their petals. When the negro girl knelt down before the grate, with her back to the bed and the soles of her shoes set up straight side by side like two gray bricks, the eyes were softly opened again. Gabriella had never seen a head like this negro girl's, that is, never until the autumn before last, when she had come out into this neighborhood of plain farming people to teach a district school. Whenever she was awake early enough to see this curiosity, she never failed to renew her study of it with unflagging zest. It was such a mysterious, careful arrangement of knots, and pine cones, and the strangest-looking little black sticks wrapped with white packing thread, and the whole system of coils seemingly connected with a central mental battery, or idea, or plan, within. She studied it now, as the fire was being kindled, and the kindler, with inflammatory blows of the poker on the bars of the grate, told her troubles over audibly to herself: "Set free, and still making fires of winter mornings; how was *that?* Where was any freedom in *that?* Her wages? Didn't she *work* for her wages? Didn't she *earn* her wages? Then where did freedom come in?"

One must look low for high truth sometimes, as we gather necessary fruit on nethermost boughs and dig the dirt for treasure. The Anglo-Saxon girl lying in the bed and the young African girl kindling her fire—these two, the highest and the humblest types of womanhood in the American republic—were inseparably connected in that room that morning as children of the same Revolution. It had cost the war of the Union, to enable this African girl to cast away the cloth enveloping her head—that detested sign of her slavery—and to arrange her hair with ancestral taste, the true African beauty sense. As long as she had been a slave, she had been compelled by her Anglo-Saxon mistress to wear her head-handkerchief; as soon as she was set free, she, with all the women of her race in the South, tore the head-handkerchief indignantly off. In the same way, it cost the war of the Union to enable Gabriella to teach school. She had been set free also, and the bandage removed from her liberties. The negress had been empowered to demand wages for her toil; the Anglo-Saxon girl had been empowered to accept without reproach the wages for hers.

(1900)

119

From

THE BATTLE-GROUND
by Ellen Glasgow

That was an autumn of burning political conditions, and the excited slavery debates in the North were reëchoing through the Virginia mountains. The Major, like the old war horse that he was, had already pricked up his ears, and determined to lend his tongue or his sword, as his state might require. That a fight could go on in the Union so long as Virginia or himself kept out of it, seemed to him a possibility little less than preposterous.

"Didn't we fight the Revolution, sir? and didn't we fight the War of 1812? and didn't we fight the Mexican War to boot?" he would demand. "And, bless my soul, aren't we ready to fight all the Yankees in the universe, and to whip them clean out of the Union, too? Why, it wouldn't take us ten days to have them on their knees, sir."

The Governor did not laugh now; the times were too grave for that. His clear eyes had seen whither they were drifting, and he had thrown his influence against the tide, which, he knew, would but sweep over him in the end. "You are out of place in Virginia, Major," he said seriously. "Virginia wants peace, and she wants the Union. Go south, my dear sir, go south."

During the spring before he had gone south himself to a convention at Montgomery, and he had spoken there against one of the greatest of the Southern orators. His state had upheld him, but the Major had not. He came home to find his old neighbour red with resentment, and refusing for the first few days to shake the hand of "a man who would tamper with the honour of Virginia." At the end of the week the Major's hand was held out, but his heart still bore his grievance, and he began quoting William L. Yancey, as he had once quoted Mr. Addison. In the little meetings at Uplands or at Chericoke, he would now declaim the words of the impassioned agitator as vigorously as in the old days he had recited those of the polished gentleman of letters. The rector and the doctor would sit silent and abashed, and only the Governor would break in now and then with: "You go too far, Major. There is a step from which there is no drawing back, and that step means ruin to your state, sir."

"Ruin, sir? Nonsense! nonsense! We made the Union, and we'll unmake it when we please. We didn't make slavery; but, if Virginia wants slaves, by God, sir, she shall have slaves!"

It was after such a discussion in the Governor's library that the old gentleman rose one evening to depart in his wrath. "The man who sits up in my presence and questions my right to own my slaves is a damned black abolitionist, sir,'' he thundered as he went, and by the time he reached his coach he was so blinded by his rage that Congo, the driver, was obliged to lift him bodily into his seat. "Dis yer ain' no way ter do, Ole Marster," said the negro, reproachfully. "How I gwine teck cyar you like Ole Miss done tole me; w'en you let yo' bile git ter yo' haid like dis? 'Tain' no way ter do, suh.''

The Major was too full for silence; and, ignoring the Governor, who had hurried out to beseech him to return, he let his rage burst forth.

"I can't help it, Congo, I can't help it!" he said. "They want to take you from me, do you hear? and that black Republican party up north wants to take you, too. They say I've no right to you, Congo,—bless my soul, and you were born on my own land!''

"Go 'way, Ole Marster, who gwine min' w'at dey say?'' returned Congo, soothingly. "You des better wrop dat ar neck'chif roun' yo' thoat er Ole Miss'll git atter you sho' es you live!''

The Major wiped his eyes on the end of the neckerchief as he tied it about his throat. "But, if they elect their President, he may send down an army to free you," he went on, with something like a sob of anger, "and I'd like to know what we'd do then, Congo.''

"Lawd, Lawd, suh," said Congo, as he wrapped the robe about his master's knees. "Did you ever heah tell er sech doin's!'' then, as he mounted the box, he leaned down and called out reassuringly, "Don' you min', Ole Marster, we'll des loose de dawgs on 'em, dat's w'at we'll do," and they rolled off indignantly, leaving the Governor half angry and half apologetic upon his portico.

It was on the way home that evening that Congo spied in the sassafras bushes beside the road a runaway slave of old Rainy-day Jones's, and descended, with a shout, to deliver his brother into bondage.

"Hi, Ole Marster, w'at I gwine tie him wid?'' he demanded gleefully.

The Major looked out of the window, and his face went white.

"What's that on his cheek, Congo?'' he asked in a whisper.

"Dat's des whar dey done hit 'im, Ole Marster. How I gwine tie 'im?''

But the Major had looked again, and the awful redness rose to his brow.

"Shut up, you fool!'' he said with a roar, as he dived under his seat and brought out his brandy flask. "Give him a swallow of that—be quick, do you hear? Pour it into your cup, sir, and give him that corn pone in your pocket. I see it sticking out. There, now hoist him up beside you, and, if I meet that rascal Jones, I'll blow his damn brains out!''

The Major doubtless would have fulfilled his oath as surely as his twelve peers would have shaken his hand afterwards; but, by the time they came up with Rainy-day a mile ahead, his wrath had settled and he had decided that "he didn't want such dirty blood upon his hands.''

So he took a different course, and merely swore a little as he threw a roll of banknotes into the road. "Don't open your mouth to me, you hell hound,'' he cried, "or I'll have you whipped clean out of this county, sir, and there's not a gentleman in Virginia that wouldn't lend a hand. Don't open your mouth to me, I tell you; here's the price of your property, and you can stoop in the dirt to pick it up. There's no man alive that shall question the divine right of slavery in my presence; but—but it is an institution for gentlemen, and you, sir, are a damned scoundrel!"

With which the Major and old Rainy-day rode on in opposite ways.

(1902)

From

THE LITTLE SHEPHERD OF KINGDOM COME

by John Fox, Jr.

On that day the crisis came at the Deans', and on that day Chad Buford made up his mind. When the Major and Miss Lucy went to bed that night, he slipped out of the house and walked through the yard and across the pike, following the little creek half unconsciously toward the Deans', until he could see the light in Margaret's window, and there he climbed the worm fence and sat leaning his head against one of the forked stakes with his hat in his lap. He would probably not see her again. He would send her word next morning to ask that he might, and he feared what the result of that word would be. Several times his longing eyes saw her shadow pass the curtain, and when her light was out, he closed his eyes and sat motionless—how long he hardly knew; but, when he sprang down, he was stiffened from the midnight chill and his unchanged posture. He went back to his room then, and wrote Margaret a letter and tore it up and went to bed. There was little sleep for him that night, and when the glimmer of morning brightened at his window, he rose listlessly, dipped his hot head in a bowl of water and stole out to the barn. His little mare whinnied a welcome as he opened the barn door. He patted her on the neck.

"Good-by, little girl," he said. He started to call her by name and stopped. Margaret had named the beautiful creature "Dixie." The servants were stirring.

"Good-mawnin', Mars Chad," said each, and with each he shook hands, saying simply that he was going away that morning. Only old Tom asked him a question.

"Foh Gawd, Mars Chad," said the old fellow, "old Mars Buford can't git along widout you. You gwine to come back soon?"

"I don't know, Uncle Tom," said Chad, sadly.

"Whar you gwine, Mars Chad?"

"Into the army."

"De ahmy?" The old man smiled. "You gwine to fight de Yankees?"

"I'm going to fight *with* the Yankees."

The old driver looked as though he could not have heard aright.

"You foolin' this ole nigger, Mars Chad, ain't you?"

Chad shook his head, and the old man straightened himself a bit.

"I'se sorry to heah it, suh," he said, with dignity, and he turned to his work.

Miss Lucy was not feeling well that morning and did not come down to breakfast. The boy was so pale and haggard that the Major looked at him anxiously.

"What's the matter with you, Chad? Are you sick?"

"I didn't sleep very well last night, Major."

The Major chuckled. "I reckon you ain't gettin' enough sleep these days. I reckon I wouldn't, either, if I were in your place."

Chad did not answer. After breakfast he sat with the Major on the porch in the fresh, sunny air. The Major smoked his pipe, taking the stem out of his mouth now and then to shout some order as a servant passed under his eye.

"What's the news, Chad?"

"Mr. Crittenden is back."

"What did old Lincoln say?"

"That Camp Dick Robinson was formed for Kentuckians by Kentuckians, and he did not believe that it was the wish of the State that it should be removed."

"Well, by——! after his promise. What did Davis say?"

"That if Kentucky opened the Northern door for invasion, she must not close the Southern door to entrance for defence."

"And dead right he is," growled the Major with satisfaction.

"Governor Magoffin asked Ohio and Indiana to join in an effort for a peace Congress," Chad added.

"Well?"

"Both governors refused."

"I tell you, boy, the hour has come."

The hour had come.

"I'm going away this morning, Major."

The Major did not even turn his head.

"I thought this was coming," he said quietly. Chad's face grew even paler, and he steeled his heart for the revelation.

"I've already spoken to Lieutenant Hunt," the Major went on. "He expects to be a captain, and he says that, maybe, he can make you a lieutenant. You can take that boy Brutus as a body servant.'' He brought his fist down on the railing of the porch. ''God, but I'd give the rest of my life to be ten years younger than I am now.''

''Major, I'm *going into the Union army.*''

The Major's pipe almost dropped from between his lips. Catching the arms of his chair with both hands, he turned heavily and with dazed wonder, as though the boy had struck him with his fist from behind, and, without a word, stared hard into Chad's tortured face. The keen old eye had not long to look before it saw the truth, and then, silently, the old man turned back. His hands trembled on the chair, and he slowly thrust them into his pockets, breathing hard through his nose. The boy expected an outbreak, but none came. A bee buzzed above them. A yellow butterfly zigzagged by. Blackbirds chattered in the firs. The screech of a peacock shrilled across the yard, and a ploughman's singing wailed across the fields:

Trouble, O Lawd!
Nothin' but trouble in de lan' of Canaan.

The boy knew he had given his old friend a mortal hurt.

''Don't, Major,'' he pleaded. ''You don't know how I have fought against this. I tried to be on your side. I thought I was. I joined the Rifles. I found first that I couldn't fight *with* the South, and—then—I—found that I had to fight *for* the North. It almost kills me when I think of all you have done——''

The Major waved his hand imperiously. He was not the man to hear his favors recounted, much less refer to them himself. He straightened and got up from his chair. His manner had grown formal, stately, coldly courteous.

''I cannot understand, but you are old enough, sir, to know your own mind. You should have prepared me for this. You will excuse me a moment.'' Chad rose and the Major walked toward the door, his step not very steady, and his shoulders a bit shrunken—his back, somehow, looked suddenly old.

''Brutus!'' he called sharply to a black boy who was training rosebushes in the yard. ''Saddle Mr. Chad's horse.'' Then, without looking again at Chad, he turned into his office, and Chad, standing where he was, with a breaking heart, could hear, through the open window, the rustling of papers and the scratching of a pen.

In a few minutes he heard the Major rise and he turned to meet him. The old man held a roll of bills in one hand and a paper in the other.

''Here is the balance due you on our last trade,'' he said, quietly. ''The mare is yours—Dixie,'' he added, grimly. ''The old mare is in foal. I will keep her and send you your due when the time comes. We are quite even,'' he went on in a level tone of business. ''Indeed, what you have done about the place more than exceeds any expense that you have ever caused me. If anything, I am still in your debt.''

''I can't take it,'' said Chad, choking back a sob.

"You will have to take it," the Major broke in, curtly, "unless——"
the Major held back the bitter speech that was on his lips and Chad understood.
The old man did not want to feel under any obligations to him.

"I would offer you Brutus, as was my intention, except that I know you
would not take him——" again he added, grimly, "and Brutus would run away
from you."

"No, Major," said Chad, sadly, "I would not take Brutus," and he stepped
down one step of the porch backward.

"I tried to tell you, Major, but you wouldn't listen. I don't wonder, for
I couldn't explain to you what I couldn't understand myself. I——" the boy
choked and tears filled his eyes. He was afraid to hold out his hand.

"Good-by, Major," he said, brokenly.

"Good-by, sir," answered the Major, with a stiff bow, but the old man's
lip shook and he turned abruptly within.

Chad did not trust himself to look back but, as he rode through the pasture to the pike gate, his ears heard, never to forget, the chatter of the blackbirds, the noises around the barn, the cry of the peacock, and the wailing of
the ploughman:

> Trouble, O Lawd!
> Nothin' but trouble——

At the gate the little mare turned her head toward town and started away
in the easy swinging lope for which she was famous. From a cornfield Jerome
Conners, the overseer, watched horse and rider for a while, and then his lips
were lifted over his protruding teeth in one of his ghastly, infrequent smiles.
Chad Buford was out of his way at last. At the Deans' gate, Snowball was just
going in on Margaret's pony and Chad pulled up.

"Where's Mr. Dan, Snowball?—and Mr. Harry?"

"Mars Dan he gwine to de wah—an' I'se gwine wid him."

"Is Mr. Harry going, too?" Snowball hesitated. He did not like to gossip
about family matters, but it was a friend of the family who was questioning
him.

"Yessuh! But Mammy say Mars Harry's teched in de haid. He gwine to
fight wid de po' white trash."

"Is Miss Margaret at home?"

"Yessuh."

Chad had his note to Margaret, unsealed. He little felt like seeing her
now, but he had just as well have it all over at once. He took it out and looked
it over once more—irresolute.

"I'm going away to join the Union army, Margaret. May I come to tell
you good-by? If not, God bless you always.

CHAD."

"Take this to Miss Margaret, Snowball, and bring me an answer here as
soon as you can."

"Yessuh."

The black boy was not gone long. Chad saw him go up the steps, and in
a few moments he reappeared and galloped back.

"Ole Mistis say dey ain't no answer."

"Thank you, Snowball." Chad pitched him a coin and loped on toward
Lexington with his head bent, his hands folded on the pommel, and the reins
flapping loosely. Within one mile of Lexington he turned into a cross-road and
set his face toward the mountains.

(1903)

From

THE CLANSMAN
by Thomas Dixon, Jr.

The excitement which preceeded the first Reconstruction election in the South
paralysed the industries of the country. When demagogues poured down from
the North and began their raving before crowds of ignorant negroes, the plow
stopped in the furrow, the hoe was dropped, and the millenium was at hand.

Negro tenants, working under contracts issued by the Freedman's Bureau, stopped work, and rode their landlords' mules and horses around the county,
following these orators.

*   *   *   *   *

At noon Ben and Phil strolled to the polling-place to watch the progress
of the first election under Negro rule. The Square was jammed with shouting,
jostling, perspiring negroes, men, women, and children. The day was warm,
and the African odour was supreme even in the open air.

A crowd of two hundred were packed around a peddler's box. There were
two of them—one crying the wares, and the other wrapping and delivering the
goods. They were selling a new patent poison for rats.

"I've only a few more bottles left now, gentlemen," he shouted, "and
the polls will close at sundown. A great day for our brother in black. Two years
of army rations from the Freedman's Bureau, with old army clothes thrown in,
and now the ballot—the priceless glory of American citizenship. But better still
the very land is to be taken from these proud aristocrats and given to the poor
down-trodden black man. Forty acres and a mule—think of it! Provided, mind
you—that you have a bottle of my wonder-worker to kill the rats and save your

corn for the mule. No man can have the mule unless he has corn; and no man can have corn if he has rats—and only a few bottles left——''

"Gimme one," yelled a negro.

"Forty acres and a mule, your old masters to work your land and pay his rent in corn, while you sit back in the shade and see him sweat."

"Gimme er bottle and two er dem pictures!" bawled another candidate for a mule.

The peddler handed him the bottle and the pictures and threw a handful of his labels among the crowd. These labels happened to be just the size of the ballots, having on them the picture of a dead rat lying on his back, and, above, the emblem of death, the cross-bones and skull.

"Forty acres and a mule for every black man—why was I ever born white? I never had no luck, nohow!"

Phil and Ben passed on nearer the polling-place, around which stood a cordon of soldiers with a line of negro voters two hundred yards in length extending back into the crowd.

The negro Leagues came in armed battalions and voted in droves, carrying their muskets in their hands. Less than a dozen white men were to be seen about the place.

The negroes, under the drill of the League and the Freedman's Bureau, protected by the bayonet, were voting to enfranchise themselves, disfranchise their former masters, ratify a new constitution, and elect a legislature to do their will. Old Aleck was a candidate for the House, chief poll-holder, and seemed to be in charge of the movements of the voters outside the booth as well as inside. He appeared to be omnipresent, and his self-importance was a sight Phil had never dreamed. He could not keep his eyes off him.

"By George, Cameron, he's a wonder!" he laughed.

Aleck had suppressed as far as possible the story of the painted stakes and the deed, after sending out warnings to the brethren to beware of two enticing strangers. The surveyors had reaped a rich harvest and passed on. Aleck made up his mind to go to Columbia, make the laws himself, and never again trust a white man from the North or South. The agent of the Freedman's Bureau at Piedmont tried to choke him off the ticket. The League backed him to a man. He could neither read nor write, but before he took to whiskey he had made a specialty of revival exhortation, and his mouth was the most effective thing about him. In this campaign he was an orator of no mean powers. He knew what he wanted, and he knew what his people wanted, and he put the thing in words so plain that a wayfaring man, though a fool, couldn't make any mistake about it.

As he bustled past, forming a battalion of his brethren in line to march to the polls, Phil followed his every movement with amused interest.

Besides being so bow-legged that his walk was a moving joke, he was so striking a negro in his personal appearance, he seemed to the young Northerner almost a distinct type of man.

His head was small and seemed mashed on the sides until it bulged into a double lobe behind. Even his ears, which he had pierced and hung with red earbobs, seemed to have been crushed flat to the side of his head. His kinked hair was wrapped in little hard rolls close to the skull and bound tightly with dirty thread. His receding forehead was high and indicated a cunning intelligence. His nose was broad and crushed flat against his face. His jaws were strong and angular, mouth wide, and lips thick, curling back from rows of solid teeth set obliquely in their blue gums. The one perfect thing about him was the size and setting of his mouth—he was a born African orator, undoubtedly descended from a long line of savage spell-binders, whose eloquence in the palaver houses of the jungle had made them native leaders. His thin spindle-shanks supported an oblong, protruding stomach, resembling an elderly monkey's, which seemed so heavy it swayed his back to carry it.

The animal vivacity of his small eyes and the flexibility of his eyebrows, which he worked up and down rapidly with every change of countenance, expressed his eager desires.

He had laid aside his new shoes, which hurt him, and went barefooted to facilitate his movements on the great occasion. His heels projected and his foot was so flat that what should have been the hollow of it made a hole in the dirt where he left his track.

He was already mellow with liquor, and was dressed in an old army uniform and cap, with two horse-pistols buckled around his waist. On a strap hanging from his shoulder were strung a half-dozen tin canteens filled with whiskey.

A disturbance in the line of voters caused the young men to move forward to see what it meant.

Two negro troopers had pulled Jake out of the line, and were dragging him toward old Aleck.

The election judge straightened himself up with great dignity:

"What wuz de rapscallion doin'?"

"In de line, tryin' ter vote."

"Fetch 'im befo' de judgment bar," said Aleck, taking a drink from one of his canteens.

The troopers brought Jake before the judge.

"Tryin' ter vote, is yer?"

" 'Lowed I would."

"You hear 'bout de great sassieties de Gubment's fomentin' in dis country?"

"Yas, I hear erbout 'em."

"Is yer er member er de Union League?"

"Na-sah. I'd rudder steal by myself. I doan' lak too many in de party!"

"En yer ain't er No'f Ca'liny gemmen, is yer—yer ain't er member er de 'Red Strings'?"

"Na-sah, I come when I'se called—dey doan' hatter put er string on me— ner er block, ner er collar, ner er chain, ner er muzzle——''

"Will yer 'splain ter dis cote——" railed Aleck.

"What cote? Dat ole army cote?" Jake laughed in loud peals that rang over the square.

Aleck recovered his dignity and demanded angrily:

"Does yer belong ter de Heroes ob Americky?"

"Na-sah. I ain't burnt nobody's house ner barn yet, ner hamstrung no stock, ner waylaid nobody atter night—honey, I ain't fit ter jine. Heroes ob Americky! Is you er hero?"

"Ef yer doan' b'long ter no s'iety," said Aleck with judicial deliberation, "what is you?"

"Des er ole-fashun all-wool-en-er-yard-wide nigger dat stan's by his ole marster 'cause he's his bes' frien', stays at home, en tends ter his own business."

(1905)

NIGGER
by Carl Sandburg

I AM the nigger.
Singer of songs,
Dancer . . .
Softer than fluff of cotton . . .
Harder than dark earth
Roads beaten in the sun
By the bare feet of slaves . . .
Foam of teeth . . . breaking crash of laughter . . .
Red love of the blood of woman,
White love of the tumbling pickaninnies . . .
Lazy love of the banjo thrum . . .
Sweated and driven for the harvest-wage,
Loud laughter with hands like hams,
Fists toughened on the handles,
Smiling the slumber dreams of old jungles,
Crazy as the sun and dew and dripping, heaving life of the jungle,
Brooding and muttering with memories of shackles:

> I am the nigger.
> Look at me.
> I am the nigger.

(1916)

HERITAGE
by Countee Cullen

What is Africa to me:
Copper sun or scarlet sea,
Jungle star or jungle track,
Strong bronzed men, or regal black
Women from whose loins I sprang
When the birds of Eden sang?
One three centuries removed
From the scenes his fathers loved,
Spicy grove, cinnamon tree,
What is Africa to me?

So I lie, who all day long
Want no sound except the song
Sung by wild barbaric birds
Goading massive jungle herds,
Juggernauts of flesh that pass
Trampling tall defiant grass
Where young forest lovers lie
Plighting troth beneath the sky.
So I lie, who always hear
Though I cram against my ear
Both my thumbs, and keep them there,
Great drums beating through the air.
So I lie, whose fount of pride,
Dear distress, and joy allied,
Is my sombre flesh and skin,
With the dark blood dammed within
Like great pulsing tides of wine
That, I fear, must burst the fine
Channels of the chafing net
Where they surge and foam and fret.

Africa? A book one thumbs
Listlessly, till slumber comes.
Unremembered are her bats
Circling through the night, her cats
Crouching in the river reeds,

Stalking gentle flesh that feeds
By the river brink; no more
Does the bugle-throated roar
Cry that monarch claws have leapt
From the scabbards where they slept.
Silver snakes that once a year
Doff the lovely coats you wear,
Seek no covert in your fear
Lest a mortal eye should see;
What's your nakedness to me?
Here no leprous flowers rear
Fierce corollas in the air;
Here no bodies sleek and wet,
Dripping mingled rain and sweat,
Tread the savage measures of
Jungle boys and girls in love.

What is last year's snow to me,
Last year's anything? The tree
Budding yearly must forget
How its past arose or set—
Bough and blossom, flower, fruit,
Even what shy bird with mute
Wonder at her travail there,
Meekly labored in its hair.
One three centuries removed
From the scenes his fathers loved,
Spicy grove, cinnamon tree,
What is Africa to me?

So I lie, who find no peace
Night or day, no slight release
From the unremittent beat
Made by cruel padded feet
Walking through my body's street.
Up and down they go, and back,
Treading out a jungle track.
So I lie, who never quite
Safely sleep from rain at night—
I can never rest at all
When the rain begins to fall;
Like a soul gone mad with pain
I must match its weird refrain;
Ever must I twist and squirm,

Writhing like a baited worm,
While its primal measures drip
Through my body, crying, "Strip!
Doff this new exuberance.
Come and dance the Lover's Dance!"
In an old remembered way
Rain works on me night and day.

Quaint, outlandish heathen gods
Black men fashion out of rods,
Clay, and brittle bits of stone,
In a likeness like their own,
My conversion came high-priced;
I belong to Jesus Christ,
Preacher of humility;
Heathen gods are naught to me.

Father, Son, and Holy Ghost,
So I make an idle boast,
Jesus of the twice turned cheek,
Lamb of God, although I speak
With my mouth thus, in my heart
Do I play a double part.
Ever at thy glowing altar
Must my heart grow sick and falter,
Wishing He I served were black,
Thinking then it would not lack
Precedent of pain to guide it,
Let who would or might deride it;
Surely then this flesh would know
Yours had borne a kindred woe.
Lord, I fashion dark gods, too,
Daring even to give to You
Dark despairing features where,
Crowned with dark rebellious hair,
Patience wavers just so much as
Mortal grief compels, while touches
Quick and hot, of anger, rise
To smitten cheek and weary eyes.
Lord, forgive me if my need
Sometimes shapes a human creed.

All day long and all night through,
One thing only must I do:
Quench my pride and cool my blood,

Lest I perish in the flood.
Lest a hidden ember set
Timber that I thought was wet
Burning like the dryest flax,
Melting like the merest wax,
Lest the grave restore its dead.
Not yet has my heart or head
In the least way realized
They and I are civilized.

(1925)

BLACK TAMBOURINE
by Hart Crane

The interests of a black man in a cellar
Mark tardy judgment on the world's closed door.
Gnats toss in the shadow of a bottle,
And a roach spans a crevice in the floor.

Æsop, driven to pondering, found
Heaven with the tortoise and the hare;
Fox brush and sow ear top his grave
And mingling incantations on the air.

The black man, forlorn in the cellar,
Wanders in some mid-kingdom, dark, that lies,
Between his tambourine, stuck on the wall,
And, in Africa, a carcass quick with flies.

(1926)

From

JOHN BROWN'S BODY
by Stephen Vincent Benét

They stray from the lost plantations like children strayed,
Grinning and singing, following the blue soldiers,
They steal from the lonesome cabins like runaways
Laden with sticks and bundles and conjur-charms;

A huge black mother carries her sucking child
Wrapped in a quilt, a slim brown girl and her lover
Wander November woods like Adam and Eve,
Living on roots and rabbits and liberty,
An old grey field hand dimly plods through the mud,
Looking for some vague place he has heard about
Where Linkum sits at a desk in his gold silk hat
With a bag of silver dollars in either hand
For every old grey field hand that comes to him,
All God's chillun got shoes there and fine new clothes,
All God's chillun got peace there and roastin'-ears,
Hills of barbecue, rivers of pot-licker,
Nobody's got to work there, never no more.

His feet are sore with the road but he stumbles on,
A hundred, a thousand others stumble as he,
Chanting, dizzied, drunken with a strange fever,
A child's delight, a brightness too huge to grasp,
The hidden nation, untaught, unrecognized,
Free at last, but not yet free with the free,
Ignorant, joyful, wronged, child-minded and searching,
Searching the army's road for this new wild thing
That means so much but can't be held in the hand,
That must be there, that yet is so hard to find,
This dream, this pentecost changing, this liberty.

Some wander away to strange death or stranger life,
Some wander awhile and starve and come back at last,
Some stay by the old plantation but will not work
To the great disgust of masters and mistresses,
Sing idly, gamble, sleep through the lazy hours,
Waiting for friendly heaven to rain them down
The mule and the forty acres of their desire.
Some, faithful beyond the bond that they never signed,
Hold to that bond in ruin as in the sun,
Steal food for a hungry mistress, keep her alive,
Keep the house alive, try to pick the weeds from the path,
Gather the wood and chop it and make the fire,
With pitying scorn for the runaway sheep of freedom,
Freedom's a ghost and freedom's a foolish talk,
What counts is making the fire as it should be made. . . .
Oh, blackskinned epic, epic with the black spear,
I cannot sing you, having too white a heart,
And yet, some day, a poet will rise to sing you

And sing you with such truth and mellowness,
—Deep mellow of the husky, golden voice
Crying dark heaven through the spirituals,
Soft mellow of the levee roustabouts,
Singing at night against the banjo-moon—
That you will be a match for any song
Sung by old, populous nations in the past,
And stand like hills against the American sky,
And lay your black spear down by Roland's horn.

(1926–27)

From

MULES AND MEN
by Zora Neale Hurston

Joe Wiley says: "Y'all might as well make up yo' mind to bear wid me, 'cause Ah feel Ah got to tell a lie on Ole Massa for my mamma. Ah done lied on him enough for myself. So Ah'm gointer tell it if I bust my gall tryin'.

> Ole John was a slave, you know. And there was Ole Massa and Ole Missy and de two li' children—a girl and a boy.
>
> Well, John was workin' in de field and he seen de children out on de lake in a boat, just a hollerin'. They had done lost they oars and was 'bout to turn over. So then he went and tole Ole Massa and Ole Missy.
>
> Well, Ole Missy, she hollered and said: "It's so sad to lose these 'cause Ah ain't never goin' to have no more children." Ole Massa made her hush and they went down to de water and follered de shore on 'round till they found 'em. John pulled off his shoes and hopped in and swum out and got in de boat wid de children and brought 'em to shore.
>
> Well, Massa and John take 'em to de house. So they was all so glad 'cause de children got saved. So Massa told 'im to make a good crop dat year and fill up de barn, and den when he lay by de crops nex' year, he was going to set him free.
>
> So John raised so much crop dat year he filled de barn and had to put some of it in de house.
>
> So Friday come, and Massa said, "Well, de day done come that I said I'd set you free. I hate to do it, but I don't like to make myself out a lie. I hate to git rid of a good nigger lak you."
>
> So he went in de house and give John one of his old suits of clothes to put on. So John put it on and come in to shake hands and tell 'em goodbye. De children they cry and Ole Missy she cry. Didn't want to see John go. So John took his bundle and put it on his stick and hung it crost his shoulder.
>
> Well, Ole John started on down de road. Well, Ole Massa said, "John, de children love yuh."

"Yassuh."

"John, I love yuh."

"Yassuh."

"And Missy *like* yuh!"

"Yassuh."

"But 'member, John, youse a nigger."

"Yassuh."

Fur as John could hear 'im down de road he wuz hollerin', "John, Oh John! De children loves you. And I love you. De Missy *like* you."

John would holler back, "Yassuh."

"But 'member youse a nigger, tho!"

Ole Massa kept callin' 'im and his voice was pitiful. But John kept right on steppin' to Canada. He answered Old Massa every time he called 'im, but he consumed on wid his bag.

(1935)

THE WITNESS
by Katherine Anne Porter

Uncle Jimbilly was so old and had spent so many years bowed over things, putting them together and taking them apart, making them over and making them do, he was bent almost double. His hands were closed and stiff from gripping objects tightly, while he worked at them, and they could not open altogether even if a child took the thick black fingers and tried to turn them back. He hobbled on a stick; his purplish skull showed through patches in his wool, which had turned greenish gray and looked as if the moths had got at it.

He mended harness and put half soles on the other Negroes' shoes, he built fences and chicken coops and barn doors; he stretched wires and put in new window panes and fixed sagging hinges and patched up roofs; he repaired carriage tops and cranky plows. Also he had a gift for carving miniature tombstones out of blocks of wood; give him almost any kind of piece of wood and he could turn out a tombstone, shaped very like the real ones, with carving, and a name and date on it if they were needed. They were often needed, for some small beast or bird was always dying and having to be buried with proper ceremonies: the cart draped as a hearse, a shoe-box coffin with a pall over it, a profuse floral outlay, and, of course, a tombstone. As he worked, turning the long blade of his bowie knife deftly in circles to cut a flower, whittling and smoothing the back and sides, stopping now and then to hold it at arm's length and examine it with one eye closed, Uncle Jimbilly would talk in a low, broken, abstracted, murmur, as if to himself; but he was really saying something he meant one to hear. Sometimes it would be an incomprehensible ghost story; listen ever so carefully, at the end it was impossible to decide whether Uncle

Jimbilly himself had seen the ghost, whether it was a real ghost at all, or only another man dressed like one; and he dwelt much on the horrors of slave times.

"Dey used to take 'em out and tie 'em down and whup 'em," he muttered, "wid gret big leather strops inch thick long as yo' ahm, wid round holes bored in 'em so's evey time dey hit 'em de hide and de meat done come off dey bones in little round chunks. And wen dey had whupped 'em wid de strop till dey backs was all raw and bloody, dey spread dry cawnshucks on dey backs and set 'em afire and pahched 'em, and den dey poured vinega all ovah 'em . . . Yassuh. And den, the ve'y nex' day dey'd got to git back to work in the fiels or dey'd do the same thing right ovah agin. Yassah. Dat was it. If dey didn't git back to work dey got it all right ovah agin."

The children—three of them: a serious, prissy older girl of ten, a thoughtful sad looking boy of eight, and a quick flighty little girl of six—sat disposed around Uncle Jimbilly and listened with faint tinglings of embarrassment. They knew, of course, that once upon a time Negroes had been slaves; but they had all been freed long ago and were now only servants. It was hard to realize that Uncle Jimbilly had been born in slavery, as the Negroes were always saying. The children thought that Uncle Jimbilly had got over his slavery very well. Since they had known him, he had never done a single thing that anyone told him to do. He did his work just as he pleased and when he pleased. If you wanted a tombstone, you had to be very careful about the way you asked for it. Nothing could have been more impersonal and faraway than his tone and manner of talking about slavery, but they wriggled a little and felt guilty. Paul would have changed the subject, but Miranda, the little quick one, wanted to know the worst. "Did they act like that to you, Uncle Jimbilly?" she asked.

"No, *mam*," said Uncle Jimbilly. "Now whut name you want on dis one? Dey nevah did. Dey done 'em dat way in the rice swamps. I always worked right here close to the house or in town with Miss Sophia. Down in the swamps . . ."

"Didn't they ever die, Uncle Jimbilly?" asked Paul.

"Cose dey died," said Uncle Jimbilly, "cose dey died—dey died," he went on, pursing his mouth gloomily, "by de thousands and tens upon thousands."

"Can you carve 'Safe in Heaven' on that, Uncle Jimbilly?" asked Maria in her pleasant, mincing voice.

"To put over a tame jackrabbit, Missy?" asked Uncle Jimbilly indignantly. He was very religious. "A heathen like dat? No, *mam*. In de swamps dey used to stake 'em out all day and all night, and all day and all night and all day wid dey hans and feet tied so dey couldn't scretch and let de muskeeters eat 'em alive. De muskeeters 'ud bite 'em tell dey was all swole up like a balloon all over, and you could heah 'em howlin and prayin all ovah the swamp. Yassuh. Dat was it. And nary a drop of watah noh a moufful of braid . . . Yassuh, dat's it. Lawd, dey done it. Hosanna! Now take dis yere tombstone and don' bother me no more . . . or I'll . . ."

Uncle Jimbilly was apt to be suddenly annoyed and you never knew why. He was easily put out about things, but his threats were always so exorbitant that not even the most credulous child could be terrifed by them. He was always going to do something quite horrible to somebody and then he was going to dispose of the remains in a revolting manner. He was going to skin somebody alive and nail the hide on the barn door, or he was just getting ready to cut off somebody's ears with a hatchet and pin them on Bongo, the crop-eared brindle dog. He was often all prepared in his mind to pull somebody's teeth and make a set of false teeth for Ole Man Ronk . . . Ole Man Ronk was a tramp who had been living all summer in the little cabin behind the smokehouse. He got his rations along with the Negroes and sat all day mumbling his naked gums. He had skimpy black whiskers which appeared to be set in wax, and angry red eyelids. He took morphine, it was said; but what morphine might be, or how he took it, or why, no one seemed to know . . . Nothing could have been more unpleasant than the notion that one's teeth might be given to Ole Man Ronk.

The reason why Uncle Jimbilly never did any of these things he threatened was, he said, because he never could get round to them. He always had so much other work on hand he never seemed to get caught up on it. But some day, somebody was going to get a mighty big surprise, and meanwhile everybody had better look out.

(1935)

From

FREEDOM'S A HARD-BOUGHT THING
by Stephen Vincent Benét

A long time ago, in times gone by, in slavery times, there was a man named Cue. I want you to think about him. I've got a reason.

He got born like the cotton in the boll or the rabbit in the pea patch. There wasn't any fine doings when he got born, but his mammy was glad to have him. Yes. He didn't get born in the Big House, or the overseer's house, or any place where the bearing was easy or the work light. No, Lord. He came out of his mammy in a field hand's cabin one sharp winter, and about the first thing he remembered was his mammy's face and the taste of a piece of bacon rind and the light and shine of the pitch-pine fire up the chimney. Well, now, he got born and there he was.

His daddy worked in the fields and his mammy worked in the fields when she wasn't bearing. They were slaves; they chopped the cotton and hoed the corn. They heard the horn blow before the light came and the horn blow that meant the day's work was done. His daddy was a strong man—strong in his back and his arms. The white folks called him Cuffee. His mammy was a good woman, yes, Lord. The white folks called her Sarah, and she was gentle with her hands and gentle with her voice. She had a voice like the river going by in the night, and at night when she wasn't too tired she'd sing songs to little Cue. Some had foreign words in them—African words. She couldn't remember what some of them meant, but they'd come to her down out of time.

Now, how am I going to describe and explain about that time when that time's gone? The white folks lived in the Big House and they had many to tend on them. Old Marster, he lived there like Pharaoh and Solomon, mighty splendid and fine. He had his flocks and his herds, his butler and his baker; his fields ran from the river to the woods and back again. He'd ride around the fields each day on his big horse, Black Billy, just like thunder and lightning, and evenings he'd sit at his table and drink his wine. Man, that was a sight to see, with all the silver knives and the silver forks, the glass decanters, and the gentlemen and ladies from all over. It was a sight to see. When Cue was young, it seemed to him that Old Marster must own the whole world, right up to the edge of the sky. You can't blame him for thinking that.

There were things that changed on the plantation, but it didn't change. There were bad times and good times. There was the time young Marse Edward got bit by the snake, and the time Big Rambo ran away and they caught him with the dogs and brought him back. There was a swivel-eyed overseer that beat folks too much, and then there was Mr. Wade, and he wasn't so bad. There was hog-killing time and Christmas and springtime and summertime. Cue didn't wonder about it or why things happened that way; he didn't expect it to be different. A bee in a hive don't ask you how there come to be a hive in the beginning. Cue grew up strong; he grew up smart with his hands. They put him in the blacksmith shop to help Daddy Jake; he didn't like it, at first, because Daddy Jake was mighty cross-tempered. Then he got to like the work; he learned to forge iron and shape it; he learned to shoe a horse and tire a wagon wheel, and everything a blacksmith does. One time they let him shoe Black Billy, and he shod him light and tight and Old Marster praised him in front of Mr. Wade. He was strong; he was black as night; he was proud of his back and his arms.

Now, he might have stayed that way—yes, he might. He heard freedom talk, now and then, but he didn't pay much mind to it. He wasn't a talker or a preacher; he was Cue and he worked in the blacksmith shop. He didn't want to be a field hand, but he didn't want to be a house servant either. He'd rather be Cue than poor white trash or owned by poor white trash. That's the way he felt; I'm obliged to tell the truth about that way.

Then there was a sickness came and his mammy and his daddy died of it. Old Miss got the doctor for them, but they died just the same. After that, Cue felt lonesome.

He felt lonesome and troubled in his mind. He'd seen his daddy and his mammy put in the ground and new slaves come to take their cabin. He didn't repine about that, because he knew things had to be that way. But when he went to bed at night, in the loft over the blacksmith shop, he'd keep thinking about his mammy and his daddy—how strong his daddy was and the songs that his mammy sang. They'd worked all their lives and had children, though he was the only one left, but the only place of their own they had was the place in the burying ground. And yet they'd been good and faithful servants, because Old Marster said so, with his hat off, when he buried them. The Big House stayed, and the cotton and the corn, but Cue's mammy and daddy were gone like last year's crop. It made Cue wonder and trouble.

He began to take notice of things he'd never noticed. When the horn blew in the morning for the hands to go to the fields, he'd wonder who started blowing that horn, in the first place. It wasn't like thunder and lightning; somebody had started it. When he heard Old Marster say, when he was talking to a friend, "This damned epidemic! It's cost me eight prime field hands and the best-trained butler in the state. I'd rather have lost the Flyaway colt than Old Isaac," Cue put that down in his mind and pondered it. Old Marster didn't mean it mean, and he'd sat up with Old Isaac all night before he died. But Isaac and Cue and the Flyaway colt, they all belonged to Old Marster and he owned them, hide and hair. He owned them, like money in his pockets. Well, Cue had known that all his life, but because he was troubled now, it gave him a queer feeling.

Well, now, he was shoeing a horse for young Marster Shepley one day, and he shod it light and tight. And when he was through, he made a stirrup for young Marster Shepley, and young Marster Shepley mounted and threw him a silver bit, with a laughing word. That shouldn't have bothered Cue, because gentlemen sometimes did that. And Old Marster wasn't mean, he didn't object. But all night Cue kept feeling the print of young Marster Shepley's heel in his hands. And yet he liked young Marster Shepley. He couldn't explain it at all.

Finally, Cue decided he must be conjured. He didn't know who had done it or why they'd done it. But he knew what he had to do. He had to go see Aunt Rachel.

Aunt Rachel was an old, old woman, and she lived in a cabin by herself, with her granddaughter, Sukey. She'd seen Old Marster's father and his father, and the tale went she'd seen George Washington with his hair all white, and General Lafayette in his gold-plated suit of clothes that the King of France gave him to fight in. Some folks said she was a conjure and some folks said she wasn't, but everybody on the plantation treated her mighty respectful, because, if she put her eye on you, she mightn't take it off. Well, his mammy had been friends with Aunt Rachel, so Cue went to see her.

She was sitting alone in her cabin by the low light of a fire. There was a pot on the fire, and now and then you could hear it bubble and chunk, like a bullfrog chunking in the swamp, but that was the only sound. Cue made his obleegances to her and asked her about the misery in her back. Then he gave her a chicken he happened to bring along. It was a black rooster, and she seemed pleased to get it. She took it in her thin black hands and it fluttered and clucked a minute. So she drew a chalk line from its beak along a board, and then it stayed still and frozen. Well, Cue had seen that trick done before. But it was different, seeing it done in Aunt Rachel's cabin, with the big pot chunking on the fire. It made him feel uneasy and he jingled the bit in his pocket for company.

After a while, the old woman spoke. "Well, Son Cue," said she, "that's a fine young rooster you've brought me. What else did you bring me, Son Cue?"

"I brought you trouble," said Cue, in a husky voice, because that was all he could think of to say.

She nodded her head as if she'd expected that. "They mostly brings me trouble," she said. "They mostly brings trouble to Aunt Rachel. What kind of trouble, Son Cue? Man trouble or woman trouble?"

"It's my trouble," said Cue, and he told her the best way he could. When he'd finished, the pot on the fire gave a bubble and a croak, and the old woman took a long spoon and stirred it.

"Well, Son Cue, son of Cuffee, son of Shango," she said, "you've got a big trouble, for sure."

"Is it going to kill me dead?" said Cue.

"I can't tell you right about that," said Aunt Rachel. "I could give you lies and prescriptions. Maybe I would, to some folks. But your Granddaddy Shango was a powerful man. It took three men to put the irons on him, and I saw the irons break his heart. I won't lie to you, Son Cue. You've got a sickness."

"Is it a bad sickness?" said Cue.

"It's a sickness in your blood," said Aunt Rachel. "It's a sickness in your liver and your veins. Your daddy never had it that I knows of—he took after his mammy's side. But his daddy was a Corromantee, and they is bold and free, and you takes after him. It's the freedom sickness, Son Cue."

"The freedom sickness?" said Cue.

"The freedom sickness," said the old woman, and her little eyes glittered like sparks. "Some they break and some they tame down," she said, "and some is neither to be tamed or broken. Don't I know the signs and the sorrow—me, that come through the middle passage on the slavery ship and seen my folks scattered like sand? Ain't I seen it coming, Lord—O Lord, ain't I seen it coming?"

"What's coming?" said Cue.

"A darkness in the sky and a cloud with a sword in it," said the old woman, stirring the pot, "because they hold our people and they hold our people."

Cue began to tremble. "I don't want to get whipped," he said. "I never been whipped—not hard."

"They whipped your Granddaddy Shango till the blood ran twinkling down his back," said the old woman, "but some you can't break or tame."

"I don't want to be chased by dogs," said Cue. "I don't want to hear the dogs belling and the paterollers after me."

The old woman stirred the pot.

"Old Marster, he's a good marster," said Cue. "I don't want to do him no harm. I don't want no trouble or projecting to get me into trouble."

The old woman stirred the pot and stirred the pot.

"O God, I want to be free," said Cue. "I just ache and hone to be free. How am I going to be free, Aunt Rachel?"

"There's a road that runs underground," said the old woman. "I never seen it, but I knows of it. There's a railroad train that runs, sparking and snorting, underground through the earth. At least that's what they tell me. But I wouldn't know for sure," and she looked at Cue.

Cue looked back at her bold enough, for he'd heard about the Underground Railroad himself—just mentions and whispers. But he knew there wasn't any use asking the old woman what she wouldn't tell.

"How I going to find that road, Aunt Rachel?" he said.

"You look at the rabbit in the brier and you see what he do," said the old woman. "You look at the owl in the woods and you see what he do. You look at the star in the sky and you see what she do. Then you come back and talk to me. Now I'm going to eat, because I'm hungry."

That was all the words she'd say to him that night; but when Cue went back to his loft, her words kept boiling around in his mind. All night he could hear that train of railroad cars, snorting and sparking underground through the earth. So, next morning, he ran away.

He didn't run far or fast. How could he? He'd never been more than twenty miles from the plantation in his life; he didn't know the roads or the ways. He ran off before the horn, and Mr. Wade caught him before sundown. Now, wasn't he a stupid man, that Cue?

When they brought him back, Mr. Wade let him off light, because he was a good boy and never run away before. All the same, he got ten, and ten laid over the ten. Yellow Joe, the head driver, laid them on. The first time the whip cut into him, it was just like a fire on Cue's skin, and he didn't see how he could stand it. Then he got to a place where he could.

After it was over, Aunt Rachel crope up to his loft and had her granddaughter, Sukey, put salve on his back. Sukey, she was sixteen, and golden-skinned and pretty as a peach on a peach tree. She worked in the Big House and he never expected her to do a thing like that.

"I'm mighty obliged," he said, though he kept thinking it was Aunt Rachel got him into trouble and he didn't feel as obliged as he might.

"Is that all you've got to say to me, Son Cue?" said Aunt Rachel, looking down at him. "I told you to watch three things. Did you watch them?"

"No'm," said Cue. "I run off in the woods just like I was a wild turkey. I won't never do that no more."

"You're right, Son Cue," said the old woman. "Freedom's a hard-bought thing. So, now you've been whipped, I reckon you'll give it up."

"I been whipped," said Cue, "but there's a road running underground. You told me so. I been whipped, but I ain't beaten."

(1940)

From

FREEDOM ROAD
by Howard Fast

As Gideon was leaving the Military Adjustment Offices, he was stopped by a well-dressed, light-complexioned colored man who introduced himself as Francis L. Cardozo. He said:

"You're a member of the Convention?"

"Uh huh."

"Mind if I walk along with you?"

"Don't know as I mind that," Gideon said uncertainly, troubled somewhat by the ease with which this well-dressed, well-mannered stranger had insinuated himself. They started off down the street, Gideon glancing sidewise at the other again and again, until finally Cardozo, with a slight nod of his head, asked, "And what is your name, sir, if I may inquire?"

"Gideon Jackson."

Cardozo said that he was also a member of the Convention, from the district of Charleston, and would Gideon care to meet with some of the other members? They would be at Cardozo's home that afternoon at about three o'clock, to talk about matters pertaining to the Convention. Had Gideon met any of the delegates?

"Guess I ain't," Gideon said.

"Well, of course you will, once the Convention convenes. This, however, may make some things clear. These are good people, I assure you, Mr. Jackson."

"I'd mighty well like to come," Gideon said.

"Do come then, and I'll write down the address for you."

He wrote it down on a card, which he gave to Gideon. They shook hands, and then Gideon walked away with the salutation ringing in his ears, Mr. Jackson, the nice rounded sound of it and the increasing wonder of it. Like Church singing to glory were all the things that happened to him; and here only a little while ago he was afraid to present his papers. Tomorrow a day, the Convention would begin. The hammering, unnatural pace of Gideon's heart was almost a constant factor now; he walked briskly through the streets, telling himself, "There's a sunshine brightness in the world. Jesus Christ walks. I was born a slave and a slave until maybe yesterday. My little ones, they was born slaves. Look at now—just look at now!"

A white man, walking down the street, facing Gideon and on a line with him, came toward him with the compact assurance that Gideon would give way. Gideon was inside himself, and the world didn't exist. They would have met head on, but at the last moment, the man swerved aside, lashing at Gideon with the cane he carried, catching him full across the back; and Gideon, plucked back to reality by the blow, stood there, surprised, tense, shamed, the welt on his back burning, rage growing inside him; rage and shame and the desire to spring after the white man, but a sense of something that held him back and talked to him until the white man had turned a corner and was out of sight.

Gideon walked on, and the world returned to a place that still needed patching here and there, not perfect yet, Gideon asking himself, "Why for did he had to do that?"

In Gideon's pocket was still twenty-five cents. Money went a long way; money was not like rice or potatoes, crops of the ground that went into a rigid calculation, so much eaten each day and finally the supply exhausted; there was a flexibility to money—one could use it for this or that, or one could not use it at all. The brisk, cool weather had given him an appetite, and he stopped at a stand in the covered market where they were selling rice and onions, five cents for a steaming plate. Then he bought another newspaper, went down to the docks and sat on a bale of cotton, spread the paper, the sting in his back almost gone now, the wonder of print reoccurring and in a certain sense erotic, making his skin tighten and prickle with excitement as he read,

"Georgia reports give promise of a more *stabilizing*—" a word his mind underlined for the future, a mystery he moved his lips over, "Stab—stalabl— no, stay-billy—" And as his eyes shifted, "Cotton futures on the New York market—" What was a *future?* The word "market" he could comprehend, a place where they sold things, a homely word; but what sort of a market was this in New York where cotton became cotton futures? His eyes ached and he became drowsy; he dozed a little there in the warming afternoon, coming awake every so often and looking at the newspaper again. Stray words caught his eyes. "Black savages from the Congo—" The stevedores were shouting and singing as they toted their great loads. Was the Congo in Carolina or Georgia? Savages was a familiar word; make a nigger out to be a red, wild Indian. Out in the bay a full-rigged ship tacked back and forth, and all the gulls raced after it. Gideon looked up at the sun and estimated that it was close to three o'clock.

He came to Cardozo's house with his paper folded neatly under his arm, and bowed correctly as he was introduced to Mr. Nash, Mr. Wright, and Mr. Delany, middle-aged Negroes of Charleston, each of them raising a brow at Gideon's clothes, at his soft, slurred back-country slave speech. Gideon was impressed; these were educated men, well-dressed in dark clothes. He was beginning to understand that certain circles preferred dark clothes to the bright, gay colors some of the delegates wore. Mr. Nash said:

"I presume, Mr. Jackson, you come with some instruction from your constituents?"

"We recognize the need of a formulated program," Mr. Delany added.

"I don't know," Gideon muttered.

There was a more gentle understanding in Cardozo. "This is high-falutin' talk, Mr. Jackson," he smiled. "Becoming a legislator, a man leaves half his brain in his pants pocket and tries to operate with an unused half he never knew he possessed."

Gideon nodded, making up his mind to keep his mouth shut and listen. Mr. Wright expressed complete hopelessness about the future. He said to Cardozo:

"But when you come down to it, Francis, there are at least thirty delegates who can neither read nor write!"

Gideon was glad he had the folded newspaper under his arm. What did they think of him, and why had they asked him here?

"So much the better," Cardozo nodded.

"But make sense, please!"

"I'm inclined to agree with Francis," Nash said. "The literate people of this world have worked no wonders."

"That, of course, is sophistry. We're faced with the problem of field-hands participating in the making of a Constitution. Not to mention the anger this is raising among the white population, we're faced with the very real question of the field-hands themselves. What will they do?"

"They can be managed."

Cardozo said lightly, "Do you feel that you can be managed, Mr. Jackson?"

"Sir?" Gideon had the feeling that he was being the butt of something; the bewilderment was changing into anger.

"But don't be angry, Mr. Jackson," Cardozo said. "You were a slave."

"I was."

"A field-hand?"

"That's right."

"How do you see this business of a Constitution? I mean that seriously. What will you want in a Constitution you have a part in making?"

Gideon looked at them, the heavy-set Nash, the slim, almost courtly Cardozo, Wright, round and suave, like a well-fed house servant. And the room they sat in, a room that to Gideon seemed elegant almost beyond belief, upholstered chairs, a stuffed squirrel, even a rug on the floor, and three crayon pictures on the walls. How does a black man come by all this? Where did he fit into it? And the other delegates who had plodded across the state in their shapeless cottonfield boots?

"Don't be offended, Mr. Jackson," Cardozo persisted.

Gideon nodded. "I ain't high. I guess you want an answer. Talk about a man can't read, can't write, just an old nigger come walking out of the cotton fields, that's me. What I want from Constitution? Maybe it ain't what you folks want—want learning, want it for all, black and white. Want a freedom that's sure as an iron fencepost. Want no man should push me off the street. Want a little farm where a nigger can put in a crop and take out a crop all his days. That's what I want."

Then there was a silence, and Gideon felt embarrassed, provocative and high and mighty without reason, a man who said a lot, none of it making sense. A little later, the others made their goodbyes, but when Gideon rose to go, Cardozo plucked at his sleeve and begged him to wait a moment. And when the others had left, said to Gideon:

"Have some tea, please, and we can talk. It wasn't so clever of me bringing you into this, was it?"

"That all right," Gideon nodded, wanting to go, but too unsure of himself to know how to go about his leave-taking. Cardozo's wife came in then, a small, pretty brown woman. Gideon loomed over her like a giant.

"Are they all as big as that in the hills?" she asked, in the way of making conversation, and Gideon, quick to take offense at anything now, answered, "I ain't from the hills, ma'am, but from the middle country."

Cardozo said, "Won't you stay? There's a lot for us to talk about."

Gideon nodded.

"Then look at it this way," Cardozo said. "Here were a few of us who have been free Negroes, maybe not as close to our people as we should have been. Just a few of us, against the four million slaves. But the books were opened to us, and we learned a little; but believe me, in a way we were more slaves than you. Now there comes a situation so strange, so open in its implications, that the world cannot fully realize it. The Union government, backed with a military machine it built during the war, says to the people of the south, white and black, build a new life. From the beginning. A new Constitution, new laws, a new society. The white planters rebel against this, but they are the defeated. Yet they stay away from the voting, and as a result here in this state black men, slaves only yesterday, choose their own people and send them to the Convention. Do you know, Gideon, that we, the blacks, are in the majority, that seventy-six out of one hundred and twenty-four elected delegates are Negroes? That over fifty of these are former slaves? This is the year eighteen sixty-eight; how long have we been out of bondage? The Children of Israel wandered in the wilderness for forty years.''

After a moment, Gideon murmured, ''I don't quote Scripture when I'm afraid. I'm a God-fearing man, but when the fright was strongest inside of me, I took a gun in my hands and fought for my freedom.''

''And what will these field-hands do in the courts of law?''

''What they do? They ain't no black savages, like newspaper say. They got a wife and child and love in their heart. They say what is good for me, for woman, for the child, and they vote that in. They got a hunger for learning, and they vote for that. They know about slavery, and they vote for freedom. They ain't going to be uppity; you lead them by the hand, and by God, they come. But you don't take no lash to their back no more. They know how it taste to be free man.''

Thoughtfully, Cardozo said, ''That'll take courage from me, Gideon.''

''Took courage from me to come to this Convention.''

''I suppose so. Tell me something about yourself, Gideon.''

The telling came slow and stumblingly from Gideon; it was nightfall when he had finished. He felt dry and used up. But before he left, Cardozo gave him two books, one *Geldon's Basic Speller* and the other *Usage of the English Language* by Fitzroy and James. They were the first real books Gideon ever had; he held them gently in his big hands, as if they were made of eggshell. Plucking a name from his memory, he asked:

''You got the Shakespeare book?''

For a moment, Cardozo hesitated; then, without smiling, he went to his little shelf of books, took *Othello,* and handed it to Gideon.

''Thank you,'' Gideon said.

And Cardozo nodded, and after Gideon had left, said to his wife, ''If I had laughed—if I had! God help me, I almost laughed! What animals we are!''

Gideon asked Carter to tell him something about Cardozo. In a way, a purely social way, that Gideon could not as yet comprehend, Carter was impressed by the fact that Gideon had been to Cardozo's home.

''He's part Jew,'' Carter said. ''That's how he come by the name. He's a proud nigger.''

Gideon, who had never seen a Jew before, said, ''Looks the same like any black man.''

''But uppity,'' Carter said.

(1944)

ON THE FRONTIER
Cultures in Conflict

He who would wish to see America in its proper light, and have a true idea of its feeble beginnings and barbarous rudiments, must visit our extended line of frontiers where the last settlers dwell. . . .

St. Jean de Crèvecoeur
Letters from an American Farmer

Stand at Cumberland Gap and watch the procession of civilization, marching single file—the buffalo following the trail to the salt springs, the Indian, the fur-trader and hunter, the cattle-raiser, the pioneer farmer—and the frontier has passed by. Stand at South Pass in the Rockies a century later and see the same procession. . . .

Frederick Jackson Turner
The Frontier in American History

From

MY LIFE AS AN INDIAN
by J. W. Schultz

"Why don't you get a woman?" Weasel Tail abruptly asked one evening as Talks-with-the-buffalo and I sat smoking with him in his lodge.

"Yes," my other friend put in. "Why not? You have the right to do so, for you can count a coup; yes, two of them. You killed a Cree, and you took a Cree horse in the fight at the Hairy Cap."

"I took a horse," I replied, "and a good one he is; but you are mistaken about the Cree; you will remember that he escaped by running into the pines on Hairy Cap."

"Oh!" said Talks-with-the-buffalo, "I don't mean that one; we all know he got away, I mean one of those who first fell when we all fired into them. That tall one, the man who wore a badger-skin cap; you killed him. I saw the bullet wound in his body; no ball from any of our rifles could have made such a small hole."

This was news to me; I remembered well having shot several times at that particular warrior, but I never had thought that my bullet ended his career. I did not know whether to feel glad or sorry about it, but finally concluded that it was best to feel glad, for he would have killed me if he could have done so. I was turning the matter over in my mind, when my host aroused me from my reverie: "I said, Why don't you take a woman? Answer."

"Oh!" I replied. "No one would have me. Isn't that a good reason?"

"Kyai-yo'!" exclaimed Madame Weasel Tail, clapping her hand to her mouth, the Blackfoot way of expressing surprise or wonder. "Kyai-yo'! What a reason! I well know that there isn't a girl in this camp but would like to be his woman. Why, if it wasn't for this lazy one here—" giving Weasel Tail's hand an affectionate squeeze—"if he would only go away somewhere and never come back, I'd make you take me. I'd follow you around until you would have to do so."

"Mah'-kah-kan-is-tsi!" I exclaimed, which is a flippant and slangy term, expressing doubt of the speaker's truthfulness.

"Mah'-kah-kan-is-tsi yourself," she rejoined. "Why do you think you

151

are asked to all these Assiniboin dances, where all the young women wear their best clothes, and try to catch you with their robes? Why do you think they put on their best things and go to the trading post with their mothers or other relatives every chance they get? What, you don't know? Well, I'll tell you: they go, each one, hoping that you will notice her, and send a friend to her parents to make a proposal."

"It is the truth," said Weasel Tail.

"Yes, the truth," Talks-with-the-buffalo and his woman joined in.

I thought over the matter a good deal. All the long winter I had rather envied my good friends Berry and Sorrel Horse, who seemed to be so happy with their women. Never a cross word, always the best of good fellowship and open affection for each other. Seeing all this, I had several times said to myself: "It is not good that the man should be alone." The Blackfeet have much the same expression: "Mat'-ah-kwi täm-äp-i-ni-po-ke-mi-o-sin—not found (is) happiness without woman."

After that evening I looked more closely at the various young women I met in the camp or at the trading post, saying to myself: "Now, I wonder what kind of a woman that would make? Is she neat, good-tempered?" All the time, however, I knew that I had no right to take one of them. I did not intend to remain long in the West; my people would never forgive me for making an alliance with one. They were of old, proud Puritan stock, and I could imagine them holding up their hands in horror at the mere hint of such a thing.

"No," I said to myself: "no, it will not do; hunt, go to war, do anything but take a woman, and in the fall go home to your people." This is the line of conduct I meant to follow. But——

One morning the Crow Woman and I were sitting out under a shade she had constructed of a couple of travois and a robe or two. She was busy as usual, embroidering a moccasin with colored quills, and I was cleaning my rifle, preparatory to an antelope hunt. A couple of women came by on their way to the trade room with three or four robes. One of them was a girl of sixteen or seventeen; good-looking, fairly tall, and well-formed, she had fine large, candid, expressive eyes, white, even teeth and heavy braided hair which hung almost to the ground. "Who is that?" I asked the Crow Woman.

"Don't you know? She comes here often; she is a cousin of Berry's woman."

I went away on my hunt, but I was thinking all the time about the cousin. That evening I spoke to Berry about her; I learned that her father was dead; that her mother was a medicine lodge woman, and noted for her goodness of character. "I'd like to have the girl," I said. "What do you think about it?"

"We'll see," Berry replied. "I'll talk with my old woman."

A couple of days went by and nothing was said by either of us about the matter, and then one afternoon Mrs. Berry told me that I was to have the girl, providing I would promise to be always good and kind to her. I readily agreed to that.

"Very well, then," said Mrs. Berry; "go into the trade room and select a shawl, some dress goods, some bleached muslin—no, I'll select the outfit and make her some white women's dresses like mine."

"But, hold on!" I exclaimed. "What am I to pay? How many horses, or whatever?"

"Her mother says there is to be no pay, only that you are to keep your promise to be good to her daughter."

Usually a lot of horses were sent to the parents, sometimes fifty or more. Sometimes the father demanded so many head, but if no number was specified, the suitor gave as many as he could. Again, it was not unusual for a father to request some promising youth, good hunter and bold raider, to become his son-in-law. In that case he was the one to give horses, and even a lodge and household goods, with the girl.

Well, I got the girl. It was an embarrassing time for us both when she came in one evening, shawl over her face, while we were eating supper. Sorrel Horse and his woman were there, and with Berry and his woman they made things interesting for us with their jokes, until Berry's mother put a stop to it. We were shy for a long time, she especially. "Yes" and "no" were about all that I could get her to say. But my room underwent a wonderful transformation; everything was kept so neat and clean, my clothes were so nicely washed, and my "medicine" was carefully taken out every day and hung on a tripod. I had purchased a war bonnet, shield, and various other things which the Blackfeet regard as sacred. I had them handled with due pomp and ceremony.

As time passed this young woman became more and more a mystery to me. I wondered what she thought of me, and if she speculated upon what I might think of her. I had no fault to find, she was always neat, always industrious about our little household affairs, quick to supply my wants. But that wasn't enough. I wanted to know her, her thoughts and beliefs. I wanted her to talk and laugh with me, and tell stories, as I could often hear her doing with the Berrys. Instead of that, when I came around, the laugh died on her lips, and she seemed to shrink within herself.

The change came when I least expected it. I was down in the Piegan camp one afternoon and learned that a war party was being made up to raid the Crows. Talks-with-the-buffalo and Weasel Tail were going, and asked me to go with them. I readily agreed, and returned to the post to prepare for the trip.

"Nät-ah'-ki," I said, bursting into our room, "give me all the moccasins I have, some clean socks, some pemmican. Where is my little brown canvas bag? Where have you put my gun case? Where—"

"What are you going to do?"

It was the first question she had ever asked me.

"Do? I'm going to war; my friends are going, they asked me to join them—"

I stopped, for she suddenly arose and faced me, and her eyes were very bright. "You are going to war!" she exclaimed. "You, a white man, are going with a lot of Indians sneaking over the plains at night to steal horses, and perhaps kill some poor prairie people. You have no shame!''

"Why," I said, rather faintly, "I thought you would be glad. Are not the Crows your enemies? I have promised, I must go.''

"It is well for the Indians to do this," she went on, "but not for a white man. You, you are rich; you have everything you want; those papers, that yellow hard rock (gold) you carry will buy anything you want; you should be ashamed to go sneaking over the plains like a coyote. None of your people ever did that.''

"I have given my promise to go.''

Then Nät-ah'-ki began to cry, and she came nearer and grasped my sleeve. "Don't go," she pleaded, "for if you do, I know you will be killed, and I love you so much.''

I was never so surprised. All these weeks of silence, then, had been nothing but a veil to cover her feelings. I was pleased and proud to know that she did care for me, but underlying that thought was another one: I had done wrong in taking this girl, in getting her to care for me, when in a short time I must return her to her mother and leave for my own country.

I readily promised not to accompany the war party, and then, her point gained, Nät-ah'-ki suddenly felt that she had been over-bold and tried to assume her reserve again. But I would not have it that way. I grasped her hand and made her sit down by my side, and pointed out to her that she was wrong; that to laugh, to joke, to be good friends and companions was better than to pass our days in silence, repressing all natural feeling. After that, the sun always shone.

(1907)

From

THE BOOK OF
THE AMERICAN INDIAN
by Hamlin Garland

Big nose was an inveterate gambler. Like all the plains tribes the Shi-an-nay are a social people. They love companionship and the interchange of jest and story. At evening, when the day's hunt is over, they come together to tell stories and joke and discuss each others' affairs precisely as the peasants of a French village do. And when amusement is desired they dance or play games.

It is this feeling on their part which makes it so difficult for the Government to carry out its theories of allotment. It is difficult to uproot a habit of life which has been thousands of years forming. It is next to impossible to get one of these people to leave the village group and go into his lonely little cabin a mile or two from a neighbor. And the need of amusement is intensified by the sad changes in the life of these people. Games of chance appeal to them precisely as they do to the negro and to large classes of white people. They play with the same abandon with which the negro enters into a game of craps.

One evening Big Nose was in company with three or four others in the midst of Charcoal's camp playing The Hand game. He had been doing some work for the Post and had brought with him to the camp a little heap of silver dollars. He was therefore in excellent temper for a brisk game. But luck was against him. His little store of money melted away and then he began taking his ponies, his gun, and finally his blankets and his tepee; all went into the yawning gulf of his bad luck. Before midnight came he had staked everything but the clothing on his back and had reached a condition of mind bordering on frenzy.

Nothing was too small for his opponents to accept and nothing was too valuable for him to stake. He began putting his moccasins up on the chance and ended by tearing off his Gee string which represented his absolute impoverishment. A reasonable being would have ended the game here but with a desperation hitherto unknown to the gamblers of his tribe, he sat naked on the ground and gambled both his wives away.

When he realized what had happened to him, that he was absolutely without home or substance in the world, naked to the cold and having no claim upon a human being, his frenzy left him and he sank into pitiful dejection. Walking naked through the camp, he began to cry his need, "Take pity on me, my friends. I have nothing. The wind is cold. I have no blanket. I am hungry. I have no tepee."

For a long time no one paid any heed to him, for they were disgusted with his foolishness and they would not allow his wives to clothe him or give him shelter. However, at last, his brother came out and gave him a blanket and took him into his tepee. "Let this be a lesson to you," he said. "You are a fool. Yet I pity you."

Next day a council was called to consider his case, which was the most remarkable that had ever happened in the tribe. There were many who were in favor of letting him take care of himself, but in the end it was decreed that he should be clothed and that he should have a tepee and the absolute necessities of life.

The question of restoring him to his wives was a much more serious one, the general opinion being that a man who would gamble his wives away in this way had no further claim upon a woman.

At last, old Charcoal arose to speak. He was a waggish old fellow whose eye twinkled with humor as he said, "Big Nose has two wives as you know.

One of them is young. She is industrious. She is very quiet, saying little and speaking in a gentle voice. The other is old and has a sharp tongue. Her tongue is like a whip. It makes her husband smart. Now let us restore him to his old wife. She will be good discipline for him. She will not let him forget what he has done.''

This suggestion made every one laugh and it was agreed with. And the news was carried to Big Nose. "I don't wany my old wife,'' he said. "I want my young wife.''

"The council has decreed,'' was the stern answer, "and there is no appeal.''

Big Nose accepted the ruling of the tribe and resolutely turned his face in the right direction. He gave up gambling and became one of the most progressive men of the tribe. By hard work he acquired a team and a wagon and worked well, freighting for the Agency and for the Post traders.

His old wife, however, grew more and more unsatisfactory as the years went by. For some inscrutable reason, she did not care to make a home, but was always moving about from camp to camp, full of gossip and unwelcome criticism. All this Big Nose patiently endured for four years. But one day he came to Seger, the superintendent of the school near him, and said:

"My friend, you know I am walking the white man's road. You see that I want to do right. I have a team. I work hard. I want a home where I can live quietly. But my old wife is trifling. She is good for nothing. She wants to gad about all the time and never stay home and look after the chickens. I want to put her away and take another and better wife.

Seger was very cautious. "What do the old chiefs say about it?''

Big Nose looked a little discouraged, but he answered defiantly, "Oh, I am walking the white man's road these days. I don't care what they say. I am listening to what you say.''

"I'll consider the matter,'' he replied evasively, for he wished to consult the head men. When he had stated the matter to White Shield, he said, "Now, of course, whatever you think best in this matter will be acceptable. I don't know anything about the circumstances, but if this old woman is as bad as Big Nose says, she is of no account.''

White Shield, very quietly, replied, "Big Nose can never marry again.''

"Why not?'' inquired Seger, being interested in White Shield's brevity and decision of utterance.

White Shield replied, "Haven't you heard how Big Nose gambled his wives away? That thing he did. Gambled away his tepees, his clothing, and walked naked through the camp. We gave him clothes. We gave back one wife, but we marked out a road and he must walk in it. He cannot marry again.''

And from this decree there was no appeal.

(1923)

THE LAST THUNDER SONG
by John G. Neihardt

The summer of 1900 debilitated all thermal adjectives. It was not hot; it was *Saharical!* It would hardly have been hyperbole to have said that the Old Century lay dying of a fever. The untilled hills of the reservation thrust themselves up in the August sunshine like the emaciated joints of one bedridden. The land lay as yellow as the skin of a fever patient, except in those rare spots where the melancholy corn struggled heartlessly up a hillside, making a blotch like a bedsore!

The blood of the prairie was impoverished, and the sky would give no drink with which to fill the dwindling veins. When one wished to search the horizon for the cloud that was not there, he did it from beneath an arched hand. The small whirlwinds that awoke like sudden fits of madness in the sultry air, rearing yellow columns of dust into the sky—these alone relieved the monotony of dazzle.

Every evening the clouds rolled flashing about the horizon and thundered back into the night. They were merely taunts, like the holding of a cool cup just out of reach of a fevered mouth; and the clear nights passed, bringing dewless dawns, until the ground cracked like a parched lip!

The annual Indian powwow was to be ended prematurely that year, for the sun beat uninvitingly upon the flat bottom where the dances were held, and the Indians found much comfort in the shade of their summer tepees. But when it was noised about that, upon the next day, the old medicine-man Mahowari (Passing Cloud) would dance potent dances and sing a thunder song with which to awaken the lazy thunder spirits to their neglected duty of rain-making, then the argument of the heat became feeble.

So the next morning, the bronze head of every Indian tepeehold took his pony, his dogs, his squaw, and his papooses of indefinite number to the powwow ground. In addition to these, the old men carried with them long memories and an implicit faith.

The young men, who had been away to Indian school, and had succeeded to some extent in stuffing their brown skins with white souls, carried with them curiosity and doubt, which, if properly united, beget derision.

The old men went to a shrine; the young men went to a show. When a shrine becomes a show, they say the world advances a step.

About the open space in which the dances were held, an oval covering had been built with willow boughs, beneath which the Indians lounged in sweating groups. Slowly about the various small circles went the cumbersome stone pipes.

To one listening, drowsed with the intense sunshine, the *buzzle* and mutter and snarl of the gossiping Omahas seemed the grotesque echoes from a vanished age. Between the fierce dazzle of the sun and the sharply contrasting blue shade, there was but a line of division; yet a thousand years lay between one gazing in the sun and those dozing in the shadow. It was as if God had flung down a bit of the young world's twilight into the midst of the old world's noon. Here lounged the masterpiece of the toiling centuries—a Yankee! There sat the remnant of a race as primitive as Israel. And the white man looked on with contempt of superiority.

Before ten o'clock everybody had arrived and his family with him. A little group, composed of the Indian Agent, the Agency Physician, the Mission Preacher, and a newspaper man, down from the city for reportorial purposes, waited and chatted, sitting upon a ragged patch of available shadow.

"These Omahas are an exceptional race," the preacher was saying in his ministerial tone of voice; "an exceptional race!"

The newspaper man mopped his face, lit a cigarette and nodded assent with a hidden meaning twinkling in his eye.

"Quite exceptional!" he said, tossing his head in the direction of an unusually corpulent bunch of steaming, sweating, bronze men and women. "God, like some lesser master-musicians, has not confined himself to grand opera, it seems!"

With severe unconcern the preacher mended the broken thread of his discourse. "Quite an exceptional race in many ways. The Omaha is quite as honest as the white man."

"That is a truism!" The pencil-pusher drove this observation between the minister's words like a wedge.

"In his natural state he was much more so," uninterruptedly continued the preacher; he was used to continuous discourse. "I have been told by many of the old men that in the olden times an Indian could leave his tepee for months at a time, and on his return would find his most valuable possessions untouched. I tell you, gentlemen, the Indian is like a prairie flower that has been transplanted from the blue sky and the summer sun and the pure winds into the steaming, artificial atmosphere of the hothouse! A glass roof is not the blue sky! Man's talent is not God's genius! That is why you are looking at a perverted growth.

"Look into an Indian's face and observe the ruins of what was once manly dignity, indomitable energy, masterful prowess! When I look upon one of these faces, I have the same thoughts as, when traveling in Europe, I looked upon the ruins of Rome.

"Everywhere broken arches, fallen columns, tumbled walls! Yet through these as through a mist one can discern the magnificence of the living city. So in looking upon one of these faces, which are merely ruins in another sense. They were once as noble, as beautiful as——"

In his momentary search for an eloquent simile, the minister paused.

"As pumpkin pies!" added the newspaper man with a chuckle; and he whipped out his notebook and pencil to jot down this brilliant thought, for he had conceived a very witty "story" which he would pound out for the Sunday edition.

"Well," said the Agency Physician, finally sucked into the whirlpool of discussion, "it seems to me that there is no room for crowing on either side. Indians are pretty much like white men; livers and kidneys and lungs, and that sort of thing; slight difference in the pigment under the skin. I've looked into the machinery of both species and find just as much room in one as the other for a soul!"

"And both will go upward," added the minister.

"Like different grades of tobacco," observed the Indian Agent, "the smoke of each goes up in the same way."

"Just so," said the reporter; "but let us cut out the metaphysics. I wonder when this magical *cuggie* is going to begin his humid evolutions. Lamentable, isn't it, that such institutions as rain prayers should exist on the very threshold of the twentieth century?"

"I think," returned the minister, "that the twentieth century has no intention of eliminating God! This medicine-man's prayer, in my belief, is as sacred as the prayer of any churchman. The difference between Wakunda and God is merely orthographical."

"But," insisted the cynical young man from the city, 'I had not been taught to think of God as of one who forgets! Do you know what I would do if I had no confidence in the executive ability of my God?"

Taking the subsequent silence as a question, the young man answered: "Why, I would take a day off and whittle one out of wood!"

"A youth's way is the wind's way," quoted the preacher, with a paternal air.

"And the thoughts of youth are long, long thoughts; but what is all this noise about?" returned the reporter.

A buzz of expectant voices had grown at one end of the oval, and had spread contagiously throughout the elliptical strip of shade. For with slow, majestic step the medicine-man, Mahowari, entered the enclosure and walked toward the center. The fierce sun emphasized the brilliancy of the old man's garments and glittered upon the profusion of trinkets, the magic heirlooms of the medicine-man. It was not the robe nor the dazzling trinkets that caught the eye of one acquainted with Mahowari. It was the erectness of his figure, for he had been bowed with years, and many vertical suns had shone upon the old man's back since his face had been turned toward the ground. But now with firm step and form rigidly erect he walked.

Any sympathetic eye could easily read the thoughts that passed through the old man's being like an elixir infusing youth. Now in his feeble years would come his greatest triumph! To-day he would sing with greater power than ever he had sung. Wakunda would hear the cry. The rains would come! Then the white men would be stricken with belief!

Already his heart sang before his lips. In spite of the hideous painting of his face, the light of triumph shone there like the reflection of a great fire.

Slowly he approached the circle of drummers who sat in the glaring center of the ellipse of sunlight. It was all as though the first century had awakened like a ghost and stood in the very doorway of the twentieth!

When Mahowari had approached within a yard of the drums, he stopped, and raising his arms and his eyes to the cloudless sky, uttered a low cry like a wail of supplication. Then the drums began to throb.

With a slow, majestic bending of the knees and an alternate lifting of his feet, the medicine-man danced in a circle about the snarling drums. Then like a faint wail of winds toiling up a wooded bluff, his thunder song began.

The drone and whine of the mysterious, untranslatable words pierced the drowse of the day, lived for a moment with the echoes of the drums among the surrounding hills, and languished from a whisper into silence. At intervals the old man raised his face, radiant with fanatic ecstasy, to the meridian glare of the sun, and the song swelled to a supplicating shout.

Faster and faster the old man moved about the circle; louder and wilder grew the song. Those who watched from the shade were absorbed in an intense silence, which, with the drowse of the sultry day, made every sound a paradox! The old men forgot their pipes and sat motionless.

Suddenly, at one end of the covering, arose the sound of laughter! At first an indefinite sound like the spirit of merriment entering a capricious dream of sacred things; then it grew and spread until it was no longer merriment, but a loud jeer of derision! It startled the old men from the intenseness of their watching. They looked up and were stricken with awe. The young men were jeering this, the holiest rite of their fathers!

Slower and slower the medicine-man danced; fainter and fainter grew the song and ceased abruptly. With one quick glance, Mahowari saw the shattering of his hopes. He glanced at the sky; but saw no swarm of black spirits to avenge such sacrilege. Only the blaze of the sun, the glitter of the arid zenith!

In that one moment, the temporary youth of the old man died out. His shoulders drooped to their wonted position. His limbs tottered. He was old again.

It was the Night stricken heart-sick with the laughter of the Dawn. It was the audacious Present jeering at the Past, tottering with years. At that moment, the impudent, cruel, brilliant youth called Civilization snatched the halo from the gray hairs of patriarchal Ignorance. Light flouted the rags of Night. A clarion challenge shrilled across the years.

Never before in all the myriad moons had such a thing occurred. It was too great a cause to produce an effect of grief or anger. It stupefied. The old men and women sat motionless. They could not understand.

With uneven step and with eyes that saw nothing, Mahowari passed from among his kinsmen and tottered up the valley toward his lonesome shack and tepee upon the hillside. It was far past noon when the last of the older Omahas left the scene of the dance.

The greater number of the white men who had witnessed the last thunder dance of the Omahas went homeward much pleased. The show had turned out quite funny indeed. "Ha, ha, ha! Did you see how surprised the old *cuggie* looked? He, he, he!"

But as the minister rode slowly toward his home there was no laughter in his heart. He was saying to himself: "If the whole fabric of my belief should suddenly be wrenched from me, what then?" Even this question was born of selfishness, but it brought pity.

In the cool of the evening the minister mounted his horse and rode to the home of Mahowari, which was a shack in the winter and a tepee in the summer. Dismounting, he threw the bridle reins upon the ground, and raised the door flap of the tepee. Mahowari sat cross-legged upon the ground, staring steadily before him with unseeing eyes.

"How!" said the minister.

The old Indian did not answer. There was no expression of grief or anger or despair upon his face. He sat like a statue. Yet, the irregularity of his breathing showed where the pain lay. An Indian suffers in his breast. His face is a mask.

The minister sat down in front of the silent old man and, after the immemorial manner of ministers, talked of a better world, of a pitying Christ, and of God, the Great Father. For the first time the Indian raised his face and spoke briefly in English:

"God? He dead, guess!"

Then he was silent again for some time.

Suddenly his eyes lit up with a light that was not the light of age. The heart of his youth had awakened. The old memories came back and he spoke fluently in his own tongue, which the minister understood.

"These times are not like the old times. The young men have caught some of the wisdom of the white man. Nothing is sure. It is not good. I cannot understand. Everything is young and new. All old things are dead. Many moons ago, the wisdom of Mahowari was great. I can remember how my father said to me one day when I was yet young and all things lay new before me: 'Let my son go to a high hill and dream a great dream'; and I went up in the evening and cried out to Wakunda and I slept and dreamed.

"I saw a great cloud sweeping up from under the earth, and it was terrible with lightning and loud with thunder. Then it passed over and disappeared. And when I awoke and told my people of my dream, they rejoiced and said: 'Great things shall come to this youth. We shall call him Passing Cloud, and he shall be a thunder man, keen and quick to know, with the keenness and

quickness of the lightning; and his name shall be as thunder for men to hear.'
And I grew and believed in these sayings and I was strong. But now I can see
the meaning of the dream—a great light and a great noise and a passing."

The old man sighed and the light passed out of his eyes. Then he looked
searchingly into the face of the minister, speaking in English:

"You white medicine man. You pray?"

The minister nodded.

Mahowari turned his gaze to the ground and said wearily:

"White god dead too, guess."

(1926)

From

WOLF SONG
by Harvey Fergusson

Black Wolf rode his small spotted pony which had no speed. He rode in a saddle of buffalo hide stretched over a frame made of two forked willow sticks.
Its willow stirrups were covered with rawhide. On his left arm he wore a round
shield of buffalo hide which he had borrowed from old Standing Horse, for
young men do not own shields. This shield was hung with eagle feathers and
it had the magic power of turning bullets. In his right hand he carried a lance
eight feet long with a tip made from a butcher knife his father had taken off
the body of a white man killed in battle. Over his shoulder in a case of glossy
otterskin, hung with tails, he carried his four foot bow and twenty new arrows.
With his rawhide lariat he led a tall rawboned sorrel mare. She carried nothing
but a buffalo-hide pad stuffed with grass and a pack containing a few pounds
of pemmican and some extra moccasins. For this was his running horse, to be
reserved for battle and hunting. She was an excellent buffalo horse and fast for
a short run but her wind was none too good. Black Wolf longed above all for
a horse that was faster than anything else on four legs and sound of wind and
knee. However strong and brave a man may be he is no better than the horse
he rides.

When he struck the Cimarron near the foot of the mountains he rode slowly
and sang no more but watched on all sides and studied the ground for he was
now in a country where he might meet anything. Mexican, gringo, Ute, Apache,
Pawnee and Rapaho passed and camped here every summer.

Black Wolf camped in the edge of the timber, keeping both himself and his horses hidden. At dusk when smoke does not show far he made a fire no bigger than his two hands under a bower of brush and cooked meat on the coals, putting out the flame as soon as it was done. When dark came he picketed his horses on good grass, wrapped himself in his one blanket and lay down. He would not sleep until after midnight when his horses would be full and he could hide them among the trees. Meantime he lay looking at the stars gravely and thinking.

His body lay there but his spirit went back to the camp of his tribe for he belonged to it as a bee belongs to its hive and it was always in his mind.

He saw it as it would look in the morning when the lodges stand in a white circle beside the shining river. He saw the women going to fill their water jars and men and boys running in naked shouting groups to bathe while smoke of morning fires hung in blue wisps before the sun and yellow dust clouds on the hilltops showed where boys were driving down the horses.

While he lay there still and lonely he pictured all the happy stir of a beginning day when men rode away on their best horses to hunt and women set out to gather firewood and groups of young girls, laughing and playing tricks, climbed the hills with their long staves for digging roots. Children were scattered along the river, paddling in shallow water, making animal figures out of mud, playing games and practicing with tiny bows and arrows as he had done such a few years ago.

For a while the camp would belong to women and to old men who sat in the shade smoking and telling tales of battles long ago and of gods and monsters, but late in the afternoon it was alive again as men came riding home on blood-stained horses and girls shouted a challenge from the hilltops. . . . He was among the young men who galloped out to meet them and fight a sham battle for their spoil of roots and berries and again he heard the ringing laughter of Ameertschee and again he caught her hand in play. . . .

Darkness fell upon the camp but it was not the awful empty darkness of night to a man alone. Fires now were akindle and those inside the lodges made them glow like moons spotted with moving shadows.

Now he was among the young men who stood outside the lodge doors waiting to court the girls while shouted invitations to feasts and storytellings went round the circle and children ran to summon those who might not hear. Above the murmur of many voices rose the music of flutes, of dance songs and gambling songs, and the droning chant of a medicine man. By this time all were gathered in warm groups inside the lodges, some to dance and sing and some to sit in polite circles and hear the words of famous storytellers. In some lodges men pledged themselves to the truth and told tales of war and hunting and challenged each other to tell better ones. In some lodges funny stories were told to shouts of mirth and in some the unchanging words of sacred legend fell upon a reverent hush—gods became visible, monsters lifted awful heads from lakes and rivers, beasts and birds spoke human words. . . . Slowly fires and voices died and the camp became quiet save for a few low tones from unseen couples and the weird notes of a flute from the hills where some lovesick boy roamed and played as they sometimes did all night. . . .

All night Black Wolf had roamed in the hills with his flute in the days when Ameertschee loved him. He walked in the dark and sat alone on hilltops thinking sometimes only of Ameertschee and sometimes only of the music he made. He heard ghosts run and whisper and spirit voices call. Wolves and wild cats came near and looked at him with eyes of green and yellow fire. Once Ameertschee heard him and came out of her lodge and called to him with the voice of an owl. . . .

Far from his people and alone for the first time in his life, Black Wolf loved them as he never had loved before. They had the magic quality of people in a story and the days of his happiness among them seemed hardly real. He wondered if ever he would sit safe in his lodge, the father of many children, the owner of many horses, telling tales of his prowess. . . . The wind spirit moaned in the forest and sleep came to Black Wolf sadly, like a prophecy of death.

(1927)

INDIAN EARTH
by Witter Bynner

1

They think they have won you to their foreign god.
They put you in their churches. On your necks
They hang their little symbols of remorse.
And all the while your hearts go up a hill
To other priests of whom you never speak
In your confessional. You sin your sins,
Your little sins, and weep. But oh, the sin
Of tearing your heart out to the perfect sun!

2

It is the earth itself that hems you round
Against intruders alien to the earth,
That brings you heaven under a shadowy tree,
Curves heaven to your arm and lets you lie

Close to its living thorn. The crown is yours,
Not theirs. You know the one divinity,
The only death, the offering of the heart
To the cruel earth, the love, the consummation.

3

Your houses are made of it. They come and go,
Arise from it and crumble back to it.
In your old graves your intimate images
Are made of it, mother and sire and son,
Infant in arms, each with his earthen face.
Anyone who has taken once a handful
Of Indian earth out from among your bones
Feels in his hand the fusing of your will.

4

No need of priests with knives for trespassers.
Let come who may with an estranging hand,
Let touch who will this earth so deeply yours,
None of it ever goes away from you.
Your gods are here, deeper than any spade;
And when you lie on the earth under the sun,
They whisper up to you ancestral spells
From your own roots, to rot these foreign hearts.

(1929)

THE SAD INDIAN
by Hart Crane

Sad heart, the gymnast of inertia, does not count
Hours, days—and scarcely sun and moon—
The warp is in his woof—and his keen vision
Spells what his tongue has had—and only that—
How more?—but the lash, lost vantage and the prison
His fathers took for granted ages since—and so he looms

Farther than his sun-shadow—farther than wings
Their shadows even—now can't carry him.
He does not know the new hum in the sky
And—backwards—is it thus the eagles fly?

(1933)

WILDWEST*

by Archibald MacLeish

There were none of my blood in this battle:
There were Minneconjous, Sans Arcs, Brules,
Many nations of Sioux: they were few men galloping.

This would have been in the long days in June:
They were galloping well deployed under the plum-trees:
They were driving riderless horses: themselves they were few.

Crazy Horse had done it with few numbers.
Crazy Horse was small for a Lakota.
He was riding always alone thinking of something:

He was standing alone by the picket lines by the ropes:
He was young then, he was thirty when he died:
Unless there were children to talk he took no notice.

When the soldiers came for him there on the other side
On the Greasy Grass in the villages we were shouting
"Hoka Hey! Crazy Horse will be riding!"

They fought in the water: horses and men were drowning:
They rode on the butte: dust settled in sunlight:
Hoka Hey! they lay on the bloody ground.

No one could tell of the dead which man was Custer . . .
That was the end of his luck: by that river.
The soldiers beat him at Slim Buttes once:

*Black Elk's memories of Crazy Horse recorded by Neihardt [MacLeish's note].

They beat him at Willow Creek when the snow lifted:
The last time they beat him was the Tongue.
He had only the meat he had made and of that little.

Do you ask why he should fight? It was his country:
My God should he not fight? It was his.
But after the Tongue there were no herds to be hunting:

He cut the knots of the tails and he led them in:
He cried out "I am Crazy Horse! Do not touch me!"
There were many soldiers between and the gun glinting . . .

And a Mister Josiah Perham of Maine had much of the
land Mister Perham was building the Northern Pacific
railroad that is Mister Perham was saying at lunch that

forty say fifty millions of acres in gift and
government grant outright ought to be worth a
wide price on the Board at two-fifty and

later a Mister Cooke had relieved Mister Perham and
later a Mister Morgan relieved Mister Cooke:
Mister Morgan converted at prices current:

It was all prices to them: they never looked at it:
why should they look at the land? they were Empire Builders:
it was all in the bid and the asked and the ink on their books . . .

When Crazy Horse was there by the Black Hills
His heart would be big with the love he had for that country
And all the game he had seen and the mares he had ridden

And how it went out from you wide and clean in the sunlight

(1933)

From

THE SURROUNDED
by D'Arcy McNickle

Archilde Leon had been away from his father's ranch for nearly a year, yet when he left the stage road and began the half-mile walk to the house he did not hurry. When he emerged from behind a clump of thornbush and cotton-wood and caught his first glimpse of the cluster of buildings before him, he looked once, and that was all.

He avoided the front of the big house, where his father would most likely be sitting, and made for the dirt-roofed log cabin which occupied lower ground, down toward the creek. Two dogs, one yellow and one black and white, leaped and howled, but they were the only ones to meet him.

He walked past the big house, which was his father's, and went to the cabin, his mother's. There she was, as he knew she would be, sitting in the shade. If she heard him she did not look up at once. But she was a little deaf and a little blind—perhaps she had not sensed his approach. He let the heavy suitcase slip from his sweating hand.

Then she looked up. A sigh escaped her and a quick smile multiplied the many fine lines in her wrinkled brown face.

Here he was, the best of her sons, and the youngest, home again after a year—but would he stay? She had only a faint idea of where he had been; the world out that way was so unlike Sniél-emen; she had even less of an idea of what he did when he went away. But never mind. Here he was again. She smiled quickly, a little at a distance; she did not wish to embarrass him with her attention.

"So you have come back," she said.

"Yes, I am here." He turned his suitcase over on its side for a seat.

"Where have you been this time?"

"To Portland. That's where the stinking water is."

She let the word echo in her ears, saying nothing herself, but it had no meaning. If he had said he had been down toward the mouth of the Snpoilshi (Columbia) River, she would have known what he meant. But Portland! Her red-rimmed eyes gazed toward the timber which came down to the far bank of the creek. Two boys were splashing in the water down there.

"You have been gone a long time."

"I had a job. I played my fiddle in a show house. I can always get a job now any time I go away."

She looked at him quickly, taking him in. He wore a blue suit and a white shirt and his tan shoes were new and polished. So he could go away any time now? He did not have to be fed at home?

"They paid me this money. Look!" She barely glanced at the offered money. It was all strange, she could not make it into a picture. An Indian boy, she thought, belonged with his people.

They sat in silence for some time. It was useless to speak of fiddle-playing, and for a while Archilde could think of nothing that was not equally useless. When you came home to your Indian mother you had to remember that it was a different world. Anyhow you had not come to show your money and talk about yourself. There would be fishing, riding, climbing a mountainside—those things you wanted to do one more time. Why talk of fiddle-playing?

The heat of the afternoon lingered. The three horses in the pasture below the house were bothered by the flies. They had been in the timber across the creek since midday and had come out only a short while before. As they ate, they moved along, stopping now and then to rub their muzzles on their forelegs or to kick themselves under the belly.

His gaze returned to his mother. How did she look after a year? No different. He had not expected her to look any different. Her eyes, which were getting weaker each year, were watery slits in the brown skin. She wore a handkerchief around her head and her calico dress was long and full and held in at the waist by a beaded belt. Her buckskin moccasins gave off a pungent odor of smoke. Nothing was any different. He knew it without looking. He had not come all the way from Portland to these mountains in Montana to satisfy himself on that score.

"No one fishes when you are away. My bones groan so loud when I walk the fish stay under their rocks."

It seemed impossible that no one cared to fish. The creek was full of swift, cunning trout. He got excited just thinking about it. Tomorrow he would cut himself a pole and try it.

The old lady was saying something else. "I will have some people here. We will make a feast and my friends will see you again."

That was something he had forgotten to include in his visit—the old lady and her feasts! You gorged yourself on meat until you felt sick, and a lot of old people told tiresome stories. He frowned. He ought to refuse. He had not come for a feast. She ought to be told that. But it was a small matter. His mother was old. It was a small matter.

"How is everybody?" He had begun to smoke a cigarette which he took ready rolled out of a package.

The question made the old lady sigh. Eheu! It was bad!

"Louis stole some horses last week. I think no one knows it yet. He's in the mountains."

"He'll go to pen if they find him."

"He'll go to hell!"

Already he was hearing the old stories—quarreling, stealing, fighting. His brothers knew nothing else. And his mother knew nothing but the fear of hell, for herself and for her sons.

A small girl, his niece, came to the corner of the cabin. Her hair was braided, with white strings tied to the end of each braid. She was bashful and kept her chin on her breast.

"Gran'pa wants to see you," she announced when she was still a dozen paces away.

"Come and shake hands, Annie!"

She looked at him but hugged the cabin wall.

Archilde got to his feet and stretched himself. He looked toward the mountains in the east, and then upward to the fleckless sky. Nowhere in the world, he imagined, was there a sky of such depth and freshness. He wanted never to forget it, wherever he might be in times to come. Yes, wherever he might be!

Down by the creek his two nephews were standing uncertainly and watching the house. They had just seen Archilde. Their shouts died away and they went behind the brush to dress.

As Archilde picked up his suitcase and walked toward the house he realized of a sudden that he dreaded meeting his father, Max Leon, the Spaniard. That dread was something which went back a long time, and Archilde, who was growing into a man now, was disturbed by it. It ought not to be.

*　　*　　*　　*　　*

Why he had gone to live with the Indians Max could not explain, except to say that he wanted a free life and they had it. He knew that wasn't enough of an explanation. A free life might mean much to an Old World man, but hardly enough by itself to win him from his loyalty to the past and what it had made of him. Some men went to the Indians because they were lazy, physically and morally, and saw in these simple people a chance to satisfy all their appetites with a minimum of effort. But Max hardly belonged in that class. He tired quickly of their footloose and improvident existence, and as soon as he married Catharine, the daughter of the only Indian he ever really admired, old Running Wolf, he settled down and began to build up his ranch. And on that he labored strenuously. He cut logs for his houses and barns, put up wild hay for winter feeding and, with rails of his own splitting, snake-fenced a large home lot. In the work of those early years he rarely had anyone to help.

It was not laziness, and it was not romanticism. He never thought the Indians were "noble" or children of a lost paradise. While it was true that the old life was much cleaner than the present existence, it was still hard for a white man to stomach. They were like any other people in this respect—that individuals varied exceedingly; some you admired and some you detested on sight. People were always asking him what he thought of the Indians, what were their chief characteristics, and it was nonsense. He didn't know. You could say that jack-rabbits had long legs and were swift runners, hoppers rather, but there was no single trait he knew of to describe all Indians. Even the first thing you thought of, color, had almost as many variations as there were single Indians. The one thing he had never seen was a red Indian. There were all shades of brown, some almost black ones, and a good many were as olive-skinned as a Spaniard.

No, as far as he could make out, the thing that had attracted him was the land. He came of Spanish peasant stock and he had an instinctive attachment to the land. It was all right to turn trapper and roam at will, more or less. He had had two years of that before stumbling upon Sniél-emen. That was enough. He was so disgusted with wandering, half-starved, through gameless country, with the risks one took in meeting unfriendly Indians, and most of all with the loneliness of those nameless rivers and mountains, that he was ready to give up. If he had been nearer to Spain he would have gone back to the ancestral home and settled into the life for which he was intended. But western Montana, especially in 1870, was a long journey from the homeland. He had mounted that treeless, grass-blown, unnamed hill on a day in early June, having no notion what he would find on the other side—and at the summit he literally fell on his knees and prayed. There was the end of his wandering. He knew it at once.

(1936)

From

CHILDREN OF GOD
by Vardis Fisher

Soon Utah Indians, seeing the smoke of fires and hearing the industry, came to the settlement to trade or steal. They were dwarfed and ragged and half-naked creatures who looked craftily at everything in sight and tried to make off with anything they could get their dirty hands on. Shoshonis came too, with whom the Utahans seemed to be at war; and one afternoon Brigham saw a terrific fight between two painted braves. One of the Utah rascals had stolen a horse from a Shoshoni buck and then traded it for a rifle. Discovered in the theft, he was unwilling to yield the rifle or return the horse; whereupon his exasperated foe broke a gun over the Utahan's skull.

Brigham expected the blow to lay the fellow out. It did stagger him and make him grunt but it did not by any means vanquish him. With blood streaming down his face, he went for his enemy like a wild beast. While the two warriors fought, an old Indian came up with a whip and laid it impartially over the heads of both. A stinging lash across the Utahan's face made him turn from his foe to strike the old man. That made the old warrior mad. With murder in his eye, he seized a pole and broke it over the Utahan's head.

Did all Indians, Brigham wondered, have skulls as thick as that? The old man now turned to the other warrior, who was his own son, and knocked him down; and then he lectured both of them and told them to do their trading away from camp. The Utahan looked abashed but he still plotted. When, a few minutes later, he saw a horse belonging to the Shoshonis, he leapt to its back and set off into the mountains as if a hundred devils were after him. With a howl of astonishment and rage, four Shoshoni warriors went in pursuit. A few hours later they returned with the horse and with blood on one of their rifles.

Satisfied with that vengeance, they built a fire and made ready for supper. When word of it went through camp, all the men came to stare in amazement; for these Indian warriors, sitting imperturbably around their fire, were catching the big-bellied crickets and roasting them alive. They ate them from their fingers, and licked their fingers and palms after each mouthful.

"By the God of Israel!" cried Porter. "I wonder what they taste like."

"I don't think," said another, "I could ever make the riffle with one of them things. Look how they wizzle up when they fry! My old stomach would come up and stick right out of my mouth."

A few of the men turned away, sickened; but most of them stared, fascinated, while the warriors, indifferent to curious eyes, thrust sharp twigs through the writhing black bodies and held them above the flame. After roasting a wriggling insect and shoving it into his mouth, a buck would turn calmly and pick another off the sagebrush.

"By God, I'd eat roots first."

"Me, I'd eat my harness tugs."

"They might taste fine," said Porter. "We might be eatun some ourselves before a year rolls by."

"Are they too dodgasted lazy to hunt deer or do they like them things?"

"The way they waller them down I'd say they like them."

"Look, you see him over there? By God, he's et seventeen since I been standun here and watchun him."

The Indians preferred sugar and bacon and flour. After midnight, they would creep stealthily through the camp, intent on stealing not only food but ammunition and guns; and they became such a pest that Brigham told his men not to admit them to wagons or tents or houses. Foreseeing possible trouble in the months ahead, he rushed the building of the stockade. It was true, he reflected, that the Lamanites were, as the Book of Mormon said, a degenerate people.

(1939)

From

THE FOREST AND THE FORT
by Hervey Allen

Mary Calahan was a white witch. She was a poor Celtic bogtrotter sold out of Ireland into the plantations by some London snatchers, and later "captivated" by the Indians along with her American mistress and her daughter near Frederick, in the province of Maryland. It was she, and her mistress and *her* daughter, who had gone along to do the squaw work for Kaysinata on the western hunting of the summer before.

"Malycal," as the Indians called her, could neither read, write, nor speak much English. She spoke Erse as though it were a living liturgy, and her life mostly had been bright, age-old misery. But for all that she was a wisewoman from the hills of Munster with half an eye at times into the past or the future. It was a trick she had of cocking her eye into the mist. She foresaw the death of her mistress in detail, and foretold it with tears. But to no avail. For Mistress Jessica Lloyd was a proud, tireless woman, who despised the Irish even more than the Indians. Mary was left behind for her trouble when Mistress Lloyd and Miss Eva tried to escape in a bark canoe to Fort Pitt. They were drowned on the falls in the Beaver, and wolves tore their faces after they were dead.

The next day William Wilson, a trader, came from Maryland and offered to ransom the Lloyds from the Shawnees. Wilson then wanted to take Mary back to Maryland, and offered Kaysinata four hundred blue wampum shells and his tow bag for her, but Mary did not want to go. She had five years to serve yet at Lloyds. She said the work was easier with the Indians, and that she hated the bloody English, who were cruel and cold as the Western Sea. Kaysinata let her have her way and refused to part with her. So she stayed on to make hominy for his lodge and foretell the weather and the hunting and certain select deaths.

That had been in the early fall and Wilson was still able to get back to the fort. He was the last trader to visit the villages on the Beaver till the war was over, and his scalp prickled, for he felt the hatchet raised in the air over his head.

When Mawakis died at the beginning of winter, Malycal had taken her place and did all the chief's work for him, taking better care of the lodge than any squaw, though she would sleep in no man's blanket. Her fleas did their own hopping. She preferred to scratch alone, she said. No one troubled her.

All the other women in the village were afraid of Malycal, both white and Indian. She knew when they were going to die. Sometimes she laughed to herself, and sometimes she told them. She came and went pretty much as she pleased. People gave her tobacco when she needed it, so she would not think ill of them. When she drank she sang long songs in Irish. She sang the "Cattle Drive." She was afraid of McArdle because he spoke Latin like a mass priest. He forbade her to mutter at him. On the whole, and considering, they got along together in the lodge not badly. And it was well they did, for it came on to be one of the worst winters ever known.

Malycal foretold the great snow that lasted nearly a month.

It was her business to inform Kaysinata of the weather and he valued her much for it, because it helped the hunters. She would go out into a clearing, lie down, and look up at the sky for a long time. Presently she would stop winking and her face went dead. In the evening she would come back into the lodge, eat, and speak of the weather.

Salathiel learned to believe her. He wrote down what she had said would happen on certain days, and it came out her way. Even McArdle was half convinced. Before the great snow came they roofed in the lodge of Kaysinata with pine slabs, and Malycal stuffed moss and clay between the logs of the walls like sod in a Munster shebang. She also brought in some coal which she had dug out of the streambank, like peat. It made the first coal fire Salathiel ever saw. It was so hot McArdle had to build a clay and stick chimney to contain it.

Many now came to see the coals glowing, until Malycal began to bid them farewell as soon as they poked their heads into the chief's house. Some thought, afterward, she put the *kibosh** on those she said good-bye to then. At last Kaysinata began throwing the hatchet at visitors and they stayed away both day and night.

Then the snow came.

Great black clouds of ducks and other wildfowl from the lake regions, flying south, began to darken the sun the day before. Next the sky came down close to the forest and turned pearl grey. The third day it grew dark as evening. Then it began to snow. It snowed for nineteen days.

Sometimes it stopped at night when the wind died down, and the wolves could be heard howling. They gathered on the tops of the hills to sing. Otherwise the wind came steadily from the north. The forest began to lean towards the south. High trees finally collapsed quietly. At last no one could go out, the snow was so deep. They stayed in the lodges and ate what they had, and waited. The Shawnees did not make snowshoes then like the Ottawas. They were the people of the south and it was not done. Everybody along the Beaver was soon pretty hungry.

There was also an earthquake that winter before the snow went. It broke the ice on the river in places. The ground rumbled. Frozen catfish were thrown

*That is, *the cap of Death* [Allen's note].

up out of the mud. It was a great help to those on the Beaver Creek, for no one could hunt in the soft drifts, and the fish saved many from starving. They came alive on the fire. Large, white horned owls came from the far north and sang to the villages till men's blood froze. Some people went to the fort to beg from George Croghan. They got salt beef there, but no powder. The commandant, Captain Ecuyer, said he would give them plenty of powder and shot when they came in the spring. He laughed when he said it.

When a hard crust at last formed on the snow, it was Salathiel and McArdle who did most of the hunting. What little fresh meat there was that winter they brought in. They took sleeping bears out of hollow trees. The deer had gone over the river. Even rabbits were scarce, for the owls and wolves lived on them. They shot grey wolves for their coats, and trapped otters. One day about midwinter they killed a young elk. It was great luck. But they had ranged far to find him, and it took them two days to get the carcass home over the snow. They hung it on trees at night and stood the wolves off with a leaping fire. At that they were nearly frozen, but the meat was desperately needed. In fact, it came in too late. When they got back to the village they heard Malycal keening, giving the Irish death howl.

Most of the white captives had been done away with in a massacre.

There was nothing for them to eat and they would have died anyway, said Kaysinata. It was a measure well meant, to save trouble. The useful and strong had been saved. Now there would be enough meat to go around. Those who had been done away with were stuffed into the river through a hole in the ice. If anyone came looking for them they would not be found. Kaysinata was anxious the news should not be taken to the fort.

McArdle listened sadly to the chief and then went outside of the lodge to weep. He crossed off eleven names on his bark tablets and put a little hatchet after them. Salathiel saw there was now quite a bundle of these bark tablets with prisoners' names, wrapped in deerskin. It was the record of most of the Indian captives held west of Fort Pitt. McArdle had been at great pains to get the names set down. Salathiel had helped write down many of them himself. He could remember the lists, too. McArdle and he had memorized them together. So many prisoners among the Delawares, so many among the Mingoes, the Shawnees, and the Illinois—so many. The Little Turtle made a singsong of all the names. He was to say nothing of the lists on the bark tablets. They were to go sometime to the fort. McArdle was afraid he would be killed and the names lost. If so, young Albine and the song would remember them. It would be time to take the list to the fort in the spring, McArdle said.

Salathiel had made up his mind to go to the fort in the spring, anyhow. He would tell them that he was English and sing the song of the lists to the captain-commandant. Mawakis was gone now. He was tired of the gloomy life in the lodge. Kaysinata was getting old and demanding. Salathiel would not stay to go on the warpath against his own people. He would leave and go clear back to the inhabitants. Maybe he could find him a girl there. He was beginning to be much troubled under his breechclout. Black Hawk laughed at him. He took the young squaws into the woods and tried them out. He boasted often. He laughed at the Little Turtle for wanting a white girl. "What is the difference?" he asked.

"To me, but not to you," said Salathiel. "You are an Indian."

(1943)

From

RABBLE IN ARMS
by Kenneth Roberts

We slid out into the lake, set a course between the point of Grand Isle and the high shores of Valcour Island, and were off on our long journey to the northward—a journey that we hoped, as do all those who go off to war, would bring us nothing but comradeship and gay adventure, and perhaps a little glory.

When Cap had indiscreetly aired his opinions of the financial abilities of Congress, he questioned Verrieul in a hoarse and angry voice concerning the Indians who might be used against us by the English—provided we had heard correctly in London from Marie de Sabrevois.

"You want to listen to this, Cap'n Peter," he told me, while Verrieul pondered. "You never can tell when information about these red weasels might come in handy." Cap was profane, and put no curb on his tongue where Indians were concerned when he was with me; though in Nason's presence he sometimes contented himself with looking contemptuous when red men were mentioned.

"Weasels?" Verrieul asked. "Which ones do you call weasels?"

"All of 'em!" Cap said. "They're all a lot of dirty, thieving, red weasels! Cut your throat quick as a wink, and can't hold their liquor!"

"How about your friend Natanis of whom I've heard you speak?" Verrieul asked. "How many throats has *he* cut?"

Cap was indignant. "Don't get the wrong idea about Natanis. He's a friend. He's different, Natanis is. Stevie saved his life once. We've all kind of helped each other a few times."

"But dirty, eh?"

"I told you he was different," Cap said. "He really ain't an Indian, except for having an Indian father and mother and a red hide. He don't even drink, the poor iggorollamus: he don't understand nothing about pleasure at all!"

Verrieul nodded thoughtfully. "Yes, that's a strange thing about Indians. We find them peculiar because, although they are called savage, they are often as civilized as white men, and sometimes more so."

"Like hell they are!" Cap said. "How are they?"

"Because," Verrieul said, "in every Indian nation, even the worst, there are many good men, and more honest ones, and even some that are merciful toward their enemies, which is against all common sense. White men, being civilized and not at all savage, avoid common sense as much as possible; but all Indians, whether good or bad, are taught to have a high regard for common sense. Those that are merciful, therefore, are merciful in spite of their teachings; whereas white men, who are forever taught to be merciful, are often the opposite."

Cap scratched his head. "I don't see no sense to what you say! Why is it against common sense to be merciful to an enemy?"

"Look," Verrieul said. "We're making war against the English. We make war against them in order to kill them, do we not?"

"For sure we do!"

"That's why Indians fight, too," Verrieul said. "To kill their enemies. They can't understand it, many of them, when they're asked to go out and kill enemies, and are then told it's cruel to kill them when the opportunity presents. The way to kill enemies is not to be merciful to them, they say, but to kill them."

"They're a lot of dirty, underhanded red stinks," Cap said.

"There's another thing," Verrieul explained. "The nations change a good deal. It depends on the Manitousiou—*m'téoulin*—or whatever a nation calls the man whose words it finds most acceptable. Sorcerer, maybe, you'd call him; or maybe magician. Shaman, the western nations say. The nations are almost like trading companies: under good men they're better than under bad men. And as the years pass, they learn how to do things better. Even the Montagnais have learned to make leggins that don't fall apart in a gale. I guess we were pretty bad three hundred years ago. I guess we were dirty, and superstitious, too, maybe; cruel, even. The Revrint Dr. Wheelock told me that when the Holy Catholic Church tortured people, it thought up worse tortures than any Indian ever imagined. Catholics have changed, the Revrint Wheelock said, and so have Indians. They're better than they were a hundred and fifty years ago—better than when the Jesuit fathers first lived among them."

"Just a lot of red stinks!" Cap insisted.

"One thing I quickly learned when I traveled with James Deane," Verrieul said, "was that if you live with Hurons, you're sure they're the kindest people on earth, and Iroquois the most terrible; whereas if you live with Iroquois, you feel that no man ever had truer friends than the Iroquois, and that Hurons are wild beasts."

"Buzzards!" Cap remarked. "Red buzzards!"

"Well," Verrieul said, "if they're buzzards, how do you account for the white children who have been captured by Indian nations, and liked them so well they refused to go back to live with white men again?''

''Listen!'' Cap said. ''When a man gets used to buzzards, he ain't going to where there's buzzards he ain't used to, is he? He likes the buzzards he's got used to now better than the buzzards he used to be used to, don't he? Don't it stand to reason? You answer me that!''

''Now I have become confused,'' Verrieul said. ''But in spite of what you say, Captain Huff—or maybe not in spite of it—I don't know which—James Deane is no buzzard. It is true, though, that after he had spent some years with the Oneidas, it was with great difficulty he was persuaded to come to Hanover with the Revrint Dr. Wheelock. The sachem of St. Francis, Joseph Gill: he was a white captive, and so was his wife. He's a wise man—no buzzard at all; but he wouldn't go back to live with white people, nor his wife either; by no means! In Dartmouth there are three from Caughnawaga, all grandchildren of white captives who would never go back among white people—the grandson of Mr. Stacy from Ipswich, the grandson of Mr. Tarbull from Groton, and the grandson of Eunice Williams from Deerfield.''

Cap Huff tapped me on the knee. ''You don't want to take too much stock in what he says, Cap'n Peter.'' He eyed Verrieul indignantly. ''You're like all the rest of these friends of the Indians! Ask 'em something straightforward and honest about the red weasels, and they tell you everything but what you want to know. All I want to know is which of these red buzzards we'll have to fight; all I get is a lot of yap about white men that want to be Irryquartz or Onudders!''

That was Cap Huff's way when the talk turned on Indians. He would ask for information about them; but it seemed impossible for him to believe anything he heard, or even to listen to the information for which he asked. It was plain that Verrieul would have answered Cap's questions as well as he could if Cap had let him; but the more Verrieul tried, the louder Cap grumbled, so that Verrieul finally had to give it up.

(1947)

NOBLE SAVAGE
Exotic Primitive

I saw the marriage of the trapper in the open air in the far
 west, the bride was a red girl,
Her father and his friends sat near cross-legged and
  dumbly smoking, they had moccasins to their feet
  and large thick blankets hanging from their shoulders,
On a bank lounged the trapper, he was drest mostly in
  skins, his luxuriant beard and curls protected his
  neck, he held his bride by the hand,
She had long eyelashes, her head was bare, her coarse
  straight locks descended upon her voluptuous
  limbs and reach'd to her feet.

      Walt Whitman
      Song of Myself

Be ever foreign, beautiful and strange!
  Nor naturalize (wild word!) that rebel blood:
Docility and use must never change
  Your sweet enchanting reckless alienhood.

      Christopher Morley
      To a Foreigner

The Indian in Baptiste performed the deed with neatness
and despatch, so that Olaf for an instant knew only a face
before him—high cheek bones, thin straight lips, and comic
eyes that were sad. The Spanish in Baptiste dug the grave
and the French tossed a rose on it.

      Ada Jack Carver
      Redbone

THE LITTLE COYOTE
by Mary Austin

Without doubt a man's son is his son, whether the law has spoken or no, and that the Little Coyote was the son of Moresco was known to all Maverick and the Campoodie beyond it. In the course of time it became known to the Little Coyote. His mother was Choyita, who swept and mended for Moresco in the room behind the store, which was all his home. In those days Choyita was young, light of foot, and pretty,—very pretty for a Piute.

The Little Coyote was swart and squat, well-knit but slow-moving, reputed dull of wit, though that, people said, he did not get from Moresco. Moresco was a Hebrew of the Hebrews, and sharp, so that they said at Maverick "as sharp as Moresco," and there was an end of comparison. Land and goods gravitated to Moresco. His Bed Rock Emporium was the centre of their commercial world, running out threads of influence to the farthest corners of the desert hills. Everybody at Maverick owed or had owed Moresco, and would be glad, if opportunity offered, to owe him again.

Moresco dealt in merchandise and miners' supplies at a profit that made men swear as they continued to buy. Moresco grubstaked prospectors, and outfitted miners for the working of prospect holes, for a lion's share of the findings. To do him justice, if there were no findings he was not heard to complain. Moresco had always the cash in hand for the backing of new enterprises, for a consideration. In short, Moresco was the burning glass that focused at Maverick whatever of bustle and trade was left in the depleted hills.

What the people perceived chiefly was, that as the country grew poorer Moresco waxed richer, and they grumbled accordingly. But the real sore spot in Maverick was his relation to the Campoodie.

It was said, and believed, that Moresco dealt brotherly by the Piutes. He gave them plain terms, forbore to haggle, preferred them for small employments, warmed them at his fire, gave them good-morrow and good-night. The fact was, Moresco had the instincts of a patriarch. To outwit Maverick was business, to despoil the Gentile might be religion; but the hapless, feckless people who dwelt gingerly beside them were his dependents, his beneficiaries,—in a word, his children. In reality they cost him very little. He was amused, he was diverted, he expanded with paternal graciousness. For their part, the Indians revered him, and Choyita was envied of the women to have borne him a son.

Not that Moresco admitted anything of the kind, but there are no secrets in a Campoodie. Choyita left the child behind when she went to clean and mend for Moresco. What was she or her son that her lord should be mindful of them? Once, when the child was about a year old, and she sat with the Mahalas by the sun-warmed wall, watching the daily pageant of white life as it passed through the streets of Maverick, Moresco called her into the store, and gave her a pair of shoes for the child, and red calico for a frock. Thereafter Choyita walked proudly. To her mind the child was acknowledged, and so it was received in the Campoodie. Happy was she among women, though her son should be called the Coyote.

Among Piutes, Coyote as a name to be called by is a matter for laughter or killing, as the case may be. For the coyote, though evilly bespoken, is of all beasts the most gullible; the butt, the cat's-paw, the Simple Simon, of four-footed things,—the Jack Dullard of Piute folk lore. So from the time he stumbled witlessly about the Campoodie on his fat, bowed legs, Choyita's son was the Little Coyote; and the time is past when a man may win a new name for himself,—long past with the time when there were deeds worth naming. The Little Coyote he remained when he was come to his full size, which was something short of the stature of a man.

By that time, Choyita, who had lost her prettiness and grown fat, had gone to keep house for a miner down Panniment way, and Moresco had married a wife, who bore him only daughters, and spent much of her time and most of his money in San Francisco. By that time, too, the Coyote knew whose son he was. It came to him as a revelation, about the time his slow wit perceived that the other children mocked him for his tainted blood.

"Nana," he asked, when the savory smell of the cooking pots drew the children in from their long day's playing,—"Nana, whose son am I?"

"Moresco's," she answered, and there fell a long silence between them. If she had said the alpenglow had fathered him, he would not have been more amazed. It lay all about them now, the diurnal benediction of high altitudes, the transfiguration of the rifted hills, and the boy at the heart of it thought of Moresco,—Moresco, who stood for power and pleasance, the quintessence of all things desired or feared, the little god of the Piutes.

"Moresco, Moresco," he repeated softly, under his breath. He did not call him "father," and he told no man, but he never forgot.

When the Little Coyote was, as nearly as he could guess, about seventeen, he killed his first big game. It was a deer, shot at the time of piñons, when all the tribe went up to the annual harvest. The Coyote made next to nothing of it, for he had the good manners of his tribe; but he put by the best cut, wrapped in fern leaves, and the next day walked the eleven miles to Maverick that he might bring it to Moresco. He stood at the door of the Bed Rock Emporium until the merchant noticed him.

"Vell, Kyode, vat you wandt?" said Moresco.

"That you should have this," said the Coyote, and then he went away.

A few days later the merchant called him into the store, and gave him a box of sardines and two tins of corn. Nobody understood the etiquette of present-giving better that Moresco.

After that, when it began to be observed there was a kindliness between the Hebrew and the Coyote, people crooked one finger to the curve of an aquiline nose and winked slyly.

Although Maverick could not deny Moresco's ultimate winnings in the financial game, it permitted itself the luxury of questioning the several moves by which he achieved them. Never, in the opinion of Maverick, had he behaved more foolishly than in the matter of Jean Rieske's sheep. Jean Rieske was a sheep-owner in a small way, shepherding his own flock in the windy passes of the hills, made his exclusive pasture by the strip of barrenness that encompassed them. Jean Rieske had been several other things in a small way, and had thoughts other than belong properly to sheep-herding. He collected bits of ledges and outcrops, and carried them to Maverick to be assayed, until at last he conceived that he had made a "strike." Forthwith he would be a miner.

Making a mine out of a prospect hole is an expensive business, but if Moresco was willing to risk the money, Jean Rieske would risk his sheep. He worked at it ten months, and at the end of that time he discovered that he had no mine and no flock. So he went a-shepherding again, and to the same flock, but as a hireling, not an owner,—at which he considered himself aggrieved, and was comforted with strong waters. At the end of other ten months Moresco discharged him, and gave his place to the Little Coyote.

Whatever Jean Rieske swore and Maverick prophesied, the Coyote proved himself born for it. He knew the hills; he scented pasture from afar; he had an instinct for short cuts like a homing pigeon; he was weather-wise as—an Indian. The flock prospered. The Little Coyote was happy: he did a man's work, and he served Moresco. Two or three times in a year he came in to replenish his stores and to make report. He stood at the door of the store, grave and still, until Moresco came out and spoke to him: "Vell, vat you wandt, Kyode?" The shepherd gave the tale of his flock in straight-spoken words and few, with long pauses. When he had quite done, Moresco would say, with his hand withdrawn from his left breast pocket, "Take a cigar, Kyode." Then he would light his own, and they smoked together, the man and his son, for a sign of good understanding, and went each his own way.

The flock increased and became notable. Moresco trusted his shepherd. It was a responsible employment, and there were men in Maverick who coveted it. Persons who felt the situation to be indefensible probed it a little, gingerly. Why should the likes of that job fall to a Piute, when there were better men wanting it? "Vell, for one ting, id is cheaber," said the merchant, with his bland, inclusive smile. And that was as much as most people got out of Moresco.

Three, four, five years the Little Coyote worked the flock from Keynot across the summit to Rose Springs, and in all the foodful hollows that lie between. He saw little of men, and missed them not at all. If in the wickiups beyond Maverick there were young breasts and bright, desirous eyes, he took no thought of them: he thought only of Moresco and the flock, how he might prosper it. All the slow heat of his being burned in a passion of service for the man who treated him as if he were white. He ran at the head of his flock; he lay down with it by night; he carried the lambs in his bosom. He lived as simply as one of his own sheep, and looked a young god, walking clear on the skyline with the nimble flock, or coming up out of streams on summer mornings, with the sun shining on his fine gold-colored limbs. And oh, but he was a silent one, was the Little Coyote. He had no pipes to play, nor any song; but at times, as he walked in the full tide of the spring, near naked and unashamed, throwing up the tall stalk of some hillside flower and catching it, his lips moved in the minor croon of his people, the *"he-na, ah-na, há-na,"* that is the burden of their songs,—an old word of a forgotten tongue, never to be laid aside. It seemed as if the morning prime of earth persisted in him with that word.

By this time the flock had trebled, and the Coyote, going down to make report, so far forgot his Indian training as to admit his pride.

"Id is too much for you, Kyode," said Moresco. "I vill ged Chopo to helb you."

"Chopo is a fool," said the Coyote. "I would rather have another dog."

"Two dogs, if you like," returned Moresco.

The Coyote considered. "No," he said, "one, if I may choose him."

So Moresco's shepherd had one of the famous dogs of Del Mar, and Maverick outdid itself guessing the price Moresco paid for it. Maverick had other things to talk about before the season was over, for that was the winter of the "great snow." Snows came occasionally to Maverick, in the wake of storms fleeting over from ridge to crest. They whitened the hills, crusted the streams, and snuggled away into the roots of the pines by the bare rock gullies. They came in a swirl of wind sometimes, that packed them deep in the cañons, and left the high places bare to days of twinkling cold, but afforded nothing by way of contrast to the great snow. For two days the sky lowered and brooded, and the valleys filled and filled with a white murk, dry, and warmer than should be for the time of year. The moon of nights showed sickly white and cast no shadow.

The Little Coyote smelled snow in the air, and began to move the flock toward the Marionette. The Marionette was the hole in the ground that Jean Rieske hoped would turn out a mine. It was a deep, wide gouge in the face of the hill, at the head of a steep gully. The Coyote had built corrals in the gully, and used it at lambing time. The Indian's instinct proved him right. The third morning snow fell, wet and clogging. It increased with the day, and grew colder. The man and the dogs put all their skill to the proof, but the sheep huddled and stumbled. They were half a day's journey from the mine in the best of weather, and every hour the storm thickened. Crossing Cedar Flat, two miners, going hastily down from a far, solitary mine, gave the Coyote a friendly hail.

"Leave the sheep to the dogs, and get out of this!" they cried. "It's going to be a hell of a storm."

But that the cold had stiffened his face into immobility the Coyote would have smiled. They to talk to him of the weather and the sheep!

He saw what his work was to be, and settled to it. He lightened the camp burro of his pack and let him go. The little beast trudged doggedly beside him, until presently they came to a wind-tilted cedar in the lee of a hill. The burro considered; he looked at the shepherd, and put his nose to the thick, sodden snow; he backed under the cedar and dropped his head. It was a hard shift, but he would see what came of it. The shepherd spoke to his dogs: they lagged and wimpered, but they heard his voice. He who had been chary of words grew voluble: he shouted, he urged, he adjured them; he wrestled with them in the white silence of the snow. The Piute had none of the white man's gift for expedients to save himself and as many of the sheep as he could. The sheep were Moresco's, and Moresco trusted him: he must bring them all in. If one halted and stumbled, the Coyote carried it until it was warmed and rested a little. They floundered in a drift, and he lifted them out upon his shoulders, the dogs whining a confession of helplessness. It grew dark, and the snow still fell, sharp, and fine, and most bitter cold. The wind came up and snatched his breath from him; but there was no longer any need for crying out,—the dogs understood. They had passed the first revolt of physical terror, and remembered their obligations; their spirits touched the man's spirit and grappled with their work. They were no longer dogs, but heroes. Moreover, they knew now where they went, and helped him with their finer sense. Happen what would to the man and the dogs, the sheep would all come in.

Late, late they found the ravine of the Marionette. The Little Coyote had lost all sense of time and feeling. He drowsed upon his feet, but moved steadily about the flock. The dogs bayed, and he heard the sharper clang of the bells given back by the rocks as the sheep began to pour into the cavern of the mine. His head floated in space; he was warm and comforted, and he knew what these things might mean. His feet slipped in the yielding drifts.

"Moresco! Moresco!" he cried, as a man might call, in extremity, on God.

The morning broke steely blue and cold upon a white wonder. At Maverick, people looked up from their path-shoveling to ask if the men from the mines had all come in, and what was to be done for those who had not. Two miners, arriving late the previous day, had told redoubtable tales of the trail and the wind and the snow. Incidentally, they mentioned having seen the Little Coyote. By ten o'clock it was known in all the saloons that Moresco was offering inducements for men to go to the rescue of his shepherd. Opinion gained ground that the Coyote was a fool for not looking out for himself better, and that cold never hurt a Piute anyway, and if he was at the Marionette he was all right.

"Yes," said a man nursing a frozen foot,—"yes, if he got in."

Within an hour there were three found willing to start,—Salty Bill, an Indian called Jim, and one Duncan, a miner from Panniment way,—and who else but Moresco! People said it was ridiculous; Moresco was short and fat, and turned fifty. The barkeeper at the Old Corner wanted to know if anybody thought Moresco would trust the counting of his sheep to any other.

It is fifteen miles from Maverick to the Marionette, and all uphill. By the time they came to the turn of the trail they were knee-deep in the snow. It was soft and shifty, and balled underfoot. They kept as much as possible to the high places; this avoided the drifts, but made more climbing. Crossing the flats they floundered hip-deep, wide of the trail. Perspiration rolled from their foreheads and froze upon their beards. Their bodies were warm and wet, and their lungs wheezing; they had lost the sense of their feet under them. The sun on the snow made them blind and sick. They had been out four hours, and were little more than halfway. The white men cursed with what breath they had; only the Indian kept a stolid front. Moresco was purple and gasping.

"Give up," cried Salty Bill,—"give up, Moresco! We'll never make it. Such a peck of trouble about a Piute and a parcel of sheep. Better for the Coyote to freeze than us four. Give up, I say."

"Ah yes, der Kyode," said Moresco, dazed and feebly,—"der Liddle Kyode. He vas my son," and he burrowed on through the snow.

The men stared, but they followed. Salty Bill kept the lead; he was in a ferment to have the thing over with, that he might go home and tell his wife.

Six hours out, quite spent, and drunk with fatigue, they came to the ravine of the Marionette. They heard the sheep bleat and the dogs yelp, trailing frozen-footed across the snow. At the foot of the gully a white heap lay, covered but well defined, spread out in the symbol of a sacrifice that the Hebrew repudiated and the Indian had never known. Moresco brushed the snow from it with his hands, and, as he stooped above it, tears fell upon a face grown white in death and strangely like his own. It was the Little Coyote.

(1902)

From

MELANCTHA
by Gertrude Stein

Rose Johnson made it very hard to bring her baby to its birth.

Melanctha Herbert who was Rose Johnson's friend, did everything that any woman could. She tended Rose, and she was patient, submissive, soothing, and untiring, while the sullen, childish, cowardly, black Rosie grumbled and fussed and howled and made herself to be an abomination and like a simple beast.

The child though it was healthy after it was born, did not live long. Rose Johnson was careless and negligent and selfish, and when Melanctha had to leave for a few days, the baby died. Rose Johnson had liked the baby well enough and perhaps she just forgot it for awhile, anyway the child was dead and Rose and Sam her husband were very sorry but then these things came so often in the negro world in Bridgepoint, that they neither of them thought about it very long.

Rose Johnson and Melanctha Herbert had been friends now for some years. Rose had lately married Sam Johnson a decent honest kindly fellow, a deck hand on a coasting steamer.

Melanctha Herbert had not yet been really married.

Rose Johnson was a real black, tall, well built, sullen, stupid, childlike, good looking negress. She laughed when she was happy and grumbled and was sullen with everything that troubled.

Rose Johnson was a real black negress but she had been brought up quite like their own child by white folks.

Rose laughed when she was happy but she had not the wide, abandoned laughter that makes the warm broad glow of negro sunshine. Rose was never joyous with the earth-born, boundless joy of negroes. Hers was just ordinary, any sort of woman laughter.

Rose Johnson was careless and was lazy, but she had been brought up by white folks and she needed decent comfort. Her white training had only made for habits, not for nature. Rose had the simple, promiscuous unmorality of the black people.

Rose Johnson and Melanctha Herbert like many of the twos with women were a curious pair to be such friends.

Melanctha Herbert was a graceful, pale yellow, intelligent, attractive negress. She had not been raised like Rose by white folks but then she had been half made with real white blood.

She and Rose Johnson were both of the better sort of negroes, there, in Bridgepoint.

"No, I ain't no common nigger," said Rose Johnson, "for I was raised by white folks, and Melanctha she is so bright and learned so much in school, she ain't no common nigger either, though she ain't got no husband to be married to like I am to Sam Johnson."

Why did the subtle, intelligent, attractive, half white girl Melanctha Herbert love and do for and demean herself in service to this coarse, decent, sullen, ordinary, black childish Rose, and why was this unmoral, promiscuous, shiftless Rose married, and that's not so common either, to a good man of the negroes, while Melanctha with her white blood and attraction and her desire for a right position had not yet been really married.

Sometimes the thought of how all her world was made, filled the complex, desiring Melanctha with despair. She wondered, often, how she could go on living when she was so blue.

Melanctha told Rose one day how a woman whom she knew had killed herself because she was so blue. Melanctha said, sometimes, she thought this was the best thing for her herself to do.

Rose Johnson did not see it the least bit that way.

"I don't see Melanctha why you should talk like you would kill yourself just because you're blue. I'd never kill myself Melanctha just 'cause I was blue. I'd maybe kill somebody else Melanctha 'cause I was blue, but I'd never kill myself. If I ever killed myself Melanctha it'd be by accident, and if I ever killed myself by accident Melanctha, I'd be awful sorry."

(1909)

From
THE SOUL OF THE INDIAN
by Charles A. Eastman

That solitary communion with the Unseen which was the highest expression of our religious life is partly described in the word *hambeday,* literally "mysterious feeling," which has been variously translated "fasting" and "dreaming." It may better be interpreted as "consciousness of the divine."

The first *hambeday,* or religious retreat, marked an epoch in the life of the youth, which may be compared to that of confirmation or conversion in Christian experience. Having first prepared himself by means of the purifying vapor-bath, and cast off as far as possible all human or fleshly influences, the young man sought out the noblest height, the most commanding summit in all the surrounding region. Knowing that God sets no value upon material things, he took with him no offerings or sacrifices other than symbolic objects, such as paints and tobacco. Wishing to appear before Him in all humility, he wore no clothing save his moccasins and breech-clout. At the solemn hour of sunrise or sunset he took up his position, overlooking the glories of earth and facing the "Great Mystery," and there he remained, naked, erect, silent, and motion-less, exposed to the elements and forces of His arming, for a night and a day to two days and nights, but rarely longer. Sometimes he would chant a hymn without words, or offer the ceremonial "filled pipe." In this holy trance or ec-stasy the Indian mystic found his highest happiness and the motive power of his existence.

When he returned to the camp, he must remain at a distance until he had again entered the vapor-bath and prepared himself for intercourse with his fel-lows. Of the vision or sign vouchsafed to him he did not speak, unless it had included some commission which must be publicly fulfilled. Sometimes an old man, standing upon the brink of eternity, might reveal to a chosen few the or-acle of his long-past youth.

The native American has been generally despised by his white conquerors for his poverty and simplicity. They forget, perhaps, that his religion forbade the accumulation of wealth and the enjoyment of luxury. To him, as to other single-minded men in every age and race, from Diogenes to the brothers of Saint Francis, from the Montanists to the Shakers, the love of possessions has appeared a snare, and the burdens of a complex society a source of needless peril and temptation. Furthermore, it was the rule of his life to share the fruits of his skill and success with his less fortunate brothers. Thus he kept his spirit free from the clog of pride, cupidity, or envy, and carried out, as he believed, the divine decree—a matter profoundly important to him.

It was not, then, wholly from ignorance or improvidence that he failed to establish permanent towns and to develop a material civilization. To the untu-tored sage, the concentration of population was the prolific mother of all evils, moral no less than physical. He argued that food is good, while surfeit kills; that love is good, but lust destroys; and not less dreaded than the pestilence following upon crowded and unsanitary dwellings was the loss of spiritual power inseparable from too close contact with one's fellow-men. All who have lived much out of doors know that there is a magnetic and nervous force that accu-mulates in solitude and that is quickly dissipated by life in a crowd; and even his enemies have recognized the fact that for a certain innate power and self-poise, wholly independent of circumstances, the American Indian is unsur-passed among men.

(1911)

From

PENROD

by Booth Tarkington

Across the alley was a cottage which a thrifty neighbour had built on the rear line of his lot and rented to negroes; and the fact that a negro family was now in process of "moving in" was manifested by the presence of a thin mule and a ramshackle wagon, the latter laden with the semblance of a stove and a few other unprentious household articles.

A very small darky boy stood near the mule. In his hand was a rusty chain, and at the end of the chain the delighted Penrod perceived the source of the special smell he was tracing—a large raccoon. Duke, who had shown not the slightest interest in the rats, set up a frantic barking and simulated a ravening assault upon the strange animal. It was only a bit of acting, however, for Duke was an old dog, had suffered much, and desired no unnecessary sorrow, wherefore he confined his demonstrations to alarums and excursions, and presently sat down at a distance and expressed himself by intermittent threatenings in a quavering falsetto.

"What's that 'coon's name?" asked Penrod, intending no discourtesy.

"Aim gommo mame," said the small darky.

"What?"

"Aim gommo mame."

"What?"

The small darky looked annoyed.

"Aim *gommo* mame, I hell you," he said impatiently.

Penrod conceived that insult was intended.

"What's the matter of you?" he demanded advancing. "You get fresh with *me*, and I'll——"

"Hyuh, white boy!" A coloured youth of Penrod's own age appeared in the doorway of the cottage. "You let 'at brothuh mine alone. He ain' do nothin' to you."

"Well, why can't he answer?"

"He can't. He can't talk no better'n what he *was* talkin'. He tongue-tie'."

"Oh," said Penrod, mollified. Then, obeying an impulse so universally aroused in the human breast under like circumstances that it has become a quip, he turned to the afflicted one.

"Talk some more," he begged eagerly.

"I hoe you ackoom aim gommo mame," was the prompt response, in which a slight ostentation was manifest. Unmistakable tokens of vanity had appeared upon the small, swart countenance.

"What's he mean?" asked Penrod, enchanted.

"He say he tole you 'at 'coon ain' got no name."

"What's *your* name?"

"I'm name Herman."

"What's his name?" Penrod pointed to the tongue-tied boy.

"Verman."

"What!"

"Verman. Was three us boys in ow fam'ly. Ol'est one name Sherman. 'N'en come me; I'm Herman. 'N'en come him; he Verman. Sherman dead. Verman, he de littles' one."

"You goin' to live here?"

"Umhuh. Done move in f'm way outen on a fahm."

He pointed to the north with his right hand, and Penrod's eyes opened wide as they followed the gesture. Herman had no forefinger on that hand.

"Look there!" exclaimed Penrod. "You haven't got any finger!"

"*I* mum map," said Verman, with egregious pride.

"*He* done 'at," interpreted Herman, chuckling. "Yessuh; done chop 'er spang off, long 'go. He's a playin' wif a ax an' I lay my finguh on de do'-sill an' I say, 'Verman, chop 'er off!' So Verman he chop 'er right spang off up to de roots! Yessuh."

"What *for*?"

"Jes' fo' nothin'."

"He hoe me hoo," remarked Verman.

"Yessuh, I tole him to," said Herman, "an' he chop 'er off, an' ey ain't airy oth' one evuh grown on wheres de ole one use to grow. Nosuh!"

"But what'd you tell him to do it for?"

"Nothin'. I jes' said it 'at way—an' he jes' chop 'er off!"

Both brothers looked pleased and proud. Penrod's profound interest was flatteringly visible, a tribute to their unusualness.

"Hem bow goy," suggested Herman eagerly.

"Aw ri'," said Herman. "Ow sistuh Queenie, she a growed-up woman; she got a goituh."

"Got a what?"

"Goituh. Swellin' on her neck—grea' big swellin'. She heppin' mammy move in now. You look in de front-room winduh wheres she sweepin'; you kin see it on her."

Penrod looked in the window and was rewarded by a fine view of Queenie's goitre. He had never before seen one, and only the lure of further conversation on the part of Verman brought him from the window.

"Verman say tell you 'bout pappy," explained Herman. "Mammy an' Queenie move in town an' go git de house all fix up befo' pappy git out."

"Out of where?"

"Jail. Pappy cut a man, an' de police done kep' him in jail evuh sense Chris'mus-time; but dey goin' tuhn him loose ag'in nex' week."

"What'd he cut the other man with?"

"Wif a pitchfawk."

Penrod began to feel that a lifetime spent with this fascinating family were all too short. The brothers, glowing with amiability, were as enraptured as he. For the first time in their lives they moved in the rich glamour of sensationalism. Herman was prodigal of gesture with his right hand; and Verman, chuckling with delight, talked fluently, though somewhat consciously. They cheerfully agreed to keep the raccoon—already beginning to be mentioned as "our 'coon" by Penrod—in Mr. Schofield's empty stable, and, when the animal had been chained to the wall near the box of rats and supplied with a pan of fair water, they assented to their new friend's suggestion (inspired by a fine sense of the artistic harmonies) that the heretofore nameless pet be christened Sherman, in honour of their deceased relative.

At this juncture was heard from the front yard the sound of that yodelling which is the peculiar accomplishment of those whose voices have not "changed." Penrod yodelled a response; and Mr. Samuel Williams appeared, a large bundle under his arm.

"Yay, Penrod!" was his greeting, casual enough from without; but, having entered, he stopped short and emitted a prodigious whistle. *"Ya-a-ay!"* he then shouted. "Look at the 'coon!"

"I guess you better say, 'Look at the 'coon!' " Penrod returned proudly. "They's a good deal more'n him to look at, too. Talk some, Verman." Verman complied.

Sam was warmly interested. "What'd you say his name was?" he asked.

"Verman."

"How d'you spell it?"

"V-e-r-m-a-n," replied Penrod, having previously received this information from Herman.

"Oh!" said Sam.

"Point to sumpthing, Herman," Penrod commanded, and Sam's excitement, when Herman pointed was sufficient to the occasion.

Penrod, the discoverer, continued his exploitation of the manifold wonders of the Sherman, Herman, and Verman collection. With the air of a proprietor he escorted Sam into the alley for a good look at Queenie (who seemed not to care for her increasing celebrity) and proceeded to a dramatic climax— the recital of the episode of the pitchfork and its consequences.

The cumulative effect was enormous, and could have but one possible result. The normal boy is always at least one half Barnum.

"Let's get up a SHOW!"

(1914)

From

THE RAINBOW TRAIL
by Zane Grey

. . . . Shefford, with time on his hands and poignant memory to combat, decided to recall his keen interest in the Navajo, and learn, if possible, what the Indian's life was like. What would a day of his natural life be?

In the gray of dawn, when the hush of the desert night still lay deep over the land, the Navajo stirred in his blanket and began to chant to the morning light. It began very soft and low, a strange, broken murmur, like the music of a brook, and as it swelled that weird and mournful tone was slowly lost in one of hope and joy. The Indian's soul was coming out of night, blackness, the sleep that resembled death, into the day, the light that was life.

Then he stood in the door of his hogan, his blanket around him, and faced the east.

Night was lifting out of the clefts and ravines; the rolling cedar ridges and the sage flats were softly gray, with thin veils like smoke mysteriously rising and vanishing; the colorless rocks were changing. A long, horizon-wide gleam of light, rosiest in the center, lay low down in the east and momentarily brightened. One by one the stars in the deep-blue sky paled and went out and the blue dome changed and lightened. Night had vanished on invisible wings and silence broke to the music of a mockingbird. The rose in the east deepened; a wisp of cloud turned gold; dim distant mountains showed dark against the red; and low down in a notch a rim of fire appeared. Over the soft ridges and valleys crept a wondrous transfiguration. It was as if every blade of grass, every leaf of sage, every twig of cedar, the flowers, the trees, the rocks came to life at sight of the sun. The red disk rose, and a golden fire burned over the glowing face of that lonely waste.

The Navajo, dark, stately, inscrutable, faced the sun—his god. This was his Great Spirit. The desert was his mother, but the sun was his life. To the keeper of the winds and rains, to the master of light, to the maker of fire, to the giver of life the Navajo sent up his prayer:

> Of all the good things of the Earth let me always have plenty.
> Of all the beautiful things of the Earth let me always have plenty.
> Peacefully let my horses go and peacefully let my sheep go.
> God of the Heavens, give me many sheep and horses.
> God of the Heavens, help me to talk straight.
> Goddess of the Earth, my Mother, let me walk straight.
> Now all is well, now all is well, now all is well, now all is well.

Hope and faith were his.

A chief would be born to save the vanishing tribe of Navajos. A bride would rise from a wind—kiss of the lilies in the moonlight.

He drank from the clear, cold spring bubbling from under mossy rocks. He went into the cedars, and the tracks in the trails told him of the visitors of night. His mustangs whistled to him from the ridge-tops, standing clear with heads up and manes flying, and then trooped down through the sage. The shepherd-dogs, guardians of the flocks, barked him a welcome, and the sheep bleated and the lambs pattered round him.

In the hogan by the warm, red fire his women baked his bread and cooked his meat. And he satisfied his hunger. Then he took choice meat to the hogan of a sick relative, and joined in the song and the dance and the prayer that drove away the evil spirit of illness. Down in the valley, in a sandy, sunny place, was his corn-field, and here he turned in the water from the ditch, and worked awhile, and went his contented way.

He loved his people, his women, and his children. To his son he said: "Be bold and brave. Grow like the pine. Work and ride and play that you may be strong. Talk straight. Love your brother. Give half to your friend. Honor your mother that you may honor your wife. Pray and listen to your gods."

Then with his gun and his mustang he climbed the slope of the mountain. He loved the solitude, but he was never alone. There were voices on the wind and steps on his trail. The lofty pine, the lichened rock, the tiny bluebell, the seared crag—all whispered their secrets. For him their spirits spoke. In the morning light Old Stone Face, the mountain, was a red god calling him to the chase. He was a brother of the eagle, at home on the heights where the winds swept and the earth lay revealed below.

In the golden afternoon, with the warm sun on his back and the blue cañons at his feet, he knew the joy of doing nothing. He did not need rest, for he was never tired. The sage-sweet breath of the open was thick in his nostrils, the silence that had so many whisperings was all about him, the loneliness of the wild was his. His falcon eye saw mustang and sheep, the puff of dust down on the cedar level, the Indian riding on a distant ridge, the gray walls, and the blue clefts. Here was home, still free, still wild, still untainted. He saw with the eyes of his ancestors. He felt them around him. They had gone into the elements from which their voices came on the wind. They were the watchers on his trails.

At sunset he faced the west, and this was his prayer:

Great Spirit, God of my Fathers,
Keep my horses in the night.
Keep my sheep in the night.
Keep my family in the night.
Let me wake to the day.
Let me be worthy of the light.
Now all is well, now all is well,
Now all is well, now all is well.

And he watched the sun go down and the gold sink from the peaks and the red die out of the west and the gray shadows creep out of the cañons to meet the twilight and the slow, silent, mysterious approach of night with its gift of stars.

Night fell. The white stars blinked. The wind sighed in the cedars. The sheep bleated. The shepherd-dogs bayed the mourning coyotes. And the Indian lay down in his blankets with his dark face tranquil in the starlight. All was well in his lonely world. Phantoms hovered, illness lingered, injury and pain and death were there, the shadow of a strange white hand flitted across the face of the moon—but now all was well—the Navajo had prayed to the god of his Fathers. Now all was well!

And this, thought Shefford in revolt, was what the white man had killed in the Indian tribes, was reaching out now to kill in this wild remnant of the Navajos. The padre, the trapper, the trader, the prospector, and the missionary—so the white man had come, some of him good, no doubt, but more of him evil; and the young brave learned a thirst that could never be quenched at the cold, sweet spring of his forefathers, and the young maiden burned with a fever in her blood, and lost the sweet, strange, wild fancies of her tribe.

(1915)

INDIAN SKY
by Alfred Kreymborg

The old squaw
is one
with the old stone behind her.
Both have squatted there—
ask mesa
or mountain, how long?
The bowl she holds—
clay ritual of her faith—
is one
with the thought of the past,
and one with the now,
though dim, a little old, strange.
The earth holds her
as she holds the bowl—
ask kiva

or shrine, how much longer?
No titan
or destroyer
or future thought
can part
earth and this woman,
woman and bowl:
the same shawl
wraps them around.

(1917–20)

ADVENT OF THE SLAVES
by William Carlos Williams

The colored men and women whom I know intimately add a quality, that is delightful, to the life about me.

There is little use, after all—save in a title—of speaking of the advent of the slaves; these were just men of a certain mettle who came to America in ships, like the rest. The minor differences of condition were of no importance—the mere condition of their coming is of no importance—

The colored men and women whom I have known intimately have a racial character which has impressed me. I have not much bothered to know why, exactly, this has been so—

The one thing that never seems to occur to anybody is that the negroes have a quality which they have brought to America. It is not important that it is available or not to us for any special use—

Poised against the *Mayflower* is the slave ship—manned by Yankees and Englishmen—bringing another race to try upon the New World, that will prove its tenacity and ability to thrive by seizing upon the Christian religion—a thing to replace their own elephant-, snake- and gorilla-filled jungles—on which to fasten for stability, blowing into it the soul of their own darkness, where, as were the Aztecs in their bloody chapels, they are founded—

They helped to build "a society that was rich and in some ways sumptuous and curiously oriental." "Puritan Massachusetts, unable to rid itself of the idea of man's essential wickedness, could not envision this earthly paradise, Georgia—" "In many families every child had his individual slave: great gentlemen almost openly kept their concubines: great ladies half dozed through the long summer afternoons on their shaded piazzas mollified by the slow fan-

ning of their black attendants, and by the laving of their feet in water periodi-
cally fetched anew from the spring house''—it is a sunken quality, or it is a
living quality—it is no matter which.

All the rest is to keep from having to say anything more—like a nigger:
it is their beauty. When they try to make their race an issue—it is nothing. In
a chorus singing *Trovatore,* they are nothing. But saying *nothing,* dancing
nothing, "NOBODY," it is a quality—

Bert Williams, author of a Russian ballet, *The Kiss;* that's worse than
nothin'. But "Somewhere the sun am shinin'—for ME . . .'' That's SOME-
THIN'. Taking his shoes off; that's SOMETHIN'. . . . dancing, singing with the
wild abandon of being close, closer, closest together; waggin', wavin', weavin',
shakin'; or alone, in a cabin, at night, in the stillness, in the moonlight—bein'
nothin'—with gravity, with tenderness—they arrive and "walk all over God's
heaven—''

There is a solidity, a racial irreducible minimum, which gives them poise
in a world where they have no authority—

Or a ramshackle "castle," peaked with doll's house gables, all awry, by
the railroad; where the boys came with their "brides" in those good days JUST
before the war; old shoes and a shambling independence: a tigerish life, lived
in defiance over a worthless son, by virtue of fierce courage, a heavy fearless
voice and a desperate determination to be let alone—with two reminiscent,
shrewd, remembering eyes stamping authenticity upon her words—and long
gorilla arms to deal a heavy blow upon man or woman who may threaten her,
with a shouted threat of knife-thrust or hatchet stroke if that fails. She was
knocked down, bellowing like a buffalo, maltreated—by whom? You wouldn't
get it out of her. But she announced to whoever has ears, in this place or the
next, that it wouldn't happen another time—and it hasn't. On a Saturday night
shuffling along absorbed, with slow, swinging gait, or staring into odd corners,
or settling back on her heels with a belligerent scowl if greeted—ready to talk:
"Why how are ya?"—anywhere. "Go ahead, kill me, I ain't afraid of ya."

I remember with thrilling pleasure and deep satisfaction E. K. Means'
tale, *Diada Daughter of Discord,* an outstanding story of a wild nigger wench,
billeted upon a friend's family by her owner while he went for a short boat trip
without her. Read *Diada*—cutting cane stalks, sharpening them with lightning
speed and driving them through the attacking hounds.

"faces like
old Florentine oak.

Also

the set pieces
of your faces stir me—
leading citizens—
but not
in the same way.''

Nothin' makes much difference—to Otie: Butcher knife, butcher knife, Mr. Gould wants you.

It's a quality, the same as "Sweet everlasting voices be still."

Of the colored men and women whom I have known intimately, the most loquacious is M.—who can't eat eggs because it gives him the hives. Language grows in the original from his laughing lips, "You know that bloom of youth stuff," his shy crooked smile, weary, slow, topping his svelte figure, his straight, slim six feet of willowy grace, drooping from the shoulders, smiling sleepy eyes. "White blood and colored blood don't mix," said he nursing his injury, "Doc, I got a hemorrhage of the FLUTE," he said. "Cocaine for horses, cocaine for mules, IN THE *TRENCHES!*" he yelled as I removed the bandage. "I'm going to feed this to the ducks," he said. The relief is never ending, never failing. It is water from a spring to talk with him—it is a quality. I wish I might write a book of his improvisations in slang. I wish I might write a play in collaboration with him.

His old man is a different sort: I once made several pages of notes upon his conversation—but I lost them; he was an able fisherman along the North Atlantic shore, resistant as an eel. In the hold of the vessel when they were packing porgies, ice and fish filling the hold of the schooner in heavy layers, it was he who could stay down there at work longest—

For sheer sordidness we never touch them, the desperate drunkenness, upon foul stuff, in which they nearly die in a heap of rags under the eaves in the attic of some revolting, disease-ridden female's dump—fly-covered, dazed—

For purity of religious devotion, in the simplicity of their manoeuvres, they exceed our greatest application. Personal cleanliness becomes them with an oriental grace before which our ablutions pale to insignificance.

They wear the BEST fabrics that money can buy, man and woman alike.

It is nothing, nothing.

There was Georgie Anderson whom I remember as some female who walked upon air and light—in her wild girlhood.

And there was "Dudu," gentle as the dew or rain in April—but I knew she had a temper for those who offended her—

And there are many others.

Put them on a ship, under any circumstances you may fancy and you have them coming, coming. Why for?

Nothin'—

As old man Hemby said to me at the door: "I'm here. I come after you yesterday but I couldn't find you. Doctor, I'm in a bad fix; I want you to do something for me."

(1925)

From

REDBONE

by Ada Jack Carver

It is lazy and sweet along the Côte Joyeuse and on into the piney red-clay hills—a land which for nearly four hundred years has been held enthralled by a river. And here among the whites and blacks there dwell in ecstatic squalor a people whom, in the intricate social system of the South, strangers find it difficult to place. For although they may be bartered with, jested with, enjoyed, despised, made friends and enemies of—yet in the eyes of those born to the subtle distinction they are forever beyond the pale.

They are a mixture of Spanish, French, and Indian, and God only knows what besides; and along the Côte Joyeuse, a region given to phrase and to fable, they are dubbed "redbones" because of their dusky skins so oddly, transparently tinted. They are shiftless and slovenly, childlike and treacherous; and yet from somewhere, like a benediction, they have been touched with something precious.

Of this hybrid and tragic tribe was Baptiste Grabbo, planter, and his the story of a man who desired and obtained a son.

One summer morn at a peep-o-day hour this Baptiste set out for Natchitoches, riding his little red pony. His mission was three-fold: first, of course, to get drunk; second, to make a thank-offering to his patron saint, whose business it was to look after him and who did it rather well, all things considered; third, in accordance with a custom that still prevails, to purchase in tribute a gift for his wife, who had been delivered of a fine and lusty son—a man-child born in the crook of a horned moon and destined for great good fortune.

Baptiste rode hard, like a centaur. Above him the frail enchantment of budding clematis filled the woods with light and, reflecting on his fortune, he recalled complacently the insults and insinuations with which since his marriage his relatives had derided his childless estate. Bah! He would make 'em swallow their words, the yellow chinquapin-eaters! He accursed of Heaven?

The glory of fatherhood gave him a heart a-tune to the tumult of summer. There were flowers purple with adoration praying in the grass; wings brushed his cheek; and Baptiste, his mind still full of the night's travail, thought of birth. He thought of The Birth, and an immense and terrible holiness shook him as with an ague. Why, God was right up in that tree. God—benignant, amused. He could talk with God if he cared to. He spread his hands in a little prayer, like a child that laughs and prays. He was shaken and spent with rapture.

Conceive of Baptiste if you can: an uncouth, oafish little man, thin and pointed and sly; but with something about him grotesque and delightful, for all the world like a clown—something of quaint buffoonery that charmed little children, even the little boys and girls who lived in the fine old houses along the river front and walked abroad so sweetly with their nurses.

"Hi, Baptiste!" they would squeal when they saw him; "Howdy, *Mister* Baptiste!"

And then they would laugh with an elfin delight as if they shared some wanton secret with him. And their nurses—respectable, coal-black "mammies"—would pull them away, disgruntled; "Lawd, white chillun, come along. Dat triflin', low-down redbone—"

But this heaven-lent quality, whatever it was, that endeared him to children caused the women of his race to stick out their tongues at him. His love tale, how for a fabulous sum he bought from her father the prettiest maid in all the Indian pinewoods, was the talk of a region already famous far and wide for its romance. Baptiste—through no effort of his own, of course—was rich, as occasionally redbones get to be when their luscious acres fringe the winding Cane; and the slim and blossomy Clorinda had pleased him mightily. She was a lovely thing with sea-green eyes and the chiseled beauty her women possess for a season; and Baptiste thought of babies when he looked at her—he who could pipe to children and trill like a bird in a tree. They would come one right after the other, of course, as was right for babies to come: brown little stairsteps of children.

He had even gone so far as to hail old Granny Loon one time as she hobbled past the courthouse; Granny who brought her babies in baskets (white ones and black ones and yellow and red ones!) and charged a fortune a day.

"Hey, Granny, what you got in there?" he wheedled in a voice that had the drawling music of the sluggish old witch-river. "You give him to me for my wife, old Granny. Yessir, we need us a son."

But Granny, disdainful, made no reply; and shifting her mysterious basket, passed with dignity down the shaded street. She could be high-and-mighty when it pleased her and, "blue-gummed" African though she was—and proud of her pure descent—she was by virtue of her calling above and beyond all race distinction. Granny Loon was dedicated, consecrated, sacred. But the greasy old mulatto women around their coffee stalls, who were shrewdly informed as to Granny's comings and goings, broke out into ribald laughter, shaking their fat gingham sides.

"Huh!" they snorted, "dat chile Granny got ain't fo' no ornery redbone. Dat chile is fo' white folks, yessir. Baptiste, he better go find his se'f one in de briar-patch."

He had swaggered away, Baptiste, pretending not to hear; but his face had burned and his heart had ached. Ah, but now he would show them. . . .

Baptiste, whose thoughts were prayerful if he but stumped his toe, had that very day taken up the matter with High Heaven. You slipped into the dim cathedral where God was all about you and your bony knees sank richly down into passionate crimson velvet.

"A son, sweet Saint. A lil' son. Send us a son, sweet Mother—"

And then to make assurance doubly sure, on emerging he had crossed two sticks to fling at a chance stray cat.

The creed of the redbone is past understanding: things vaguely heard and remembered; things felt and but dimly divined; superstitions drilled into him by the wrinkled old crones of his race. His religion is compounded of Catholic altars where candles burn through the thick dim smoke from the swinging incense bowls; of pinewoods tremulous like a sounding organ; of forest fires and thunders and winds; of fetishes against the powers of darkness; of a moon that comes up red from the swamp; of a wilful river that doles out life and death.

Sometimes when Baptiste lay prone on a hillside things came to him, ancient things, and he knew what people had known when the earth was young— something stirring in him that had swung a papoose in the treetops. Sometimes when the moon was thin and the cotton greening in the fields was beginning to square, something lifted his soul that had strummed a guitar under a lady's window. Sometimes when that same young moon had grown sullen with orange fire, sometimes when he lay on the hot black earth and heard the negroes singing, something ached within him like the curse of a voodoo witch.

His patron saint he had chosen for reasons best known to himself, not the least significant of which was the little saint's unobtrusiveness; for he was an ecstatic little blue fellow who lived in a niche of the church, in so dim and distant a corner that one might pray to him without exciting comment. The redbone, you must know, is secretive in matters religious; and pagan as he is at heart, is chary of dogma and fixed belief—his erratic worship being tolerated rather than condoned by the priesthood.

To this adopted saint, then, Baptiste told his beads, beseeching intercession: three masses a week, so many "Hail Marys," the Way of the Cross for a baby. Since he always returned from his orisons uplifted and slightly unsteady, Baptiste's mysterious pilgrimages had provoked his relatives to what was to them an obvious and foregone conclusion: Baptiste was drinking and gambling *awful!* He had better stay home with his wife.

Baptiste, jogging the deep-rutted roads, suddenly laughed and smacked at his pony. Now that a son had been born to him he would pour the shining dollars into his little saint's outstretched paws, the little saint who had moved Heaven and earth in his, Baptiste's, behalf. And then across the young day's joy a wavering shadow passed, and then another. Bats! From the swamp near by. The creatures came flickering, velvet-black and crazy, with the uncertain, chittering, sweezy sound that their wings make in the air; and when Baptiste struck out to fend them off, one of the gibbety things fell to the earth, stricken. Aghast that he had unwittingly wounded the devil's own, Baptiste turned straight about, although fully two miles from home. The sweet havoc in his heart had chilled into dreadful foreboding—for what man in his senses would flaunt such disaster?

Could it mean that his child was ill, perhaps at this moment dead?

When he rode into the back yard he saw his wife's pink petticoat a-hanging in the sun. His throat was dry and parched as he opened the kitchen door.

Granny was in the kitchen, crouching over the stove and stirring a viscous substance in a kettle. Her sacred basket hung above her on a nail. Her snowy white head was bound with a red bandanna, and she wore a spotless apron in the pocket of which was a buckeye to ward off the dread swamp fever. From a cord around her neck hung a curious carved African stone that dangled against her breasts. She turned and squinted at him as he entered.

"The lil' feller . . . is he . . . do he still breathe? Answer me, old woman."

Granny shrugged her shoulders. Her scorn of men was instinctive, she who assisted them into the world and first clothed their nakedness. There was not a midwife in all that neck of the woods who could hold a candle to her. When not "waiting" on a woman she lived alone on the edge of the Indian pinewoods in a shack half hidden with splashy sunflowers. There was a rail fence around it and toadstools at the door; and in the back yard an iron pot that looked like a cauldron. She was age-old and deathless, and all her movements were soft as if timed to the sleeping of children.

She gave Baptiste a mystic look; and then from above, down the rickety stairs, there sounded a thin little wail. Baptiste listened, woe in his eyes. It sounded so strange and so young.

"Mon Dieu!" he implored, "what was that?"

"De good Lawd he'p us," Granny answered, stirring and tasting, tasting and stirring. "Fo' shame, Mister Baptiste Grabbo. Dat up dere's yo'son, man, a-cryin' fo' his dinner."

"And her? Is she well?—Clorinda—"

His agonized eyes searched the old woman's face, but Granny was muttering incantations over her ill-smelling brew: runes for the newborn babe and his mother; spells against milk-leg and childbed-fever. It was a full minute before she turned to him her sybil face, wrinkled with a thousand tragedies.

"Gawd-a-mighty!" she grumbled, "how many time yo' come runnin' back to ask 'bout dat wife an' dat child? How come yo' don't go an' git outer my way? I done brung a many a baby, to white folks an' niggers an' mixed blood too. But I ain't nebber seen no daddy take on like dat befo'. Nussir, not since I been bo'n."

She looked at him and relented. "Heylaw—wait, I go make yo' a cup—"

Baptiste sat down, still shaking, and Granny poured for him hot black comforting coffee. Behind her somewhere in the dim old house she heard a door open and close. But her gaze held Baptiste's eye.

"Now, go long wid yo' se'f, Mister Grabbo," she said when he had drained the last drop. "A fine strappin' son yo' got, an' yo' all a-tremblin' and shakin'. I oughter brung yo' a lil' ole puny gal. Now yo' go on to town an' git drunk like a man."

(1925)

From

LET'S GO TO HINKY-DINK'S
by Louis Bromfield

It was midnight when George and Betty and the Harry Spencers fought their way through the hot crowd to a table at Hinky-Dink's.

"I won't have any trouble," boasted Harry Spencer. "I knew Hinky-Dink when he was just a nigger bartender in Harlem."

And, sure enough, there before them stood Hinky-Dink, an immense coal-black negro, showing his expanse of white teeth in a broad grin at the approach of Harry Spencer. Above the sound of "Red-Hot Mamma!" blared out by a half-dozen saxophones, the big negro led them to a little table at one side, where they seated themselves, very hot and a little deafened, with their backs touching the backs of other Americans who sat squeezed into the little room.

"This is the real stuff!" screamed Helen Spencer above the din. She shook her tousled blonde hair. "I guess George and Betty are seeing life for the first time in Paris." Then she seized her husband by the arm and shouted in his ear, "They ought to meet Mazie. Go over and fetch her!"

So Harry Spencer, while the others ordered drinks concocted of gin and whisky, went uncertainly across the crowded floor and brought a mulatto girl in a short skirt with a tail attached to emphasize her resemblance to a monkey. She was introduced.

"When are you going to dance?" screamed Helen Spencer.

"Right away . . . Miss . . . right away," said the mulatto girl. "As soon as they turn down the lights."

The lights went down and Mazie, stepping into the glow of a red calcium light, thrust out her stomach and began to dance wildly, a barbaric dance that revealed to the hot, tired crowd all the muscles that lay beneath the satiny yellow skin. It was a wild dance, born in the jungles and translated into new figures and patterns through a whole century-old corridor of barrooms and brothels.

Above the whine of the saxophones, Harry Spencer leaned close to Betty and said, "Let's go for a ride. We can slip out now and tell George and Helen we've gone for some air. They can get home all right."

There was a little struggle, for into the eyes of Betty there had come a strange look of fright at something which lay beyond her understanding. It was a vague, nameless terror of the crowd and the noise, the heat and the sight of the dancer's bare rippling skin. The negroes were shouting now, urging Mazie into a frenzy of contortions. She was frightened as if she had been caught by something from which she could not escape.

"You promised," said Harry Spencer.

And silently Betty rose and followed him through the darkness into the street where the big red motor stood waiting at the curb.

(1927)

From

THE ENORMOUS ROOM
by E. E. Cummings

On a certain day, the ringing of the bell and accompanying rush of men to the window facing the entrance gate was supplemented by an unparalleled volley of enthusiastic exclamations in all the languages of La Ferté Macé—provoking in me a certainty that the queen of fair women had arrived. This certainty thrillingly withered when I heard the cry: "Il y a un noir!" Fritz was at the best peephole, resisting successfully the onslaughts of a dozen fellow-prisoners, and of him I demanded in English, "Who's come?"—"Oh a lot of girls" he yelled, "and there's a NIGGER too"—hereupon writhing with laughter.

I attempted to get a look, but in vain; for by this at least two dozen men were at the peep-hole, fighting and gesticulating and slapping each other's backs with joy. However, my curiosity was not long in being answered. I heard on the stairs the sound of mounting feet, and knew that a couple of plantons would before many minutes arrive at the door with their new prey. So did everyone else—and from the farthest beds uncouth figures sprang and rushed to the door, eager for the first glimpse of the nouveau: which was very significant, as the ordinary procedure on arrival of prisoners was for everybody to rush to his own bed and stand guard over it.

Even as the plantons fumbled with the locks I heard the inimitable unmistakable divine laugh of a negro. The door opened at last. Entered a beautiful pillar of black strutting muscle topped with a tremendous display of the whitest teeth on earth. The muscle bowed politely in our direction, the grin remarked musically; "Bo'jour, tou'l'monde"; then came a cascade of laughter. Its effect on the spectators was instantaneous: they roared and danced with joy. "Comment vous appelez-vous?" was fired from the hubbub.—"J'm'appelle Jean, moi" the muscle rapidly answered with sudden solemnity, proudly gazing to left and right as if expecting a challenge to this statement: but when none appeared, it relapsed as suddenly into laughter—as if hugely amused at itself and everyone else including a little and tough boy, whom I had not previously noted although his entrance had coincided with the muscle's.

Thus into the misère of La Ferté Macé stepped lightly and proudly Jean Le Nègre.

Of all the fine people in La Ferté, Monsieur Jean ("le noir" as he was entitled by his enemies) swaggers in my memory as the finest.

Jean's first act was to complete the distribution (begun, he announced, among the plantons who had escorted him upstairs) of two pockets full of Cubebs. Right and left he gave them up to the last, remarking carelessly "J'ne veux, moi."

Après la soupe (which occurred a few minutes after le noir's entry), B and I and the greater number of prisoners descended to the cour for our afternoon promenade. The Cook spotted us immediately and desired us to "catch water"; which we did, three cartfulls of it, earning our usual café sucré. On quitting the cuisine after this delicious repast (which as usual mitigated somewhat the effects of the swill that was our official nutriment) we entered the cour. And we noticed at once a well-made figure standing conspicuously by itself, and poring with extraordinary intentness over the pages of a London Daily Mail which it was holding upside-down. The reader was culling choice bits of news of a highly sensational nature, and exclaiming from time to time—"Est-ce vrai! V'là, le roi d'Angleterre est malade. Quelque chose!—Comment? La reine aussi? Bon Dieu! Qu'est-ce que c'est?—Mon père est mort! Merde!—Eh, b'en! La guerre est fini. Bon."—It was Jean Le Nègre, playing a little game with Himself to beguile the time.

When we had mounted à la chambre, two or three tried to talk with this extraordinary personage in French; at which he became very superior and announced: "J'suis anglais, moi. Parlez anglais. Comprends pas français, moi." At this a crowd escorted him over to B and me—anticipating great deeds in the English language. Jean looked at us critically and said "Vous parlez anglais? Moi parlez anglais."—"We are Americans, and speak English" I answered.— "Moi anglais" Jean said. "Mon père, capitaine de gendarmerie, Londres. Comprends pas français, moi. SPEE-Kingliss"—he laughed all over himself.

At this display of English on Jean's part the English speaking Hollanders began laughing. "The son of a bitch is crazy" one said.

And from that moment B and I got on famously with Jean.

His mind was a child's. His use of language was sometimes exalted fibbing, sometimes the purely picturesque. He courted above all the sound of words, more or less disdaining their meaning. He told us immediately (in pidgin French) that he was born without a mother because his mother died when he was born, that his father was (first) sixteen (then) sixty years old, that his father gagnait cinq cent francs par jour (later, par année), that he was born in London and not in England, that he was in the French army and had never been in any army.

He did not, however, contradict himself in one statement: "Les français sont des cochons"—to which we heartily agreed, and which won him the approval of the Hollanders.

The next day I had my hands full acting as interpreter for "le noir qui comprends pas français." I was summoned from the cour to elucidate a great grief which Jean had been unable to explain to the Gestionnaire. I mounted with a planton to find Jean in hysterics; speechless; his eyes starting out of his head. As nearly as I could make out, Jean had had sixty francs when he arrived, which money he had given to a planton upon his arrival, the planton having told Jean that he would deposit the money with the Gestionnaire in Jean's name (Jean could not write). The planton in question who looked particularly innocent denied this charge upon my explaining Jean's version; while the Gestionnaire puffed and grumbled, disclaiming any connection with the alleged theft and protesting sonorously that he was hearing about Jean's sixty francs for the first time. The Gestionnaire shook his thick piggish finger at the book wherein all financial transactions were to be found—from the year one to the present year, month, day, hour and minute (or words to that effect). "Mais c'est pas là" he kept repeating stupidly. The Surveillant was uh-ahing at a great rate and attempting to pacify Jean in French. I myself was somewhat fearful for Jean's sanity and highly indignant at the planton. The matter ended with the planton's being sent about his business; simultaneously with Jean's dismissal to the cour, whither I accompanied him. My best efforts to comfort Jean in this matter were quite futile. Like a child who had been unjustly punished he was inconsolable. Great tears welled in his eyes. He kept repeating "sees-tee franc—planton voleur," and—absolutely like a child who in anguish calls itself by the name which has been given itself by grownups—"steel Jean munee." To no avail I called the planton a menteur, a voleur, a fils de chienne and various other names. Jean felt the wrong itself too keenly to be interested in my denunciation of the mere agent through whom injustice had (as it happened) been consummated.

But—again like an inconsolable child who weeps his heart out when no human comfort avails and wakes the next day without an apparent trace of the recent grief—Jean Le Nègre, in the course of the next twenty-four hours, had completely recovered his normal buoyancy of spirit. The sees-tee franc were gone. A wrong had been done. But that was yesterday. Today—

and he wandered up and down, joking, laughing, singing

"après la guerre finit" . . .

In the cour Jean was the mecca of all female eyes. Handkerchiefs were waved to him; phrases of the most amorous nature greeted his every appearance. To all these demonstrations he by no means turned a deaf ear; on the contrary. Jean was irrevocably vain. He boasted of having been enormously popular with the girls wherever he went and of having never disdained their admiration. In Paris one day—(and thus it happened that we discovered why le gouvernement français had arrested Jean)—

One afternoon, having rien à faire, and being flush (owing to his success as a thief, of which vocation he made a great deal, adding as many ciphers to the amounts as fancy dictated) Jean happened to cast his eyes in a store window where were displayed all possible appurtenances for the militarie. Vanity was rooted deeply in Jean's soul. The uniform of an English captain met his eyes. Without a moment's hesitation he entered the store, bought the entire uniform including leather puttees and belt (of the latter purchase he was especially proud), and departed. The next store contained a display of medals of all descriptions. It struck Jean at once that a uniform would be incomplete without medals. He entered this store, bought one of every decoration—not forgetting the Colonial, nor yet the Belgian Cross (which on account of its size and colour particularly appealed to him)—and went to his room. There he adjusted the decorations on the chest of his blouse, donned the uniform, and sallied importantly forth to capture Paris.

Everywhere he met with success. He was frantically pursued by women of all stations from les putains to les princesses. The police salaamed to him. His arm was wearied with the returning of innumerable salutes. So far did his medals carry him that, although on one occasion a gendarme dared to arrest him for beating-in the head of a fellow English officer (who being a mere lieutenant, should not have objected to Captain Jean's stealing the affections of his lady), the sergent de gendarmerie before whom Jean was arraigned on a charge of attempting to kill refused to even hear the evidence, and dismissed the case with profuse apologies to the heroic Captain. " 'Le gouvernement français, Monsieur, extends to you through me its profound apology for the insult which your honour has received.' Ils sont des cochons, les français'' said Jean, and laughed throughout his entire body.

Having had the most blue-blooded ladies of the capital cooing upon his heroic chest, having completely beaten up with the full support of the law whosoever of lesser rank attempted to cross his path or refused him the salute—having had "great fun" saluting generals on les grands boulevards and being in turn saluted ("tous les généraux, tous, salute me, Jean have more medel''), and this state of affairs having lasted for about three months—Jean began to be very bored ("me très ennuyé"). A bit of temper ("me très fâché") arising from this ennui led to a rixe with the police, in consequence of which (Jean, though outnumbered three to one, having almost killed one of his assailants) our hero was a second time arrested. This time the authorities went so far as to ask the heroic captain to what branch of the English army he was at present attached; to which Jean first replied "parle pas français, moi'' and immediately after announced that he was a Lord of the Admiralty, that he had committed robberies in Paris to the tune of sees meel-i-own franc, that he was a son of the Lord Mayor of London by the Queen, that he had lost a leg in Algeria, and that the French were cochons. All of which assertions being duly disproved, Jean was remanded to La Ferté for psychopathic observation and safe keeping on the technical charge of wearing an English officer's uniform.

Jean's particular girl at La Ferté was "LOO-Loo.'' With Lulu it was the same as with les princesses in Paris—"me no travaille, ja-MAIS. Les femmes travaillent, geev Jean mun-ee, sees, sees-tee, see-cent francs. Jamais travaille, moi.'' Lulu smuggled Jean money; and not for some time did the woman who slept next Lulu miss it. Lulu also sent Jean a lace embroidered handkerchief, which Jean would squeeze and press to his lips with a beatific smile of perfect contentment. The affair with Lulu kept Mexique and Pete The Hollander busy writing letters; which Jean dictated, rolling his eyes and scratching his head for words.

At this time Jean was immensely happy. He was continually playing practical jokes on one of the Hollanders, or Mexique, or The Wanderer, or in fact anyone of whom he was particularly fond. At intervals between these demonstrations of irrepressibility (which kept everyone in a state of laughter) he would stride up and down the filth-sprinkled floor with his hands in the pockets of his stylish jacket, singing at the top of his lungs his own version of the famous song of songs—

> après la guerre finit,
> soldat anglais parti,
> mademoiselle que je laissais en France
> avec des pickaninee. PLENTY!

and laughing till he shook and had to lean against a wall.

(1930)

From

AMERICAN BEAUTY
by Edna Ferber

Summer, Temmie decided, was a fine thing in Connecticut. She had arrived in the last blaze of October splendor, soon faded. That first winter had been bitter, strange, often lonely, more than a little frightening. The spring had been blighted by the tragedy of Polcia. But now here was summer, hot, sweet-smelling, with fresh early morning breezes dispelling the mists that hung low on the pastures and over the Housatonic, creeping along the meadow brooks in curling wisps. The dews were heavy, so that it was like walking through water to cross the early morning fields. In the cool of the evening the shadows lengthened across Pequot Ridge and stalked, long-legged giants, into the valley.

Polcia's brief American interlude was almost forgotten. When Temmie or Ondy went to the Smentkowskis to see the dark-eyed Rozia, they somehow did not associate her with the bewildered and desperate woman whose life had ended when hers began.

Temmie was sixteen and over; she was healthy, the sun shone, there was work, there was food, there were friendly human beings to talk to, and young; Ondy, strong, genial, kind; Jot, running about, with his short-legged rolling gait, like a jolly little pirate; stocky Stas, a serious, stolid child. With these at home, and the red-cheeked Rozia to be visited at the Smentkowskis, life at Oakes Farm was not so bad, in spite of the caustic and fault-finding Jude. The farm itself was going well enough—better, surely, than it had in fifty years and more. Ondy's feeling for the land was too inherent not to serve it well, even though no clod of it belonged to him. He made no secret of his determination to buy a piece of land for himself somewhere in the valley as soon as he had money enough put by. Other Poles of longer standing in the community were buying, acre by acre. Under their slavish tending the valley was taking on a second youth; blooming like a widow wooed.

Jude and Ondy were forever bickering about the way in which the farm should be run. Jude seemed to enjoy these tiffs.

"And I'll thank you to remember I'm boss here," she was always saying. Her sallow cheeks would be flushed, her eyes bright behind the glasses. She was pleasantly stimulated by these emotional battles with one of the opposite sex.

"Sure Miss Oakes is boss. Ondy he know to run farm."

"If you're so all-fired smart at it, why didn't you run your own farm in Poland?"

"Is big here, is fine here, is land for everybody. Ondy he makes Oakes Farm rich like anything. You see you have more fine tobacco November as in your life, I betcha."

"I'm not complaining about the way you work. But you've got such crazy notions. I never heard anything so crazy. Speak about the water and the land and the very fire in the stove as if they were folks. And the cows in the barn."

"Sure is like folks. Cow he is know things peoples not know."

Just the day before, Jude had come to Temmie in considerable agitation. "I stepped into the barn, unbeknownst, and there was Ondy with the red heifer that's sick, and talking to the animal as polite as a pair of sugar tongs. Not just so-bossy, so-bossy, as a body sometimes does, to soothe, but talking. It gave me a turn."

Temmie did not seem surprised at this. "Ondy is like that Aunt Jude. He told me. He says all Polack farmers are like that. He says the fire and the water and the earth and the animals aren't just things. They're like people, only better."

"Don't you ever let me catch you talking such nonsense. I'm beginning to believe John Veal was right. They're heathen, those Polacks."

Certainly Ondy, and all the other Poles of the region, had outlandish customs and beliefs connected with the business of plowing, planting, sowing, reaping. Earth, fire, water, plants, animals—all were associated with Old World myths in Ondy's mind.

When the red heifer fell sick Jude was for using such customary methods as she and Big Bella and the other farmers of the neighborhood had always relied upon.

Ondy shook his head. "I fix him." He spent half a day searching in the woods and fields for a certain plant. He tried to explain to Big Bella what it was he sought. When he came upon it he bent it down, fastened its top to the ground with a stone, and said aloud, in Polish, "I will release you when you make my cow well."

"To-night," he told Miss Jude, on his return, "cow he is well. You wait. You see."

Next morning, sure enough, the cow had recovered. Ondy hastened to the spot, three miles away, where he had found the plant, removed the stone, released the plant; for if he failed to do this the cow would fall sick again, and die.

Ondy was for planting in the dark of the moon all seed whose fruit is under the ground—potatoes, onions, turnips, and the like—and in the full of the moon the others—beans, tomatoes, pumpkins, cucumbers, peas. Beans, especially, were planted on Good Friday. There was simply no moving him in that.

"The man's daft as a loon."

Hail, in the sudden cold of late spring, is the great terror of the tobacco grower, when the tender young plants may be battered to death in a few brief minutes. Ondy assured the scoffing Miss Jude that a furrow drawn around a field by a pair of twin oxen would insure that field against hail.

"You're safe enough saying that, Olszak. Go find yourself a pair of twin oxen in all the county, to prove it." Still, to Temmie or to Big Bella she sometimes admitted, with grudging admiration, "He's a knowing kind of cattle, that Olszak."

Temmie, brought up on the superstitions and childish beliefs common to the wagon shows and the carnival companies, accepted, wide-eyed, all that Ondy told her. Jot believed him, too, like a simple child.

Once, when Jude Oakes, in anger against Ondy, had confided to Temmie her suspicion that Olszak was scheming to get her land away from her, Temmie denied the accusation earnestly. "Oh, no, Aunt Jude. He wouldn't. He couldn't, you see. Even if he wanted to, he wouldn't."

"Why not, I'd like to know!"

"Because every field knows its real owner, and if somebody else tries to take it away it won't yield any crops."

Temmie understood now why Ondy loved the land. She, too, began to love Oakes Farm and all that was on it. Not the house alone, but all that was on the farm and of it. She heard and believed—or thought she did, because she wanted to.

Water should never be wantonly dirtied or dried up. Nothing bad should be said or done near it, because it knows, and can betray. Swallows and lizards know herbs that can revive the dead. Fires lighted on the Eve of St. John—June 24th—make the crops succeed. There are all about us witches, goblins, devils, vampires, water spirits, earth spirits, giants, dwarfs, invisible. A *potud-nica,* the midday woman, strangles anyone who sleeps in a field at noon. Water spirits, *boginki,* have human bodies but can become invisible at will. They often try to change their children for human ones, stealing a child from a household and putting their own in its place. A child changed thus can be recognized by its bad temper, its growing ugliness, and its enormous appetite. Sometimes Ondy, jestingly, called little Stas a *boginka's* child, and Stas, at this, stuck out a tremendous lower lip in protest. Cloud beings, *planetniki,* dwell in the clouds and bring rain, hail, thunderstorms. Bees will never stay with a thief. The swallows will leave a farm where some evil deed has been committed. If fruit trees grow well, if crops succeed, it is not the result of man's activity; the plants and trees are conscious of being well treated and show their gratitude. Fire is a superior being. Ondy blessed it when he lighted it in the morning; when he covered it with ashes at night. Snakes and wild birds are the most knowing of creatures, but all four-footed animals understand some things better than men.

Now Temmie understood Ondy's way with the cattle. On cold, bright winter noondays he would turn the cows out of the dark, noisome barn, and they would stand gratefully in the barnyard, their nostrils smoking. He would put his strong gentle hand on their flanks, on their necks, and they would turn their soft eyes on him. Every day he gave each cow two ears of corn, lovingly, tenderly. Good corn, he seemed to be saying. Kind corn.

During that summer a certain peace and contentment settled down upon Oakes Farm. Even into Jude's face there came a kind of nipped blooming. Ondy throve with the crops. He had had the baby, Rozia, baptized by Father Scully, the handsome young Irish priest of the big church at Fenwick. There were now so many Poles settling throughout the valley that they had sent him—a student priest—to Warsaw, and there at school for three years he had learned the language, so that now, when he addressed the Irish-born members of the thriving congregation in English, or the Polish members in Polish, it was with a trace of the brogue in both tongues.

(1931)

BLACK TROUBADOUR
by David L. Cohn

Joe Moss is a harp-blowing black man. When he bears down hard on his two-bit harmonica he can make trouble leave your weary mind, set your tired feet to stomping, bring Sweet Jesus to your backsliding soul. Joe Moss is a one-harp, two-harp, three-harp-blowing man. Sometimes on hot nights in summer when folks are sitting out on the front porch catching air, talking, or sleeping on a mattress stuck in the front doorway to get the benefit of the draft blowing through the open back door and at the same time to keep the dog from leaving the house, Joe takes a stand on the corner of Redbud Street and Cately Avenue. He draws a harp out of the belt that holds up his red corduroy trousers and slowly eases up on the blues just like a lonesome man sidling up to talk to a lady who has a mean and jealous husband.

The first notes of the long, lonesome, mournful tune scarcely seem to disturb the stillness of the night. They merge with it. For a little while you are unaware that anything new has come into the night; that music must always have been there. It must always have been part of the dusty road in the moonlight; of the smoky coal-oil lamps in the shacks; the querulous whine of mosquitoes; the howling of dogs lost in the anguish of mating under the street light at the corner; the slow, reptilian crawling of crayfish in the muddy ditches; the pools of shadow between the close-packed shotgun houses; the broken picket fences and the fecund sunflowers heavy with dust and seed; the quiet voices talking, giggling; the sweaty hands, seeking, searching; the black, oily clouds scudding past the moon; and the far-off rumbling of the Cannon Ball train rounding the curve up above the oil mill. Joe bears down harder and harder. The notes of his harp tremble sadly on the air like a weary sinner laying his head at last on the bosom of Sweet Jesus. Gawd, save us sinners on Judgment Day.

Joe Moss is a rambling, rolling, train-riding, harp-blowing man. They know him on Rampart Street in New Orleans; in the hot-cat parlors and dice dens of Beale Street in Memphis; in Natchez, Vicksburg, Greenville, Helena; in all the river towns up to Cape Girardeau; as far west as Dallas, Texas. Winter and summer, fall and spring, Joe rambles the land, a sweat shirt and red corduroy trousers covering his nakedness, and a ragged hat on his nappy head. It ain't no need to work. It ain't no need to have no one woman and no one home. A man with music in his body can win hisself a woman and a home wherever he lights. A nigger ain't gonna have nothin' nohow, so it ain't no need to try to have nothin'. And it sho' ain't no sense to stay in no one place 'cause when yo' foots itches to travel they's trains goin' whichever way you wants, and somebody, white or black, to feed you when you's hungry.

Joe was born to be a harp-blowing man, but he didn't know it until he was past twenty-one and the Albino Preacher told him right out in church before all the folks that he had the gift of song and music. Up to that time he had worked on Deep Snow Plantation just like any common man, chopping cotton, hoeing grass, ditching, clearing land for the white people, never going farther from home than Greenville, fourteen miles away, and living with only three women from the time he was fifteen years old until he became twenty-one. Nowadays Joe laughs when he sees people chopping cotton in the hot sun; picking cotton on frosty mornings in the fall; felling trees in icy swamps. He rares back and laughs when they flash by him as he crouches on the blinders of that Pan-

American train leaving out from New Awleens for Birmingham, Alabamer; when he rides that Manifest Freight from Memphis to Fulton, Kentucky.

As Joe plays the lonesome blues, up and down Redbud Street folks stop talking. Across the road in the jailhouse prisoners come to the windows of their cells and stick their heads close to the bars to drink in the music lingering on the air. Two high-yellow young couples driving down the street in a V-8 Ford automobile, on their way to the Chinaman's store to get something t' eat, pull up and stop. By this time everybody in the neighborhood knows that Joe Moss, the harp-blowingest man in Mississippi, is back in town. Suddenly Joe sticks the harp in his belt and begins to sing in a warm, rich barytone that can be heard two blocks away:—

> "It's a po' boy long way from home.
> I ain't got no money,
> Ain't got nowhere to go,
> Just stand at de railroad crossin',
> Waitin' to hear de whistle blow."

Up and down the street women cock their ears to catch every word, every note, every tiny evocation of sound. Men listen, too, their souls wooed by the song, their hearts touched with jealousy and vague, uneasy stirrings. The song ends. The night is given over again to the whining of mosquitoes, the brittle crashing of heavy-bodied insects against the dazzling street lamp on the corner, the howling of dogs, and the rumbling of the Cannon Ball as it moves slowly through New Africa on its way to the near-by station. The air is heavy with heat. There is a ring around the moon. Gwine rain to-morrow sho'. Lawd Jesus, he'p us. We's heavy laden.

Then Joe pulls two harps out of his belt. Once, long ago, when he was a fatherless chile and got religion, he promised the Lawd that he would quit blowing the blues and play nothing but church songs. But Joe is a man who is messed up in his weary mind, and he can't always remember what he promised the Lawd and what he did n't promise. But shucks. If you blows the blues now and then and plays church songs now and then, the Lawd sho' ain't gwine be vexed with you.

He stands now under the street light, two harps gleaming silver in the great black gash of his mouth, and blows like Gabriel on Judgment Mawnin'. Tiny rivulets of sweat chase one another through his kinky hair and roll down his neck and throat to merge in little streams lost in the sea of his broad back and thick chest. His torso moves in slow circles on his hips; his feet tap time in the dust; his neck moves in convulsive jerks while his hands tremble on the harps, and the pupils of his eyes dilate until they become spots of black in pools of cream-white. Jesus, come take me home.

> "Well, don't you mind me dyin',
> Lawd, don't you mind me dyin',
> Lawd, don't you mind me dyin',
> Jesus gwine make up my dyin' bed.

"Well, I'll be sleepin' easy,
Well, I'll be sleepin' easy,
Well, I'll be sleepin' easy,
Jesus gwine make up my dyin' bed."

Across the street in the jailhouse, Mankind Armstrong stands with an ear hard against the iron bars of his cell listening. He knows that Joe is singing the gospel truth. His mama told him it was the truth long ago when he was a little boy on Sunup Plantation. Reverem Green, the pastor of his church, told him it was so when he was baptized in Possum Slough. Even the white folks—and they ain't got much sense no matter if the Law is on they side—believe you're going to Jesus when you die. Now Mankind is on his way—on his way to know the truth beyond all dispute; on his way to Jesus; on his way unscarred from his life on earth except for a tiny dislocation of his vertebræ that will occur when he drops through the trapdoor of the newly erected gallows that stands in the back yard of the jailhouse. Mankind listens to Joe Moss blowing on his harps, laughs out loud, and shouts to the prisoner in the adjoining cell: "Nigger, ain't dat de beatin'est, harp-blowin'est man you ever has heerd?"

Once more silence falls on Redbud Street as Joe's song is ended. Then the Law walks up on him out of the darkness—the white-faced Law in a sweaty shirt, dust-stained shoes, gleaming badge beneath sagging suspenders, and black-and-silver pistol stuck in a sweat-stained holster.

Joe takes off his hat as the Law approaches and holds it respectfully in his hand. It was n't no need to run, and besides Joe had n't done nothin'.

"Good evenin', Cap'm," Joe said.

"Good evenin', Joe," the Law said.

"Boss Man, how come you knows my name?" Joe asked.

" 'Cause every nigger in New Africa say they gonna kill you if you keep comin' around here blowin' them harps and monkeyin' round with their women."

Joe smiled complacently. "Cap'm," he said, looking at the ground, "I'm a man don't never kick in no other man's stall."

"Well, maybe you do and maybe you don't. That ain't no skin off my teeth, and if you get killed messin' around here that won't be nothin' new. Anyhow, it ain't gonna be to-night. You been givin' me the creeps with them songs you been singin'. Now let's hear somethin' lively."

"Yassuh, Boss," replied Joe energetically, a note of vast relief in his voice. This was not the first time he had played for the Law, but it was the first time as a free man. Once, down in Natchez, Joe had been arrested and had blown himself clean out of police court. Judge Patterson had asked him to play a tune to see if he was just a jackleg musician, and then had kept him playing all morning long while the other prisoners awaiting trial joined in the singing, and when it was all over the Judge told Joe to come back to see him whenever he was in town and gave him a dollar bill to boot. It ain't no way on earth to tell what white folks will do even if you's a two-headed man. And here Joe was facing the Law again under novel circumstances. "Cap'm," he said, "how 'bout a mess of dem 'Saint Louis Blues'?"

"Go 'head," said the Law, as it whittled a match into a toothpick and began to explore the cavities of its teeth.

Joe took three harps out of his belt, put them in his mouth, and began passionately to celebrate the immortal fame of that Saint Louis woman who tied men to her apron strings. Up and down the length of Redbud Street the music ran. Up and down the length of the street bare feet, shoed feet, stockinged feet, black feet, brown feet, chocolate feet, tan feet, café-au-lait feet, smooth feet, splay feet, flat feet, calloused feet, began to beat time. Up and down the length of the street bodies swayed. Fat bodies, thin bodies, fecund bodies, sterile bodies, old bodies, young bodies, flat-chested bodies, full-breasted bodies, swayed with the music. Bodies moved closer to bodies; lips to lips; chests to breasts; legs to legs; thighs to thighs—moved closer, swayed, beat time. Up and down the length of the street, children stirred in their sleep; stirred, awoke, and crept to the front door sensing rather than hearing something strange in the night. Up and down the street, women hissed to their children to git back in bed 'fo' I busts you wide open. Up and down Redbud Street, old men and old women dreamed of their hot lost youth when they could have talked under their clothes with the strongest in the land.

The harps stopped blowing. The Law walked away, moonlight on its badge, moonlight on its black-and-silver pistol, moonlight on its dusty-silver shoes, moonlight on its wet shirt sloping over rounded shoulders. The hot air pressed closer on Redbud Street. The ring around the moon pressed closer on the moon. Frogs croaked in the stagnant ditches; an automobile coughed in the far distance and was suddenly still. From the river came the mournful wail of the whistle of the *Tennessee Belle* as she backed out into the stream bound down for way landings and New Awleens. Silence and heat and moonlight lay heavily on Redbud Street.

Then doors up and down the length of the street began to bang. Doors popped, screeched, slammed, and boomed as they were violently shut. Porch swings, suddenly deserted, swayed for a moment or two and then were still. Mattresses vanished inside the shacks. Soon the street was deserted save for old men and women who remained rocking in their chairs catching little puffs of breeze that came up from the river, and slapping with weary hands at the mosquitoes that sang about their ears and legs.

Joe Moss stuck three harps into the belt that held up his red corduroy trousers, and walked slowly over to Mee Hop's café on Nelson Street to get him a can of sardine-fish and crackers. Chinermens was funny. Funnier even than white folks. They wouldn't give you nothing for no music if you blowed yo' lungs out. But it might be some niggers there and them sardine-fish could be turned into a mess of chitlins.

A few minutes later the chitlins were frying on Mee Hop's stove, and Joe sat smoking a Two Orphans cigar, voluptuously sniffing the rich, satisfying, mingled aromas of fat entrails and tobacco. Around Joe clustered a little group of his admirers. He took the cigar out of his mouth, spat on the floor, and laughed. "I swears to Gawd," he said, "de way dem niggers banged dey doors sounds like de time Wetherbee's Hardware Store caught on fire and fawty thousand shotgun shells went off at de same time. I does n't keer where de niggers at or who dey is, when Joe Moss tears off a piece on his harps de mens shuts dey doors and tells dey wimmens to stay way back in de kitchen to I done passed by."

"Hit's sho' de truth," said Virgie Mae Jones, as she put twenty cents on the counter and Joe Moss lifted a forkful of steaming chitlins from the plate.

(1938)

From

POWERHOUSE
by Eudora Welty

Powerhouse is playing!

He's here on tour from the city—"Powerhouse and His Keyboard"— "Powerhouse and His Tasmanians"—think of the things he calls himself! There's no one in the world like him. You can't tell what he is. "Nigger man"?—he looks more Asiatic, monkey, Jewish, Babylonian, Peruvian, fanatic, devil. He has pale gray eyes, heavy lids, maybe horny like a lizard's, but big glowing eyes when they're open. He has African feet of the greatest size, stomping, both together, on each side of the pedals. He's not coal black—beverage colored—looks like a preacher when his mouth is shut, but then it opens—vast and obscene. And his mouth is going every minute: like a monkey's when it looks for something. Improvising, coming on a light and childish melody— smooch—he loves it with his mouth.

Is it possible that he could be this! When you have him there performing for you, that's what you feel. You know people on a stage—and people of a darker race—so likely to be marvelous, frightening.

This is a white dance. Powerhouse is not a show-off like the Harlem boys, not drunk, not crazy—he's in a trance; he's a person of joy, a fanatic. He listens as much as he performs, a look of hideous, powerful rapture on his face. Big arched eyebrows that never stop traveling, like a Jew's—wandering-Jew eyebrows. When he plays he beats down piano and seat and wears them away.

He is in motion every moment—what could be more obscene? There he is with his great head, fat stomach, and little round piston legs, and long yellow-sectioned strong big fingers, at rest about the size of bananas. Of course you know how he sounds—you've heard him on records—but still you need to see him. He's going all the time, like skating around the skating rink or rowing a boat. It makes everybody crowd around, here in this shadowless steel-trussed hall with the rose-like posters of Nelson Eddy and the testimonial for the mind-reading horse in handwriting magnified five hundred times. Then all quietly he lays his finger on a key with the promise and serenity of a sibyl touching the book.

Powerhouse is so monstrous he sends everybody into oblivion. When any group, any performers, come to town, don't people always come out and hover near, leaning inward, about them, to learn what it is? What is it? Listen. Remember how it was with the acrobats. Watch them carefully, hear the least word, especially what they say to one another, in another language—don't let them escape you; it's the only time for hallucination, the last time. They can't stay. They'll be somewhere else this time tomorrow.

Powerhouse has as much as possible done by signals. Everybody, laughing as if to hide a weakness, will sooner or later hand him up a written request. Powerhouse reads each one, studying with a secret face: that is the face which looks like a mask—anybody's; there is a moment when he makes a decision. Then a light slides under his eyelids, and he says, "92!" or some combination of figures—never a name. Before a number the band is all frantic, misbehaving, pushing, like children in a schoolroom, and he is the teacher getting silence. His hands over the keys, then says sternly, "You-all ready? You-all ready to do some serious walking?"—waits—then, STAMP. Quiet. STAMP, for the second time. This is absolute. Then a set of rhythmic kicks against the floor to communicate the tempo. Then, O Lord! say the distended eyes from beyond the boundary of the trumpets, Hello and good-bye, and they are all down the first note like a waterfall.

This note marks the end of any known discipline. Powerhouse seems to abandon them all—he himself seems lost—down in the song, yelling up like somebody in a whirlpool—not guiding them—hailing them only. But he knows, really. He cries out, but he must know exactly. "Mercy! . . . What I say! . . . Yeah!" And then drifting, listening—"Where that skin beater?"—wanting drums, and starting up and pouring it out in the greatest delight and brutality. On the sweet pieces such a leer for everybody! He looks down so benevolently upon all our faces and whispers the lyrics to us. And if you could hear him at this moment on "Marie, the Dawn is Breaking"! He's going up the keyboard with a few fingers in some very derogatory triplet-routine, he gets higher and higher, and then he looks over the end of the piano, as if over a cliff. But not in a show-off way—the song makes him do it.

He loves the way they all play, too—all those next to him. The far section of the band is all studious, wearing glasses, every one—they don't count.

Only those playing around Powerhouse are the real ones. He has a bass fiddler from Vicksburg, black as pitch, named Valentine, who plays with his eyes shut and talking to himself, very young: Powerhouse has to keep encouraging him. "Go on, go on, give it up, bring it on out there!" When you heard him like that on records, did you know he was really pleading?

He calls Valentine out to take a solo.

"What you going to play?" Powerhouse looks out kindly from behind the piano; he opens his mouth and shows his tongue, listening.

Valentine looks down, drawing against his instrument, and says without a lip movement, " 'Honeysuckle Rose.' "

He has a clarinet player named Little Brother, and loves to listen to anything he does. He'll smile and say, "Beautiful!" Little Brother takes a step forward when he plays and stands at the very front, with the whites of his eyes like fishes swimming. Once when he played a low note, Powerhouse muttered in dirty praise, "He went clear downstairs to get that one!"

After a long time, he holds up the number of fingers to tell the band how many choruses still to go—usually five. He keeps his directions down to signals.

It's a bad night outside. It's a white dance, and nobody dances, except a few straggling jitterbugs and two elderly couples. Everybody just stands around the band and watches Powerhouse. Sometimes they steal glances at one another, as if to say, Of course, you know how it is with *them*—Negroes—band leaders—they would play the same way, giving all they've got, for an audience of one. . . . When somebody, no matter who, gives everything, it makes people feel ashamed for him.

(1941)

From

OTHER VOICES, OTHER ROOMS
by Truman Capote

With a cut of cornbread, Joel mopped bone-dry the steaming plate of fried eggs and grits, sopping rich with sausage gravy, that Missouri had set before him.

"It sure do gimme pleasure to see a boy relish his vittels," she said. "Only don't spec no refills cause I gotta pain lickin my back like to kill me: didn't sleep a blessed wink last night; been sufferin with this pain off and on since I'm a wee child, and done took enough medicine to float the whole entire United

States Navy: ain't nona it done me a bita good nohow. There was a witch woman lived a piece down the road (Miz Gus Hulie) usta make a fine magic brew, and that helped some. Poor white lady. Miz Gus Hulie. Met a terrible accident: fell into an ol Injun grave and was too feeble for to climb out.'' Tall, powerful, barefoot, graceful, soundless, Missouri Fever was like a supple black cat as she paraded serenely about the kitchen, the casual flow of her walk beautifully sensuous and haughty. She was slant-eyed, and darker than the charred stove; her crooked hair stood straight on end, as if she'd seen a ghost, and her lips were thick and purple. The length of her neck was something to ponder upon, for she was almost a freak, a human giraffe, and Joel recalled photos, which he'd scissored once from the pages of a *National Geographic,* of curious African ladies with countless silver chokers stretching their necks to improbable heights. Though she wore no silver bands, naturally, there was a sweat-stained blue polka-dot bandanna wrapped round the middle of her soaring neck. ''Papadaddy and me's countin on you for our Service,'' she said, after filling two coffee cups and mannishly straddling a chair at the table. ''We got our own little place backa the garden, so you scoot over later on, and we'll have us a real good ol time.''

''I'll come if I can, but this being my first day and all, Dad will most likely expect me to visit with him,'' said Joel hopefully.

Missouri emptied her coffee into a saucer, blew on it, dumped it back into the cup, sucked up a swallow, and smacked her lips. ''This here's the Lord's day,'' she announced. ''You believe in Him? You got faith in His healin power?''

Joel said: ''I go to church.''

''Now that ain't what I'm speakin of. Take for instance, when you thinks about the Lord, what is it passes in your mind?''

''Oh, stuff,'' he said, though actually, whenever he had occasion to remember that a God in heaven supposedly kept his record, one thing he thought of was money: quarters his mother had given him for each Bible stanza memorized, dimes diverted from the Sunday School collection plate to Gabaldoni's Soda Fountain, the tinkling rain of coins as the cashiers of the church solicited among the congregation. But Joel didn't much like God, for He had betrayed him too many times. ''Just stuff like saying my prayers.''

''When I thinks bout Him, I thinks bout what I'm gonna do when Papadaddy goes to his rest,'' said Missouri, and rinsed her mouth with a big swallow of coffee. ''Well, I'm gonna spread my wings and fly way to some swell city up north like Washington, D.C.''

''Aren't you happy here?''

''Honey, there's things you too young to unnerstan.''

''I'm thirteen,'' he declared. ''And you'd be surprised how much I know.''

''Shoot, boy, the country's just fulla folks what knows everythin, and don't understand nothin, just fullofem,'' she said, and began to prod her upper teeth: she had a flashy gold tooth, and it occurred to Joel that the prodding was designed for attracting his attention to it. ''Now one reason is, I get lonesome: what I all the time say is, you ain't got no notion what lonesome is till you stayed a spell at the Landin. And there ain't no mens round here I'm innersted in, leastwise not at the present: one time there was this mean buzzard name of Keg, but he did a crime to me and landed hisself on the chain gang, which is sweet justice considerin the lowdown kinda trash he was. I'm only a girl of fourteen when he did this bad thing to me.'' A fist-like knot of flies, hovering over a sugar jar, dispersed every whichaway as she swung an irritated hand. "Yessir, Keg Brown, that's the name he go by.'' With a fingertip she shined her gold tooth to a brighter luster while her slanted eyes scrutinized Joel; these eyes were like wild foxgrapes, or two discs of black porcelain, and they looked out intelligently from their almond slits. "I gotta longin for city life poisonin my blood cause I was brung up in St. Louis till Papadaddy fetched me here for to nurse him in his dyin days. Papadaddy was past ninety then, and they say he ain't long for this world, so I come. That be thirteen year ago, and now it look to me like Papadaddy gonna outlive Methusaleh. Make no mistake, I love Papadaddy, but when he gone I sure aimin to light out for Washington, D.C., or Boston, Coneckikut. And that's what I thinks bout when I thinks bout God.''

"Why not New Orleans?'' said Joel. "There are all kinds of good-looking fellows in New Orleans.''

"Aw, I ain't studyin no New Orleans. It ain't only the mens, honey: I wants to be where they got snow, and not all this sunshine. I wants to walk around in snow up to my hips: watch it come outa the sky in gret big globs. Oh, pretty . . . pretty. You ever see the snow?''

Rather breathlessly, Joel lied and claimed that he most certainly had; it was a pardonable deception, for he had a great yearning to see bona fide snow: next to owning the Koh-i-noor diamond, that was his ultimate secret wish. Sometimes, on flat boring afternoons, he'd squatted on the curb of St. Deval Street and daydreamed silent pearly snowclouds into sifting coldly through the boughs of the dry, dirty trees. Snow falling in August and silvering the glassy pavement, the ghostly flakes icing his hair, coating rooftops, changing the grimy old neighborhood into a hushed frozen white wasteland uninhabited except for himself and a menagerie of wonder-beasts: albino antelopes, and ivory-breasted snowbirds; and occasionally there were humans, such fantastic folk as Mr. Mystery, the vaudeville hypnotist, and Lucky Rogers, the movie star, and Madame Veronica, who read fortunes in a Vieux Carré tearoom. "It was one stormy night in Canada that I saw the snow,'' he said, though the farthest north he'd ever set foot was Richmond, Virginia. "We were lost in the mountains, Mother and me, and snow, tons and tons of it, was piling up all around us. And we lived in an ice-cold cave for a solid week, and we kept slapping each other to stay awake: if you fall asleep in snow, chances are you'll never see the light of day again.''

"Then what happened?'' said Missouri, disbelief subtly narrowing her eyes.

"Well, things got worse and worse. Mama cried, and the tears froze on her face like little BB bullets, and she was always cold. . . .'' Nothing had warmed her, not the fine wool blankets, not the mugs of hot toddy Ellen fixed.

"Each night hungry wolves howled in the mountains, and I prayed. . . ." In the darkness of the garage he'd prayed, and in the lavatory at school, and in the first row of the Nemo Theatre while duelling gangsters went unnoticed on the magic screen. "The snow kept falling, and heavy drifts blocked the entrance to the cave, but uh . . ." Stuck. It was the end of a Saturday serial that leaves the hero locked in a slowly filling gas chamber.

"*And?*"

"And a man in a red coat, a Canadian mountie, rescued us. . . . only me, really: Mama had already frozen to death."

Missouri denounced him with considerable disgust. "You is a gret big story."

"Honest, cross my heart," and he x-ed his chest.

"Uh uh. You Mama die in the sick bed. Mister Randolph say so."

Somehow, spinning the tale, Joel had believed every word; the cave, the howling wolves, these had seemed more real than Missouri and her long neck, or Miss Amy, or the shadowy kitchen. "You won't tattle, will you, Missouri? About what a liar I am."

She patted his arm gently. "Course not, honey. Come to think, I wish I had me a two-bit piece for every story I done told. Sides, you tell good lies, the kind I likes to hear. We gonna get along just elegant: me, I ain't but eight years older'n you, and you been to the school." Her voice, which was like melted chocolate, was warm and tender. "Les us be friends."

"O.K.," said Joel, toasting her with his coffee cup, "friends."

"And somethin else is, you call me Zoo. Zoo's my rightful name, and I always been called by that till Papadaddy let on it stood for Missouri, which is the state where is located the city of St. Louis. *Them,* Miss Amy 'n Mister Randolph, they so proper: Missouri this 'n Missouri t'other, day in, day out. Huh! You call me Zoo."

(1948)

THE
GHETTO
Haven and Hell

Eventually they entered into a dark region where, from a careening building, a dozen gruesome doorways gave up loads of babies to the street and the gutter. A wind of early autumn raised yellow dust from cobbles and swirled it against an hundred windows. Long streamers of garments fluttered from fire-escapes. In all unhandy places there were buckets, brooms, rags and bottles. In the street infants played or fought with other infants or sat stupidly in the way of vehicles. Formidable women, with uncombed hair and disordered dress, gossiped while leaning on railings, or screamed in frantic quarrels. Withered persons, in curious postures of submission to something, sat smoking pipes in obscure corners. A thousand odors of cooking food came forth to the street. The building quivered and creaked from the weight of humanity stamping about in its bowels.

> Stephen Crane
> *Maggie: A Girl of the Streets*

A young coloured buck and his doe dolled up on Sunday afternoon in the Easter rutting season, parading the pavement of Amsterdam Avenue, is nearly the most divinely comic sight in life.

> Christopher Morley
> *Inward Ho!*

. . . the white man walking through Harlem is not at all likely to find it sinister and no more wretched than any other slum.

> James Baldwin
> The Harlem Ghetto: Winter, 1948

From

THE AMERICAN SCENE
by Henry James

New York really, I think, is all formidable foreground; or, if it be not, there is
more than enough of this pressure of the present and the immediate to cut out
the close sketcher's work for him. These things are a thick growth all round
him, and when I recall the intensity of the material picture in the dense Yiddish
quarter, for instance, I wonder at its not having forestalled, on my page, mere
musings and, as they will doubtless be called, moonings. There abides with
me, ineffaceably, the memory of a summer evening spent there by invitation of
a high public functionary domiciled on the spot—to the extreme enhancement
of the romantic interest his visitor found him foredoomed to inspire—who was
to prove one of the most liberal of hosts and most luminous of guides. I can
scarce help if it this brilliant personality, on that occasion the very medium itself through which the whole spectacle showed, so colours my impressions that
if I speak, by intention, of the facts that played into them I may really but reflect the rich talk and the general privilege of the hour. That accident moreover
must take its place simply as the highest value and the strongest note in the
total show—so much did it testify to the quality of appealing, surrounding life.
The sense of this quality was already strong in my drive, with a companion,
through the long, warm June twilight, from a comparatively conventional
neighbourhood; it was the sense, after all, of a great swarming, a swarming that
had begun to thicken, infinitely, as soon as we had crossed to the East side and
long before we had got to Rutgers Street. There is no swarming like that of
Israel when once Israel has got a start, and the scene here bristled, at every
step, with the signs and sounds, immitigable, unmistakable, of a Jewry that had
burst all bounds. That it has burst all bounds in New York, almost any combination of figures or of objects taken at hazard sufficiently proclaims; but I
remember how the rising waters, on this summer night, rose, to the imagination, even above the housetops and seemed to sound their murmur to the pale
distant stars. It was as if we had been thus, in the crowded, hustled roadway,
where multiplication, multiplication of everything, was the dominant note, at
the bottom of some vast sallow aquarium in which innumerable fish, of over-

developed proboscis, were to bump together, for ever, amid heaped spoils of the sea.

The children swarmed above all—here was multiplication with a vengeance; and the number of very old persons, of either sex, was almost equally remarkable; the very old persons being in equal vague occupation of the doorstep, pavement, curbstone, gutter, roadway, and every one alike using the street for overflow. As overflow, in the whole quarter, is the main fact of life—I was to learn later on that, with the exception of some shy corner of Asia, no district in the world known to the statistician has so many inhabitants to the yard—the scene hummed with the human presence beyond any I had ever faced in quest even of refreshment; producing part of the impression, moreover, no doubt, as a direct consequence of the intensity of the Jewish aspect. This, I think, makes the individual Jew more of a concentrated person, savingly possessed of everything that is in him, than any other human, noted at random—or is it simply, rather, that the unsurpassed strength of the race permits of the chopping into myriads of fine fragments without loss of race-quality? There are small strange animals, known to natural history, snakes or worms, I believe, who, when cut into pieces, wriggle away contentedly and live in the snippet as completely as in the whole. So the denizens of the New York Ghetto, heaped as thick as the splinters on the table of a glass-blower, had each, like the fine glass particle, his or her individual share of the whole hard glitter of Israel. This diffused intensity, as I have called it, causes any array of Jews to resemble (if I may be allowed another image) some long nocturnal street where every window in every house shows a maintained light. The advanced age of so many of the figures, the ubiquity of the children, carried out in fact this analogy; they were all there for race, and not, as it were, for reason: that excess of lurid meaning, in some of the old men's and old women's faces in particular, would have been absurd, in the conditions, as a really directed attention—it could only be the gathered past of Israel mechanically pushing through. The way, at the same time, this chapter of history did, all that evening, seem to push, was a matter that made the ''ethnic'' apparition again sit like a skeleton at the feast. It was fairly as if I could see the spectre grin while the talk of the hour gave me, across the board, facts and figures, chapter and verse, for the extent of the Hebrew conquest of New York. With a reverence for intellect, one should doubtless have drunk in tribute to an intellectual people; but I remember being at no time more conscious of that merely portentous element, in the aspects of American growth, which reduces to inanity any marked dismay quite as much as any high elation. The portent is one of too many—you always come back, as I have hinted, with your easier gasp, to *that:* it will be time enough to sigh or to shout when the relation of the particular appearance to all the other relations shall have cleared itself up. Phantasmagoric for me, accordingly, in a high degree, are the interesting hours I here glance at content to remain—setting in this respect, I recognize, an excellent example to all the rest of the New York phantasmagoria. Let me speak of the remainder only as phantasmagoric too, so that I may both the more kindly recall it and the sooner have done with it.

I have not done, however, with the impression of that large evening in the Ghetto; there was too much in the vision, and it has left too much the sense of a rare experience. For what did it all really come to but that one had seen with one's eyes the New Jerusalem on earth? What less than that could it all have been, in its far-spreading light and its celestial serenity of multiplication? There it was, there it is, and when I think of the dark, foul, stifling Ghettos of other remembered cities, I shall think by the same stroke of the city of redemption, and evoke in particular the rich Rutgers Street perspective—rich, so peculiarly, for the eye, in that complexity of fire-escapes with which each housefront bristles and which gives the whole vista so modernized and appointed a look. Omnipresent in the ''poor'' regions, this neat applied machinery has, for the stranger, a common side with the electric light and the telelphone, suggests the distance achieved from the old Jerusalem. (These frontal iron ladders and platforms, by the way, so numerous throughout New York, strike more New York notes than can be parenthetically named—and among them perhaps most sharply the note of the ease with which, in the terrible town, on opportunity, ''architecture'' goes by the board; but the appearance to which they often most conduce is that of the spaciously organized cage for the nimbler class of animals in some great zoological garden. This general analogy is irresistible—it seems to offer, in each district, a little world of bars and perches and swings for human squirrels and monkeys. The very name of architecture perishes, for the fire-escapes look like abashed afterthoughts, staircases and communications forgotten in the construction; but the inhabitants lead, like the squirrels and monkeys, all the merrier life.) It was while I hung over the prospect from the windows of my friend, however, the presiding genius of the district, and it was while, at a later hour, I proceeded in his company, and in that of a trio of contributive fellow-pilgrims, from one ''characteristic'' place of public entertainment to another: it was during this rich climax, I say, that the city of redemption was least to be taken for anything less than it was. The windows, while we sat at meat, looked out on a swarming little square in which an ant-like population darted to and fro; the square consisted in part of a ''district'' public garden, or public lounge rather, one of those small backwaters or refuges, artfully economized for rest, here and there, in the very heart of the New York whirlpool, and which spoke louder than anything else of a Jerusalem disinfected. What spoke loudest, no doubt, was the great overtowering School which formed a main boundary and in the shadow of which we all comparatively crouched.

But the School must not lead me on just yet—so colossally has its presence still to loom for us; that presence which profits so, for predominance, in America, by the failure of concurrent and competitive presences, the failure of any others looming at all on the same scale save that of Business, those in particular of a visible Church, a visible State, a visible Society, a visible Past; those of the many visibilities, in short, that warmly cumber the ground in older countries. Yet it also spoke loud that my friend was quartered, for the interest of the thing (from his so interesting point of view), in a ''tenement-house''; the

New Jerusalem would so have triumphed, had it triumphed nowhere else, in the fact that this charming little structure *could* be ranged, on the wonderful little square, under that invidious head. On my asking to what latent vice it owed its stigma, I was asked in return if it didn't sufficiently pay for its name by harbouring some five-and-twenty families. But this, exactly, was the way it testified—this circumstance of the simultaneous enjoyment by five-and-twenty families, on "tenement" lines, of conditions so little sordid, so highly "evolved." I remember the evolved fire-proof staircase, a thing of scientific surfaces, impenetrable to the microbe, and above all plated, against side friction, with white marble of a goodly grain. The white marble was surely the New Jerusalem note, and we followed that note, up and down the district, the rest of the evening, through more happy changes than I may take time to count. What struck me in the flaring streets (over and beyond the everywhere insistent, defiant, unhumorous, exotic face) was the blaze of the shops addressed to the New Jerusalem wants and the splendour with which these were taken for granted; the only thing indeed a little ambiguous was just this look of the trap too brilliantly, too candidly baited for the wary side of Israel itself. It is not *for* Israel, in general, that Israel so artfully shines—yet its being moved to do so, at last, in that luxurious style, might be precisely the grand side of the city of redemption. Who can ever tell, moreover, in any conditions and in presence of any apparent anomaly, what the genius of Israel may, or may not, really be "up to"?

(1907)

THE NEGRO MIGRATION
by Carl Sandburg

At Michigan avenue and East 31st street comes along the street a colored woman and three of her children. Two months ago they lived in Alabama, in a two room hut with a dirt floor and no running water and none of the things known as "conveniences." Barefooted and bareheaded, the children walk along with the mother, casually glancing at Michigan avenue's moving line of motor cars. Suddenly, as in a movie play, a big limousine swings to the curb. A colored man steps out, touches his hat to the mother and children and gives them the surprise of their lives. This is what he says:

"We don't do this up here. It isn't good for us colored folks to send our children out on the streets like this. We're all working together to do the best we can. One thing we're particular about is the way we take the little ones out on the streets.

"They ought to look as if they're washed clean all over. And they ought to have shoes and stockings and hats and clean shirts on. Now you go home and see to that. If you haven't got the money to do it, come and see me. Here's my card.''

He gives her the card of a banker and real estate man at an office where they collect rent monthly from over 1,000 tenants, and where they hold titles in fee simple to the rented properties.

This little incident gives some idea of the task of assimilation Chicago took in the last five years in handling the more than 70,000 colored people who came here in that time, mostly from southern states.

A big brown stone residence in Wabash avenue, of the type that used to be known as "mansions," housed five families from Alabama. They threw their dinner leavings from the back porch. And one night they sat on the front steps and ate watermelon and threw the rinds out past the curbstone. In effect, they thought they were going to live in the packed human metropolis of Chicago just as they had lived "down in Alabam'.''

Now they have learned what garbage cans are for. From all sides the organized and intelligent forces of the colored people have hammered home the suggestion that every mistake of one colored man or woman may result in casting a reflection on the whole group. The theory is, "Be clean for your own sake, but remember that every good thing you do goes to the credit of all of us.''

It must not be assumed, of course, that the types thus far mentioned are representative of all who come from Alabama or other states of the south. Among the recent arrivals, for example, are a banker, the managing editor of a weekly newspaper, a manual training instructor in the public schools and several men who have made successes in business. It is possible now for Chicago white people to come into contact with colored men who have had years of experience in direct co-operation with Tuskegee and Hampton institutes and with the workings in southern states of the theories of Booker T. Washington, W. E. B. Du Bois and others. The application of these theories is being continued in Chicago.

Willis N. Huggins, an intensely earnest and active worker for the interests of the colored people, is an instructor in manual training at the Wendell Phillips high school. He came from Alabama in 1917.

"I was making a social survey of the northern counties of Alabama through the financial aid of Mrs. Emmons Blaine of Chicago," he said to me. "My work was discontinued because our information collected in that territory would be useless. About one-fourth of the colored people migrated to the north.

"There were 12,000 colored people in Decatur, Ala., before the war. The migration took away 4,000, judging by a house to house canvass I made in various sections of that one city. When they took the notion they just went. You could see hundreds of houses where mattresses, beds, wash bowls and pans were thrown around the back yard after the people got through picking out what they wanted to take along.

"All the railroad trains from big territory farther south came on through Decatur. Some days five and six of these trains came along. The colored people in Decatur would go to the railroad station and talk with these other people about where they were going. And when the moving fever hit them there was no changing their minds.

"Take Huntsville, only a few miles from Decatur, on a branch line. There they didn't see these twelve coach trains coming through loaded with emigrants. So from Huntsville there was not much emigration.

"In many localities the educated negroes came right along with their people. I rode in September, 1917, with a minister from Monroe, La. This was his second trip. He had been to Boston and organized a church with 100 members of his Louisiana congregation. Now he was taking fifty, all in one coach. I hear that later he made a third trip and has now moved the whole of his original congregation of 300 members up to Boston. He told me that the first group he took to Boston were all naturally inclined to go. The second group made up their minds more slowly. He said that probably they would not have gone at all if it had not been for fears of lynching. A series of lynchings in Texas at that time gave him examples from which to argue that the north was safer for colored people.

"With many who have come north, the attraction of wages and employment is secondary to the feeling that they are going where there are no lynchings. Others say that while they know they would never be lynched in the south and they are not afraid on that score, they do want to go where they are sure there is more equality and opportunity than in the south. The schools in the north are an attraction to others.

"I make these observations from having personally talked with my people in Madison county, Alabama, where there were 10,000 negroes, of whom 5,000 came north in two years."

(1919)

From

HARLEM

by William Rose Benét

Oh, I want to sing Harlem wild alive
In Nineteen Hundred Twenty Five;
The Negro City, the dream-book town,
Metropolis of black and brown;

Number-gambling round the clock,
Bones and razors on every block,
Coon-can raging, thirst assuaging,
Egypt-rouged and all-engaging,
Drinking, dancing on till day,
Swarming to church or *cabaret,*
Whirlwind-gay with leopard power,
Rolling eyes in a Holy Ghost shower,
Lazing, laughing 'long the street,
Stepping high, stepping high,
Shaken with the shuffles from head to feet,—
Mansions in the sky!

(1925)

From

NIGGER HEAVEN
by Carl Van Vechten

Anatole Longfellow, alias the Scarlet Creeper, strutted aimfully down the east side of Seventh Avenue. He wore a tight-fitting suit of shepherd's plaid which thoroughly revealed his lithe, sinewy figure to all who gazed upon him, and all gazed. A great diamond, or some less valuable stone which aped a diamond, glistened in his fuchsia cravat. The uppers of his highly polished tan boots were dove-coloured suède and the buttons were pale blue. His black hair was sleek under his straw hat, set at a jaunty angle. When he saluted a friend—and his acquaintanceship seemed to be wide—two rows of pearly teeth gleamed from his seal-brown countenance.

It was the hour when promenading was popular—about eleven o'clock in the evening. The air was warm, balmy for June, and not too humid. Over the broad avenue, up and down which multi-hued taxicabs rolled, hung a canopy of indigo sky, spangled with bright stars. The shops, still open, were brilliantly illuminated. Slouching under the protecting walls of the buildings, in front of show-windows, or under the trees, groups of young men congregated, chattering and laughing. Women, in pairs, or with male escorts, strolled up and down the ample sidewalk.

Hello, 'Toly! A stalwart black man accosted the Creeper.

Hello, Ed. How you been?

Po'ly, thank you. How *you* been?

No complaints. Nummer come out. Drew sixty-seven bucks.

Holy Kerist!

Yeh. Anatole displayed his teeth.

What nummer?

Seven-Nine-Eight.

Whah you found et?

Off'n a gal's fron' do'.

Comin' out?

Goin' in. Ah went out duh back winder. Her daddy done come home widout writin'.

Hush mah mouf!

Ah doan mean mebbe.

As Anatole walked on, his self-esteem flowered. Unbuttoning his coat, he expanded his chest, dangerously stretching the gold watch-chain which extended from pocket to pocket across his muscular belly.

Howdy.

Howdy.

He greeted in passing Leanshanks Pescod, a mulatto lightweight who, in successive Saturday sessions at the Commonwealth Club, had defeated two white comers.

Is you enjoyin' de air, Mr. Longfellow?

'Deed, Ah is, Mrs. Guckeen. How you been? The Creeper's manner became slightly flirtatious.

Thank you, Mr. Longfellow, an' pretty well.

Mrs. Imogene Guckeen was the proprietor of a popular beauty parlour further up the avenue. It was Anatole's custom to indulge in a manicure at this parlour every afternoon around five. As a wide circle of admiring women was cognizant of this habit, five was the rush hour at Mrs. Guckeen's establishment. She was fully aware of the important rôle this customer played in her affairs and, as a consequence, made no effort to collect his always considerable bill. Occasionally, moreover, the Creeper would slip her five or ten dollars on account, adding a chuck under her drooping chin and a devastating smile.

Turning about at One hundred and twenty-seventh Street, Anatole faced north and resumed his leisurely promenade. Now, however, despite the apparently careless flipping and twisting of his ebony cane, tipped with a ball of ivory, his air was more serious. He peered into the faces of the women he encountered with an expression that was almost anxious. Once, so eagerly did he seek a pair of eyes which obstinately refused to return his stare, he bumped into an elderly black man with a long white beard, who limped, supported by a cane. Anatole caught the old fellow only in time to prevent his falling.

Ah sartainly beg yo' pahdon, he said with his most enchanting smile.

The octogenarian returned the smile.

'Pears to me, he squeaked, dat you's mos' unnacherly perlite fo' dis street at dis hour.

The Creeper's breast expanded a full two inches, causing his watch-chain, stretched to capacity, to drag a ring of jangling keys from his waistcoat pocket. Replacing the keys, he reflected that he could afford to be agreeable, even magnanimous, to harmless old gentlemen. Was there another sheik in Harlem who possessed one-tenth his attraction for the female sex? Was there another of whose muscles the brick-pressers, ordinarily quite free with their audible, unflattering comments about passers-by, were more afraid? As he meditated in this wise, his pride received an unexpected jolt. Under the bright lights in front of the Lafayette Theatre, he discerned a pompous figure whose presence obliterated the smug cheerfulness from his heart.

A few years earlier Randolph Pettijohn had made his start in Harlem as a merchant of hot-dogs. His little one-storey shop, hugged between two towering buildings, had rapidly become popular. His frankfurters were excellent; his buns were fresh; his mustard beyond reproach. In a short time Pettijohn's business was so successful, the overhead expense so light—he was his own cook and he personally served his customers over the counter—that he had saved a sufficient sum of money to invest in real-estate, an investment which increased in value over-night. Next, with the proceeds of a few judicious sales, he opened a cabaret which shortly became the favourite resort in Harlem. Now, his Bolito game had made him so rich that his powerfully exerted influence began to be felt in political circles.

Unreasoningly, Anatole hated him. He had never inimically crossed the Creeper's path, but somehow, subconsciously, Anatole was aware that such an eventuality was by no means impossible. Besides, it irked the Creeper to realize that any one else possessed power of whatever kind. The feeling was not reciprocated. Anatole was frequently a spectacular figure at the Winter Palace, Pettijohn's cabaret, where he was welcome because he was known to be a particular favourite with jig-chasers from below the line.

How you been, 'Toly? The Bolito King greeted the Creeper warmly, even affectionately.

Hello, Ran.

Lookin' 'em over?

Ah'm takin' 'em in. The Creeper was reticent.

You sartainly are one dressin' up fool, Creeper, one of the King's companions inserted.

Heavy lover, too, another added.

The King offered his accolade: Nobody like duh Creeper fo' close an' women, nobody a-tall.

Anatole exposed his pearls. Bottle et, he suggested.

Come in an' see me, Pettijohn invited. Mah Winter Palace is open winter an' summer.

Completely at his ease again, the Creeper strutted on, swinging his cane, expanding his chest, and humming to himself:

Mah man's got teeth lak a lighthouse on duh sea,
An' when he smiles he throws dem lights on me.

Howdy, 'Toly!

As Anatole looked into the unwelcome eyes of a high yellow boy whose suit was shiny and whose boots were patched, his manner became a trifle patronizing.

How you been, Duke?

Not so good, 'Toly. Duh show done went broke.

Dere'll be annudder.

Sho'. How's Ah gwine live till den?

The Creeper proffered no advice.

You lookin' mighty lucky, 'Toly. The Duke's tone was one of whining admiration.

The Creeper preserved his discreet silence.

Ah nebber did see no sheik what had yo' gif' fo' dressin'.

The Creeper's chest was the thermometer of the effect of this compliment.

Ah's hungry, 'Toly. Hones'. Gimme duh price of a dog.

Drawing a handful of loose change from his trouser-pocket, with great deliberation the Creeper selected a quarter from this heap and passed it to his indigent acquaintance.

Heah you is, Duke. . . . He had the air of a munificent benefactor. . . . Now why ain' you git mo' providen'?

Ah is, 'Toly, when Ah gits duh chance. 'T'ain' mah fault duh show done went broke. Inserting the quarter in his mouth, the boy made a sudden dash down a side-street.

Han' full o' gimme, mouf full o' much oblige, mused the Creeper.

At the corner of One hundred and thirty-seventh Street, surrounded by a numerous group of spectators, many of whom clapped their hands rhythmically, a crowd of urchins executed the Charleston. Apparently without intent, Anatole joined these pleasure-seekers. His eyes, however, quickly shifted from the dancers and stole around the ring of onlookers, in hasty but accurate inspection. Suddenly he found that for which he had been searching.

She was a golden-brown and her skin was clear, as soft as velvet. As pretty a piece, he reflected, as he had seen around these parts for some time, and he had not happened to see her before. Her slender body was encased in coral silk, the skirt sufficiently short to expose her trim legs in golden-brown stockings. A turquoise-blue cloche all but covered her straight black shingled hair. Her soft, brown eyes seemed to be begging. Withdrawing his own gaze almost immediately, so swift had been his satisfactory appraisal, he was nevertheless aware that she was contriving, without appearing to do so, without, indeed, appearing to look at him at all, to edge nearer to him. Never once, while she carried out her design, did her hands refrain from the rhythmic clapping which accompanied the juvenile dancers. When at last, she stood by his side, so close that he might touch her, she continued to pretend that she was only interested in the intricate steps of the Charleston. Anatole, outwardly, gave no sign whatever that he was aware of her presence.

After they had played this game of mutual duplicity for some time, she, losing patience or acquiring courage, accosted him.

Hello, 'Toly.

He turned, without a smile, and stared at her.

Ah doan seem to recerllec' dat Ah got duh honour o' yo' acquaintance.

You ain', Mr. 'Toly, an' dat's a fac'. Mah name's Ruby.

He did not encourage her to proceed.

Ruby Silver, she completed.

He remained silent. Presently, in an offhand way, he began to clap his hands. A particularly agile lad of six was executing some pretty capers. Hey! Hey! Do that thing!

Everybody knows who you is, Mr. 'Toly, *everybody!* Her voice implored his attention.

The Creeper continued to clap.

Ah been jes' nacherly crazy to meet you.

The Creeper was stern. What fo'? he shot out.

You knows, Mr. 'Toly. I guess you knows.

He drew her a little apart from the ring.

How much you got?

Oh, Ah been full o' prosperity dis evenin'. Ah met an ofay wanted to change his luck. He gimme a tenner.

The Creeper appeared to be taking the matter under consideration. Ah met a gal las' night dat offer me fifteen, he countered. Nevertheless, it could be seen that he was weakening.

Ah got annuder five in mah lef' stockin', an' Ah'll show you lovin' such as you never seen.

The Creeper became more affable. Ah do seem to remember yo' face, Miss Silver, he averred. Will you do me duh favour to cling to mah arm.

As they strolled, their bodies touching, down a dark side-street, his hand freely explored her flesh, soft and warm under the thin covering of coral silk.

Wanna dance? he demanded.

Luvvit, she replied.

Come across.

She stooped to fumble in her stockings, first the right, then the left. Presently she handed him two bills which he stuffed into his waistcoat pocket without the formality of examination.

Winter Palace? she inquired.

A nasty shadow flitted across Anatole's face.

Naw, he retorted. Too many ofays an' jig-chasers.

Bowie Wilcox's is dicty.

Too many monks.

Atlantic City Joe's?

Too many pink-chasers an' bulldikers.

Where den?

Duh Black Venus.

A few moments later they were swallowed by an entrance on Lenox Avenue, flanked by two revolving green lights. Arm in arm, they descended the stairs to the basement. As they walked down the long hallway which led to the dance-floor, the sensual blare of jazz, slow, wailing jazz, stroked their ears. At the door three waiters in evening clothes greeted the Creeper with enthusiasm.

Why, dat's sartainly Mr. 'Toly.

Good evenin'.

Gwine sit at mah table?

Mine?

Mine, Mr. 'Toly?

Expanding his chest, Anatole gazed down the length of the hall. Couples were dancing in such close proximity that their bodies melted together as they swayed and rocked to the tormented howling of the brass, the barbaric beating of the drum. Across each woman's back, clasped tight against her shoulder blades, the black hands of her partner were flattened. Blues, smokes, dinges, charcoals, chocolate browns, shines, and jigs.

Le's hoof, Ruby urged.

Le's set down, Anatole commanded. Passing his straw hat to the hat-check girl, he followed a waiter to an empty table, pushing Ruby ahead of him.

Hello, 'Toly! A friend hailed him from an adjoining table.

Hello, Licey.

A pint, the Creeper ordered.

The waiter Charlestoned down the floor to the intoxicating rhythm, twirling his tray on palm held high overhead.

Put ashes in sweet papa's bed so as he can' slip out, moaned Licey in the Creeper's ear. Ah knows a lady what'll be singing, Wonder whah mah easy rider's gone!

Bottle et.

Licey chuckled. Hush mah mouf ef Ah doan!

The waiter came back, like a cat, shuffling ingeniously from one side of the room to the other, in and out of the throng of dancers. Charleston! Charleston! Do that thing! Oh boy!

On his tray were two glasses, two splits of ginger ale, and a bowl of cracked ice. From his hip-pocket he extracted a bottle containing a transparent liquid. He poured out the ginger ale. Anatole poured out the gin.

Tea fo' two! he toasted his companion, almost jovially.

She gulped her glassful in one swallow, and then giggled, 'Toly, you's mah sho' 'nough daddy an' Ah sho' does love you wid all mah h'aht.

Everybody loves mah baby, tooted the cornet.

But mah baby doan love nobody but me, Ruby chimed in. She tentatively touched the Creeper's arm. As he did not appear to object to this attention, she stroked it tenderly.

Jes' once 'roun', she pleaded.

He humoured her. Embracing her closely, he rocked her slowly around the hall. Their heels shuffled along the floor. Their knees clicked amorously. On all sides of the swaying couple, bodies in picturesque costumes rocked, black bodies, brown bodies, high yellows, a kaleidoscope of colour transfigured by the amber searchlight. Scarves of bottle green, cerise, amethyst, vermilion, lemon. The drummer in complete abandon tossed his sticks in the air while he shook his head like a wild animal. The saxophone player drew a dilapidated derby over the bowl of his instrument, smothering the din. The banjos planked deliriously. The band snored and snorted and whistled and laughed like a hyena. This music reminded the Creeper of the days when he worked as a bootblack in a Memphis barbershop. Hugged closely together, the bodies rocked and swayed, rocked and swayed. Sometimes a rolling-eyed couple, caught in the whirlpool of aching sound, would scarcely move from one spot. Then the floor-manager would cry, Git off dat dime!

Unexpectedly it was over. The saxophone player substituted the stub of a black cigar for the tube of his instrument. As if they had been released from some subtle enchantment the dancing couples broke apart, dazed, and lumbered towards their tables. Now that music was lacking their bodies had lost the secret of the magic rhythm. Normal illumination. A new mood. Laughter and chatter. A woman shrieked hysterically. The Creeper drew the bottle from his hip-pocket and poured out two more drinks.

Again Ruby drained her portion at one gulp. This time she had repudiated the ginger ale. Again she caressed her companion's arm. Again she sought his eyes, his great brown eyes, like a doe's.

Ah sho' will show you some lovin', daddy, she promised.

The Creeper grunted his approval.

Does you know what Ah calls dis? she continued rapturously.

Calls what?

Dis place, where Ah met you—Harlem. Ah calls et, specherly tonight, Ah calls et Nigger Heaven! I jes' nacherly think dis heah is Nigger Heaven!

On the floor a scrawny yellow girl in pink silk, embroidered with bronze sequins in floral designs, began to sing:

Mah daddy rocks me with one steady roll;
Dere ain' no slippin' when he once takes hol' . . .

The Creeper sipped his gin meditatively.

(1926)

From

JEWS WITHOUT MONEY

by Michael Gold

1

What a crazy mingling of races and religions on my street. I heard most of the
languages when I was a child. Germans, Poles, Russians, Armenians, Irish,
Chinese; there were always a few of these aliens living among our Jews. Once
my father fetched a Negro to supper. My father beamed with pride.

"Katie, do not be frightened," he said. "This black man is one of us.
He is an African Jew. I met him in the synagogue. Imagine, he prays in Hebrew like the rest of us!"

The Negro, tall, stiff, unsmiling, mysterious as death in a black suit of
clothes, kissed the *mezzuzah* over our door. Then he salaamed until his forehead almost touched the floor. He greeted my mother solemnly:

"*Sholem Aleichem!* Peace be with you!"

"*Aleichem Sholem!*" my mother answered. "With you, Peace!"

Before sitting down to eat, the Negro stranger washed his hands piously
and muttered a Hebrew prayer. Before each course that was served he recited
the proper Hebrew blessing. What an ultra-pious Jew. My mother was thrilled
by such orthodoxy in a black man. She stole out between the soup and the fish
to inform the neighbors. Reb Samuel and others came in to witness the miracle.

They questioned the stranger after supper. He proved to be a Tartar. Before the evening was over he had quarreled with every one. Harshly and firmly,
he insisted that he was a better Jew than any one present. He was an Abys-
sinian Jew, descended from the mating of King Solomon and the Queen of Sheba.
We others had wandered among the Gentiles, he said, and had been corrupted.
But his people had kept the faith pure. For instance, we prayed only at morning
and evening. His congregation prayed four times a day. We used seven twists
in binding on the phylacteries. His people used nine. And so on, and so on. He
was very dogmatic. He out-talked every one. Reb Samuel was dumbfounded.
My father hung his head in shame. At last the Negro left haughtily, kissing the
mezzuzah again. By his manner one could see he despised us all as backsliders,
as mere pretenders to the proud title of Jew.

2

Gypsies camped one winter in a vacant store on our street. Twelve men and women, and some twenty lusty, filthy children, they added a gala note to the drab street. I could see their way of living from our back windows. They had no furniture. They slept on the floor at night, and ate their meals from newspapers spread on the floor. They squatted in three circles while eating. The men sat in the first ring nearest the food, the women behind them, and then the children. The gamins roamed around restlessly, and snatched like dogs at tidbits thrown them. Every one shouted, fought, laughed while they grabbed meat from the common bowl.

These gypsies made a lot of trouble on our street. They visited grocery stores and butchers. While a gypsy woman talked the most astonishing nonsense to the proprietor, and held him hypnotized, the others would steal things. The gypsy men mended pots and pans for the East Side housewives. The women told fortunes with cards and read palms. Several visitors to the gypsy store lost their watches in there; an old woman lost her purse. Every one got to fear the gypsies in our midst, yet chuckled and smiled fondly when they passed in their gay, flaming dresses. Ach, it was like Europe. It made my mother homesick to see them. My mother had known gypsies in Hungary, and could speak a few gypsy words.

Late one night all the kerosene lamps were lit in the gypsy store. I looked in and saw a party. The children were crowded against the wall, and a gypsy woman in a brilliant red shawl danced for them. She sang as she danced. The children clapped their hands in time, and called to her.

My mother, like all the mothers along the street, warned me against the gypsy children. "Don't play with them; they are filthy with lice." But she herself had played with gypsies when a child in Hungary; she told me so herself.

A day came in spring, warm and luring. A closed wagon drew up before the store. The gypsies piled into it laughing and chattering, with all their pots, pans, bedding, filth. They drove off while the crowd on the sidewalk booed them good-naturedly.

3

We were near Chinatown. At various times Chinese lived in our tenement. Once a group of fifteen chop suey waiters moved into one of the flats. They were a nuisance from the start. They never seemed to sleep. All night long one heard a Chinese phonograph whining and banging horribly. The waiters held long explosive conversations all night. They quarreled, played cards, cooked queer dishes that filled the tenement with sweet, nauseating smells. An opium den, some of the neighbors said. A gambling house, said others. One morning there was a crash. Then the police came and found the house in wreckage. The young Chinese had disappeared. The nude body of a white girl lay on the floor. She had swallowed rat-poison.

4

Negroes, Chinese, Gypsies, Turks, Germans, Irish, Jews—and there was even an American on our street.

She was Mary Sugar Bum; she came from Boston. She was an old vagabond woman who sometimes worked as a scrubwoman in office buildings. But most of her days were spent in being violently drunk and disorderly.

Mary slept in an empty stall in the livery stable. Vassa, the night watchman, was a kind, pock-marked old Polack with one eye; his other eye had been kicked out by a funeral horse. He saw to it that Mary always had clean straw for her stall, and a blanket in winter.

Some of the most sodden bums made love to Mary. They bought her a five-cent hooker of rotgut whisky and took her into an alley while she cursed them and bargained for more whisky. We children watched this frequent drama.

Every one knew Mary. With bonnet tipped over her eyes, her gray hair streaming down her shawl, her skirt tripping her floppy comical old feet, she appeared screaming on our street, prima donna for an afternoon. There was an audience at once. Heads popped out of tenement windows, a crowd assembled, every one laughed.

In a weird voice, shrill as a cat's, Mary sang old ballads. She pirouetted, holding her skirts out daintily. Sometimes she kicked them high with a chorus girl's squeal, exposing her horrible underthings. Every one laughed. Then she flopped in the mud, and cursed, and could not rise again. She was too drunk. And we children formed a circle, and taunted her, singing gayly:

Lazy Mary, will you get up,
Will you get up to-day?

This infuriated her. She chased us, flopping again and again, like a bird with broken wings. Her face was spotted with mud; her blue eyes blazed; the rose on her bonnet teetered.

"Where's your wedding suit, Mary?" we yelled. "Where's your husband, Mary?"

This made her rave. When Mary was sober, she liked to talk about her first husband, and the elegant "wedding suit" he gave her when she married him at sixteen. This was her life's romance. Every one knew it, even the children. The worst taunt of all was to remind her of it. It made her rave.

In her worst frenzies, she would pull a knife from her bosom, and scream:

"I'll cut the heart out of every goddamned man in the world!" Then five coach drivers had to grab her, and take her into the stable, where they put the American woman to sleep in her stall.

5

The red Indians once inhabited the East Side; then came the Dutch, the English, the Irish, then the Germans, Italians and Jews. Each group left its deposits, as in geology.

At Second Avenue and 5th Street there remained a German landmark among the Jews. It was a Lutheran church, a brick building with an old-fashioned porch. One summer morning I saw a curious sight there. A crowd had gathered in front of the church, jeering and booing. There were venerable Jews among them with white beards. They were giggling like boys. What amused the crowd was something almost too metaphysical for words.

The owlish little sexton was scrubbing on the porch with soap and water a tall wooden statue of Jesus.

"Jesus is taking a bath!" the crowd jeered. "Their idol is dirty, he needs a bath!"

The elder Jews were especially cynical. "For this stick of wood we were slaughtered in Europe," one graybeard said to another. The crowd grew bigger and more hilarious each minute. At last a policeman arrived, and shooed it away. There might have been some unpleasant explosion—a stoning, a riot. Such riots had been known in the past.

Once a crowd of young Jewish atheists paraded before the synagogues on Yom Kippur. This is a fast day, the most sacred holiday in the year. The atheists ate ham sandwiches, and shouted blasphemous slogans. Six of them were taken to the hospital with severe wounds.

Another time a mob of religious Jews attacked the funeral of a Jewish girl who married an Italian, and had become a convert. She was being buried in the Catholic Church. Led by her distracted father, the crowd tried to capture her body from the profanation. They were beaten off by the police. Religion was a fervent affair on the East Side. Every persecuted race becomes a race of fanatics.

(1930)

From

THE AUTOBIOGRAPHY OF LINCOLN STEFFENS
by Lincoln Steffens

One day as I was standing beside the doorman waiting for something to happen, we saw a reporter come running out of the basement and dart across into his office. The doorman winked at me and I stepped down to the telegraph bureau. A woman had been killed in Mulberry Bend. I came out and called, "Max!" Out he ran from his office, and we hurried down to the address in Little Italy. There was a crowd standing watching some children dancing beautifully around an organ-grinder who was playing a waltz.

"There's your story," said Max, pointing at the street scene. "Mine is inside."

Max understood. I went inside with him. We saw the dead woman, the blood, the wretched tenement apartment, and we talked to the neighbors, who told us how the murderer came into the court with the organ-grinder, and while the organ played and the children danced, he had seen the woman's face at the window, recognized her, rushed up, and cut her all to pieces; the crowd gathered and were about to beat the man to death when the police came, saved and arrested him. The poker-playing reporters came tearing up, asked for names, ages, and—details. Theirs was the sensational story of the day, all blood and no dancing. Riis wrote it as a melodrama with a moral, an old cry of his: "Mulberry Bend must go." And, by the way, it went. Such was the power of Riis! There's a small park now where Mulberry Bend was.

I wrote the murder as a descriptive sketch of Italian character, beginning with the dance music, bringing the murder in among the children whose cries called the mob; the excitement, the sudden rage, the saving arrest; and ending with the peaceful afterscene of the children dancing in the street, with the mob smiling and forgetting out in the street.

(1931)

From

SUMMER IN WILLIAMSBURG
by Daniel Fuchs

The Maujer Street gang came out of nowhere, armed with onion-bags of stones and helmeted with milk-can covers, ready for battle. Davey saw them a block off and he had little time to marshal his gang at full strength and run for the ammunition caches they had planted in yards and lots for emergencies like this. Davey lined the best men up in front, protected behind wash-kettle and ash-can covers for shields and supplied with little piles of rocks at the sides. The younger boys had the menial job of picking up stones as they fell from the enemy and rushing them forward to their own front-line men.

The fight began at the corner of Hooper Street and at the outset looked like an easy conquest for the Maujers. They had taken Davey's men by surprise, had given them little time to build up an effective morale for the battle. Davey's gang were being pushed back steadily, some of the more timid were already deserting into hallways, and the worst of it was that they were soon lacking ammunition. For the further they retreated the more they fell on territory that had not been visited by the enemy's hail of stones. Then Natie the Buller, next in command, a highly imaginative fellow who owed his importance to the gaudy stories he told, conferred with Davey on a plan of action. They decided to surround the Maujers. Davey remained fast at the front while Natie dived down the cellar steps of the nearest house. Gradually the boys at the rear slipped down after him, one at a time to attract no attention, until about fifteen were gone. They climbed over fences, reached South Third Street through the opposite tenement and marched down Hooper. There was a short wait until Natie had gathered all his men. Then with a concerted whoop they fell upon the back of the enemy. With the Maujers thrown into confusion the rest was simple. They ran off in panic, scattering through the yards and scuttling over fences while Davey's men relentlessly pegged away at them until they were out of sight.

In the calm of victory Natie's group and Davey's division walked slowly up to one another in the middle of the street.

"One thing about these goyim," Davey said with the triumph that marks the strong, "they never got no brains."

He enjoyed the victory. The Maujers were comparatively a weak outfit but he hated them particularly for one nasty trick they alone used. When one of his gang, usually to get to the Leonard Street library, entered their territory they would not jump on him and give him his beating forthwith. Instead they would send a kid of four or five who would start a fight with him. Naturally the Rippler would hit back, only to find himself instantly surrounded by Maujers popping out of hallways. "You dirty Jew kike," they would say with painful deliberation, "you cheap Jew bastard, hitting a kid below your size. Well, we'll show you." The dozen or so true defenders of proper sportsmanship would proceed to show him.

Actually, Davey's gang was a pretty anemic bunch, never venturing on any attack, often declining to accept battle when it was proffered. Instead, they ran up to the roofs of their houses. Davey, a recent importation from the East Side, owed his leadership to his vigor, his swagger, and the bold tales he narrated of his former neighborhood. He came to displace one called Coke whose frail body was the subject of fascinating shivers and jerky movements. Davey had refused to be impressed by this boy's talents, provoked a fist-fight and established himself within his first week. Coke languished until his family delivered him by removing themselves to the swell elegance of Brownsville.

The only Jewish gang of importance was the Havemeyer Streeters, all newcomers from the East Side. They furnished fierce opposition, to the Italians especially, and as more Jews settled in the neighborhood the Havemeyers often boasted that it was they who had compelled the Italian migration to Bensonhurst and Bay Ridge. One of the Havemeyers' specialties was to smash repeatedly the windows of the Williamsburg Mission for Jews. This was an organization on the Bridge Plaza for converting Jews to Christianity, and anathema to every Jewish mother. The worst Davey's gang had done in this connection was to parade inside of the meeting house in a rapid snake dance, chanting:

"We'll all stand up for Jesus,
We'll all stand up for Jesus,
We'll all stand up for Jesus,
For the love of Christ sit down!"

Natie the Buller and Davey swaggered up and down the street.
"Well," said Natie, "I guess that showed 'em."

(1934)

From

THE BIG MONEY
by John Dos Passos

Dick couldn't help grinning and nodding. He felt better since he'd eaten. He ordered another round of drinks and began to talk about going up to Harlem to dance at Small's Paradise. He said he couldn't go to bed, he was too tired, he had to have some relaxation. Pat Doolittle said she loved it in Harlem but that she hadn't brought any money. "My party," said Dick. "I've got plenty of cash on me."

They went up with a flask of whiskey in each of the girls' handbags and in Dick's and Reggie's back pockets. Reggie and Pat sang *The Fireship* in the taxi. Dick drank a good deal in the taxi to catch up with the others. Going down the steps to Small's was like going underwater into a warm thicklygrown pool. The air was dense with musky smells of mulatto powder and perfume and lipstick and dresses and throbbed like flesh with the smoothlybalanced chugging of the band. Dick and Pat danced right away, holding each other very close. Their dancing seemed smooth as cream. Dick found her lips under his and kissed them. She kissed back. When the music stopped they were reeling a little. They walked back to their table with drunken dignity. When the band started again Dick danced with Jo. He kissed her too. She pushed him off a little. "Dick, you oughtn't to." "Reggie won't mind. It's all in the family. . . ." They were dancing next to Reggie and Pat hemmed in by a swaying blur of couples. Dick dropped Jo's hand and put his hand on Reggie's shoulder. "Reggie, you don't mind if I kiss your future wife for you just once." "Go as far as you like, senator," said Reggie. His voice was thick. Pat was having trouble keeping him on his feet. Jo gave Dick a waspish look and kept her face turned away for the rest of the dance. As soon as they got back to the table she told Reggie that it was after two and she'd have to go home, she for one had to work in the morning.

When they were alone and Dick was just starting to make love to Pat she turned to him and said, "Oh, Dick, do take me some place low . . . nobody'll ever take me any place really low." "I should think this would be quite low enough for a juniorleaguer," he said. "But this is more respectable than Broadway, and I'm not a juniorleaguer . . . I'm the new woman." Dick burst out laughing. They both laughed and had a drink on it and felt fond of each other again and Dick suddenly asked her why couldn't they be together always. "I think you're mean. This isn't any place to propose to a girl. Imagine remem-

bering all your life that you'd got engaged in Harlem. . . . I want to see life.''
''All right, young lady, we'll go . . . but don't blame me if it's too rough for
you.'' ''I'm not a sissy,'' said Pat angrily. ''I know it wasn't the stork.''

Dick paid and they finished up one of the pints. Outside it was snowing.
Streets and stoops and pavements were white, innocent, quiet, glittering under
the streetlights with freshfallen snow. Dick asked the whiteeyed black doorman
about a dump he'd heard of and the doorman gave the taximan the address.
Dick began to feel good. ''Gosh, Pat, isn't this lovely,'' he kept crying. ''Those
kids can't take it. Takes us grownups to take it. . . . Say, Reggie's getting too
fresh, do you know it?'' Pat held his hand tight. Her cheeks were flushed and
her face had a taut look. ''Isn't it exciting?'' she said. The taxi stopped in front
of an unpainted basement door with one electriclightbulb haloed with snow-
flakes above it.

They had a hard time getting in. There were no white people there at all.
It was a furnaceroom set around with plain kitchen tables and chairs. The
steampipes overhead were hung with colored paper streamers. A big brown
woman in a pink dress, big eyes rolling loose in their dark sockets and twitch-
ing lips, led them to a table. She seemed to take a shine to Pat. ''Come right
on in, darlin','' she said. ''Where's you been all my life?''

Their whiskey was gone so they drank gin. Things got to whirling round
in Dick's head. He couldn't get off the subject of how sore he was at that little
squirt Reggie. Here Dick had been nursing him along in the office for a year
and now he goes smartaleck on him. The little twirp.

The only music was a piano where a slimwaisted black man was tickling
the ivories. Dick and Pat danced and danced and he whirled her around until
the sealskin browns and the highyallers cheered and clapped. Then Dick slipped
and dropped her. She went spinning into a table where some girls were sitting.
Dark heads went back, pink rubber lips stretched, mouths opened. Gold teeth
and ivories let out a roar.

Pat was dancing with a pale pretty mulatto girl in a yellow dress. Dick
was dancing with a softhanded brown boy in a tightfitting suit the color of his
skin. The boy was whispering in Dick's ear that his name was Gloria Swanson.
Dick suddenly broke away from him and went over to Pat and pulled her away
from the girl. Then he ordered drinks all around that changed sullen looks into
smiles again. He had trouble getting Pat into her coat. The fat woman was very
helpful. ''Sure, honey,'' she said, ''you don't want to go on drinkin' tonight,
spoil your lovely looks.'' Dick hugged her and gave her a tendollar bill.

In the taxi Pat had hysterics and punched and bit at him when he held her
tight to try to keep her from opening the door and jumping out into the snow.
''You spoil everything. . . . You can't think of anybody except yourself,'' she
yelled. ''You'll never go through with anything.'' ''But, Pat, honestly,'' he
was whining, ''I thought it was time to draw the line.'' By the time the taxi
drew up in front of the big square apartment house on Park Avenue where she
lived she was sobbing quietly on his shoulder. He took her into the elevator

and kissed her for a long time in the upstairs hall before he'd let her put the key in the lock of her door. They stood there tottering clinging to each other rubbing up against each other through their clothes until Dick heard the swish of the rising elevator and opened her door for her and pushed her in.

When he got outside the door he found the taxi waiting for him. He'd forgotten to pay the driver. He couldn't stand to go home. He didn't feel drunk, he felt immensely venturesome and cool and innocently excited. Patricia Doolittle he hated more than anybody in the world. "The bitch," he kept saying aloud. He wondered how it would be to go back to the dump and see what happened and there he was being kissed by the fat woman who wiggled her breasts as she hugged him and called him her own lovin' chile, with a bottle of gin in his hand pouring drinks for everybody and dancing cheek to cheek with Gloria Swanson who was humming in his ear: Do I get it now . . . or must I he . . . esitate.

It was morning. Dick was shouting the party couldn't break up, they must all come to breakfast with him. Everybody was gone and he was getting into a taxicab with Gloria and a strapping black buck he said was his girlfriend Florence. He had a terrible time getting his key in the lock. He tripped and fell towards the paleblue light seeping through his mother's lace curtains in the windows. Something very soft tapped him across the back of the head.

He woke up undressed in his own bed. It was broad daylight. The phone was ringing. He let it ring. He sat up. He felt lightheaded but not sick. He put his hand to his ear and it came away all bloody. It must have been a stocking full of sand that hit him. He got to his feet. He felt tottery but he could walk. His head began to ache like thunder. He reached for the place on the table he usually left his watch. No watch. His clothes were neatly hung on a chair. He found the wallet in its usual place, but the roll of bills was gone.

(1936)

THE WAY IT IS
by Ralph Ellison

The boy looked at me through the cracked door and stood staring with his large eyes until his mother came and invited me in. It was an average Harlem apartment, cool now with the shift in the fall weather. The room was clean and furnished with the old-fashioned furniture found so often up our way, two old upholstered chairs and a divan upon a faded blue and red rug. It was painfully clean, and the furniture crowded the narrow room.

"Sit right there, sir," the woman said. "It's where Wilbur use to sit before he went to camp, it's pretty comfortable."

I watched her ease herself tiredly upon the divan, the light from the large red lamp reflected upon her face from the top of a mirrored side table.

She must have been fifty, her hair slightly graying. The portrait of a young soldier smiled back from the top of a radio cabinet beside her.

She pointed. "That's my boy Wilbur right there," she said proudly. "He's a sergeant."

"Wilbur's got a medal for shooting so good," the boy said.

"You just be quiet and go eat your supper," she said. "All you can think about is guns and shooting." She spoke with the harsh tenderness so often used by Negro mothers.

The boy went, reluctantly opening the door. The odor of peas and rice and pork chops drifted through.

"Who was it, Tommy?" shrilled a voice on the other side.

"You two be quiet in there and eat your supper now," Mrs. Jackson called. "Them two just keeps my hands full. They just get into something *all* the time. I was coming up the street the other day and like to got the fright of my life. There was Tommy hanging on the back of a streetcar! But didn't I tan his bottom! I bet he won't even *look* at a streetcar for a long, long time. It ain't really that he's a *bad* child, it's just that he tries to do what he sees the other boys do. I wanted to send both him and his sister away to camp for the summer, but things was so tight this year that I couldn't do it. Raising kids in Harlem nowadays is more than a notion."

As is true so often in Negro American life, Mrs. Jackson, the mother, is the head of her family. Her husband had died several years ago; the smaller children were babies. She had kept going by doing domestic work and had kept the family together with the help of the older boy.

There is a quiet courage about Mrs. Jackson. And yet now and then the clenching and unclenching of her work-hardened fingers betray an anxiety that does not register in her face. I offer to wait until after she has eaten, but she says no, that she is too tired right now and she would rather talk than eat.

"You finding the writing business any better since the war?" she asked.

"I'm afraid not," I said.

"Is that so? Well, I don't know nothing about the writing business. I just know that don't many colored go in for it. But I guess like everything else, some folks is doing good while others ain't. The other day I was over on 126th Street and saw them dispossessing a lawyer! Yes, sir, it was like back in the thirties. Things piled all over the sidewalk, the Negroes a-hanging out of the windows, and the poor man rushing around trying to get his stuff off the streets before it got dark, and everything."

I remembered the incident myself, having passed through the street that afternoon. Files, chest of drawers, bedsteads, tables and barrels had been piled

along the sidewalk; with pink, blue, and white mattresses and bundles of table
linen and bedclothing piled on top. And the crowd had been as she described:
some indignant, some curious, and all talking in subdued tones so as not to
offend the evicted family. Law books had been piled upon the sidewalk near
where a black and white kitten—and these are no writer's details—played games
with itself in the coils of an upright bedspring. I told her I had seen the incident.

"Lord," she said. "And did you see all those law books he had? Looks
like to me that anybody with all those books of law oughtn't to never get dispossessed.

"I was dispossessed, myself, back in thirty-seven, when we were all out
of work. And they threatened me once since Wilbur's been in the Army. But I
stood up for my rights and when the government sent the check we pulled
through. Anybody's liable to get dispossessed though." She said it defensively.

"Just how do you find it otherwise?" I asked.

"Things is mighty tight, son. . . . You'll have to excuse me for calling
you 'son,' because I suspect you must be just about Wilbur's age."

She sat back abruptly. "How come you not in the Army?" she asked.

"I've a wife and dependents," I said.

"I see," she pondered. "Wilbur would have got married too, but he was
helping me with the kids."

"That's the way it goes," I said.

"Things is tight," she said again. "With food so high and everything I
sometimes don't know what's going to happen. Then, too, with Wilbur in the
Army we naturally misses the money he use to bring in."

She regarded me shrewdly. "So you want to know about how we're doing?
Don't you live in Harlem?"

"Oh, yes, but I want to know what *you* think about it."

"So's you can write it up?"

"Some of it, sure. But I won't use your name."

"Oh I don't care 'bout that. I *want* them to know how I feel."

She became silent. Then, "You didn't tell me where you live, you know,"
she said cagily. I had to laugh and she laughed too.

"I live up near Amsterdam Avenue," I said.

"You telling me the truth?"

"Honest."

"And is your place a nice one?"

"Just average. You know how they go," I said.

"I bet you live up there on Sugar Hill."

"Not me," I said.

"And you're sure you're not one of these investigators?"

"Of course not."

"I bet you are too." She smiled.

I shook my head and she laughed.

"They always starting something new," she said. "You can't keep up with them."

But now she seemed reassured and settled down to talk, her hands clasped loosely in her lap against the checkered design of her dress.

"Well, we're carrying on somehow. I'm still working and I manage to keep the young uns in school, and I pays the rent too. I guess maybe it would be a little better if the government would send the checks on time. . . ."

She paused and pointed across the room to the picture of a young woman. "And it would be even better if Mary, that's my next oldest after Wilbur—if she could get some of that defense training so she could get a job what pays decent money. But don't look like she's going to get anything. She was out to the Western Electric plant in Kearney, New Jersey, the other day and they give her some kind of test, but that was the end of that."

"Did she pass the test?" I asked.

"Sure she passed. But they just put her name down on a card and told her they would keep her in mind. They always do that. They ask her a lot of questions, then they want to know if she ever had any experience in running machines, and when she says she ain't, they just take down her name. Now where is a colored girl going to get any experience in running all these kinds of machines they never even seen before?"

When I could not answer she threw up her hands.

"Well, there you have it, they got you any which way you turn. A few gets jobs, but most don't."

"Things are much better outside of New York," I said.

"So I hear," she said. "Guess if I was younger I'd take the kids and move to Jersey or up to Connecticut, where I hear there's some jobs for colored. Or even down South. Only I keep hearing about the trouble they're having down there. And I don't want the kids to grow up down there nohow. Had enough of that when I was a kid. . . ."

"Have any of your friends gotten work through the F.E.P.C.?"

She thought for a moment.

"No, son. It seems to me that that committee is doing something everywhere but here in New York. Maybe that's why it's so bad for us—and you know it's bad 'cause you're colored yourself."

As I heard the clatter of dishes coming from the kitchen, her face suddenly assumed an outraged expression.

"Now you take my sister's boy, William. God bless his poor soul. William went to the trade schools and learned all about machines. He got so he could take any kind of machine apart and fix it and put it together again. He was machine-crazy! But he was a smart boy and a good boy. He got good marks in school too. But when he went to get a job in one of those factories where they make war machines of some kind, they wouldn't take him 'cause he was colored—*and they told him so!*"

She paused for breath, a red flush dyeing her skin. The tinted portrait of a brown mother holding a brown, shiny-haired baby posed madonna-like from a calendar above her head.

"Well, when they wouldn't take him some of the folks over to the church told him to take his case to the F.E.P.C., and he did. But they had so many cases and it took so long that William got discouraged and joined up in the Merchant Marine. That poor boy was just so disgusted that he said that he would have enlisted in the Army, only that his mamma's got two little ones like I have. So he went out on that boat 'cause it paid good money and a good bonus. It was real good money and he helped his mamma a heap. But it didn't last long before one of those submarines sunk the boat."

Her eyes strayed to the window, where a line of potted plants crowded the sill: a profusion of green things, slowly becoming silhouettes in the fading light. Snake plants, English ivy, and others, a potato plant in a glass jar, its vines twining around a cross of wood and its thousand thread-fine roots pushing hungrily against the wall of glass. A single red bloom pushed above the rest, and in one corner a corn plant threatened to touch the ceiling from the floor with its blade-like leaves.

The light was fading and her voice had slipped into the intense detachment of recent grief. "It was just about four months yesterday," she said. "He was such a fine boy. Everybody liked William."

She shook her head silently, her fingers gripping her folded arms as she swallowed tensely.

"It hurts to think about it," she said, getting up and snapping on another light, revealing a child's airplane model beneath the table. "Well, the folks from his union is being very nice to my sister, the whites as well as the colored. And you know," she added, leaning toward me, "it really makes you feel a little better when they come round—the white ones, I mean—and really tries to help. Like some of these ole relief investigators who come in wanting to run your life for you, but really like they interested in you. Something like colored folks in a way. We used to get after William for being with white folks so much, but these sure have shown themselves to be real friends."

She stared at me as though it was a fact which she deeply feared to accept.

"Some of them is going to try and see that my sister gets some sort of defense work. But what I'm trying to tell you is that it's a sin and a shame that a fine boy like William had to go fooling round on them ships when ever since he was a little ole boy he'd been crazy about machines."

"But don't you think that the Merchant Marine is helping to win the war?" I said. "It takes brave men to go out there, and they've done a lot."

"Sure they have," she said. "Sure they have. But I'm not talking about that. Anybody could do what they had him doing on that boat. Anybody can wait tables who's got sense enough to keep his fingernails clean! Waiting tables, when he could *make* things on a machine!

"You see that radio there? Well, William made that radio. It ain't no store set, no, sir, even though it looks like one. William made it for the kids. Made everything but the cabinet, and you can hear way down to Cuba and Mexico with it. And to think of that boy! Oh, it makes me so mad I don't know what to do! He ought to be here right now helping his mamma and lil brother and sister. But what can you do? You educated, son, you one of our educated Negroes that's been to college and everything. Now you tell me, *what can we do?*" She paused. "I'm a colored woman, and colored women can take it. I can hit the chillies to the subway every morning and stand in the white folks' kitchen all day long, but so much is happening in the world that I don't know which way to turn. First it's my sister's boy and then they sends my own boy down to Fort Bragg. I tells you I'm even afraid to open Wilbur's letters, some of the things he tells is so awful. I'm even afraid to open letters that the *government* sends sometimes about his insurance or something like that, 'cause I'm afraid it might be a message that Wilbur's been beaten up or killed by some of those white folks down there. Then I gets so mad I don't know what to do. I use to pray, but praying don't do no good. And too, like the union folks was telling us when we was so broken up about William, we got to fight the big Hitler over yonder even with all the little Hitlers over here. I wish they'd hurry up and send Wilbur on out of the country 'cause then maybe my mind would know some ease. Lord!" she sighed. "If it wasn't so serious I'd break down and laugh at my ownself."

She smiled now and the tension eased from her face and she leaned back against the divan and laughed. Then she became serious again.

"But, son, you really can't laugh about it. Not honestly laugh like you can about some things. It reminds me of that crazy man what's always running up and down the streets up here. You know, the one who's always hollering at the cars and making out like he's throwing bombs?"

"Of course, I've seen him often," I said.

"Sure you have. Well, I use to laugh at that poor man when he'd start acting the fool—you know how it is, you feel sorry for him but you can't help but laugh. They say he got that way in the last war. Well, I can understand him better now. Course I ain't had no bombs bursting in my ears like he had. But yet and still, with things pulling me thisaway and thataway, I sometimes feel that I'm going to go screaming up and down the streets just like that poor fellow does."

"He's shell-shocked," I said. "Sometimes I've seen him talking and acting just as normal as anyone."

"Is that so?" she said. "I always thought it was funny he never got hit by a car. I've seen them almost hit him, but he goes right back. One day I heard a man say, Lord, if that crazy fellow really had some bombs he'd get rid of every car in Harlem!"

We laughed and I prepared to go.

"Sorry you found me so gloomy today, son. But you know, things have a way of just piling up these days and I just had to talk about them. Anyway, you asked for me to tell you what I thought.''

She walked with me to the door. Street lamps glowed on the avenue, lighting the early dark. The after-school cries of children drifted dimly in from the sidewalk.

She shivered close beside me.

''It's getting chilly already,'' she said. ''I'm wondering what's going to happen this winter about the oil and coal situation. These ole holes we have to live in can get mighty cold. Now can't they though?''

I agreed.

''A friend of mine that moved up on Amsterdam Avenue about a month ago wanted to know why I don't move out of Harlem. So I told her it wouldn't do no good to move 'cause anywhere they let us go gets to be Harlem right on. I done moved round too much not to know that. Oh yes!''

She shook her head knowingly.

''Harlem's like that old song says:

It's so high you can't get over it
So low, you can't get under it,
And so wide, you can't get round it. . . .

''That's the way it really is,'' she said. ''Well, good-bye, son.''

And as I went down the dimmed-out street the verse completed itself in my mind, *You must come through by the living gate. . . .*

So there you have Mrs. Jackson. And that's the way ''it really is'' for her and many like her who are searching for the gate of freedom. In the very texture of their lives there is confusion, war-made confusion. And the problem is to get around, over, under, and through this confusion. They do not ask for a lighter share of necessary war sacrifices than other Americans have to bear. But they do ask for equal reasons to believe that their sacrifices are worthwhile, and they *do* want to be rid of the heavy resentment and bitterness which has been theirs for long before the war.

Forced in normal times to live at standards much lower than those the war has brought to the United States generally, they find it emotionally difficult to give their attention to the war. The struggle for existence constitutes a war in itself. The Mrs. Jacksons of Harlem offer one of the best arguments for the stabilization of prices and the freezing of rents. For twenty-five percent of those still on relief come from our five percent of New York's population. Mrs. Jackson finds it increasingly difficult to feed her children. She must pay six cents more on the dollar for food than do the mothers of similar-income sections of the city. And with the prospect of a heatless winter, Harlem, with its poor housing and high tuberculosis death rate, will know an increase of hardship.

It is an old story. Touch any phase of urban living in our democracy and its worst aspects are to be found in Harlem. Our housing is the poorest, and our rents the highest. Our people are the sickest, and Harlem Hospital the most overcrowded and understaffed. Our unemployment is the greatest, and our cost of food the most exorbitant. Our crime the most understandable and easily corrected, but the policemen sent among us the most brutal. Our desire to rid the world of fascism the most burning, and the obstacles placed in our way the most frustrating. Our need to see the war as a struggle between democracy and fascism the most intense, and our temptation to interpret it as a "color" war the most compelling. Our need to believe in the age of the "common man" the most hope-inspiring, and our reasons to doubt that it will include us the most disheartening (this is no Whitmanesque catalogue of democratic exultations, while more than anything else we wish that it could be). And that's the way it is.

Many of Mrs. Jackson's neighbors are joining in the fight to freeze rents and for the broadening of the F.E.P.C., for Negroes and all other Americans. Their very lives demand that they back the President's stabilization program. That they must be victorious is one of the necessities upon which our democratic freedom rests. The Mrs. Jacksons cannot make the sacrifices necessary to participate in a total war if the conditions under which they live, the very ground on which they must fight, continues its offensive against them. Nor is this something to be solved by propaganda. Morale grows out of realities, not out of words alone. Only concrete action will be effective—lest irritation and confusion turn into exasperation, and exasperation change to disgust and finally into anti-war sentiment (and there is such a danger). Mrs Jackson's reality must be democratized so that she may clarify her thinking and her emotions. And that's the way it really is.

(1942)

From

A TREE GROWS IN BROOKLYN
by Betty Smith

The mystery of mysteries to Francie was the Chinaman's one-windowed store. The Chinaman wore his pigtail wound around his head. That was so he could go back to China if he wanted to, mama said. Once he cut it off, they would never let him return. He shuffled back and forth silently in his black felt slippers and listened patiently to instructions about shirts. When Francie spoke to him, he folded his hands in the wide sleeves of his nankeen shirt coat and kept his eyes on the ground. She thought that he was wise and contemplative and listened with all his heart. But he understood nothing of what she said, having little English. All he knew was *tickee* and *shirtee*.

When Francie brought her father's soiled shirt there, he whisked it under the counter, took a square of mysteriously textured paper, dipped a thin brush into a pot of India Ink, made a few strokes and gave her this magic document in exchange for a common dirty shirt. It seemed a wonderful barter.

The inside of the store had a clean warm but fragile scent, like odorless flowers in a hot room. He did the washing in some mysterious recess and it must have been in the dead of night because all day, from seven in the morning until ten at night, he stood in the store at his clean ironing board pushing a heavy black iron back and forth. The iron must have had a tiny gasoline arrangement inside it to keep it hot. Francie did not know this. She thought it part of the mystery of his race that he could iron with an iron never heated on a stove. She had a vague theory that the heat came from something he used in place of starch in the shirts and collars.

When Francie brought a ticket and a dime back and pushed them across the counter, he gave her the wrapped shirt and two lichee nuts in exchange. Francie loved these lichee nuts. There was a crisp easily broken shell and the soft sweet meat inside. Inside the meat was a hard stone that no child had ever been able to break open. It was said that this stone contained a smaller stone and that the smaller stone contained a smaller stone which contained a yet smaller stone and so on. It was said that soon the stones got so small you could only see them with a magnifying glass and those smaller ones got still smaller until you couldn't see them with anything but they were always there and would never stop coming. It was Francie's first experience with infinity.

The best times were when he had to make change. He brought out a small wooden frame strung with thin rods on which were blue, red, yellow and green balls. He slid the balls up the brass rods, pondered swiftly, clicked them all back into place and announced "dirty-nine cent." The tiny balls told him how much to charge and how much change to give.

Oh, to be a Chinaman, wished Francie, and have such a pretty toy to count on; oh, to eat all the lichee nuts she wanted and to know the mystery of the iron that was ever hot and yet never stood on a stove. Oh, to paint those symbols with a slight brush and a quick turn of the wrist and to make a clear black mark as fragile as a piece of a butterfly wing! That was the mystery of the Orient in Brooklyn.

(1943)

From

THE DARK STAIN
by Benjamin Appel

Suddenly he realized that he knew nothing about Negroes as human beings like himself. Absolutely nothing. All he had known were the statistics of a people: So many lynched. So many millions in tenements and cabins. So many in the spot news: Robeson, Yergan, Wright, Davis, Randolph, Louis. But what went on inside their hearts? They were like the inhabitants of a city he had never seen, a city read about, and now he had come to the gates. Downstairs, on One Hundred and Twenty-Fifth, he stared at the passing Negroes, stirred by a tremendous groping curiosity. What were they all thinking of, hoping for, praying for?

*   *   *   *   *

He walked west, never noticing the white faces in the going-home crowds, the Harlem Finns and Swedes, the Irish, Italians, Jews. There were only black faces; black women with linoleum shopping bags, roller-skating kids with bruised brown knees, laborers in work shoes crusted with plaster. He had boarded the crosstown street as a man gets on a subway, shuttling now between these Harlem flats and stores. And all these people? What did they want? How did they feel about the war when they were among themselves and no whites were listening?

On Seventh Avenue, Sam pushed into the Aventine Grill. He stepped to the bar, ordered a beer from a big Italian bartender with bushy black eyebrows. It was a small place, the walls painted olive green and decorated with the lithographs distributed gratis by the whiskey manufacturers. He was the only white customer, he observed. A half dozen or so Negroes were leaning on the bar, glasses at elbow. Sam winked at the bartender, who wiped his hands on his apron and slowly, his shoulders swinging, eased over. Sam said, "I want to talk to Mr. Carlucci."

The bartender looked him over. "I'm him." He spoke out of the corner of his mouth as if he had been reared in some Irish neighborhood.

"Are you the boss?"

"Who wants to know?"

Sam jerked his thumb towards the rear. Beyond a pinball game, there were a half a dozen tables with wire legs; at one of them a middle-aged man was sitting. "Is that the boss?"

"I ast you who wants to know?"

"The Harlem Equality League sent me over."

"I guess it's okay, mister. That's the boss. He's my uncle so we got the same name." The bartender's face, wooden and impersonal as a beer barrel suddenly opened two worried eyes. "Maybe you guys can do somethin'?"

Sam hurried over to Mr. Carlucci's table. "You phoned the Harlem Equality League and they sent me over."

Mr. Carlucci was thin and bald and he had a toothpick between his teeth. Without removing it, he said, "Yes?"

"We want to help you."

"Yeh?"

"What happened?"

"You don't look colored."

"I'm not. I'm white."

"You look like a wop like me?"

Sam smiled. "What happened, Mr. Carlucci?"

"But you work for the colored?"

"You could say that."

"They must pay you good money?"

"What happened?"

"I don't expect nothin', mister. I don't expect a single thing from no-body. Not from you, not from the cops. Didn't I phone the station house and the desk sarge sends a cop over who guzzles three beers which I mark down on his account—" He wrote on air with his forefinger. "Then, he blows out so a colored man here a good customer o' mine, good as a white man, lemme tell you, he sees the cop guzzlin' my beer and when the cop blows out, he says why don't I get the Harlem Equalities." He pronounced the name swiftly like the name of a ball team. "And I says who are they and he says they can help me. I don't take his word, see. I'll tell you the unvarnished, mister. I don't take nobody's word in Harlem so I call the desk sarge and I ask him about the Harlem Equalities and he say you're Reds. See, mister, I tell you just how it is. But the desk sarge tells me you got influence among the colored and that's good enough for me." He had removed the toothpick and now glared up front at the Negroes at the bar. They would drink a beer or two or a small whiskey and leave and other Negroes would come in. It didn't seem to Sam as if there had ever been any trouble. "I don't expect a single thing, mister. That's Harlem for you. Don't I know how the colored feel about the wops? It's been n.g. since the Doochay jumped on Selassie so they take it out on me. I'm Mussolini! A hell of a Mussolini I am! Maybe the colored gotta right with the big bars where there's a dozen guys workin' and all of 'em white except maybe the porter who cleans out the can and all the dough, colored dough. But I'm a small joint like you see. The barkeep's my nephew. Just the two of us. So what the hell they want of me?"

"Who started the trouble today?"

"Who you think? The colored."

"I'm trying to get at the facts, Mr. Carlucci. What time was it?"

"About five o'clock it was. In comes this big nigger—" He glanced at Sam. "It slipped the tongue, mister. You ain't gonna hold it against me?"

"Go on."

"There was about six guys at the bar like now. I never got it busy. This big colored begins to holler like a son-of-a-bitch. 'Call yourself colored,' he says or somethin' like that. 'Some colored you are,' he says or something like that. 'Drinkin' in a wop dive.' He calls this place a dive, the big bastard."

"How big was he?"

"A six footer. Maybe bigger."

"What'd he look like?"

"Like nothin' much. A big face and he was wearin' a dark suit."

"What else did he say?"

"He said they wasn't real Negroes but yellows—that was his wisecrack and he hollers about the killing of that nut Randolph last week. And me here, you know what I was doin', of all the lamebrains! I was askin' that guy to ack like a gennelman. Should've listened to my nephew who wanted to give'm the bottle. But what the hell, who wants to be the first to start a riot? Not me. He hollers some more that I gyp 'em. I gyp 'em! I keep the best beer. You don't catch me givin' the customer rubbin' alky out of a bottle with a fancy label. I sell good stuff."

"Was this Negro alone?"

"Yeh."

"Did you see anything out of the ordinary before he showed up?"

"I don't get you."

"Was there any sign that you were going to have trouble before he showed up?"

"No."

"Have your customers been talking much about Randolph? Or the meeting or about the different leaflets?"

Mr. Carlucci looked up at the ceiling as if to say: That's all they do talk about. "I'm neutral," he declared. "I know from nothin'. I mind my own business. When some guy grouches heavy maybe I say it's too bad the nut got himself bumped, only I don't say nut to them. They're awful touchy, the colored. They're like the Jews. One for all and all for one." He leaned his head on both elbows and muttered. "I been here, you wouldn't believe it, eighteen years and I can tell that feelin'."

"What kind of a feeling?"

"Mister, ever hear of a riot? Get twenty more like that big bastard who come in here and you get yourself a riot. Think he listened when I tell'm I can't hire a colored man. What'll I do with the nephew? Five kids and a wife. But that big bastard keeps on hollerin' until the customers walk out except two guys and one of 'em tells me to call the Harlem Equalities so I done it."

"Thanks for the information, Mr. Carlucci."

"Okay. Have a drink on the house."

(1943)

From

THE STREET

by Ann Petry

There was a cold November wind blowing through 116th Street. It rattled the tops of garbage cans, sucked window shades out through the top of opened windows and set them flapping back against the windows; and it drove most of the people off the street in the block between Seventh and Eighth Avenues except for a few hurried pedestrians who bent double in an effort to offer the least possible exposed surface to its violent assault.

It found every scrap of paper along the street—theater throwaways, announcements of dances and lodge meetings, the heavy waxed paper that loaves of bread had been wrapped in, the thinner waxed paper that had enclosed sandwiches, old envelopes, newspapers. Fingering its way along the curb, the wind set the bits of paper to dancing high in the air, so that a barrage of paper swirled into the faces of the people on the street. It even took time to rush into doorways and areaways and find chicken bones and pork-chop bones and pushed them along the curb.

It did everything it could to discourage the people walking along the street. It found all the dirt and dust and grime on the sidewalk and lifted it up so that the dirt got into their noses, making it difficult to breathe; the dust got into their eyes and blinded them; and the grit stung their skins. It wrapped newspaper around their feet entangling them until the people cursed deep in their throats, stamped their feet, kicked at the paper. The wind blew it back again and again until they were forced to stoop and dislodge the paper with their hands. And then the wind grabbed their hats, pried their scarves from around their necks, stuck its fingers inside their coat collars, blew their coats away from their bodies.

The wind lifted Lutie Johnson's hair away from the back of her neck so that she felt suddenly naked and bald, for her hair had been resting softly and warmly against her skin. She shivered as the cold fingers of the wind touched the back of her neck, explored the sides of her head. It even blew her eyelashes away from her eyes so that her eyeballs were bathed in a rush of coldness and she had to blink in order to read the words on the sign swaying back and forth over her head.

Each time she thought she had the sign in focus, the wind pushed it away from her so that she wasn't certain whether it said three rooms or two rooms. If it was three, why, she would go in and ask to see it, but if it said two—why, there wasn't any point. Even with the wind twisting the sign away from her, she could see that it had been there for a long time because its original coat of white paint was streaked with rust where years of rain and snow had finally eaten the paint off down to the metal and the metal had slowly rusted, making a dark red stain like blood.

It was three rooms. The wind held it still for an instant in front of her and then swooped it away until it was standing at an impossible angle on the rod that suspended it from the building. She read it rapidly. Three rooms, steam heat, parquet floors, respectable tenants. Reasonable.

She looked at the outside of the building. Parquet floors here meant that the wood was so old and so discolored no amount of varnish or shellac would conceal the scars and the old scraped places, the years of dragging furniture across the floors, the hammer blows of time and children and drunks and dirty, slovenly women. Steam heat meant a rattling, clanging noise in radiators early in the morning and then a hissing that went on all day.

Respectable tenants in these houses where colored people were allowed to live included anyone who could pay the rent, so some of them would be drunk and loud-mouthed and quarrelsome; given to fits of depression when they would curse and cry violently, given to fits of equally violent elation. And, she thought, because the walls would be flimsy, why, the good people, the bad people, the children, the dogs, and the godawful smells would all be wrapped up together in one big package—the package that was called respectable tenants.

The wind pried at the red skullcap on her head, and as though angered because it couldn't tear it loose from its firm anchorage of bobby pins, the wind blew a great cloud of dust and ashes and bits of paper into her face, her eyes, her nose. It smacked against her ears as though it were giving her a final, exasperated blow as proof of its displeasure in not being able to make her move on.

Lutie braced her body against the wind's attack determined to finish thinking about the apartment before she went in to look at it. Reasonable—now that could mean almost anything. On Eighth Avenue it meant tenements—ghastly places not fit for humans. On St. Nicholas Avenue it meant high rents for small apartments; and on Seventh Avenue it meant great big apartments where you had to take in roomers in order to pay the rent. On this street it could mean almost anything.

She turned and faced the wind in order to estimate the street. The buildings were old with small slit-like windows, which meant the rooms were small and dark. In a street running in this direction there wouldn't be any sunlight in the apartments. Not ever. It would be hot as hell in summer and cold in winter.

"Reasonable" here in this dark, crowded street ought to be about twenty-eight dollars, provided it was on a top floor.

The hallways here would be dark and narrow. Then she shrugged her shoulders, for getting an apartment where she and Bub would be alone was more important than dark hallways. The thing that really mattered was getting away from Pop and his raddled women, and anything was better than that. Dark hallways, dirty stairs, even roaches on the walls. Anything. Anything. Anything.

Anything? Well, almost anything. So she turned toward the entrance of the building and as she turned, she heard someone clear his or her throat. It was so distinct—done as it was on two notes, the first one high and then the grunting expiration of breath on a lower note—that it came to her ears quite clearly under the sound of the wind rattling the garbage cans and slapping at the curtains. It was as though someone had said "hello," and she looked up at the window over her head.

There was a faint light somewhere in the room she was looking into and the enormous bulk of a woman was silhouetted against the light. She half-closed her eyes in order to see better. The woman was very black, she had a bandanna knotted tightly around her head, and Lutie saw, with some surprise, that the window was open. She began to wonder how the woman could sit by an open window on a cold, windy night like this one. And she didn't have on a coat, but a kind of loose-looking cotton dress—or at least it must be cotton, she thought, for it had a clumsy look—bulky and wrinkled.

"Nice little place, dearie. Just ring the Super's bell and he'll show it to you."

*   *   *   *   *

"Yes," she said firmly. "I want to look at the apartment."

"I'll get a flashlight," he said and went back into his apartment, closing the door behind him so that it made a soft, sucking sound. He said something, but she couldn't hear what it was. The whispering voice inside the apartment stopped and the dog was suddenly quiet.

Then he was back at the door, closing it behind him so it made the same soft, sucking sound. He had a long black flashlight in his hand. And she went up the stairs ahead of him thinking that the rod of its length was almost as black as his hands. The flashlight was a shiny black—smooth and gleaming faintly as the light lay along its length. Whereas the hand that held it was flesh—dull, scarred, worn flesh—no smoothness there. The knuckles were knobs that stood out under the skin, pulled out from hauling ashes, shoveling coal.

But not apparently from using a mop or a broom, for, as she went up and up the steep flight of stairs, she saw that they were filthy, with wastepaper, cigarette butts, the discarded wrappings from packages of snuff, pink ticket stubs from the movie houses. On the landings there were empty gin and whiskey bottles.

She stopped looking at the stairs, stopped peering into the corners of the long hallways, for it was cold, and she began walking faster trying to keep warm. As they completed a flight of stairs and turned to walk up another hall, and then started climbing another flight of stairs, she was aware that the cold increased. The farther up they went, the colder it got. And in summer she supposed it would get hotter and hotter as you went up until when you reached the top floor your breath would be cut off completely.

The halls were so narrow that she could reach out and touch them on either side without having to stretch her arms any distance. When they reached the fourth floor, she thought, instead of her reaching out for the walls, the walls were reaching out for her—bending and swaying toward her in an effort to envelop her. The Super's footsteps behind her were slow, even, steady. She walked a little faster and apparently without hurrying, without even increasing his pace, he was exactly the same distance behind her. In fact his heavy footsteps were a little nearer than before.

She began to wonder how it was that she had gone up the stairs first, why was she leading the way? It was all wrong. He was the one who knew the place, the one who lived here. He should have gone up first. How had he got her to go up the stairs in front of him? She wanted to turn around and see the expression on his face, but she knew if she turned on the stairs like this, her face would be on a level with his; and she wouldn't want to be that close to him.

She didn't need to turn around, anyway; he was staring at her back, her legs, her thighs. She could feel his eyes traveling over her—estimating her, summing her up, wondering about her. As she climbed up the last flight of stairs, she was aware that the skin on her back was crawling with fear. Fear of what? she asked herself. Fear of him, fear of the dark, of the smells in the halls, the high steep stairs, of yourself? She didn't know, and even as she admitted that she didn't know, she felt sweat start pouring from her armpits, dampening her forehead, breaking out in beads on her nose.

The apartment was in the back of the house. The Super fished another flashlight from his pocket which he handed to her before he bent over to unlock the door very quietly. And she thought, everything he does, he does quietly.

She played the beam of the flashlight on the walls. The rooms were small. There was no window in the bedroom. At least she supposed it was the bedroom. She walked over to look at it, and then went inside for a better look. There wasn't a window—just an air shaft and a narrow one at that. She looked around the room, thinking that by the time there was a bed and a chest of drawers in it there'd be barely space enough to walk around in. At that she'd probably bump her knees every time she went past the corner of the bed. She tried to visualize how the room would look and began to wonder why she had already decided to take this room for herself.

It might be better to give it to Bub, let him have a real bedroom to himself for once. No, that wouldn't do. He would swelter in this room in summer. It would be better to have him sleep on the couch in the living room, at least he'd get some air, for there was a window out there, though it wasn't a very big one. She looked out into the living room, trying again to see the window, to see just how much air would come through, how much light there would be for Bub to study by when he came home from school, to determine, too, the amount of air that would reach into the room at night when the window was open, and he was sleeping curled up on the studio couch.

The Super was standing in the middle of the living room. Waiting for her. It wasn't anything that she had to wonder about or figure out. It wasn't by any stretch of the imagination something she had conjured up out of thin air. It was a simple fact. He was waiting for her. She knew it just as she knew she was standing there in that small room. He was holding his flashlight so the beam fell down at his feet. It turned him into a figure of never-ending tallness. And his silent waiting and his appearance of incredible height appalled her.

With the light at his feet like that, he looked at though his head must end somewhere in the ceiling. He simply went up and up into darkness. And he radiated such desire for her that she could feel it. She told herself she was a fool, an idiot, drunk on fear, on fatigue and gnawing worry. Even while she thought it, the hot, choking awfulness of his desire for her pinioned her there so that she couldn't move. It was an aching yearning that filled the apartment, pushed against the walls, plucked at her arms.

She forced herself to start walking toward the kitchen. As she went past him, it seemed to her that he actually did reach one long arm out toward her, his body swaying so that its exaggerated length almost brushed against her. She really couldn't be certain of it, she decided, and resolutely turned the beam of her flashlight on the kitchen walls.

It isn't possible to read people's minds, she argued. Now the Super was probably not even thinking about her when he was standing there like that. He probably wanted to get back downstairs to read his paper. Don't kid yourself, she thought, he probably can't read, or if he can, he probably doesn't spend any time at it. Well—listen to the radio. That was it, he probably wanted to hear his favorite program and she had thought he was filled with the desire to leap upon her. She was as bad as Granny. Which just went on to prove you couldn't be brought up by someone like Granny without absorbing a lot of nonsense that would spring at you out of nowhere, so to speak, and when you least expected it. All those tales about things that people sensed before they actually happened. Tales that had been handed down and down and down until, if you tried to trace them back, you'd end up God knows where—probably Africa. And Granny had them all at the tip of her tongue.

Yet would wanting to hear a radio program make a man look quite like that? Impatiently she forced herself to inspect the kitchen; holding the light on first one wall, then another. It was no better and no worse than she had anticipated. The sink was battered; and the gas stove was a little rusted. The faint smell of gas that hovered about it suggested a slow, incurable leak somewhere in its connections.

Peering into the bathroom, she saw that the fixtures were old-fashioned and deeply chipped. She thought Methuselah himself might well have taken baths in the tub. Certainly it looked ancient enough, though he'd have had to stick his beard out in the hall while he washed himself, for the place was far too small for a man with a full-grown beard to turn around in. She presumed because there was no window that the vent pipe would serve as a source of nice, fresh, clean air.

One thing about it the rent wouldn't be very much. It couldn't be for a place like this. Tiny hall. Bathroom on the right, kitchen straight ahead; living room to the left of the hall and you had to go through the living room to get to the bedroom. The whole apartment would fit very neatly into just one good-sized room.

She was conscious that all the little rooms smelt exactly alike. It was a mixture that contained the faint persistent odor of gas, of old walls, dusty plaster, and over it all the heavy, sour smell of garbage—a smell that seeped through the dumb-waiter shaft. She started humming under her breath, not realizing she was doing it. It was an old song that Granny used to sing. "Ain't no restin' place for a sinner like me. Like me. Like me." It had a nice recurrent rhythm. "Like me. Like me." The humming increased in volume as she stood there thinking about the apartment.

(1946)

From

EAST RIVER
by Sholem Asch

The inhabitants of 48th Street fell into two categories. There were those who came and went, occupying for a short period the usually empty flats in one of the buildings of the long uniform row of three-story houses that lined part of both sides of the street. These were mostly down-at-the-heel theater folk, small-bit actors, musicians, and stage hands, who worked in the theatrical section farther west in Manhattan and whom poverty had driven to the cheaper neighborhood of the East River. Their places of residence changed with their "engagements." They weren't looked on as properly part of the local population; Uncle Maloney didn't even bother to try to get them to become members of the local Tammany club, or Harry to get them to vote correctly at election. Most of them were unnaturalized foreigners, but even the natives and naturalized citizens among them gave little thought to their voting rights. They were here today and gone tomorrow.

To the same category belonged the residents who were waiters in the elegant restaurants in the swanky sections of the city, and all of those who had jobs around the city's night life, over toward Broadway.

The other category was represented by the "old settlers," the permanent residents, the backbone of the block, who knew one another, loved or hated one another, but belonged together.

Mrs. Kranz's "apartment hotel" was in the middle of the block. The patrons kept constantly changing—but not the hotel nor Mrs. Kranz. Clara Kranz was a European; and she stayed one. Did she come from Vienna, from Slovakia, from Hungary? No one knew. She seemed to be the type that might belong to any of those countries, a characteristic type from the Austria of the Hapsburgs. She had the seductive figure and blonde hair of the Viennese, the good nature of Prague, and the easy acquiescence and friendliness of Budapest. Whether she was a widow, or a divorcee, or maybe an old maid, no one was quite sure. It was known that in her bedroom there was an enlarged colored photograph of a man with long, curled mustaches, dressed in a mountain-climbing costume, knee-length deerskin breeches, leather suspenders, a green hunting jacket, with a gun in his hand. Some said it was a picture of her husband, others of her sweetheart. But everyone believed he was a baron, of the Hungarian or Czech nobility. And everyone knew that he had fallen, dressed as he was in the picture, and gun in hand, from a mountain peak, and had been killed on the spot. At any rate that had all happened in the old country. In America there was nothing more of him than this handsomely colored photograph, enlarged from a small European original.

Mrs. Kranz was an independent woman, running her rooming house, which she graced with the name of apartment hotel, in two adjoining buildings which she had rented and furnished, for artists, musicians, and singers, most of them Central Europeans who had come from Austria to seek their fortunes in the world of the theater in America. Her clientele, needless to say, consisted of the type of artists who had either not yet begun or long since ended their careers on Broadway.

The musicians and singers lent color to the block, taking away the weekday bleakness of similar neighborhoods. There was always to be heard the scraping of fiddles and the tinkling of pianos through the rooming house windows. The block was bathed in the blue Danube waters of the Strauss waltzes which kept pouring through the windows into the street. In the early evenings the children of the block would dance to the rhythm of the music.

In front of the house one could see men of various ages, with long, wavy hair, in artistic knotted ties, unfamiliar European clothes, pastel-colored jackets, trousers narrow at the knees; women with unusual hair arrangements and gaily colored dresses and shawls. To the street they were "Bohemians."

It would seem that Mrs. Kranz was much attached to this sort of people, and she was said to be very good to them. She herself loved to sing and make music. It was told of her that she was once on the stage in the old country. From her appearance it would not be difficult to believe that she was once a "Bohemian" herself.

For as long as people could remember on 48th Street—and that was a matter of six or eight years—Mrs. Kranz hadn't changed so much as a hair. It was difficult to tell her age. There are natures which seem to resist the passing of the years; time seems to have no effect on them, as though they live in a sphere beyond its sway. Mrs. Kranz looked as though her appearance had remained permanently fixed in her middle thirties.

Her figure was tall, and her unlined face was carefully and heavily powdered. At all times her blonde hair was carefully braided about her head and three little curls clung close to her forehead. In a short gypsy jacket, an Indian shawl around her shoulders, and a bewildering variety of ornaments, she presented an exotic picture. Long earrings dangled from the lobes of her ears; around her throat was a coral and amber band; old European ornaments were pinned over her high breasts; on her wrists an entire arsenal of charms and amulets dangled and glittered from wide bracelets. Her fingers sparkled with rings set with imitation stones. Her whole person was surrounded with an aura of heady and heavy Oriental perfume. You could detect, too, the odor of lavender and camphor, like the faint atmosphere around an ancient wedding dress left hanging forgotten in an old wardrobe. All the cosmetics and rose waters and other feminine devices with which she sought to retain the appearance of her youth now gone could not give her tall figure and smooth cheeks the freshness of youth. There was a sort of deadly fatigue that seemed to push its way through the cosmetics. True, it gave a quality of feminine delicacy and grace to her face, but it also evoked a feeling of anxiety lest she might suddenly wither away, like a flower that has been kept in a tightly closed glass jar and is suddenly exposed to the air.

It was no secret to 48th Street—there was no secret in 48th Street about anyone on the block—that the main reason for Mrs. Kranz's heroic efforts to hold on to her youth was to entangle and hold Harry Greenstock in the net she had spread for him. Everyone knew that Harry's wife suffered from asthma and that her heart was bad—she had already had a couple of serious attacks—and that she couldn't last long. Mrs. Kranz, they were sure, was simply making preparations ahead of time. That was the reason she was such a constant visitor to Harry's house, taking care of things, washing and combing the children. It was said, too, that she was winning away the children's affections even while their mother was still alive. She was even deluding the heart of the sick woman herself with all the attentions she heaped on her, helping her during her bad days, caring for the children so generously that they loved her almost as their mother. And all in order to take over when the proper time should come.

But it wasn't altogether so. It is true that she was in love with Harry. In all the block he was the only one who reminded her of the old country. She loved his home and she loved his children, and she loved to steal away with him some evenings—when there were no prying eyes about—to sit in Neufeld's Hungarian restaurant and listen to gypsy music and watch the dancing of a Hungarian czardas. He was such a sport, was Harry Greenstock. The figure of a hussar, a Hungarian hussar. Thick black hair and black mustache. And the way he dressed. Like a count. It was a privilege and a pleasure to go out with him. You felt important sitting with Harry in a restaurant or being ushered into your theater seats. And then there were his connections with important politicians. The boss of the ward clapped him on the shoulder and the district captain was his intimate friend. He was high up in the inner circles of the lodge, and his words were listened to with respect by everyone on the block. Even the Judge, Judge Greenberg, was his friend. If there was any trouble at all, Harry was the one to come to. All Harry had to do was to call up this or that one. There wasn't a wire Harry couldn't pull.

A woman alone in the world . . . and a man, lonely too . . . with a wife sick for the last two years . . . practically without a wife since the beginning of her sickness. . . . There was really nothing to wonder at.

And therefore it was nothing to be surprised about that Mrs. Kranz, the moment she heard of the great feat of Harry's pigeons in bringing home the rare Japanese specimen, should put on one of her cinnamon-colored gypsy blouses, short-sleeved and cut low at the neck, adjust a pair of her dangling earrings, load her arms down with bracelets, pat her three blonde curls more fetchingly on her forehead, put an Indian shawl around her shoulders, and go over to Harry's yard—although she usually waited for the evening for her visits—to celebrate the unparalleled victory. Without waiting for the cover of night, she walked over in the broad daylight, with the women of the neighborhood seated on the doorsteps or the balcony fire escapes. Pairs of scornful eyes followed her, and the women, too exhausted with the heat to summon enough energy for anything else, found the strength to toss remarks to one another.

"The slut . . ."

". . . and while his wife is still alive . . ."

"It's no wonder that God sends a blistering heat like this," a Jewish woman said.

". . . and all the sicknesses the children get . . ."

Mrs. Kranz ignored the remarks. Trailing a heavy perfume after her she walked along with a coquettish swing, and even had the impudence to stop at Davidowsky's grocery store to buy corned beef, smoked tongue, a couple of loaves of bread, some sour pickles, and a laxative for the children.

"They stuffed themselves with ice cream and stale milk on the excursion. They'll probably all be sick," she said, as though she owed an explanation to Moshe Wolf, who waited on her.

Moshe Wolf made no answer. He served her without a word.

When Mrs. Kranz reached the dark basement apartment, she could hear from the yard the familiar noises of the men—the children had already left. The men were passing a flask of whisky from hand to hand, drinking from the bottle, to celebrate the victory over the captured Japanese from the 57th Street flock. The raucous, rumbling male noise was refreshing to Mrs. Kranz after the delicate sentimentality of the music and singing with which she had been surrounded all day. She didn't go directly out into the yard, but paused at Mrs. Greenstock's rocking chair, with her sympathetic and patient smile, while Mrs. Greenstock swayed back and forth, trying to take a deep breath and fanning herself.

"It's all the fault of the noise out there," Mrs. Kranz said. "Here." She took some rock candy out of a bag. "Mr. Davidowsky says it's the best thing for asthma. Even the doctors haven't been able to find anything better."

Mrs. Greenstock—she was known simply as "the Missus" in the neighborhood—took the rock candy, and like a man grasping at a straw or anything that might save him from imminent disaster, put it in her mouth without a word or a glance. With the self-centeredness characteristic of sick people, she seemed not to have any interest in anything outside her.

Mrs. Kranz turned around to see Rachel picking at her fingernails. She slapped her hand fondly, and gave her a nail file. "This is what ladies use," she scolded her. "I don't know where you learn such habits. Go and put on a clean dress, and put some water to boil. And Goldie—see the way she looks!" She lifted the youngest child onto a chair and wiped her perspiring face with a towel. "The poor child probably hasn't had anything to eat all day. And in all this heat! What are you standing there for, Rachel? Don't you see that your mother can't help herself? You out there," she called to the men in the yard, "one of you come in and help!"

"What's the trouble?" asked Harry, coming in from the yard.

"What's the trouble? Your wife can hardly catch her breath and you sit outside and have a good time! There's no one to give her a glass of water. And look at the way this room looks! And the children! They haven't had a bit of warm food all day—and all of you stay outside with your Tammany and your pigeons. You're a pack of animals. . . . ."

"All right, Clara, all right. . . ." Harry turned to his wife. "What's the matter, Sara? Don't you feel well?" He called out to the yard. "Ola Boga! Run over to Davidowsky's. Tell him I asked him to come over right away."

Moshe Wolf Davidowsky was the emergency first aid for everyone on 48th Street. Whatever the sickness, the patient would first of all go over to the grocery store to take counsel with Davidowsky. Whether it was a splinter in the finger or a cinder in the eye or a painful belly ache, it was to Davidowsky that they went. In his store could be found cures for everything. He had brought them with him from the old country, and he knew all about mixing herbs and applying ointments—all the old home remedies.

But it wasn't only for physical ailments that Davidowsky was consulted. Most of all he was the one to come to for advice in time of trouble—whether it was necessary or not to call in a doctor, whether the case called for a lawyer. He was, so to say, the first haven of refuge, in case of a family fight, or trouble with the landlord, or when it was just a person feeling lonesome and needing someone to pour out his heart to. Harry was no exception. Like everyone else in the block, he sent for Davidowsky before he sent for the doctor.

"Maybe you can do something to help her," he said to Moshe Wolf, standing over his wife's chair like a helpless child.

"I see, I see," said Moshe Wolf, stroking his beard. "I see what she needs. She needs a husband. . . ."

"What have I done now?" asked Harry angrily, but with a note of apology in his tone.

"It's what you haven't done. A woman with a bad asthma shouldn't be in New York in the summer. In America they have blue mountains, green mountains, black mountains, white mountains, all kinds of mountains. That's where a woman with asthma should be in the summer. And you keep her caged in here. And you're supposed to be such a big shot, such a politician. . . ."

"Didn't I do everything I could? Didn't I run over to the Committee? Didn't I plead with them? Judge Greenberg gave me a letter of recommendation. 'No vacancies,' they told me, 'till after Labor Day.' "

"Listen to what I'm telling you. For your pigeons and your animals you'd find a summer place if they needed mountain air. Don't forget she's your wife, the mother of your children."

"Moshe Wolf, believe me . . . may I drop dead . . ." Harry was white with anger. He bit his lip in rage.

"Who cares for your oaths! Get her to bed first, then go back to your friends. We'll manage without you. You were no good in the old country and you're no good here. Get me a glass of water. . . . Here, Sara, take this. . . ."—he took a spill of powder and poured it into the glass—"it'll make you feel better; it'll calm you. There's been too much noise and excitement. . . . What heroes! What great pigeon heroes! You'd think they'd captured the eagle of King Solomon. . . . You ought to be ashamed of yourself! You, a grown man, a Jew, a father! . . ."

Moshe Wolf was the only one who would dare talk that way to Harry, and it was only from Moshe Wolf that Harry would take it. Pale with anger and biting his lip he did everything that Moshe Wolf asked him, brought the water for the powder, dragged the bed over to the open window. The powder actually worked—probably more as a result of the sick woman's satisfaction at hearing her husband raked over the coals in the very presence of his mistress. Her coughing subsided. Moshe Wolf was able to return to his store—and Harry to the yard where his cronies were waiting for the provisions Mrs. Kranz had brought.

The ones in the yard were Harry's closest intimates. Mike Maloney, Tony the bricklayer, Maczikowicz the Polack, and Harry's errand boy Choleva—and of course, Mrs. Kranz, sitting in the doorway leading to the yard. They talked about familiar things, about horses and dogs, holdups, about the fights they had had, about policemen and politicians. Choleva was constantly occupied in running over to the saloon, where the saloonkeeper would hand him out cans of beer through the side door. He was in and out the yard a dozen times.

For Mrs. Kranz it was paradise. She loved to listen to the talk about horses, bandits, policemen, politicians. She loved the smell of whisky and beer, the sour smell of male sweat.

She sat quietly, half in and half out of the house, careful not to move, so as not to arouse the jealousy of the sick woman, who, lying on the bed near the window, kept her eyes closed and made no sound, but was aware of everything going on. Mrs. Kranz didn't say a word. She sat there in blissful satisfaction at being near real men, listening to real men's talk. She sat in the shadows, wrapped in her gypsy scarf, in silence except for the occasional tinkling of the charms and amulets dangling from her bracelets as though she wanted to give a gentle reminder of her presence. She could feel the eyes of the men peering at her. With her languid eyes she looked up at the stars in the sky. "The stars are coming out," she said, unaffectedly.

"The stars are coming out," Maloney repeated after her.

Harry was silent. He just looked at her with his keen, black sparkling eyes. Mrs. Kranz's breast heaved in a sigh. She fanned herself with her hand.

Choleva took his harmonica out of his pocket and began to play a Polish mazurka. The harmonica—like the flask of whisky and the beer can—began to pass from mouth to mouth, each of them piping out his national songs.

From the second-story windows overlooking the yard came the sounds of weeping. They were not shrieks, they were muffled, painful sobs. They all knew what it was. Patrick McCarthy, the Irishman on the second floor, was beating his daughter Mary.

"Bastard!" Harry shouted. He shook his fist in the direction of the windows.

"Sunday is McCarthy's day for handing out a beating. If it isn't his wife, it's his daughter," Maloney said.

"The bastard! He's beating Mary because she went with Rachel and Irving on the picnic," Harry shouted angrily.

Harry was right. McCarthy, with his small job in a shipping agency, was the block's official anti-Semite. He hated Jews—and, as though some weird spell had been cast over him, he couldn't bring himself to move away from them. There were plenty of places in the neighborhood where most of the people were Italian Catholics and German Protestants; but as though the devil drove him to it, he stayed on 48th Street, where most of the inhabitants were Jews. He never thought of moving away. On the contrary, he not only insisted on living in the Jewish section but in the Jewish tenements themselves, to get a whiff every Friday of the Jewish gefüllte fish and other Sabbath delicacies— and to curse and pick fights and parade his hatred. His children, like his wife, didn't share his spleen. His older daughter, Mary, had for several years been the schoolmate of Rachel Greenstock and Irving Davidowsky, and had become so accustomed to Jewish families that she spent more time in the Davidowsky home or the Greenstock home than she did in her own. Many a time she would hide from her father at Harry's house. Her own home life was unhappy. She would see her father come home drunk, his wages spent, and let out his shame and bitterness on her mother. She suffered a great deal. Her family troubles had awakened a deep religious emotion in her; it was a way of escape for her. But her piety, encouraged by the old priest of the Church of St. Boniface over on Second Avenue, did not estrange her from Jews. It seemed to give her a closer feeling of sympathy with the Jewish customs and traditions she saw practiced in Davidowsky's house. Driven out by her father's brutality, the child was grateful for the warmth and kindliness she found in the homes of her friends.

"The best thing would be to haul the bastard once for all to court," said Harry. "Judge Greenberg would fix him."

"They'll only send him to jail, and in the meantime his wife and kids will starve," commented Maloney. "The thing to do is to beat him up."

"A beating won't do that kind of guy any good," said Harry.

"It'll help for a couple of weeks, and that'll be all to the good," Maloney said quietly.

"Yes, it'll have to be done one of these days," Harry agreed.

(1946)

From

KNOCK ON ANY DOOR
by Willard Motley

On the stone step of a tenement sat a Mexican boy watching a crap game in the middle of the street. After an indecisive pause Nick sat next to him. After a while the Mexican kid pulled out a package of cigarettes, lit one, saw Nick there on the step and shoved the pack at him without saying anything. In the street the crapshooters saw nothing but the black and white cubes tangoing across the dirty pavement.

"Two bits he don't come."

"You're covered!"

Two big-shouldered men in dark suits walked along the sidewalk, in the shadows, watching. Nick looked at them uneasily and said to the Mexican boy, "They're going to be raided." The Mexican smiled and shook his head no. "You're not from around here, are you?"

"No," Nick said.

One of the dicks caught the eye of the teen-aged fellow who was running the game. The dick lifted a long, beckoning finger. The youth walked over to him with his hand in his pocket. They stood close together. Their hands touched. They walked their opposite ways.

"Come on seven, come on seven, baby needs shoes."

"See how we do things down here," the Mexican said to Nick a little proudly.

Nick, losing his way a dozen times, went home. Yes, they were smart down there.

Something pulled him back to Maxwell Street. Right after supper he got up and started for the door. "Where you going, Nick?" Ma wanted to know.

"Aw, for a walk," and outside the door, "for Christ sake!"

"You come back here! You might get lost," Ma called.

Nick had already hit the bottom step.

That was a *big* night. The crowd, gathering from all the slum houses, talked about the mayor coming to make a speech. The whole neighborhood was turning out.

They came across the cracked sidewalks and the dirty street stones.

There was music at the carnival. And laughter.

The street lamps leaned drunkenly and were an easy target for the kids' rocks. Under the now deserted Maxwell stands the cats fought their fights. In an alley a bottle of fifteen-cents-a-pint wine went the rounds. On a stand, blotted out by the darkness, a boy had his arm around a girl. They looked up, through the threading trails of smoke, at the moon. In the alley an empty bottle crashed against a brick wall and tinkled in shattered glass to the ground.

Nick walked down the carnival street, edging his way through the crowd. One end of the street had been sectioned off. Wooden horses made an uneven circle around the part that was for dancing. A crayoned sign tacked to one of the horses read: 5¢ A DANCE. A string of sickly red bulbs crossed above the dance space. There was a jukebox playing constantly. Its long electric cord went across the sidewalk to a second story window. A group of young Italian boys, fourteen to eighteen years old, loafed near the wooden horses, straddling them, laughing, joking, poking fun. The jukebox beat its drums, moaned with its saxophones, swung the music out loudly—

Come on and hear, come on and hear
Alexander's rag-time band—
Come on and hear, come on and hear,—
It's the best band in the land. . . .

The boys each grabbed another boy and, outside the circle of wooden horses, went into their wild, imitative dance.

The music said—

Come on along, come on along—
Let me take you by the hand
Up to the man, up to the man
Who's the leader of the band. . . .

The boys protruded their rear ends. They kicked their toes against the street. Some postured like girls, smirking, touching their hair, putting their cheeks up against their partners'.

A youth escorted a girl to the dance floor entrance and, embarrassed, led her out to dance on the empty pavement. The ridiculing boys, recognizing him, hurdled the horses, clapped their hands in time to the music, patted their feet to its rhythm, began chanting the words.

The boys joined hands and circled him, shouting, laughing, ribbing him.

The shuffle of feet in broken shoes, in turned-over heels, came across the night pavement and under the electric wreath of lights over the middle of the street. Nick leaned against a stand and watched them. There were women ready to drop kids into the world. There were the tough faces of boys who had known no boyhood and the broadened bodies of girls who had known everything before they were fourteen. There were little kids, looking like they belonged to no one—with just a dress pulled over their heads, with their stockings hanging down over their shoes and their shoe laces dragging. Lots of kids. And young fellows. And girls. Boys, half-grown, with arms encircled, walked down the carnival pavement. Girls in slacks, in tight-fitting sweaters, whispered together or giggled. There were a couple of drunks staggering up to beer stalls. Negro youths, black, brown, yellow, walked down the middle of the street in baseball shirts and caps. They walked loose-joined with all the ancient African grace retained. And when the sob of the music caught their ears it affected their feet.

Wheels of chance spun. Bingo games were in full swing with a loud voice coming out over the microphone to announce the numbers. At one stand Italian sausages on long, swordlike spears baked over charcoal pan-fires. The smoke curled up and was lost overhead. In the houses lining each side of the street people were leaning out the windows with their elbows on the sills.

The mayor came in a shiny new car, and a policeman opened up the wooden horses that blocked off the street to let his car pass.

The mayor said he had been raised in the neighborhood and pointed toward the street where his school was. The mayor said, "I came from the bottom and I'm still with the bottom!" And everybody cheered. The mayor said, "We can thank God for living in a great country and a great city." And everybody cheered. The mayor said, "Each boy in this neighborhood has the same chance I had to make his place in the world."

The mayor left. The crowd was good-natured and happy all over the carnival street. There was a colored orchestra by the dance floor now. It played hot music from the back of a truck. The crowd ringed a drunken Irishman who danced in the street, his hat sliding over his eyes. Then a colored boy and girl did a jitterbug dance while the crowd clapped hands, keeping time with the music. They could dance! Then a Jewish girl in a high school sweater with bumps and her skinny partner in loud-colored trousers and glasses took over. They were almost as good. Then, for a nickel you could dance inside the ring of wooden horses.

Only a few people danced. Fellows and girls stood around uncertain and half-embarrassed. A lean young Negro, black as the hat he wore, came out of the crowd and asked a pretty Italian girl in her teens for a dance. She smiled and nodded. Together they went under the strings of electric bulbs. Through the wild steps of the jitterbug dance he took her. They whirled across the dirty asphalt and back. They swayed to the music. They answered its harsh notes. The crowd, three-fourths white, watched, applauded when they were finished. The black boy escorted the Italian girl back to the fringe of the crowd, thanked her for the dance and went on his way.

Nick stayed late. When the carnival was no longer interesting he walked around the side streets. By the hot-dog stand on Newberry and Maxwell, propped against an empty stand were two women. One of them looked only about seventeen. She still had a childishness about her lips and an undefinable freshness. In the half-dark of the street they were smoking cigarettes.

One of the Maxwell Street merchants, a little round Jew in a straw hat, came along the sidewalk. When he saw the two women sitting there he tipped his hat to them. He said, "Hello, girls." Then he walked over closer, let his voice drop down and said confidentially, "Better be careful. The heat is on."

"How often do we have to pay them goddamn cops!" the older women complained, half-whining.

Nick sat near where the women were, listening and smoking a cigarette he had sneaked out of Aunt Rosa's pack. The two women kicked their heels against the stand. They lit cigarettes and complained about "business." "I can't make fifty cents. If I was getting drunk I know I'd make it," said the older one. "I'd run up and grab somebody."

"You gotta eat," said the young one, laughing, but her eyes didn't match her laugh.

A man came through the shadows. The young whore whispered loud enough for his ear, "Want to go home with me, honey?"

The man walked slow. He hung on the corner, uncertain. The young whore's heels struck against the sidewalk. She dug her elbow into the other woman's side and said, matter-of-fact, "Here I go again."

The man waited on the corner. She caught up with him, said something under her breath, walked half a step in front. He followed her with one hand in his pocket.

Nick smoked the second half of his cigarette and went home. On the way he went to see if the dog was still there.

He was.

He lay in the gutter. The grime of the street had sooted his white coat. Red spots were crusted on it. Flies had already commenced to carry bits of him away.

And newspapers swirled around him like the withered petals of flowers.

In the street in the dark ahead of Nick were the reform school grounds. Again he was staring through the little diamonds of its tall wire fence.

(1947)

HOW THE DEVIL CAME DOWN DIVISION STREET
by Nelson Algren

Last Saturday evening there was a great argument in the Polonia Bar. All the biggest drunks on Divison were there, trying to decide who the biggest drunk of them was. Symanski said he was, and Oljiec said he was, and Koncel said he was, and Czechowski said he was.

Then Roman Orlov came in and the argument was decided. For Poor Roman had been drunk so long, night and day, that when we remember living men we almost forget Poor Roman, as though he were no longer really among the living at all.

"The devil lives in a double-shot," Roman explains himself obscurely. "I got a great worm inside. Gnaws and gnaws. Every day I drown him and every day he gnaws. Help me drown the worm, fellas."

So I bought Poor Roman a double-shot and asked him frankly how, before he was thirty, he had become the biggest drunk on Division.

It took a long time, and many double-shots for him to tell. But tell it he did, between curses and sobs, and I tell it now as closely to what he told as I can. Without the sobs, of course. And of course without any cursing.

When Roman was thirteen, it seems, the Orlovs moved into three stove-heated rooms in the rear of a lopsided tenement on Noble Street. Mama O. cooked in a Division Street restaurant by day and cooked in her own home by night.

Papa O. played an accordian for pennies in Division Street taverns by night and slept alone in the rooms by day.

There were only two beds in the tiny flat, so nobody encouraged Papa O. to come home at all.

Because he was the oldest, Roman slept between the twins, on the bed set up in the front room, to keep the pair from fighting during the night as they did during the day. Every day Teresa, who was eleven and could not learn her lessons as well as some of her classmates, slept with Mama O. in the windowless back bedroom, under a bleeding heart in a gilded oval frame.

If Papa O. got in before light, as happened occasionally early in the week, he crawled uncomplainingly under Roman's bed until Roman rose and got the twins, who were seven, up with him in time for Mass.

If Udo, who was something between a collie and a St. Bernard and as big as both together, was already curled up beneath the front-room bed, Papa O. slugged him with the accordion in friendly reproach—and went on into the back bedroom to crawl under Mama O.'s bed. In such an event he slept under a bed all day. For he never crawled, even with daylight, into Mama O.'s bed. Empty or not. As though he did not feel himself worthy to sleep there even when she was gone.

It was as though, having given himself all night to his accordion, he must remain true to it during the day.

For all manner of strange things went on in Papa O.'s head, as even the twins had become aware. Things so strange that Teresa was made ashamed of them by her schoolmates, whenever they wanted someone to tease.

This, too, was why no one, not even the twins, paid Papa O. any heed when the family returned from Mass one Sunday forenoon and he told them someone had been knocking while they were away.

"Some*body* was by door," he insisted. "I say 'Hallo.' Was no*body*." He looked slyly about him at the children. "Who plays tricks by Papa?"

"Maybe was Zolewitzes," Mama O. suggested indifferently. "Mama Z. comes perhaps to borrow."

That Sunday night it was cold in all the corners. Papa O. was gone to play for pennies and drinks, Mama O. was frying *pierogi,* the twins were in bed, and Teresa was studying her catechism across the table from Roman, when someone knocked lightly twice.

To Roman it sounded like someone at the clothes-closet door; but that was foolish to think, since the twins were in bed. Yet, when he opened the hall door, only a cold wind came into the room from the long gaslit passage.

Roman, being only thirteen, did not dare look behind the door. Far less to speak of the clothes closet.

All that night a light snow fell, while Roman O. lay wakeful, fancying he saw it falling on darkened streets all over the mysterious earth, on the pointing roof tops of old-world cities, on mountain-high waves of the mid-Atlantic, and in the leaning eaves of Noble Street. He was just falling off to sleep when the knocking came again. Three times, like a measured warning.

The boy stiffened under the covers, listening with his fear. Heard the hall door squeak softly, as though Papa O. were sneaking in. But Papa O. never knocked, and Papa O. never sneaked. Papa O. came home with the accordion banging against buildings all down Noble Street, jingling his pennies proudly, singing off-key bravely, mumbling and laughing and stumbling. Papa O. never knocked. He kicked the door in happily and shouted cheerfully, "What you say, all peoples? How's t'ings, ever-body?" Papa O. pulled people out of bed and rattled pans and laughed at nothing and argued with unseen bartenders until somebody gave him sausage and eggs and coffee and bread and hung the accordion safely away.

Roman crept, barefooted, in the long underwear Mama O. had sewed on him in the early fall, to the hallway door.

The whole house slept. The windows were frosted and a thin line of ice had edged up under the front window and along the pane. The family slept. Roman shoved the door open gently. The tenement slept. Down the hall the single jet flickered feebly. No one. Nothing. The people slept.

Roman looked behind the door, shivering now with more than cold.

No one. Nothing. All night long.

He returned to bed and prayed quietly, until he heard Mama O. rise; waited till he knew she had the fire going in the big kitchen stove. Then, dressing with his back to the heat, he told Mama O. what he had heard. Mama O. said nothing.

Two mornings later, Papa O. came home without the accordion. It did not matter then to Mama O. whether he had sold it or lost it or loaned it; she knew it at last for a sign, she had felt the change coming, she said, in her blood. For she had dreamed a dream, all night, of a stranger waiting in the hall: a young man, drunken, leaning against the gaslit wall for support, with blood down the front of his shirt and drying on his hands. She knew, as all the Orlovs knew, that the unhappy dead return to warn or comfort, to plead or repent, to gain peace or to avenge.

That day, standing over steaming kettles, Mama O. went back in her mind to all those dear to her of earth who had died: the cousin drowned at sea, the brother returned from the war to die, the mother and father gone from their fields before she had married.

That night she knocked on Mama Zolewitz's door. Mama Z. sat silently, as though she had been expecting Mama O. for many evenings.

"Landlord doesn't like we should tell new tenants too soon," Mama Z. explained even before being told of the knocking, "so you shouldn't say it, I told. It was a young man lived in this place, in your very rooms. A strong young man, and good to look at. But sick, sick in the head from the drink. A sinner certainly. For here he lived with his lady without being wed, and she worked and he did not. That he did not work had little to do with what happened, and the drink had little to do. For it was being unwed that brought it on, at night, on the New Year. He returned from the taverns that night and beat her till her screams were a whimpering. Till her whimpering became nothing. A strong young man, like a bull, made violent by the drink. When the whimpering ceased, there was no sound at all. No sound until noon, when the police came with shouting.

"What was there to shout about? I could have told them before they came. The young man had hanged himself in the bedroom closet. Thus it is that one sin leads to another, and both were buried together. In unsanctified ground, with no priest near.''

Mama O. grew pale. Her very clothes closet.

"It is nothing to worry," Mama Z. told her neighbor sagely. "He does not knock to do harm. He comes only to gain a little peace that good Christian prayer for him may give. Pray for the young man, Mama O. He wishes peace."

That night after supper the Orlovs gathered in prayer about the front-room stove, and Papa O. prayed also. For now that the accordion was gone, the taverns must do without him. When the prayer was done, he went to bed with Mama O. like a good husband, and the knocking did not come again.

Each night the Orlovs prayed for the poor young man. And each night Papa O. went to bed with Mama O. for lack of his accordion.

Mama O. knew then that the knocking had been a sign of good omen, and told the priest, and the priest blessed her for a Christian. He said it was the will of God that the Orlovs should redeem the young man by prayer and that Papa O. should have a wife instead of an accordion.

Papa O. stayed at home until, for lack of music, he became the best janitor on Noble Street. Mama Z. went to the priest and told of her part in the miracle of the poor young man, and the priest blessed Mama Z. also.

When the landlord learned that his house was no longer haunted he brought the Orlovs gifts; and when the rent was late he said nothing. So the priest blessed him equally, and in time the Orlovs paid no rent at all, but prayed for the landlord instead.

Teresa became the most important person in her class, for it became known that a miracle had been done in the Orlov home. Sister Mary Ursula said the child looked more like a little saint every day. And no other child in the room ever had her lessons as well as Teresa thereafter.

The twins sensed the miracle and grew up to be fast friends, doing all things together, even wearing the same clothes and reading the same catechism. Udo, too, knew that the home was blessed. For he received no more blows from the accordion.

Only one sad aspect shadowed this great and happy change: Poor Roman was left bedless. For with Papa O. home every night like a good husband, Teresa must sleep between the twins.

Thus it came about that the nights of Roman Orlov became fitful and restless, first under the front-room bed and then under the back-room bed. With the springs overhead squeaking half the night as likely as not. The nights of Roman's boyhood were thereafter passed beneath one bed or the other, with no bed of his own at all. Until, attaining his young manhood and his seventeenth year, he took at last to sleeping during the day in order to have no need for sleep at night.

And at night, as everyone knows, there is no place to go but the taverns.

So it was, being abroad with no place to go and the whole night to kill, that Roman took his father's place. He had no accordion for excuse—only lack of a bed. He came to think of the dawn, when the taverns closed and he must go home, as the bitterest hour of the day.

This is why he still calls the dawn the bitterest hour: he must go home though he has no home.

Is this a drunkard's tale or sober truth? I can only say he told it like the truth, drinking double-shots all the while. I only know that no one argues about who the biggest drunk on Divison is if Roman O. is around.

I only know what Mama O. now tells, after many years and Papa O. in his grave and the twins scattered: that the young man who knocked was in truth the devil. For did she not give him, without knowing what she did, a good son in return for a worthless husband?

"I'm drownin' the worm t'night," Poor Roman explains, talking to his double-shot. "Help me drown the worm t'night, fellas."

Does the devil live in a double-shot? Is he the one who gnaws, all night, within?

Or is he the one who knocks, on winter nights, with blood drying on his knuckles, in the gaslit passages of our dreams?

(1947)

From

THE SEVEN STOREY MOUNTAIN
by *Thomas Merton*

It was a hot day, a rainy day, in the middle of August when I came out of the subway into the heat of Harlem. There were not many people on the streets that afternoon. I walked along the street until I came to the middle of the block, and saw one or two stores marked "Friendship House" and "Bl. Martin de Porres Center" or some such title in big blue letters. There did not seem to be anyone around.

The biggest of the stores was the library, and there I found half a dozen young Negroes, boys and girls, high school students, sitting at a table. Some of them wore glasses, and it seemed they were having some kind of an organized intellectual discussion, because when I came in they got a little embarrassed about it. I asked them if the Baroness was there, and they said no, she had gone downtown because it was her birthday, and I asked who I should see, so they told me Mary Jerdo. She was around somewhere. If I waited she would probably show up in a few minutes.

So I stood there, and took down off the shelf Father Bruno's *Life of St. John of the Cross* and looked at the pictures.

The young Negroes tried to pick up their discussion where they had left off: but they did not succeed. The stranger made them nervous. One of the girls opened her mouth and pronounced three or four abstract words, and then broke off into a giggle. Then another one opened her mouth and said: "Yes, but don't you think . . . ?" And this solemn question also collapsed in embarrassed tittering. One of the young men got off a whole paragraph or so, full of big words, and everybody roared with laughter. So I turned around and started to laugh too, and immediately the whole thing became a game.

They began saying big words just because it was funny. They uttered the most profoundly dull and ponderous statements, and laughed at them, and at the fact that such strange things had come out of their mouths. But soon they calmed down, and then Mary Jerdo came along, and showed me the different departments of Friendship House, and explained what they were.

The embarrassment of those young Negroes was something that gave me a picture of Harlem: the details of the picture were to be filled in later, but the essentials were already there.

Here in this huge, dark, steaming slum, hundreds of thousands of Negroes are herded together like cattle, most of them with nothing to eat and nothing to do. All the senses and imagination and sensibilities and emotions and sorrows and desires and hopes and ideas of a race with vivid feelings and deep emotional reactions are forced in upon themselves, bound inward by an iron ring of frustration: the prejudice that hems them in with its four insurmountable walls. In this huge cauldron, inestimable natural gifts, wisdom, love, music, science, poetry are stamped down and left to boil with the dregs of an elementally corrupted nature, and thousands upon thousands of souls are destroyed by vice and misery and degradation, obliterated, wiped out, washed from the register of the living, dehumanized.

What has not been devoured, in your dark furnace, Harlem, by marihuana, by gin, by insanity, hysteria, syphilis?

Those who manage somehow to swim to the top of the seething cauldron, and remain on its surface, through some special spiritual quality or other, or because they have been able to get away from Harlem, and go to some college or school, these are not all at once annihilated: but they are left with the dubious privilege of living out the only thing Harlem possesses in the way of an ideal. They are left with the sorry task of contemplating and imitating what passes for culture in the world of the white people.

Now the terrifying paradox of the whole thing is this: Harlem itself, and every individual Negro in it, is a living condemnation of our so-called "culture." Harlem is there by way of a divine indictment against New York City and the people who live downtown and make their money downtown. The brothels of Harlem, and all its prostitution, and its dope-rings, and all the rest are the mirror of the polite divorces and the manifold cultured adulteries of Park Avenue: they are God's commentary on the whole of our society.

Harlem is, in a sense, what God thinks of Hollywood. And Hollywood is all Harlem has, in its despair, to grasp at, by way of a surrogate for heaven.

The most terrible thing about it all is that there is not a Negro in the whole place who does not realize, somewhere in the depths of his nature, that the culture of the white men is not worth the dirt in Harlem's gutters. They sense that the whole thing is rotten, that it is a fake, that it is spurious, empty, a shadow of nothingness. And yet they are condemned to reach out for it, and to seem to desire it, and to pretend they like it, as if the whole thing were some kind of bitter cosmic conspiracy: as if they were thus being forced to work out, in their own lives, a clear representation of the misery which has corrupted the ontological roots of the white man's own existence.

The little children of Harlem are growing up, crowded together like sardines in the rooms of tenements full of vice, where evil takes place hourly and inescapably before their eyes, so that there is not an excess of passion, not a perversion of natural appetite with which they are not familiar before the age of six or seven: and this by way of an accusation of the polite and expensive and furtive sensualities and lusts of the rich whose sins have bred this abominable slum. The effect resembles and even magnifies the cause, and Harlem is the portrait of those through whose fault such things come into existence. What was heard in secret in the bedrooms and apartments of the rich and of the cultured and the educated and the white is preached from the housetops of Harlem and there declared for what it is, in all its horror, somewhat as it is seen in the eyes of God, naked and frightful.

No, there is not a Negro in the whole place who can fail to know, in the marrow of his own bones, that the white man's culture is not worth the jetsam in the Harlem River.

(1948)

SERVANT
AND MASTER
The Pecking Order

My old Mistiss promise me,
W'en she died, she'd set me free,
She lived so long dat 'er head got bal',
An' she give out'n de notion a-dyin'
     at all.
            Slave Secular

Mammy's victories over Scarlett were hard-
won and represented guile unknown to the
white mind.
            Margaret Mitchell
            Gone with the Wind

THE WHIPPING OF UNCLE HENRY

by Will N. Harben

"I do believe," said Mrs. Pelham, stooping to look through the oblong window of the milk-and-butter cellar toward the great barn across the farmyard, "I do believe Cobb an' Uncle Henry are fussin' ag'in."

"Shorely not," answered her old-maid sister, Miss Molly Meyers. She left her butter bowl and paddles, and bent her angular figure beside Mrs. Pelham, to see the white man and the black man who were gesticulating in each other's faces under the low wagon-shed that leaned against the barn.

The old women strained their ears to overhear what was said, but the stiff breeze from across the white-and-brown fields of cotton stretching toward the west bore the angry words away. Mrs. Pelham turned and drew the white cloths over her milkpans.

"Cobb will never manage them niggers in the world," she sighed. "Henry has Old Nick in 'im as big as a house ever since Mr. Pelham went off an' left Cobb in charge. Uncle Henry hain't minded one word Cobb has said, nur he won't. The whole crop is goin' to rack an' ruin. Thar's jest one thing to be done. Mr. Pelham has jest got to come home an' whip Henry. Nobody else could do it, an' he never will behave till it's done. Cobb tried to whip 'im t'other day when you was over the mountain, but Henry laid hold of a axhelve an' jest dared Cobb to tech 'im. That ended it. Cobb was afeared of 'im. Moreover, he's afeard Uncle Henry will put p'ison in his victuals, or do 'im or his family some bodily damage on the sly."

"It would be a powerful pity," returned Miss Molly, "fer Mr. Pelham to have to lay down his business in North Carolina, whar he's got so awful much to do, an' ride all that three hundred miles jest fer to whip one nigger. It looks like some other way mought be thought of. Couldn't you use your influence—"

"I've talked till I'm tired out," Mrs. Pelham interrupted. "Uncle Henry promises an' forms good resolutions, it seems like, but the very minute Cobb wants 'im to do some'n a little different from Mr. Pelham's way, Henry won't stir a peg. He jest hates the ground Cobb walks on. Well, I reckon Cobb *ain't* much of a man. He never would work a lick, an' if he couldn't git a job overseein' somebody's niggers he'd let his family starve to death. Nobody kin hate a lazy, good-for-nothin' white man like a nigger kin. Thar Cobb comes now, to complain to me, I reckon," added Mrs. Pelham, going back to the window. "An' bless your soul, Henry has took his seat out in the sun on the wagon-tongue, as big as life. I reckon the whole crop will go to rack an' ruin.

The next moment a tall, thin-visaged man with gray hair and beard stood in the cellar door.

"I'm jest about to the end o' my tether, Sister Pelham." (He always called her "Sister," because they were members of the same church.) "I can't get that black rascal to stir a step. I ordered Alf an' Jake to hold 'im, so I could give 'im a sound lashin', but they was afeared to tech 'im."

Mrs. Pelham looked at him over her glasses as she wiped her damp hands on her apron.

"You don't know how to manage niggers, Brother Cobb; I didn't much 'low you did the day Mr. Pelham left you in charge. The fust mornin', you went to the field with that hoss-whip in your hand, an' you've toted it about ever since. You mought know that would give offense. Mr. Pelham never toted one, an' yore doin' of it looks like you 'lowed you'd have a use for it."

"I acknowledge I don't know what to do," said Cobb, frowning down her reference to his whip. "I've been paid fer three months' work in advance, in the white mare an' colt Mr. Pelham give me, an' I've done sold 'em an' used the money. I'm free to confess that Brother Pelham's intrusts are bein' badly protected as things are goin'; but I've done my best."

"I reckon you have," answered Mrs. Pelham, with some scorn in her tone. "I reckon you have, accordin' to your ability an' judgment, an' we can't afford to lose your services after you've been paid. Thar is jest one thing left to do, an' that is fer Mr. Pelham to come home an' whip Henry. He's sowin' discord an' rebellion, an' needs a good, sound lashin'. The sooner it's done the better. Nobody can do it but Mr. Pelham, an' I'm goin' in now an' write the letter an' send it off. In the mean time, you'd better go on to work with the others, an' leave Henry alone till his master comes."

"Brother Pelham is the only man alive that could whip 'im," replied Cobb; "but it looks like a great pity an' expense for Brother Pel—" But the planter's wife had passed him and gone up the steps into the sitting-room. Cobb walked across the barnyard without looking at the stalwart negro sitting on the wagon-tongue. He threw his whip down at the barn, and he and half a dozen negroes went to the hayfields over the knoll toward the creek.

In half an hour Mrs. Pelham, wearing her gingham bonnet, came out to where Uncle Henry still sat sulking in the sun. As she approached him, she pushed back her bonnet till her gray hair and glasses showed beneath it.

"Henry," she said, sternly, "I've jest done a thing that I hated mightily to do."

"What's that, Mis' Liza?" He looked up as he asked the question, and then hung his head shamefacedly. He was about forty-five years of age. For one of his race he had a strong, intelligent face. Indeed, he possessed far more intelligence than the average negro. He was considered the most influential slave on any of the half-dozen plantations lying along that side of the river. He had learned to read, and by listening to the conversation of white people had (if he had acquired the colloquial speech of the middle-class whites) dropped almost every trace of the dialect current among his people. And on this he prided himself no little. He often led in prayer at the colored meeting-house on an adjoining plantation, and some of his prayers were more widely quoted and discussed than many of the sermons preached in the same church.

"I have wrote to yore master, Henry," answered Mrs. Pelham, "an' I've tol' 'im all yore doin's, an' tol' him to come home an' whip you fer disobeyin' Brother Cobb. I hated to do it, as I've jest said; but I couldn't see no other way out of the difficulty. Don't you think you deserve a whippin', Uncle Henry?"

"I don't know, Mis' Liza." He did not look up from the grass over which he swung his rag-covered leg and gaping brogan. "I don't know myself, Mis' Liza. I want to help Marse Jasper out all I can while he is off, but it seems like I jest can't work fer that man. Huh, overseer! I say overseer! Why, Mis' Liza, he ain't as good as a nigger! Thar ain't no pore white trash in all this valley country as low down as all his lay-out. He ain't fittin' fer a overseer of nothin'. He don't do anything like master did, nohow. He's too lazy to git in out of a rain. He—"

"That will do, Henry. Mr. Pelham put him over you, an' you've disobeyed. He'll be home in a few days, an' you an' him can settle it between you. He will surely give you a good whippin' when he gits here. Are you goin' to sit thar without layin' yore hand to a thing till he comes?"

"Now, you know me better'n that, Mis' Liza. I've done said I won't mind that man an' I reckon I won't; but the meadow-piece has obliged to be broken an' sowed in wheat. I'm goin' to do that jest as soon as the blacksmith fetches my bull-tongue plow."

Mrs. Pelham turned away silently. She had heard some talk of the government buying the negroes from their owners and setting them free. She ardently hoped this would be done, for she was sure they could then be hired cheaper than they could be owned and provided for. She disliked to see a negro whipped; but occasionally she could see no other way to make them do their duty.

From the dairy window, a few minutes later, she saw Uncle Henry put the gear on a mule, and, with a heavy plow-stock on his shoulder, start for the wheat-field beyond the meadow.

"He'll do two men's work over thar, jest to show what he kin do when he's let alone," she said to Miss Molly. "I hate to see 'im whipped. He's too old an' sensible in most things, an' it would jest break Lucinda's heart. Mr. Pelham had ruther cut off his right arm, too; but he'll do it, an' do it good, after havin' to come so far."

Mr. Pelham was a week in reaching the plantation. He wrote that it would take several days to arrange his affairs so that he could leave. He admitted that there was nothing left to do except to whip Uncle Henry soundly, and that they were right in thinking that Henry would not let anyone do it but himself. After the whipping he was sure that the negro would obey Cobb, and that matters would then move along smoothly.

When Mr. Pelham arrived, he left the stage at the cross-roads, half a mile from his house, and carpet-bag in hand, walked home through his own fields. He was a short, thick-set man of about sixty, round-faced, blue-eyed, and gray-haired. He wore a sack-coat, top-boots, and baggy trousers. He had a good-natured, kindly face, and walked with the quick step and general air of a busy man.

He had traveled three hundred miles, slept on the hard seat of a jolting train, eaten railroad pies and peanuts, and was covered with the grime of a dusty journey, all to whip one disobedient negro. Still, he was not out of humor, and after the whipping and lecture to his old servant he would travel back over the tiresome route and resume his business where he had left it.

His wife and sister-in-law were in the kitchen when they heard his step in the long hall. They went into the sitting-room, where he had put down his carpet-bag, and in the center of the floor stood swinging his hat and mopping his brow with his red handkerchief. He shook hands with the two women, and then sat down in his old seat in the chimney-corner.

"You want a bite to eat, an' a cup of coffee, I reckon," said Mrs. Pelham, solicitously.

"No, I kin wait till dinner. Whar's Cobb?"

"I seed 'im at the wagon-shed a minute ago," spoke up Miss Molly; "he was expectin' you, an' didn't go to the field with the balance."

"Tell 'im I want to see 'im."

Both of the women went out, and the overseer came in.

"Bad state of affairs, Brother Cobb," said the planter, as he shook hands. They both sat down with their knees to the embers.

"That it is, Brother Pelham, an' I take it you didn't count on it any more'n I did."

"Never dreamt of it. Has he been doin' any better since he heerd I was comin' to—whip 'im?"

"Not fer me, Brother Pelham. He hain't done a lick fer me; but all of his own accord, in the last week, he has broke and sowed all that meadow-piece in wheat, an' is now harrowin' it down to hide it from the birds. To do 'im jestice, I hain't seed so much work done in six days by any human bein' alive. He'll work for hisse'f, but he won't budge fer me."

Mr. Pelham broke into a soft, impulsive laugh, as if at the memory of something.

"They all had a big joke on me out in North Carolina," he said. "I tol' 'em I was comin' home to whip a nigger, an' they wouldn't believe a word of it. I reckon it is the fust time a body ever went so fur on sech business. They 'lowed I was jest homesick an' wanted a' excuse to come back.''

"They don't know what a difficult subject we got to handle," Cobb replied. "You are, without doubt, the only man in seven states that could whip 'im, Brother Pelham. I believe on my soul he'd kill anybody else that'd tech 'im. He's got the strangest notions about the rights of niggers I ever heerd from one of his kind. He's jest simply dangerous.''

"You're afeard of 'im, Brother Cobb, an' he's sharp enough to see it; that's all.''

The overseer winced. "I don't reckon I'm any more so than any other white man would be under the same circumstances. Henry mought not strike back lick fer lick on the spot—I say he mought not; an' then ag'in he mought— but he'd git even by some hook or crook, or I'm no judge o' niggers.''

Mr. Pelham rose. "Whar is he?''

"Over in the wheat-field.''

"Well, you go over thar n' tell 'im I'm here, an' to come right away down in the woods by the gum spring. I'll go down an' cut some hickory withes an' wait fer 'im. The quicker it's done an' over, the deeper the impression will be made on 'im. You see, I want 'im to realize that all this trip is jest solely on his account. I'll start back early in the mornin'. That will have its weight on his future conduct. An', Brother Cobb, I can't—I jest *can't* afford to be bothered ag'in. My business out thar at the lumber-camp won't admit of it. This whippin' has got to do fer the rest of the year. I think he'll mind you when I git through with 'im. I like 'im better'n any slave I ever owned, an' I'd a thousand times ruther take the whippin' myself; but it's got to be done.''

Cobb took himself to Henry in the wheatfield, and the planter went down into the edge of the woods near the spring. With his pocket-knife he cut two slender hickory switches about five feet in length. He trimmed off the out-shooting twigs and knots, and rounded the butts smoothly.

From where he sat on a fallen log, he could see, across the boggy swamp of bulrushes, the slight rise on which Henry was at work. He could hear Henry's mellow, resonant "Haw" and "Gee," as he drove his mule and harrow from end to end of the field, and saw Cobb slowly making his way toward him.

Mr. Pelham laid the switches down beside him, put his knife in his pocket, and stroked his chin thoughtfully. Suddenly he felt a tight sensation in his throat. The solitary figure of the negro as he trudged along by the harrow seemed vaguely pathetic. Henry had always been such a noble fellow, so reliable and trustworthy. They had really been, in one way, more like brothers than master and slave. He had told Henry secrets that he had confided to no other human being, and they had laughed and cried together over certain adventures and sorrows. About ten years before, Mr. Pelham's horse had run away and thrown him against a tree and broken his leg. Henry had heard his cries and run to him. They were two miles from the farmhouse, and it was a bitterly cold day, but the stalwart negro had taken him in his arms and carried him home and laid him down on his bed. There had been a great deal of excitement about the house, and it was not until after the doctor had come and dressed the broken limb that it was learned that Henry had fallen in a swoon in his cabin and lain there unconscious for an hour, his wife and children being away. Indeed, he had been almost as long recovering as had been his master.

Henry had stopped his mule. Cobb had called to him, and was approaching. Then Mr. Pelham knew that the overseer was delivering his message, for the negro had turned his head and was looking toward the woods which hid his master from view. Mr. Pelham felt himself flush all over. Could he be going to whip Henry—really to lash his bare back with those switches? How strange it seemed all at once! And that this should be their first meeting after a two months' separation!

In his home-comings before, Uncle Henry had always been the first to meet him with outstretched hand. But the negro had to be whipped. Mr. Pelham had said it in North Carolina; he had said it to Cobb, and he had written it to his wife. Yes, it must be done; and if done at all, of course it must be done right.

He saw Henry hitch his mule to a chestnut-tree in the field and Cobb turn to make his way back to the farm-house. Then he watched Henry approaching till the bushes which skirted the field hid him from view. There was no sound for several minutes except the rustling of the fallen leaves in the woods behind him, and then Uncle Henry's head and shoulders appeared above the broom-sedge near by.

"Howdy do, Marse Jasper?" he cried; and the next instant he broke through the yellow sedge and stood before his master.

"Purty well, Henry." Mr. Pelham could not refuse the black hand which was extended, and which caught his with a hearty grasp. "I hope you are as well as common, Henry?"

"Never better in my life, Marse Jasper."

The planter had risen, but he now sat down beside his switches. For a moment nothing was said. Uncle Henry awkwardly bent his body and his neck to see if his mule were standing where he had left him, and his master looked steadfastly at the ground.

"Sit down, Henry," he said, presently; and the negro took a seat on the extreme end of the log and folded his black, seamed hands over his knee. "I want to talk to you first of all. Something of a very unpleasant, unavoidable nature has got to take place betwixt us, an' I want to give you a sound talkin' to beforehan'."

"All right, Marse Jasper; I'm a-listenin'." Henry looked again toward his mule. "I did want to harrow that wheat down 'fore them birds eat it up; but I got time, I reckon."

The planter coughed and cleared his throat. He tried to cross his short, fat legs by sliding the right one up to the knee of the left, but owing to the lowness of the log, he was unable to do this, so he left his legs to themselves, and with a hand on either side of him, leaned back.

"Do you remember, Uncle Henry, twenty years ago, when you belonged to old Heaton Pelzer an' got to hankerin' after that yellow girl of mine jest after I bought her in South Carolina?"

"Mighty plain, Master Jasper, mighty plain." Henry's face showed a tendency to smile at the absurdity of the question.

"Lucinda was jest as much set after you, it seemed," went on the planter. "Old Pelzer was workin' you purty nigh to death on his pore, wore-out land, an' pointedly refused to buy Lucinda so you could marry her, nur he wouldn't consent to you marryin' a slave of mine. Ain't that so?"

"Yes, Marse Jasper, that's so, sir."

"I had jest as many niggers as I could afford to keep, an' a sight more. I was already up to my neck in debt, an' to buy you I knowed I'd have to borrow money an' mortgage the last thing I had. But you come to me night after night, when you could sneak off, an' begged an' begged to be bought, so that I jest didn't have the heart to refuse. So, jest to accommodate you, I got up the money an' bought you, payin' fully a third more fer you than men of yore age was goin' at. You are married now, an' got three as likely children as ever come into the world, an' a big buxom wife that loves you, an' if I haven't treated you an' them right I never heerd of it."

"Never was a better master on earth, Marse Jasper. If thar is, I hain't never seed 'im." Henry's face was full of emotion. He picked up his slouch hat from the grass and folded it awkwardly on the log beside him.

"From that day till this," the planter went on, "I've been over my head in debt, an' I can really trace it to that transaction. It was the straw that broke the camel's back, as the feller said. Well, now, Henry, six months ago, when I saw that openin' to deal in lumber in North Carolina, it seemed to me to be my chance to work out of debt, if I could jest find somebody to look after my farm. I found a man, Henry—a good, clever, honest man, as everybody said, an' a member of Big Bethel Church. For a certain consideration he agreed to take charge. That consideration I've paid in advance, an' it's gone; I couldn't git it back.

"Now, how has it turned out? I had hardly got started out thar before one of my niggers—the very one I relied on the most—has played smash with all my plans. You begun by turnin' up yore nose at Brother Cobb, an' then by openly disobeyin' 'im. Then he tried to punish you—the right that the law gives a overseer—an' you up an' dared him to tech you, an'—"

"Marse Jasper—"

"Hold yore tongue till I'm through."

"All right, Marse Jasper, but—"

"You openly defied 'im, that's enough; you broke up the order of the whole thing, an' yore mistress was so upset that she had to send fer me. Now, Henry, I hain't never laid the lash on you in my life, an' I'd ruther take it myself than to have to do it, but I hain't come three hundred miles jest to talk to you. I'm goin' to whip you, Henry, an' I'm goin' to do it right, if thar's enough strength in my arm. You needn't shake yore head an' sulk. No matter what you refused to let Cobb an' the rest of 'em do, you are a-goin' to take what I'm goin' to give you without a word, because you know it's just an' right.''

Henry's face was downcast, and his master could not see his eyes, but a strange, rebellious fire had suddenly kindled in them, and he was stubbornly silent. Mr. Pelham could not have dreamed of what was passing in his mind.

"Henry, you an' me are both religious men," said the planter, after he had waited for a moment. "Let's kneel right down here by this log an' commune with the Lord on this matter.''

Without a word the negro rose and knelt, his face in his hands, his elbows on the log. There never had been a moment when Uncle Henry was not ready to pray or listen to a prayer. He prided himself on his own powers in that line, and had unbounded respect even for the less skillful efforts of others. Mr. Pelham knelt very deliberately and began to pray:

"Our heavenly Father, it is with extreme sadness an' sorrow that we come to Thee this bright, sunny day. Our sins have been many, an' we hardly know when our deeds are acceptable in Thy sight; but bless all our efforts, we pray Thee, for the sake of Him that died for us, an' let us not walk into error in our zeal to do Thy holy will.

"Lord, Thou knowest the hearts of Thy humble supplicant an' this man beside him. Thou, through the existin' laws of this land, hast put him into my care an' keepin' an' made me responsible to a human law for his good or bad behavior. Lord, on this occasion it seems my duty to punish him for disobedience, an' we pray Thee to sanction what is about to take place with Thy grace. Let no anger or malice rest in our hearts during the performance of this disagreeable task, an' let the whole redound to Thy glory, for ever an' ever, through the mercy of Thy Son, our Lord Jesus Christ. Amen.''

Mr. Pelham rose to his feet stiffly, for he had touches of rheumatism, and the ground was cold. He brushed his trousers, and laid hold of his switches. But to his surprise, Henry had not risen. If it had not been for the stiffness of his elbows, and the upright position of his long feet, which stood on their toes erect as gate-posts, Mr. Pelham might have thought that he had dropped asleep.

For a moment the planter stood silent, glancing first at the mass of ill-clothed humanity at his feet, and then sweeping his eyes over the quiet, rolling land which lay between him and the farmhouse. How awfully still everything was! He saw Henry's cabin near the farmhouse. Lucinda was out in the yard picking up chips, and one of Uncle Henry's children was clinging to her skirts. The planter was very fond of Lucinda, and he wondered what she would do if she knew he was about to whip her husband. But why did the fellow not get up? Surely that was an unusual way to act. In some doubt as to what he ought to do, Mr. Pelham sat down again. It should not be said of him that he had ever interrupted any man's prayers to whip him. As he sat down, the log rolled slightly, the elbows of the negro slid off the bark, and Henry's head almost came in contact with the log. But he took little notice of the accident, and glancing at his master from the corner of his eye, he deliberately replaced his elbows, pressed his hands together, and began to pray aloud:

"Our heavenly Father." These words were spoken in a deep, sonorous tone, and as Uncle Henry paused for an instant the echoes groaned and murmured and died against the hill behind him. Mr. Pelham bowed his head to his hand. He had heard Henry pray before, and now he dreaded hearing him, he hardly knew why. He felt a strange creeping sensation in his spine.

"Our heavenly Father," the slave repeated, in his mellow sing-song tone, "Thou knowest that I am Thy humble servant. Thou knowest that I have brought to Thee all my troubles since my change of heart—that I have left nothing hidden from Thee, who art my Maker, my Redeemer, an' my Lord. Thou knowest that I have for a long time harbored the belief that the black man has some rights that he don't git under existin' laws, but which, Thy will be done, will come in due time, like the harvest follows the plantin'. Thou knowest, an' I know, that Henry Pelham is nigher to Thee than a dumb brute, an' that it ain't no way to lift a nigger up to beat 'im like a horse or a ox. I have said this to Thee in secret prayer, time an' ag'in, an' Thou knowest how I stand on it, if my master don't. Thou knowest that before Thee I have vowed that I would die before any man, white or black, kin beat the blood out'n my back. I may have brought trouble an' vexation to Marse Jasper, I don't dispute that, but he had no business puttin' me under that low-down, white-trash overseer an' goin' off so far. Heavenly Father, thou knowest I love Marse Jasper, an' I would work fer 'im till I die; but he is ready to put the lash to me an' disgrace me before my wife an' children. Give my arms strength, Lord, to defend myself even against him—against him who has, up to now, won my respect an' love by forbearance an' kindness. He has said it, Lord—he has said that he will whip me; but I've said, also, that no man shall do it. Give me strength to battle fer the right, an' if he is hurt—bad hurt—may the Lord have mercy on him! This I ask through the mercy an' the blood of the Lord Jesus Christ. Amen."

Henry rose awkwardly to his feet and looked down at his master, who sat silent on the log. Mr. Pelham's face was pale. There was a look of indecision under the pallor. He held one of the switches by the butt in his hand, and with its tapering end tapped the brown leaves between his legs. He looked at the imperturbable countenace of the negro for fully a minute before he spoke.

"Do you mean to say, Henry," he asked, "that you are a-goin' to resist me by force?"

"I reckon I am, Marse Jasper, if nothin' else won't do you. That's what I have promised the Lord time an' ag'in since Cobb come to boss me. I wasn't thinkin' about you then, Marse Jasper, because I didn't 'low you ever would try such a thing; but I said *any* white man, an' I can't take it back."

The planter looked up at the stalwart man towering over him. Henry could toss him about like a ball. In his imagination he had pictured the faithful fellow bowed before him, patiently submitting to his blows, but the present contingency had never entered his mind. He tried to be angry, but the good-natured face of the slave he loved made it impossible.

"Sit down thar, Henry," he said; and when the negro had obeyed, he continued, almost appealingly: "I have told the folks in North Carolina that I was comin' home to whip you, you see. I have told yore mistress, an' I have told Cobb. I'll look like a purty fool if I don't do it."

A regretful softness came into the face of the negro, and he hung his head, and for a moment picked at the bark of the log with his long thumbnail.

"I'm might sorry, Marse Jasper," he answered, after remaining silent for a while. "But you see I've done promised the Lord; you wouldn't have me—what do all them folks amount to beside the Lord? No; a body ought to be careful about what he's promised the Almighty."

Mr. Pelham had no reply forthcoming. He realized that he was simply not going to whip Uncle Henry, and he did not want to appear ridiculous in the eyes of his friends. The negro saw by his master's silence that he was going to escape punishment, and that made him more humble and sympathetic than ever. He was genuinely sorry for his master.

"You have done told 'em all you was goin' to whip me, I know, Marse Jasper; but why don't you jest let 'em think you done it? I don't keer, jest so I kin keep my word. Lucinda ain't a-goin' to believe I'd take it, no-how."

At this loophole of escape the face of the planter brightened. For a moment he felt like grasping Henry's hand: then a cloud came over his face.

"But," he demurred, "what about yore future conduct? Will you mind what Cobb tells you?"

"I jest can't do that, Marse Jasper. Me 'n him jest can't git along together. He ain't no man at all."

"Well, what on earth am I to do? I've got to have an overseer, an' I've got to go back to North Carolina."

"You don't have to have no overseer fer me, Marse Jasper. Have I ever failed to keep a promise to you, Marse Jasper?"

"No; but I can't be here."

"I'll tell you what I'll do, Marse Jasper. Would you be satisfied with my part of the work if I tend all the twenty-acre piece beyond my cabin, an' make a good crop on it, an' look after all the cattle an' stock, an' clear the woodland on the hill an' cord up the firewood?"

"You couldn't do it, Henry."

"I'll come mighty nigh it, Marse Jasper, if you'll let me be my own boss an' be responsible to you when you git back. Mr. Cobb kin boss the rest of 'em. They don't keer how much he swings his whip an' struts around."

"Henry, I'll do it. I can trust you a sight better than I can Cobb. I know you will keep yore word. But you will not say anything about—"

"Not a word, Marse Jasper. They all may 'low I'm half dead, if they want to." Then the two men laughed together heartily and parted.

The overseer and the two white women were waiting for Mr. Pelham in the backyard as he emerged from the woods and came toward the house. Mrs. Pelham opened the gate for him, scanning his face anxiously.

"I was afeard you an' Henry had had some difficulty," she said, in a tone of relief; "he has been that hard to manage lately."

Mr. Pelham grunted and laughed in disdain.

"I'll bet he was the hardest you ever tackled," ventured Cobb.

"Anybody can manage him," the planter replied—"anybody that has got enough determination. You see Henry knows me."

"But do you think he'll obey my orders after you go back?" Cobb had followed Mr. Pelham into the sitting-room, and he anxiously waited for the reply to his question.

The planter stooped to spit into a corner of the chimney, and then slowly and thoughtfully stroked his chin with his hand. "That's the only trouble, Brother Cobb," he said, thrusting his fat hands into the pockets of his trousers and turning his back to the fire-place; "that's the only drawback. To be plain with you, Brother Cobb, I'm afeard you don't inspire respect; men that don't own niggers seldom do. I believe on my soul that nigger would die fightin' before he'd obey yore orders. To tell the truth, I had to arrange a plan, an' that is one reason— one reason—why I was down thar so long. After what happened today" (Mr. Pelham spoke significantly and stroked his chin again) "he'll mind me jest as well at a distance as if I was here on the spot. He'd have a mortal dread of havin' me come so fur ag'in."

"I hope you wasn't cruel, Mr. Pelham," said Mrs. Pelham, who had just come in. "Henry's so good-hearted—"

"Oh, he'll git over it," replied the planter, ambiguously. "But, as I was goin' on to say, I had to fix another plan. I have set him a sort o' task to do while I'm away, an' believe he'll do it, Brother Cobb. So all you'll have to do will be to look after the other niggers."

The plan suited Cobb exactly; but when Mr. Pelham came home the following summer it was hard to hear him say that Uncle Henry had accomplished more than any three of the other negroes.

(1900)

From

THE GENTLE LENA
by Gertrude Stein

Lena was patient, gentle, sweet and german. She had been a servant for four years and had liked it very well.

Lena had been brought from Germany to Bridgepoint by a cousin and had been in the same place there for four years.

This place Lena had found very good. There was a pleasant, unexacting mistress and her children, and they all liked Lena very well.

There was a cook there who scolded Lena a great deal but Lena's german patience held no suffering and the good incessant woman really only scolded so for Lena's good.

Lena's german voice when she knocked and called the family in the morning was as awakening, as soothing, and as appealing, as a delicate soft breeze in midday, summer. She stood in the hallway every morning a long time in her unexpectant and unsuffering german patience calling to the young ones to get up. She would call and wait a long time and then call again, always even, gentle, patient, while the young ones fell back often into that precious, tense, last bit of sleeping that gives a strength of joyous vigor in the young, over them that have come to the readiness of middle age, in their awakening.

Lena had good hard work all morning, and on the pleasant, sunny afternoons she was sent out into the park to sit and watch the little two year old girl baby of the family.

The other girls, all them that make the pleasant, lazy crowd, that watch the children in the sunny afternoons out in the park, all liked the simple, gentle, german Lena very well. They all, too, liked very well to tease her, for it was so easy to make her mixed and troubled, and all helpless, for she could never learn to know just what the other quicker girls meant by the queer things they said.

The two or three of these girls, the ones that Lena always sat with, always worked together to confuse her. Still it was pleasant, all this life for Lena.

The little girl fell down sometimes and cried, and then Lena had to soothe her. When the little girl would drop her hat, Lena had to pick it up and hold it. When the little girl was bad and threw away her playthings, Lena told her she could not have them and took them from her to hold until the little girl should need them.

It was all a peaceful life for Lena, almost as peaceful as a pleasant leisure. The other girls, of course, did tease her, but then that only made a gentle stir within her.

Lena was a brown and pleasant creature, brown as blonde races often have them brown, brown, not with the yellow or the red or the chocolate brown of sun burned countries, but brown with the clear color laid flat on the light toned skin beneath, the plain, spare brown that makes it right to have been made with hazel eyes, and not too abundant straight, brown hair, hair that only later deepens itself into brown from the straw yellow of a german childhood.

Lena had the flat chest, straight back and forward falling shoulders of the patient and enduring working woman, though her body was now still in its milder girlhood and work had not yet made these lines too clear.

The rarer feeling that there was with Lena, showed in all the even quiet of her body movements, but in all it was the strongest in the patient, old-world ignorance, and earth made pureness of her brown, flat, soft featured face. Lena had eyebrows that were a wondrous thickness. They were black, and spread, and very cool, with their dark color and their beauty, and beneath them were her hazel eyes, simple and human, with the earth patience of the working, gentle, german woman.

Yes it was all a peaceful life for Lena. The other girls, of course, did tease her, but then that only made a gentle stir within her.

"What you got on your finger Lena," Mary, one of the girls she always sat with, one day asked her. Mary was good natured, quick, intelligent and Irish.

Lena had just picked up the fancy paper made accordion that the little girl had dropped beside her, and was making it squeak sadly as she pulled it with her brown, strong, awkward finger.

"Why, what is it, Mary, paint?" said Lena, putting her finger to her mouth to taste the dirt spot.

"That's awful poison Lena, don't you know?" said Mary, "that green paint that you just tasted."

Lena had sucked a good deal of the green paint from her finger. She stopped and looked hard at the finger. She did not know just how much Mary meant by what she said.

"Ain't it poison, Nellie, that green paint, that Lena sucked just now," said Mary. "Sure it is Lena, its real poison, I ain't foolin' this time anyhow."

Lena was a little troubled. She looked hard at her finger where the paint was, and she wondered if she had really sucked it.

It was still a little wet on the edges and she rubbed it off a long time on the inside of her dress, and in between she wondered and looked at the finger and thought, was it really poison that she had just tasted.

"Ain't it too bad, Nellie, Lena should have sucked that," Mary said.

Nellie smiled and did not answer. Nellie was dark and thin, and looked Italian. She had a big mass of black hair that she wore high up on her head, and that made her face look very fine.

Nellie always smiled and did not say much, and then she would look at Lena to perplex her.

And so they all three sat with their little charges in the pleasant sunshine a long time. And Lena would often look at her finger and wonder if it was really poison that she had just tasted and then she would rub her finger on her dress a little harder.

Mary laughed at her and teased her and Nellie smiled a little and looked queerly at her.

Then it came time, for it was growing cooler, for them to drag together the little ones, who had begun to wander, and to take each one back to its own mother. And Lena never knew for certain whether it was really poison, that green stuff that she had tasted.

During these four years of service, Lena always spent her Sundays out at the house of her aunt, who had brought her four years before to Bridgepoint.

This aunt, who had brought Lena, four years before, to Bridgepoint, was a hard, ambitious, well meaning, german woman. Her husband was a grocer in the town, and they were very well to do. Mrs. Haydon, Lena's aunt, had two daughters who were just beginning as young ladies, and she had a little boy who was not honest and who was very hard to manage.

Mrs. Haydon was a short, stout, hard built, german woman. She always hit the ground very firmly and compactly as she walked. Mrs. Haydon was all a compact and well hardened mass, even to her face, reddish and darkened from its early blonde, with its hearty, shiny, cheeks, and doubled chin well covered over with the uproll from her short, square neck.

The two daughters, who were fourteen and fifteen, looked like un-kneaded, unformed mounds of flesh beside her.

The elder girl, Mathilda, was blonde, and slow, and simple, and quite fat. The younger, Bertha, who was almost as tall as her sister, was dark, and quicker, and she was heavy, too, but not really fat.

These two girls the mother had brought up very firmly. They were well taught for their position. They were always both well dressed, in the same kinds of hats and dresses, as is becoming in two german sisters. The mother liked to have them dressed in red. Their best clothes were red dresses, made of good heavy cloth, and strongly trimmed with braid of a glistening black. They had stiff, red felt hats, trimmed with black velvet ribbon, and a bird. The mother dressed matronly, in a bonnet and in black, always sat between her two big daughters, firm, directing, and repressed.

The only weak spot in this good german woman's conduct was the way she spoiled her boy, who was not honest and who was very hard to manage.

The father of this family was a decent, quiet, heavy, and uninterfering german man. He tried to cure the boy of his bad ways, and make him honest, but the mother could not make herself let the father manage, and so the boy was brought up very badly.

Mrs. Haydon's girls were now only just beginning as young ladies, and so to get her niece, Lena, married, was just then the most important thing that Mrs. Haydon had to do.

Mrs. Haydon had four years before gone to Germany to see her parents, and had taken the girls with her. This visit had been for Mrs. Haydon most successful, though her children had not liked it very well.

Mrs. Haydon was a good and generous woman, and she patronized her parents grandly, and all the cousins who came from all about to see her. Mrs Haydon's people were of the middling class of farmers. They were not peasants, and they lived in a town of some pretension, but it all seemed very poor and smelly to Mrs. Haydon's american born daughters.

Mrs. Haydon liked it all. It was familiar, and then here she was so wealthy and important. She listened and decided, and advised all of her relations how to do things better. She arranged their present and their future for them, and showed them how in the past they had been wrong in all their methods.

Mrs Haydon's only trouble was with her two daughters, whom she could not make behave well to her parents. The two girls were very nasty to all their numerous relations. Their mother could hardly make them kiss their grandparents, and every day the girls would get a scolding. But then Mrs. Haydon was so very busy that she did not have time to really manage her stubborn daughters.

These hard working, earth-rough german cousins were to these american born children, ugly and dirty, and as far below them as were italian or negro workmen, and they could not see how their mother could ever bear to touch them, and then all the women dressed so funny, and were worked all rough and different.

The two girls stuck up their noses at them all, and always talked in English to each other about how they hated all these people and how they wished their mother would not do so. The girls could talk some German, but they never chose to use it.

It was her eldest brother's family that most interested Mrs. Haydon. Here there were eight children, and out of the eight, five of them were girls.

Mrs. Haydon thought it would be a fine thing to take one of these girls back with her to Bridgepoint and get her well started. Everybody liked that she should do so, and they were all willing that it should be Lena.

Lena was the second girl in her large family. She was at this time just seventeen years old. Lena was not an important daughter in the family. She was always sort of dreamy and not there. She worked hard and went very regularly at it, but even good work never seemed to bring her near.

Lena's age just suited Mrs. Haydon's purpose. Lena could first go out to service, and learn how to do things, and then, when she was a little older, Mrs. Haydon could get her a good husband. And then Lena was so still and docile, she would never want to do things her own way. And then, too, Mrs. Haydon, with all her hardness had wisdom, and she could feel the rarer strain there was in Lena.

Lena was willing to go with Mrs. Haydon. Lena did not like her german life very well. It was not the hard work but the roughness that disturbed her. The people were not gentle, and the men when they were glad were very boisterous, and would lay hold of her and roughly tease her. They were good people enough around her, but it was all harsh and dreary for her.

Lena did not really know that she did not like it. She did not know that she was always dreamy and not there. She did not think whether it would be different for her away off there in Bridgepoint. Mrs. Haydon took her and got her different kinds of dresses, and then took her with them to the steamer. Lena did not really know what it was that had happened to her.

Mrs. Haydon, and her daughters, and Lena traveled second class on the steamer. Mrs. Haydon's daughters hated that their mother should take Lena. They hated to have a cousin, who was to them, little better than a nigger, and then everybody on the steamer there would see her. Mrs. Haydon's daughters said things like this to their mother, but she never stopped to hear them, and the girls did not dare to make their meaning very clear. And so they could only go on hating Lena hard, together. They could not stop her from going back with them to Bridgepoint.

Lena was very sick on the voyage. She thought, surely before it was over that she would die. She was so sick she could not even wish that she had not started. She could not eat, she could not moan, she was just blank and scared, and sure that every minute she would die. She could not hold herself in, nor help herself in her trouble. She just staid where she had been put, pale, and scared, and weak, and sick, and sure that she was going to die.

Mathilda and Bertha Haydon had no trouble from having Lena for a cousin on the voyage, until the last day that they were on the ship, and by that time they had made their friends and could explain.

Mrs. Haydon went down every day to Lena, gave her things to make her better, held her head when it was needful, and generally was good and did her duty by her.

Poor Lena had no power to be strong in such trouble. She did not know how to yield to her sickness nor endure. She lost all her little sense of being in her suffering. She was so scared, and then at her best, Lena, who was patient, sweet and quiet, had not self-control, nor any active courage.

Poor Lena was so scared and weak, and every minute she was sure that she would die.

After Lena was on land again a little while, she forgot all her bad suffering. Mrs. Haydon got her the good place, with the pleasant unexacting mistress, and her children, and Lena began to learn some English and soon was very happy and content.

All her Sundays out Lena spent at Mrs. Haydon's house. Lena would have liked much better to spend her Sundays with the girls she always sat with, and who often asked her, and who teased her and made a gentle stir within her, but it never came to Lena's unexpectant and unsuffering german nature to do something different from what was expected of her, just because she would like it that way better. Mrs. Haydon had said that Lena was to come to her house every other Sunday, and so Lena always went there.

Mrs. Haydon was the only one of her family who took any interest in Lena. Mr. Haydon did not think much of her. She was his wife's cousin and he was good to her, but she was for him stupid, and a little simple, and very dull, and sure some day to need help and to be in trouble. All young poor relations, who were brought from Germany to Bridgepoint were sure, before long, to need help and to be in trouble.

The little Haydon boy was always very nasty to her. He was a hard child for any one to manage, and his mother spoiled him very badly. Mrs. Haydon's daughters as they grew older did not learn to like Lena any better. Lena never knew that she did not like them either. She did not know that she was only happy with the other quicker girls, she always sat with in the park, and who laughed at her and always teased her.

Mathilda Haydon, the simple, fat, blonde, older daughter felt very badly that she had to say that this was her cousin Lena, this Lena who was little better for her than a nigger. Mathilda was an overgrown, slow, flabby, blonde, stupid, fat girl, just beginning as a woman; thick in her speech and dull and simple in her mind, and very jealous of all her family and of other girls, and proud that she could have good dresses and new hats and learn music, and hating very badly to have a cousin who was a common servant. And then Mathilda remembered very strongly that dirty nasty place that Lena came from and that Mathilda had so turned up her nose at, and where she had been made so angry because her mother scolded her and liked all those rough cow-smelly people.

Then, too, Mathilda would get very mad when her mother had Lena at their parties, and when she talked about how good Lena was, to certain german mothers in whose sons, perhaps, Mrs. Haydon might find Lena a good husband. All this would make the dull, blonde, fat Mathilda very angry. Sometimes she would get so angry that she would, in her thick, slow way, and with jealous anger blazing in her light blue eyes, tell her mother that she did not see how she could like that nasty Lena; and then her mother would scold Mathilda, and tell her that she knew her cousin Lena was poor and Mathilda must be good to poor people.

Mathilda Haydon did not like relations to be poor. She told all her girl friends what she thought of Lena, and so the girls would never talk to Lena at Mrs. Haydon's parties. But Lena in her unsuffering and unexpectant patience never really knew that she was slighted. When Mathilda was with her girls in the street or in the park and would see Lena, she always turned up her nose and barely nodded to her, and then she would tell her friends how funny her mother was to take care of people like that Lena, and how, back in Germany, all Lena's people lived just like pigs.

The younger daughter, the dark, large, but not fat, Bertha Haydon, who was very quick in her mind, and in her ways, and who was the favorite with her father, did not like Lena, either. She did not like her because for her Lena was a fool and so stupid, and she would let those Irish and Italian girls laugh at her and tease her, and everybody always made fun of Lena, and Lena never got mad, or even had sense enough to know that they were all making an awful fool of her.

(1909)

CHILD OF THE ROMANS
by Carl Sandburg

The dago shovelman sits by the railroad track
Eating a noon meal of bread and bologna.
    A train whirls by, and men and women at tables
    Alive with red roses and yellow jonquils,
    Eat steaks running with brown gravy,
    Strawberries and cream, eclairs and coffee.
The dago shovelman finishes the dry bread and bologna,
Washes it down with a dipper from the water-boy,
And goes back to the second half of a ten-hour day's work
Keeping the road-bed so the roses and jonquils
Shake hardly at all in the cut glass vases
Standing slender on the tables in the dining cars.

(1916)

FOR A LADY I KNOW
by Countee Cullen

She even thinks that up in heaven
    Her class lies late and snores,
While poor black cherubs rise at seven
    To do celestial chores.

(1925)

UPSTAIRS DOWNSTAIRS
by Hervey Allen

The judge, who lives impeccably upstairs
With dull decorum and its implication,
Has all his servants in to family prayers,
And edifies *his* soul with exhortation.

Meanwhile his blacks live wastefully downstairs;
Not always chaste, they manage to exist
With less decorum than the judge upstairs,
And find withal a something that he missed.

This painful fact a Swede philosopher,
Who tarried for a fortnight in our city,
Remarked, one evening at the meal, before
We paralyzed him silent with our pity—

Saying the black man living with the white
Had given more than white men could requite.

(1922)

BLACK BOY
by Carl Carmer

Mark Lee was born a month before M. L.;
M. L. was named for him as nigger boys
Are often christened out of compliment
To white folks' boys who live in the Big House,
And M. L.'s daddy got a present for it.

Well, from the time that those two boys could walk
They were together always, rain or shine;
That's why we had to call the one M. L.—
To tell which boy we meant. A funny pair

They looked, for while Mark Lee was blond and pale,
M. L. was satin-black—except his teeth,
Snow-white and 'most as big as daisy petals.

I knew them first when I was a small girl:
Sometimes I used to see them playing horse,
And M. L. always was the prancing steed
While Mark Lee drove, with many rousing oaths:
But all his words and flicks of his birch whip
Just stretched M. L.'s wide grin a little wider.

One day I saw a big boy hit Mark Lee,
He hit him hard, but Mark Lee didn't wince—
He stepped aside, turned round, and said quite low,
"Hit him, M. L.," and M. L., smiling, hit,
And the boy began to cry and ran away.

Mark Lee and I were fifth-grade pupils once
(Though I was younger, he was slow to learn),
And one examination day in spring
I saw him sitting by the open window
And frowning at the questions on the board.
Then, as I looked, I saw him pass his slate
Outside and saw a yellow hand reach up
From underneath the window, snatch the slate,
And vanish. Soon it came back up again,
And teacher came and got it, and she said,
"Mark Lee, you're doing better, and I'm glad."

A few years later on an April day
Worth Dunn, a little red-haired friend, and I
Were eating ice-cream at the corner store
When, unbeknownst, Mark Lee crept softly up
And clipped an auburn curl from Worth's bright head.
She turned upon him and began to scold
As only red-heads can—she stamped her foot—
Her temper filled her mouth with scorching words.
Mark Lee stood still a moment; then he called
"M. L.," and M. L. came and took his master's place,
Stood grinning under Worth's high-voiced abuse
While Mark Lee strolled on down the shady street.

The last time that I saw the two of them
Mark Lee lay in his bed in the Big House,

His face chalk-white beneath his yellow curls.
M. L. sat by him there, alone and still,
Blacker than coal beside the tumbled sheets,
And neither boy looked up as I walked in;
Their eyes were fixed upon each other now.
M. L.'s broad grin was saying as before,
"Step back, white boy, and let me take your place,"
But the blue eyes held a stricken, staring look,
A look of puzzlement and wild despair,
For poor Mark Lee at last had come upon
One thing that M. L. couldn't do for him.

(1930)

A SEQUENCE OF SERVANTS
by James Thurber

When I look back on the long line of servants my mother hired during the years I lived at home, I remember clearly ten or twelve of them (we had about a hundred and sixty-two, all told, but few of them were memorable). There was, among the immortals, Dora Gedd, a quiet, mousy girl of thirty-two who one night shot at a man in her room, throwing our household into an uproar that was equalled perhaps only by the goings-on the night the ghost got in. Nobody knew how her lover, a morose garage man, got into the house, but everybody for two blocks knew how he got out. Dora had dressed up in a lavender evening gown for the occasion and she wore a mass of jewelry, some of which was my mother's. She kept shouting something from Shakespeare after the shooting—I forget just what—and pursued the gentleman downstairs from her attic room. When he got to the second floor he rushed into my father's room. It was this entrance, and not the shot or the shouting, that aroused father, a deep sleeper always. "Get me out of here!" shouted the victim. This situation rapidly developed, from then on, into one of those bewildering involvements for which my family had, I am afraid, a kind of unhappy genius. When the cops arrived Dora was shooting out the Welsbach gas mantles in the living room, and her gentleman friend had fled. By dawn everything was quiet once more.

There were others. Gertie Straub: big, genial, and ruddy, a collector of pints of rye (we learned after she was gone), who came in after two o'clock one night from a dancing party at Buckeye Lake and awakened us by bumping into and knocking over furniture. "Who's down there?" called mother from upstairs. "It's me, dearie," said Gertie, "Gertie Straub." "What are you *doing?*" demanded mother. "Dusting," said Gertie.

Juanemma Kramer was one of my favorites. Her mother loved the name Juanita so dearly that she had worked the first part of it into the names of all her daughters—they were (in addition to a Juanita) Juanemma, Juanhelen, and Juangrace. Juanemma was a thin, nervous maid who lived in constant dread of being hypnotized. Nor were her fears unfounded, for she was so extremely susceptible to hypnotic suggestion that one evening at B. F. Keith's theatre when a man on the stage was hypnotized, Juanemma, in the audience, was hypnotized too and floundered out into the aisle making the same cheeping sound that the subject on the stage, who had been told he was a chicken, was making. The act was abandoned and some xylophone players were brought on to restore order. One night, when our house was deep in quiet slumber, Juanemma became hypnotized in her sleep. She dreamed that a man "put her under" and then disappeared without "bringing her out." This was explained when, at last, a police surgeon whom we called in—he was the only doctor we could persuade to come out at three in the morning—slapped her into consciousness. It got so finally that any buzzing or whirling sound or any flashing object would put Juanemma under, and we had to let her go. I was reminded of her recently when, at a performance of the movie *Rasputin and the Empress,* there came the scene in which Lionel Barrymore as the unholy priest hypnotizes the Czarevitch by spinning before his eyes a glittering watch. If Juanemma sat in any theatre and witnessed that scene she must, I am sure, have gone under instantly. Happily, she seems to have missed the picture, for otherwise Mr. Barrymore might have had to dress up again as Rasputin (which God forbid) and journey across the country to get her out of it—excellent publicity but a great bother.

Before I go on to Vashti, whose last name I forget, I will look in passing at another of our white maids (Vashti was colored). Belle Giddin distinguished herself by one gesture which fortunately did not result in the bedlam occasioned by Juanemma's hypnotic states or Dora Gedd's shooting spree. Bella burned her finger grievously, and purposely, one afternoon in the steam of a boiling kettle so that she could find out whether the pain-killer she had bought one night at a tent-show for fifty cents was any good. It was only fair.

Vashti turned out, in the end, to be partly legendary. She was a comely and sombre negress who was always able to find things my mother lost. "I don't know what's become of my garnet brooch," my mother said one day. "Yassum," said Vashti. In half an hour she had found it. "Where in the world was it?" asked mother. "In de yahd," said Vashti. "De dog mussa drug it out."

Vashti was in love with a young colored chauffeur named Charley, but she was also desired by her stepfather, whom none of us had ever seen but who was, she said, a handsome but messin' round gentleman from Georgia who had come north and married Vashti's mother just so he could be near Vashti. Charley, her fiancé, was for killing the stepfather but we counselled flight to another city. Vashti, however, would burst into tears and hymns and vow she'd never leave us; she got a certain pleasure out of bearing her cross. Thus we all lived in jeopardy, for the possibility that Vashti, Charley, and her stepfather might fight it out some night in our kitchen did not, at times, seem remote. Once I went into the kitchen at midnight to make some coffee. Charley was standing at a window looking out into the back yard; Vashti was rolling her eyes. "Heah he come! Heah he come!" she moaned. The stepfather didn't show up, however.

Charley finally saved up twenty-seven dollars toward taking Vashti away but one day he impulsively bought a .22 revolver with a mother-of-pearl handle and demanded that Vashti tell him where her mother and stepfather lived. "Doan go up dere, doan go *up* dere!" said Vashti. "Mah mothah is just as rarin' as he is!" Charley, however, insisted. It came out then that Vashti didn't have any stepfather: there was no such person. Charley threw her over for a yellow gal named Nancy: he never forgave Vashti for the vanishing from his life of a menace that had come to mean more to him than Vashti herself. Afterwards, if you asked Vashti about her stepfather or about Charley she would say, proudly, and with a woman-of-the-world air, "Neither one ob 'em is messin' round *me* any mo'."

Mrs. Doody, a huge, middle-aged woman with a religious taint, came into and went out of our house like a comet. The second night she was there she went berserk while doing the dishes and, under the impression that father was the Antichrist, pursued him several times up the back stairs and down the front. He had been sitting quietly over his coffee in the living room when she burst in from the kitchen waving a bread knife. My brother Herman finally felled her with a piece of Libby's cut glass that had been a wedding present of mother's. Mother, I remember, was in the attic at the time, trying to find some old things, and, appearing on the scene in the midst of it all, got the quick and mistaken impression that father was chasing Mrs. Doody.

Mrs. Robertson, a fat and mumbly old colored woman, who might have been sixty and who might have been a hundred, gave us more than one turn during the many years that she did our washing. She had been a slave down South and she remembered "having seen the troops marching—a mess o' blue, den a mass o' gray." "What," my mother asked her once, "were they fighting about?" "Dat," said Mrs. Robertson, "Ah don't know." She had a feeling, at all times, that something was going to happen. I can see her now, staggering up from the basement with a basketful of clothes and coming abruptly to a halt in the middle of the kitchen. "Hahk!" she would say, in a deep, guttural voice. We would all hark; there was never anything to be heard. Neither, when she shouted "Look yondah!" and pointed a trembling hand at a window, was there ever anything to be seen. Father protested time and again that he couldn't stand Mrs. Robertson around, but mother always refused to let her go. It seems that she was a jewel. Once she walked unbidden, a dishpan full of wrung-out clothes under her arm, into father's study, where he was engrossed in some figures. Father looked up. She regarded him for a moment in silence. Then—"Look out!'' she said, and withdrew. Another time, a murky winter afternoon, she came flubbering up the cellar stairs and bounced, out of breath, into the kitchen. Father was in the kitchen sipping some black coffee; he was in a jittery state of nerves from the effects of having had a tooth out, and had been in bed most of the day. "Dey is a death watch downstaihs!" rumbled the old colored lady. It developed that she had heard a strange "chipping" noise back of the furnace. "That was a cricket," said father. "Um-*hm,*" said Mrs. Robertson. "Dat was uh death watch!" With that she put on her hat and went home, poising just long enough at the back door to observe darkly to father, *"Dey ain't no way!"* It upset him for days.

Mrs. Robertson had only one great hour that I can think of—Jack Johnson's victory over Mistah Jeffries on the Fourth of July, 1910. She took a prominent part in the colored parade through the South End that night, playing a Spanish fandango on a banjo. The procession was led by the pastor of her church who, Mrs. Robertson later told us, had 'splained that the victory of Jack over Mistah Jeffries proved "de 'speriority ob de race." "What," asked my mother, "did he mean by that?" "Dat," said Mrs. Robertson, "Ah don't know."

Our other servants I don't remember so clearly, except the one who set the house on fire (her name eludes me), and Edda Millmoss. Edda was always slightly morose but she had gone along for months, all the time she was with us, quietly and efficiently attending to her work, until the night we had Carson Blair and F. R. Gardiner to dinner—both men of importance to my father's ambitions. Then suddenly, while serving the entrée, Edda dropped everything and, pointing a quivering finger at father, accused him in a long rigamarole of having done her out of her rights to the land on which Trinity Church in New York stands. Mr. Gardiner had one of his "attacks" and the whole evening turned out miserably.

(1933)

From

SO RED THE ROSE
by Stark Young

At Portobello during this first half of the year 1863 life went on very much as it had always done. Two or three of the negroes had run away from the quarters and those with children had been sent to the plantation farther away in Concordia Parish. Twelve of the house servants, all women, remained. In much of the country that had fallen into Federal hands, slaves that had run away or been seized either were with the army companies or were collected into camps or in plantation houses under guard. But in Natchez itself, down by the lower town the runaway negroes were established in a kind of stockade, under the eye of a Federal gunboat; Natchez itself was as yet not occupied. The stockades were near the edge of the river, and those who died of the crowding and the epidemics breaking out among them were buried in the sand of the river bars. On the Portobello plantations, with negroes leaving and uncertain management, the working of the land had dropped to a third.

Over this whole part of the country the unrest among the negroes was growing. On January 2nd President Lincoln had made the Emancipation Proclamation. Since then agents had been travelling among the plantation hands, who now heard of Lincoln's plan to enlist 100,000 negroes in the Northern Army. It was during the siege of Vicksburg that the first negroes were enlisted in the Federal Army. The agents did not spread the information that General Sherman had done this against his will and had declared that as soldiers the negroes were a joke, nor that General Sherman sent out to corral negroes all over the country and held them prisoners, to prevent their being used in trench digging or felling trees in the Confederate blockade of creeks and rivers.

There had always been a sharp division, however, between domestic slaves and slaves under plantation overseers, and Mrs. Bedford handled her servants as if affairs were the same as always. She saw the look in their eyes sometimes, and knew that they were thinking and saying things among themselves, things they did not tell her of. She even suspected that they might have some plot hatching. But she let one day after another run its course nevertheless.

She went about her life, keeping the garden planted, with the help of Uncle Thornton, Mammy's husband. In the garden the Tom Thumb peas, the corn, okra, potatoes still flourished, and the melon patch was as large as ever. To keep the negroes from stealing the melons and to protect them from foraging soldiers who might come by, Sallie Bedford went out herself early in the mornings and sprinkled flour on the gashes she cut in the melons. She did the same with the meat in the smokehouse. The negroes were afraid to touch anything, and to the soldiers who asked if the meat was poisoned she said, "You can judge for yourselves, gentlemen."

(1934)

MISTER McGREGOR
by Andrew Lytle

"I want to speak to Mister McGregor."

Yes sir, that's what he said. Not marster, but MISTER McGREGOR. If I live to be a hundred, and I don't think I will, account of my kidneys, I'll never forget the feelen that come over the room when he said them two words: Mister McGregor. The air shivered into a cold jelly; and all of us, me, ma, and pa, sort of froze in it. I remember thinken how much we favored one of them wax-work figures Sis Lou had learnt to make at Doctor Price's Female Academy. There I was, a little shaver of eight, standen by the window a-blowen my breath on it so's I could draw my name, like chillun'll do when they're kept to the house with a cold. The knock come sudden and sharp, I remember, as I was crossen a T. My heart flopped down in my belly and commenced to flutter around in my breakfast; then popped up to my ears and drawed all the blood out'n my nose except a little sack that got left in the point to swell and tingle. It's a singular thing, but the first time that nigger's fist hit the door I knowed it was the knock of death. I can smell death. It's a gift, I reckon, one of them no-count gifts like good conversation that don't do you no good no more. Once Cousin John Mebane come to see us, and he leaned over to pat me on the head— he was polite and hog-friendly to everybody, chillun and poverty-wropped kin especial—I said, Cousin John, what makes you smell so funny? Ma all but took the hide off'n me; but four days later they was dressen him in his shroud. Then I didn't know what it was I'd smelled, but by this time I'd got better acquainted with the meanen.

Ma was rollen tapers for the mantel. She stiffened a spell like she was listenen for the North wind to rise; rolled out a taper and laid it down. She went to the door and put her hand square on the knob; hesitated like she knew what was comen; then opened it. There stood Rhears. He was the coachman. Him and his wife Della was ma's pets. The both of 'm was give to ma by her pa at the marryen; and in a way that folks don't understand no more, they somehow become a part of her. Ma liked horses that wanted to run away all the time, and Rhears was the only nigger on the place that could manage'm. He was a powerful, dangerous feller. He'd killed the blacksmith and two free niggers in the other county before ma brought him to Long Gourd. His shoulders jest but stretched across the openen, as he stood there in a respectful-arrogant sort of way with a basket-knife in his hand.

"What do you want, Rhears?" his mistress asked.

"I want to speak to Mister McGregor," he said.

Pa had been scratchen away at his secretary. At "Mister" the scratchen stopped. That last scratch made more noise in my ears than the guns at Shiloh. Without a word, without even looken behind him, pa stood up and reached for his gun. The secretary was close to the fireplace and had a mirror over it. He didn't waste no time, but he didn't hurry none either. He just got up, took off his specs, and laid them as careful on the secretary, just like he meant to set'm in one special place and no other place would do. He reached for the gun and turned.

Rhears warn't no common field hand. He was proud, black like the satin in widow-women's shirt-waists, and spoiled. And his feelens was bad hurt. The day before, pa had whupped Della, and Rhears had had all night to fret and sull over it and think about what was be-en said in the quarters and how glad the field hands was she'd been whupped. He didn't mean to run away from his home like any blue-gum nigger. He jest come a-marchen straight to the house to settle with pa before them hot night thoughts had had time to git cooled down by the frost.

Pa turned and walked towards him. He still moved as steady and solemn. I watched the even distance each boot-heel made and calculated that two more steps would put him up to the threshold. Just to look at him you might have thought he was a-goen towards the courthouse to pay his taxes or walken down the aisle to his pew. All of a sudden he come to a stop. Ma's brown silk skirt had spread out before him. I looked up. There she was, one hand tight around the gun stock, the othern around the barrel. Her left little finger, plunged like a hornet's needle where the skin drew tight over pa's knuckles, made the blood drop on the bristly hairs along his hand; hang there; then spring to the floor. She held there the time it took three drops to bounce down and splatter. That blood put a spell on me.

A gold shiver along ma's dress made me look quick at their faces. Her hair was a shade darker than the dress she was wearen and slicked down around her ears. There wasn't no direct sun on it, but a light sorghum color slipped up and down as if it was playen on grease. The light might have come from her eyes, for they was afire. She was always fine to look at, although her face wasn't soft enough to rightly claim her beautiful. But she would have taken the breeches away from any ordinary man, I tell you. She'd rather manage folks than eat. Pa ought to have let her do a sight more of it than he did. She was happier than I ever seen her the time he went to the legislature. But he didn't take to politics somehow. He said the government rooms smelled too strong of tobacco. He was a mighty clean man, the cleanest I ever come across. Took a washen once a day reg'lar. When I come to think about ma, I see her a-studyen about somethen, with a wrinkle in her eyes. She didn't have to tell the servants not to bother her then. They stayed out of her way or went tippen around if their work took'm near her.

Well, pa saw he couldn't get his gun out of her grip without acting ungentlemanly. He gave her a curious look and a low bow; then turned it loose.

Taken off his coat and folden it, he laid it across a chair. Ma was marbly-pale when she stepped out of the way, but she moved easy and steady.

For a long time I never could make out the meanen of them looks, nor why ma done what she done. And she never set us right about it. She wasn't the explainen kind, and you can bet nobody never asked. I'd just as soon've asked the devil to pop his tail. It's bothered me a heap in my time, more'n it's had any right to. I reckon it's because I always think about it when I'm taperen off. That's a time when a man gits melancholy and thinks about how he come not to be president and sich-like concerns. Well, sir, when I'd run through all my mistakes and seen where if I'd a-done this instead of that how much better off I'd be today, and cuss myself for drinken up my kidneys, I'd always end up by asken myself why that woman acted like that. I've knowed a sight of women in my day, knowed'm as the Bible saints knowed'm, as well as in a social and business way; and I'm here to say, sir, they are stuffed with dynamite, the puniest of'm.

It was a question of authority, and a time when whuppen was out of the argyment. All you had to do was look at Rhears and that basket-knife sharpened thin like a dagger, a-hangen as innocent agen his pant leg, to see he didn't mean to take no whuppen. He must have felt in his Afrykin way that pa had betrayed him. Folks jest didn't whup their house servants, and Rhears was a-meanen to teach pa his manners. Niggers can think straight up to a certain point, and beyond that the steadiest of'm let their senses fly like buckshot, high to scatter. It never struck him that Della needed her whuppen. No, sir, he was jest a-standen in the door tellen pa he warn't his marster.

Now ma might have thought that pa ought, with his proper strength, to show him who his marster was. There ain't no doubt but what he had to show it in some way, or he might as well have sold all his niggers for any work he could a got out'n them. Still it was a powerful big risk to run. And it was plain she was a-meanen for him to run it.

Anyway, that was the construction the kin put on it, and it was natural they would. But it never satisfied me. I got it in my head that Rhears warn't the only person on Long Gourd who didn't claim pa his marster. Before I tell you what I mean, give me a little taste of that shuck juice—half a glass'll do, jest enough to settle the dust in my belly. I'm about to choke to death with the drought.

Aah . . . that's sweet to the taste. Now, sir. You'll excuse me if I lean over and whisper this. *That other body was ma.* I know it ain't a-goen to sound right, for she and pa had the name of be-en a mighty loven couple. But a man and woman can fight and still love. Most of'm enjoy fighten. I ain't never seen one get wore out with it. They can go on with a fight for years. Can git fat on it. When they win out, they put the man down amongst the chillun and give him a whuppen when he forgits his manners or sasses back. But if he's stout enough to put her and keep her in her place, she don't hold it agin him. She's proud to think she picked such a game one. That's how come I never married.

I'm peaceful by nature. Ain't but one thing ever gits me fighten mad: that's putten salt in my whisky. That riles me. I'll fight a elyplant then.

Well, sir, that morning Della was late. Ma had had to send for her twice, and she come in looken like the hornets stung her. She fluffed down to her sewen and went to work in a sullen way, her lip stuck out so far it looked swole. And they ain't nothen meaner-looken than a blue-black, shiney lip of a sullen nigger woman. It looks like a devil's pillow.

Directly ma said, "Della, take out that seam and do it over again."

"Take it out yourself, if it don't suit," she flounced back.

In a second pa was on his feet: "Woman, lay down that sewen and come with me."

Them was his words; and if a nigger can git pale, Della done it. She seen right away what a mistake she'd made. She fell on the floor and commenced to grab at ma's skirts. "Don't let him whup me, Mistiss. Don't let him." For a while ma didn't say a word.

"Get up off that floor and come with me," said pa again.

"Mister McGregor, what are you going to do with this girl?"

Pa never made her no answer. He walked over and lifted Della up by the arm.

"Don't you tech me: you don't dare tech me. I belongs to Mistiss."

Pa shuck her till her teeth rattled; then she stopped her jumpen and goen on and stood there a-tremblen like a scared horse.

"Mister McGregor," come ma's even tones, "you're not going to punish that girl. She's mine."

And with that pa turned and said in a hard, polite way he never used before to ma: "And so are you mine, my dear." Then he nodded to Della to go before him, and she went.

When he came back, ma was standen in the middle of the floor just where he had left her. She hadn't moved a peg. She just stood there, stiff as a poker, her head thrown up and her eyes as wide as a hawk's.

"I have whipped Della and sent her to the field for six months. If at the end of that time she has learned not to forget her manners, she may take up again her duties here. In the meantime, so you will not want, I've sent for P'niny. If you find her too old or in any way unsuitable, you may take your choice of the young girls."

He waited a breath for her answer and when it didn't come, got on his horse and went runnen over the back road down to the fields. No other words passed between them that day. At supper the meal went off in quick order. There wasn't no good old-fashioned table talk. Everybody was as polite to one another as if they was visiten. Ma sat at the foot, froze to her chair. Pa at the head like a judge expecten shooten in the court. We knew somethen was bound to blow up and bust; and I do believe if somebody had tromped on a hog bladder, we chillun'd a jumped under the table.

Next mornen it come. That bow of pa's, as he let go of the gun, was his answer to the challenge. For you might almost say pa had whupped ma by proxy. And here was Rhears, agen by proxy, to make him answer for it . . . a nigger and a slave, his mistress's gallant, a-callen her husband and his marster to account for her. I don't reckon they'd been any such mixed-up arrangement as that before that time; and I know they ain't since.

I scrouched back in the corner and watched, so scared my eyes turned loose in their sockets. If Jesus Christ had a touched me on the shoulder and said, "Come on, little boy, and git your harp," I'd a no more looked at him than if he'd a been my dog come to lick me. For pa and Rhears was a-eyen one another. This fight was to be accorden to no rules. I saw straight off it would start fist and skull and work into a stomp and gouge. If pa didn't manage to git that knife away from the nigger, it would be cut and grunt as well.

Pa was the slimberer of the two, but he wouldn't a looked it away from Rhears. From necked heel up he was six feet—no, six feet four—and his boots raised him an ench higher. Right away he took a quick easy step forward, and both of'm tied their muscles together. Rhears tightened his fingers around the knife. I looked at pa's breeches. They fit him tight; and the meat rolled up, snapped, then quivered under the cloth. His butt give in at the sides and squeezed away its sitten-down softness. His waist drawed in and pumped the wind into his chest, a-pushen out his shoulders just as easy and slow. I don't believe you could have found a man in the whole cotton country hung together any purtier.

Pa, quick-like, sunk his hand in and around the black flesh of Rhears' neck. The knife swung backwards, but pa grabbed it with his left hand before it could do its damage. A breath, and Rhears was a-spinnen round the room. The basket-knife lay in the door as still as any of the pine floor boards. This rattled the nigger some. He had figured on gitten Mister McGregor in the door, where he could a used the knife to advantage. Fighten in his mistress's room, a place he didn't feel at home in, rattled him some more. So before he could come to himself good, pa lambed a blow into his black jaw. It was a blow fit to down a mule, but Rhears shook his head and run in to close; changed quick; dropped low and butted. Four quick butts jambed pa agen the wall, where he saved his guts by grabben Rhears' shoulders—to hold. That kinky hunk of iron slowed down. Both men shook under the strain. The noise of destruction held up. All you could hear was a heavy-pumpen blowen, like to wind-broke horses drawen a killen load . . . then a rippen cry from Rhears' coat—and it was good broadcloth—as it split both ways from the small of his back. Both men drawed in their breaths for a long second.

Sudden-like pa's head and chest went down and forward. His feet pressed agen the wall. Slow as candy pullen he broke the nigger's holt on the front muscles of his thighs. But that nigger's grip never give. No, sir. What give was two drippen hunks of leg meat. Just the second that holt was broke pa shifted neat and shoved hard. Rhears smashed a sewen table top into kindlen wood before he hit the wall. That table saved his neck, or I'm as good a man as I used to be. Before he could get his bearens, pa was a-pounden his head into the hard pine floor. I looked for the brains to go a-splatteren any time, and I begun to wonder how far they would slide on the floor's smooth polish. But God never made but one thing tougher'n a nigger's head—and that's ironwood. Slowly Rhears raised up and, with a beautiful strain of muscles, got to his feet. Then him and pa went round the room. It looked like that bangen had set the nigger crazy. A stranger comen into the room would a thought he was set on breaken up ever stick of furniture, a-usen pa for his mallet. Once the two of'm come close to ma, so close the wind they made blowed her skirts; but never a peg did she move. She held as rigid as a conjure woman.

Directly the nigger begun to wear some. All that crazy spurt of energy hadn't done him no good. Gradually pa's feet touched the floor more and more; then they didn't leave it. The panten got heavier, more like bellows. A chair got in their way. They went over it. They did a sight of rollen—up to the door crowded with house servants, all a-looken like they had fell in the ash-hopper. You could follow how far they'd rolled by the sweat on the floor. It looked like a wet mop had been run by a triflen hand. Then, sir, my hairs straightened up and drawed in to hide under the scalp. Rhears had ended up on top and was a-shiften to gouge. Pa looked all wore down. I tried to holler to ma to shoot, but my throat was as parched as it is right this minute. . . . Thank you, sir. You are very generous.

Have you ever seen a long dead limb stretched between sky and droppen sun? Well, that's how still ma held on to that gun of pa's. I couldn't stand to see them black thumbs go down. As I turned my head, I heard the nigger holler. Pa had jerked up his knee and hit him in a tender spot. He fell back and grabbed himself. It must have been an accident, for pa made no move to take advantage of the break. He just lay there and let Rhears take hold of himself and git at pa's throat. I never seen such guts in nobody, nigger or white man. Bump went pa's head on the floor. Bump and agen. Ever time he lifted pa, he squeezed tighter. Ever time he come down he pushed him forward.

It had been one of them frosty December mornens, and a fire had been burnen in the chimney since first light. The front stick had been burned in two and left between it and the back stick a heap of red and blue hickory coals. They don't make no hotter fire than that. I saw right away what Rhears had in mind. Every time he bumped my father's head against the floor, he was that much nearer the hearth. Pa wriggled and jerked, but his wind was cut and the black blood ran into his eyes. Those heavy black hands growed deep in the red, greasy flesh of pa's neck.

They moved slower towards the fire, for pa had at last clamped his legs in a way to slow'm down. Then I saw him reach for his pocket. Rhears didn't see this move. His eyes was bucked on what they had in mind to do, and the heat from the hickory logs made'm swell with a dark, dry look of battle luck. After some fumblen pa finally brought out his knife. He opened it in a feeble way over the nigger's back, and let it rip and tear through his ribs. The blood first oozed; then spouted. It fell back from the knife like dirt from a turnen plow. Then pa made a jab back of the kidneys. That done for him. He grunted, turned loose and rolled over like a hunk of meat.

Staggering to his feet, pa went over and leaned agen the mantel. Directly Rhears spoke up, so low you could hardly hear him:

"Marster, if you hadn't got me, I'd a got you."

Then he shook with a chill, straightened out, and rolled back his eyes. Mister McGregor looked at him a minute before he turned to his wife. And then no words passed his mouth. He reached out his hand and she walked over and handed him the gun. He reached over the mantel and, his arms a tremblen, set the gun back in its rack.

"Bring me a pan of warm water, the turpentine, and the things out of my medicine chest." That was ma speaken, sharp and peremptory, to the servants in the doorway. "And take this body out of here," she added in a tone she used when the girl Sally failed to dust behind the furniture.

"Sit down in that chair, Mister McGregor, so I can dress your wounds."

Pa done what she told him. She worked away at him with deft, quick fingers. Directly I hears her in a off-hand way, her head benden over and her hands busy wrappen:

"Colonel Winston will be through here on the way South. I think it would be best to sell him Della."

"I think that, my dear," said pa, "would be the most sensible thing to do."

(1935)

I THOUGHT ABOUT THIS GIRL
by Jerome Weidman

I thought about this girl quite a lot. We all did—my mother, my father, my brothers, all of us. It seemed silly to let ourselves be upset by a girl who worked for us, but we couldn't help it. She worried us. All we knew was that for a long time she was happy with us, and then suddenly she wasn't.

She said nothing, of course, right up to the end. She was too considerate and friendly and kind to say anything, but we could tell. We could tell by the way she stood behind the counter in our little bakery, by the way she served a customer. She used to laugh all the time and keep the whole store bright with her energy and her smile and her pleasant voice. People spoke about it. It was a pleasure to be served by her, they said.

"The smartest thing I ever did," my father would say with a smile as he watched her. "Hiring that girl was the smartest thing I ever did."

It wasn't that way very long, though. Not that we had any fault to find. She still came in early. She still worked hard. She still was polite and friendly and quick, but it wasn't the same. She didn't laugh any more. She stood very quietly when it wasn't busy and looked out of the window. She was worried about something.

At first we thought it would pass away, but it didn't. It got worse and worse. We did the obvious thing, of course. We asked her what was wrong.

"Nothing," she said at once, smiling quickly. "Nothing is wrong."

We asked her many times, but we still got the same answer, and knew it wasn't true.

It annoyed my mother.

"Why should we be bothered like this?" she asked sharply. "We've treated her like a daughter. Why should she be unhappy? Anyway, we didn't need her to start with."

And, of course, we didn't. We had always managed pretty well in the store. We were seldom overworked, because it is only a small bakeshop, though business is brisk and profitable. It happened very simply. A woman, a very good customer of ours, came in one day and told us about her—a poor girl from Poland, whose parents were still on the other side and who had no one here to take care of her except an old aunt, herself far from wealthy. Wouldn't it be wonderful, this customer said to my mother, if it were possible to find some sort of job for the girl, something to help her support herself and make her less of a burden to her aunt? My mother was sympathetic and interested at once—she is always like that—and the woman went on to wonder casually if we mightn't be able to find a place for this girl in our own shop. Poor Mother was too far gone in compassion to realize that she had been trapped, and said quickly that we certainly could; she would talk to my father.

At first, of course, we laughed. There was scarcely enough work in the shop to keep all of us busy. It seemed ridiculous to hire anybody else.

"We'll be waiting on each other," my father said.

In the end, however, Mother brought us around. We can afford it, she said, and think how nice it would be to have a young girl's face in the store, how nice for the customers. Her arguments weren't very impressive, but Father seldom denies Mother anything she wants, so he said all right, let's take a look at her. And then, of course, as soon as we saw her, we were lost. She was so fresh and cheerful and bright, with her round face and her ready smile and her yellow hair.

"My God," my Father said, "she looks like she was made for a bakery."

He pinched his chin between his thumb and forefinger and said well, maybe now he'd be able to have a little time for himself. There was a book on elementary chemistry that he'd been nibbling at cautiously for almost thirty years, ever since he came to America. Now, he said, he might get a chance to read it. There were also a lot of things my mother had always wanted to do. There were dishes she had yearned to make but had never dared try. Now she'd have time to experiment a little.

"You'll be able to cook," my father roared. "After thirty years you'll finally be able to cook."

It was a boisterous and happy occasion. The girl had done that for us.

After she had been with us a short while, however, we began to notice that my father hadn't made much progress with his chemistry and that there were no startling innovations at my mother's table. We knew the reason, of course. The habits of thirty years are not easily broken, and they were spending as much time as ever in the shop. But nobody seemed to mind. It was pleasant just to watch this girl with her bouncing energy and her happy laugh. Often my father would cock his head admiringly and repeat, "Smartest thing I ever did, hiring that girl."

Then suddenly he didn't say it any more. He still thought the world of her. We all did, but he was just as worried as the rest of us. What was wrong? Why was she no longer happy?

Before we could find an answer, and before our vague irritation could turn to anger, however, she came to us. She said she was leaving.

It was typical of her to wait until we were all together before she told us. She could have told my father or my mother or any one of us, but she knew how we all felt about her. It was hard for her to say it to all of us at the same time. She picked the harder way, because it seemed to her to be the right way.

"Leaving?" we asked, startled.

"Yes," she said quietly, dropping her eyes from ours. "I must leave."

Apparently it was something she had been wanting to tell us for a long time, something she had been afraid to tell us.

"But why?" we asked. "Why are you leaving?"

She didn't answer. She just shook her head and bit her lip.

"Aren't you happy here?" we asked.

"I am very happy here," she said.

"Don't we pay you enough?" we asked. "Do you want more?"

She shook her head quickly.

"No," she said. "You pay me enough."

We didn't want to make her cry, but somehow we couldn't stop asking questions.

"You have another job, maybe? A better one?"

She shook her head again.

"No, I have no other job."

"But you *need* a job, don't you?"

"Yes," she said. "I need a job."

"Then why?"

She didn't want to tell us, but we liked her too well not to insist on knowing.

"You can tell us, Mary," my mother said kindly. "We are your friends. You can tell us."

She looked up at us. She seemed confused and beaten, but she saw she would have to tell us.

"My mother," she began almost inaudibly, "my mother wrote me a letter from Poland—"

She stopped to blink away the tears, and then began again.

"My mother wrote me it isn't right," she said softly, brokenly. "She says it isn't right to—it isn't right to work for Jews."

She kept her puzzled, tearful glance upon us for another moment. Then she turned and walked away, her shoulders shaking with her sobs.

(1938)

From

KITTY FOYLE

by Christopher Morley

The old man and I were mighty close to each other. I guess it was me tagging along so far behind the rest, and then Mother dying when I was ten, and the old man being home daytimes. He was good company, I guess it was the Irish in him. Then he'd get what he called his black streak, you could see the darkness come out on his face like he'd swallowed something. "Kitty, get the hell out of here, I got to be by myself."

Myrtle would say "What's wrong honey, has he Gone Irish? You run out on the street and play." Usually I took my jacks out on the front stoop until someone came along and we'd jump hopscotch by the Methodist church.

I know more about it now. I'm never quite sure what I think about things when I'm with someone. Either I'm likely to be putting on an act, or else I'm thinking how much smarter they are than me and I better agree with them. You've got to get back into yourself to chew things over.

When Pop was feeling good he'd sing. He had a nice voice, I can drive myself crazy half remembering The Low-Backed Car, or that fool piece The Irish Jubilee. I never saw it written down but I can still hum some of the words the way he used to rattle them off—

Oh a short time ago boys, an Irishman named Dorrity
Was elected to the Senate by a very large majority,
He felt so elated that he went to Dennis Cassidy
The owner of a bar-room of a very large capacity.

With the words I can smell a whiff of whiskey and tobacco as I climbed in his lap. I didn't like it and often told him so, but anything was worth while to get that song—

Two by three they marched in the dining hall,
Young men and old men, and girls that were not men at all,
Blind men and deaf men, and men who had their teeth in pawn
Soda crackers, fire crackers, limburg cheese with tresses on,

and then something about

In came Piper Heidseck and handed him a glass of wine.

I hadn't the faintest idea who or what Piper Heidseck was. Years after, I found the name on a bottle the first time Wyn and I drank champagne together. It made me cry.

Even now, when the old man's been dead so long, I often think of him. There were things he said that I almost didn't notice at the time. Mother wasn't dead very long when one day Myrtle was hanging out wash on the line. In among his and Mac's big things were some of my pantywaists and nightgowns. He noticed them and said "I'll be glad when those clothes of yours grow up. It's lonesome washing that don't have a woman's shift among it." Lonesome washing—I think of that sometimes, the other way round. I guess there's a lot of women good and sick of nothing but feminine flimsies coming home in the bundle.

I think of Pop most for the help he might have given me when I needed it. By the time I was ready to ask his advice it was too late. The nearest he ever got to giving me a hint was a queer saying he got from grandfather who came fresh from the old country. It hurts—

In house to keep household
    When folks wish to wed
Needs something more than
    Four legs in a bed.

I wonder what happened to grandfather made that stick in his crop? He was in the Civil War and died long before I was born and thought of.

It used to make Wyn laugh when he found we lived just round the corner from Orthodox Street. That's in Frankford, and a long way from the Main Line, if you know what that means in Philly. It's freight trains and coal yards and factories and the smell of the tanneries down by Frankford Creek. The fact they were building an L out our way was comic to Wyn; it was a New York kind of thing to do, not in the Philadelphia picture.

But I'm not thinking about Wyn just now; really I'm not. I'm trying to get ready to think about him by getting the B.U. clear in my mind. B.U. was what he called Before *Us*. He was wonderful at making up a language of our own. I guess all lucky people have one, but they're not likely to tell about it.

I've pretty much gotten over the idea I had once that I was queer, different from other people. But it was a funny way to be a small girl, alone with men so much older than me and then pushed out into a different world a thousand miles away. After Mother died various people, for instance Aunt Hattie, dinned it into the old man that I should lead "a normal life." That made him obstinate. He liked having me around, he gave me free run and then suddenly he'd turn cranky. One time Lena McTaggart and I hiked all the way over to where the Barnum and Bailey circus train was parked on a siding, in North Philly. Of course we were late getting back, he and Mr McTaggart each blamed the other, it was the beginning of a regular feud. "Listen, Mac," said Pop, "there's lots of leather belting made in Frankford, why don't you use some of it on that kid of yours."

After three boys, Pop was awfully tickled at begetting a female; I don't know just why. He enjoyed going to stores with me to buy girls' clothes. It was comical to hear him consulting old black Myrtle about what I ought to wear. I overheard her: "Dat chile gwine be handsome, you should doll her up a bit. Get her some froufrou." This did me good till I heard the old man say "She aint female at all. She looks just like me from the waist up, she's got no more shape than a cricket bat."

Out of the steam of the washtubs Myrtle said: "Shape'll come. Dey bulges here and dey bulges dere, all of a sudden dey's real pleasurable."

This didn't mean anything to me but it sounded hopeful. One day I found Pop waiting outside when school let out. Kids dislike their parents to step out of routine and also I was sensitive about the old man being so crippled up and walking on a stick. I wondered what the devil he was staring at us for. He explained, he was looking to see what kind of clothes the other girls wore so he could pick something special for me. Bless his old heart! It must have been then he got the plaid dress I was so proud of. I think that was Myrtle's suggestion, she heard Lena McTaggart and me cutting out paper dolls and discussing their costumes. Myrtle was proud of the fact we were "Scotch-Irish." She figured that Irish, like colored people, were sort of on their own, secretly at odds with the rest of the world.

When you're a kid it's a big help to have someone really proud of you and show it. That was Myrtle. Things I wouldn't have thought much about come back now because that old colored woman made a fuss about them. After Mother died Myrtle came more often and she certainly kept us up to the mark. There was Pop's walking stick with the silver handle and an inscription from the Frankford Cricket Club, she always kept it polished. "Let be that cane," she shouted at Lena and me when we wanted to use it in some game we were playing. "That's your Pop's gentility cane." After I got over the shock of Mother being dead in the Front Room I used to want to go in there sometimes, but Myrtle was always driving me out of it.

Colored people don't have to stop and think in order to be wise; they just know about things naturally, it oozes out of them.

*   *   *   *   *

In spite of heat, and the smell of Myrtle in the room and the smell of chlorides in the yard it was never dull in that old kitchen. Pop would be sitting in the wicker chair under the wisteria vine wondering how he could wait until Mac got home to fetch something from the speakeasy. Myrtle and I wouldn't do that errand for him. When Myrtle had something on her mind she wanted to get across to Pop, but she didn't quite like to say it direct, she'd tell it to me in a way he could hear it. Or she'd wait till she was in the john and grumble it in there. I guess she had a notion that what you say in the closet is kind of privileged utterance.

I have the ironing board across the washtubs so I can look out the window and get a breath of air. I hear Myrtle down below in the backhouse. "That ole man better git less sociable with liquor. He ought to be ashame to encourage bootleggin' on Orthodox Street. I take note there's two ends to that street, there's a speakeasy one end and a unsane asylum the other. He better stick in the middle where that Quaker Meetin' holds forth."

I made a chink in the vine so I could look down from above and see poor old Pop's hand holding his newspaper. If it was shaking too much I'd go down and talk to him. Myrtle brings clothes in from the line and sprinkles them on the big kitchen table. That was a grand old table, white as bread from scrubbing, it was the kind the top lifts up and turns it into a settle. When the top was down I could crawl underneath when I was small and lie hidden on the bench part, watching people's feet. I remember how fast Mother's used to move, and the smell of hot jam. You got to move fast when you're boiling preserves. Myrtle's feet were quite different, a comical flat shape with the heel sticking out behind. They would forget I was under there. Once I called out "Why are colored people's feet such a funny shape?" Myrtle was so frightened she dropped the coal scuttle.

"Lucky I didn't drop that bucket on 'em, they'd be funnier yet. Honey, them's perseverin' feet. Feet tromps out flat wuhkin' in de vineyard."

We used that table for meals. It was handy, over in the far end of the kitchen where the little window looked down the side passage. Anybody came to the door we could see them before they rang and "arrange our defences" Pop said. Under that window was the oldfashioned ice-chest, the kind where the top raises up. Mac could make a long arm from the table right into the ice-chest for a bottle of beer. Over by the stove was the sink, the kind you never see any more, tall curl-over copper spigots. That kind of sink was made for gentry, Pop said, the tall curved pipes so as not to break fine china in washing it.

There's a cursing and a creaking of wicker down under the arbor, and the clatter of pipe fallen on the brick walk. I go out and give Pop a hand to ratch up from his chair. He'd go through any kind of misery to hobble round the yard, pinch off faded hollyhocks by the back fence. While he was doing that I'd fix him some hot tea and paper-thin slices of brown bread and butter. Butter with bread spread on it, Myrtle called it.

You tell that black woman, he says, there's one advantage in being Irish. If you can't get whiskey you can always make out with a cup of tea.

They both enjoyed kidding, and like sensitive people do, they knew where to stop. Myrtle said once "If yo' Pop called me nigger I'd be like to walk out and quit. But when he say Black Woman I know he mean it fo' compliment."

So Pop and I take our cup of tea in the arbor, and Myrtle has hers leaning on the washtubs over our heads, and calling down through the trellis. Sometimes Lena McTaggart came in about that time of the afternoon. She wasn't so bad when she was away from Nellie Simmons, and she brought her mah-jong set. When I was talking to her of course my mind went back to high school and I'd get a bit mixed up inside. I didn't quite know whether I was an Illinois girl or a Philadelphia girl. Then Mac would come home, and Myrtle left to look after her own family. I'd set out supper for the men, and Pop and Mac and Griscom Street were all my world and a good one.

(1939)

From
YOU CAN'T GO HOME AGAIN
by Thomas Wolfe

As Mrs. Jack stood there beside her bed, her maidservant, Nora Fogarty, knocked at the door and entered immediately, bearing a tray with a tall silver coffee pot, a small bowl of sugar, a cup, saucer, and spoon, and the morning *Times*. The maid put the tray down on a little table beside the bed, saying in a thick voice:

"Good maar-nin', Mrs. Jack."

"Oh, hello, Nora!" the woman answered, crying out in the eager and surprised tone with which she usually responded to a greeting. "How are you—hah?" she asked, as if she were really greatly concerned, but immediately adding: "Isn't it going to be a nice day? Did you ever see a more beautiful morning in your life?"

"Oh, *beautiful*, Mrs. Jack!" Nora answered. "Beautiful!"

The maid's voice had a respectful and almost unctuously reverential tone of agreement as she answered, but there was in it an undernote of something sly, furtive, and sullen, and Mrs. Jack looked at her swiftly now and saw the maid's eyes, inflamed with drink and irrationally choleric, staring back at her. Their rancor, however, seemed to be directed not so much at her mistress as at the general family of the earth. Or, if Nora's eyes did swelter with a glare of spite more personal and direct, her resentment was blind and instinctive: it just smoldered in her with an ugly truculence, and she did not know the reason for it. Certainly it was not based on any feeling of class inferiority, for she was Irish, and a papist to the bone, and where social dignities were concerned she thought she knew on which side condescension lay.

She had served Mrs. Jack and her family for more than twenty years, and had grown slothful on their bounty, but in spite of a very affectionate devotion and warmth of old Irish feeling she had never doubted for a moment that they would ultimately go to hell, together with other pagans and all alien heathen tribes whatever. Just the same, she had done pretty well by herself among these prosperous infidels. She had a "cushy" job, she always fell heir to the scarcely-worn garments of Mrs. Jack and her sister Edith, and she saw to it that the policeman who came to woo her several times a week should lack for nothing in the way of food and drink to keep him contented and to forestall any desire he might have to stray off and forage in other pastures. Meanwhile, she had laid by several thousand dollars, and had kept her sisters and nieces back in County Cork faithfully furnished with a titillating chronicle (sprinkled with pious interjections of regret and deprecation and appeals to the Virgin to watch over her and guard her among such infidels) of high life in this rich New World that had such pickings in it.

No—decidedly this truculent resentment which smoldered in her eyes had nothing to do with caste. She had lived here for twenty years, enjoying the generous favor of a very good, superior sort of heathen, and growing used to almost all their sinful customs, but she had never let herself forget where the true way and the true light was, nor her hope that she would one day return into the more civilized and Christian precincts of her own kind.

*   *   *   *   *

In fact, although the kind and jolly look on Mrs. Jack's lovely face had not changed a bit since she had greeted the maid, her eye had observed instantly all the signs of the unwholesome fury that was raging in the woman, and with a strong emotion of pity, wonder, and regret she was thinking:

"She's been at it again! This is the third time in a week that she's been drinking. I wonder what it is—I wonder what it is that happens to that kind of person."

Mrs. Jack did not know clearly what she meant by "that kind of person," but she felt momentarily the detached curiosity that a powerful, rich, and decisive character may feel when he pauses for a moment from the brilliant exercise of a talent that has crowned his life with triumphant ease and success almost every step of the way, and notes suddenly, and with surprise, that most of the other people in the world are fumbling blindly and wretchedly about, eking out from day to day the flabby substance of grey lives. She realized with regret that such people are so utterly lacking in any individual distinction that each seems to be a small particle of some immense and vicious life-stuff rather than a living creature who is able to feel and to inspire love, beauty, joy, passion, pain, and death. With a sense of sudden discovery the mistress was feeling this as she looked at the servant who had lived with her familiarly for almost twenty years, and now for the first time she reflected on the kind of life the other woman might have had.

"What is it?" she kept thinking. "What's gone wrong with her? She never used to be this way. It has all happened within the last year. And Nora used to be so pretty, too!" she thought, startled by the memory. "Why, when she first came to us she was really a very handsome girl. Isn't it a shame," she thought indignantly, "that she should let herself go to seed like this—a girl who's had the chances that she's had! I wonder why she never married. She used to have half a dozen of those big policemen on the string, and now there's only one who still comes faithfully. They were all mad about her, and she could have had her pick of them!"

All at once, as she was looking at the servant with kindly interest, the woman's breath, foul with a stale whiskey stench, was blown upon her, and she got suddenly a rank body smell, strong, hairy, female, and unwashed. She frowned with revulsion, and her face began to burn with a glow of shame, embarrassment, and acute distaste.

"God, but she stinks!" she thought, with a feeling of horror and disgust. "You could cut the smell around her with an axe! The nasty things!" she thought, now including all the servants in her indictment. "I'll bet they never wash—and here they are all day long with nothing to do, and they could at least keep clean! My God! You'd think these people would be so glad to be here in this lovely place with the fine life we've made for them that they would be a little proud of it and try to show that they appreciate it! But no! They're just not good enough!" she thought scornfully, and for a moment her fine mouth was disfigured at one corner by an ugly expression.

It was an expression which had in it not only contempt and scorn, but also something almost racial—a quality of arrogance that was too bold and naked, as if it were eager to assert its own superiority. This ugly look rested only for a second, and almost imperceptibly, about the edges of her mouth, and it did not sit well on her lovely face. Then it was gone. But the maid had seen it, and that swift look, with all its implications, had stung and whipped her tortured spirit to a frenzy.

"Oh, yes, me fine lady!" she was thinking. "It's too good fer the likes of us ye are, ain't it? Oh me, yes, an' we're very grand, ain't we? What wit' our fine clothes an' our evenin' gowns an' our forty pairs of hand-made shoes! Jesus, now! Ye'd think she was some kind of centipede to see the different pairs of shoes she's got! An' our silk petticoats an' step-ins that we have made in Paris, now! Yes! That makes us very fine, don't it? It's not as if we ever did a little private monkey-business on the side, like ordinary people, is it? Oh, me, no! We are gathered together wit' a friend fer a little elegant an' high-class entertainment durin' the course of the evenin'! But if it's some poor girl wit'out an extra pair of drawers to her name, it's different, now! It's: 'Oh! you nasty thing! I'm disgusted wit' you!' . . . Yes! An' there's many a fine lady livin' on Park Avenoo right now who's no better, if the truth was told! That I know! So just take care, me lady, not to give yerself too many airs!'' she thought with rancorous triumph. . . .

"Ah! if I told all that I know! 'Nora,' she says, "if anyone calls when I'm not here, I wish ye'd take the message yerself. Mr. Jack don't like to be disturbed.' . . . Jesus! From what I've seen there's none of 'em that likes to be disturbed. It's love and let love wit' 'em, no questions ast an' the divil take the hindmost, so long as ye do it in yer leisure hours. But if ye're twenty minutes late fer dinner, it's where the hell have ye been, an' what's to become of us when ye neglect yer family in this way? . . . Sure,'' she thought, warming with a flush of humor and a more tolerant and liberal spirit, "it's a queer world, ain't it? An' these are the queerest of the lot! Thank God I was brought up like a Christian in the Holy Church, an' still have grace enough to go to Mass when I have sinned! But then——''

As often happens with people of strong but disordered feelings, she was already sorry for her flare of ugly temper, and her affections were now running warmly in another direction:

"But then, God knows, there's not a better-hearted sort of people in the world! There's no one I'd rather work fer than Mrs. Jack. They'll give ye everything they have if they like ye. I've been here twenty years next April, an' in all that time no one has ever been turned away from the door who needed food. Sure, there's far worse that go to Mass seven days a week—yes, an' would steal the pennies off a dead man's eyes if they got the chance! It's a good home we've been given here—as I keep tellin' all the rest of 'em,'' she thought with virtuous content, "an' Nora Fogarty's not the one to turn an' bite the hand that's feedin' her—no matter what the rest of 'em may do!''

(1940)

I WOULDN'T DREAM OF IT
by Leane Zugsmith

The Charles Street police station was only a couple of blocks away, so it didn't take the detectives more than five minutes to get over. When they rang the bell Adelaide just stood and looked at Mrs. Carlisle. She was naturally a pale colored girl, but now her skin looked like bleached-out khaki and the freckles under her eyes stood out like drops of tar.

The bell rang a second time, peremptorily. "I'll go," Mrs. Carlisle said nervously. "And for goodness' sake, Adelaide, put some powder on or something and don't keep looking like something the cat dragged in."

This time she didn't even notice that Mrs. Carlisle was different; she even treated you enough like a white girl to know you used powder too. She couldn't keep back the tears again. "You don't know how they'll talk to me," she said and she put a thin shaking hand to her eyes.

Both the men looked enormous, not tall so much as bursting out of their clothes, their shoulders, their arms, their hands big enough and strong enough . . . she winced and made herself think: for their jobs. Even the sunburnt one, who couldn't be more than thirty, or anyway more than a few years older than she was, eyed her in a way that chilled her.

"Perhaps I'd better tell it first and then Adelaide can," said Mrs. Carlisle. She made the detectives sit down and handed them cigarettes. "Because Adelaide—"

The older one interrupted her. "What's her last name?"

"Morrisey," said Mrs. Carlisle. "Look, officers, Adelaide has worked for me, part-time, for nearly four years. I trust her utterly." She looked up at Adelaide standing near her and smiled. "What happened, as I said over the 'phone, was somebody rang the bell around three and Adelaide pressed the button and he came up and said he was from the cleaner. Adelaide said he said Mr. Carlisle wanted his brown suit cleaned."

"A nigger or white?" asked the older one.

"He was a Negro, Adelaide said." Mrs. Carlisle's fair face became flushed as though she were angry or embarrassed, Adelaide couldn't tell which. Anyway, it was all she could do to pretend she didn't know the young one's cold blue stare was fixed upon her.

"And she never saw him before in her life," the older one said, then he snickered.

"I never did," said Adelaide without moving. "He said, just like Mrs. Carlisle told you, he said Mr. Carlisle stopped by on his way to the office this morning and said to come get a brown suit between two and three when I'd be here, like I am every other day, I mean, Mondays, Wednesdays, and Fridays. That's the God's own truth." Her voice cracked on the last words and once more she put her hand over her brimming eyes.

"Adelaide should have asked what cleaner he came from," Mrs. Carlisle said quickly. "If I'd been home—but that's carelessness, not dishonesty."

"I would of," Adelaide said, crying harder. "Only I just took it for granted. I thought it was orders."

"Anyway," said Mrs. Carlisle, grinding out her cigarette in the ashtray, "my husband didn't stop by any cleaners and didn't plan to have his suit cleaned and it cost him eighty-five dollars less than four months ago." She suddenly looked winningly at the men. "Is there any chance of tracing it, officers? We really can't afford to lose it."

"Well, I think maybe we can." The older one got up ponderously and moved toward Adelaide. "With a little co-operation." He showed almost all his teeth. Then he said roughly: "All right. Do you want to give us his name now or would you prefer to come along with us and give it later?"

Inside her it felt as if an icy oil was coming right up into her throat. She wet her lips. "I don't know his name, I never saw him before," she said faintly. It wasn't going to be any use, she thought, it wasn't going to make the least little bit of difference that she hadn't had a thing to do with it.

The younger one was on his feet now looking at her—but that wasn't news; he hadn't ever stopped since he walked in. "Come on now, Adelaide," he said and his voice was soft and syruplike; it sounded worse to her than the other one's. "Tell us about that boy friend of yours. Let her sit down a second—" he looked at his companion—"and tell us about that fellow she thinks the world of."

"What's the nigger's name?" the older one said in a bark.

Mrs. Carlisle twirled her wedding ring fast round her finger. "I'd rather you didn't talk to Adelaide that way if you don't mind," she said in an apologetic voice. "My husband . . . and I feel, that is—" She stopped and looked helplessly at the etching of the waterfowl over the sofa. "I mean, Adelaide's been with us, part-time, for nearly four years." Mechanically she added: "I have utter trust in her."

"Well, either you want us to get him or you don't," the older one said indifferently. "We can just take her along right now; it's all the same to us." He put a big meaty hand on Adelaide's arm and she checked her impulse to pull away.

"My goodness, we want the suit back," Mrs. Carlisle said uncertainly.

"Okay." The older one used Adelaide's arm as a lever, so rapidly that she found herself before him without remembering moving. "Get your duds," he said.

As she started to move she spoke. "I didn't have a thing to do with it," she said in a dull, solemn voice. "It was the first I ever laid eyes on him."

"Get moving," said the older one.

"Of course you didn't know him," said the younger one but there wasn't any compassion in his cold eyes. "But what about your boy friend, maybe *he* knows him? Why don't you try to think back, Adelaide, you know to the night you told him about that fine brown suit the mister had?"

She lifted her head. "I never knew which was the brown suit before today," she said drearily. "I don't clean the closets but once a month and I don't take time to look at all that's in them."

The older one jabbed his thumb beneath her shoulder blade. "All right. Save it for later," he said.

"Oh, wait a minute." Mrs. Carlisle clenched her small hands into fists. "I just can't let you—my husband would never forgive me."

"It's up to you, lady." The older one closed his eyes as if he were bored, inclined his head to one side, and nipped his ear lobe between his thumb and finger.

"Don't you have a boy friend, Adelaide?" the younger one said in his soft voice.

She looked from him to Mrs. Carlisle, twisting her ring. If she said yes they'd make her give Jules' name. Then they'd go to see Jules' boss and, even though he hadn't had a thing to do with it either, they'd try to pin it on him or he'd lose his job anyway. "No, I haven't," she said, looking straight at the detective.

"All right," he said lightly.

"Let's get going," said his companion.

Mrs. Carlisle backed up to the door. "I don't want you—I'd much rather—" She looked unhappy. "I mean, you couldn't take her if I don't prefer charges or something, can you?"

The older one arched his eyebrows and half yawned. "If you want to drop the whole thing," he said elaborately, "it's your privilege."

"My goodness!" She looked from Adelaide to the two men and back again. "You see, my husband would be simply frantic to have a human being we know . . . when there isn't any *positive* basis to go on," she said, her voice dwindling away at the end.

"Okay." The older one clapped his hat on his head. At the door he said over his shoulder, "Next time you call, you might find out what you do want first." He looked at her with his lips puckered as though he were about to whistle.

The young one gave Adelaide a long look before he disappeared; it made her feel as though someone had pulled the knife out of her.

Mrs. Carlisle lighted another cigarette and, without looking at Adelaide, said in too bright a voice: "Well, we're just where we started, aren't we?"

Adelaide shifted from one foot to another before she said: "Mrs. Carlisle, I don't know how to thank you for sticking up for me, except somehow I'm going to find him. I think I'd know his face anywhere, even if it was ten years from now."

"I doubt if Mr. Carlisle's suit would be the right size for him by then." Mrs. Carlisle straightened the pottery on the mantelpiece and, with her back to Adelaide, said: "Why don't you just finish up? You've been held way over your time."

"Oh, that doesn't make a speck of difference," Adelaide said fervently.

She felt her legs wobbling as she went toward the bedroom which she had just started on when Mrs. Carlisle had come home and she had told her about the man getting the suit. Adelaide kept shaking her head sidewise as she thought of it and she turned the mattress without remembering she had turned it earlier. But Mrs. Carlisle remembered. She had followed Adelaide into the room and seemed to be fooling round in one of the dressing-table drawers for a long time.

"Are you turning it again, Adelaide?" she said.

Adelaide stared at her for a moment and then at the bed. "I guess I better put my mind down on my work," she said. "I just couldn't help think about *it.*"

Mrs. Carlisle left the room but she was back before Adelaide had started dusting. Usually she kept out of Adelaide's way but now she seemed to have a million things to do. And when Adelaide went to the living room to empty the ashtrays they had all been using, Mrs. Carlisle was never more than a few steps away. She didn't say anything, she didn't have to, Adelaide thought bitterly. There was sterling silver about; she had been polishing it for nearly four years with everybody out. Only now it was different.

When she was ready to leave Mrs. Carlisle stopped her before she reached the door. "Oh, Adelaide, I hope you don't mind," she said in an artificial voice. "I mean, leaving your key. I forgot I was expecting a friend overnight and I haven't an extra one for her."

"Yes, ma'am," said Adelaide. She fished in the cracked patent-leather handbag that Mrs. Carlisle had given her when she had finished with it. As she handed over the key she said:

"I lied once this afternoon. I said I didn't have a boy friend because I thought if I did they'd make it bad for him, no matter what. That was the one time I lied."

Mrs. Carlisle flushed. "Oh, Adelaide, please let's not. I never connected you with anything like that. I wouldn't dream of it." She waited a moment for a reply; then she said hurriedly: "It's just that this sort of thing happening makes me so nervous. Maybe we could switch hours some way so you could come in while I'm home and then you wouldn't even need a key, would you?"

She looked up at Adelaide with the same appealing face she had shown the detectives and, for a moment, Adelaide wondered what she would have done if only the soft-spoken one had appeared. Then she said carefully: "You're afraid to have me any more, I guess."

"That's such a wrong way to put it," Mrs. Carlisle said. She backed away a little as she spoke. "It's just that this is a terribly upsetting experience for me. After all—look, Adelaide, you must admit I refused to prefer charges against you."

"Yes, ma'am," Adelaide said and she thought of Mr. Carlisle who had taught his wife never to say "nigger" and who read all the books that said colored people were also human beings. "Only you don't want me back any more, I guess, do you, Mrs. Carlisle?"

"I just don't know," she answered in a distressed voice. "I just can't think right now."

I know, Adelaide thought as she quietly closed the door and walked down the apartment hall. She could even hear Mrs. Carlisle telling her husband later: "It isn't that I suspect her; I wouldn't dream of it. Darling, I snatched her away from those dreadful men. But it would make me so uncomfortable to have her around, I don't think I could stand it." And Mr. Carlisle would finally say something about mailing her maybe a day's pay. She wouldn't send it back either, she thought, as she trudged toward the subway. She only hoped they'd think to send her work shoes too. She was going to need them if she could find another place.

(1941)

BOOGIE-WOOGIE BALLADS: THE TOUCHIN' CASE OF MR. AND MRS. MASSA
by St. Clair McKelway

Oh, let's fix us a julep and kick us a houn'
(Sing "Yassah! Yassah! Yassah!")
And let's dig a place in de col', col', groun'
For Mr. and Mrs. Massa!

[Boogie-woogie]

Oh, this Mr. and Mrs. Massa have always lived in old Virginia and old North Carolina and old South Carolina and old Alabama and old Kentucky and old So Forth and old So On and nobody has ever understood the colored people the way they do because down in old So Forth and old So On is where the white folks understand the colored folks like no other white folks on earth understand colored folks. Yassah! Massa! Yassah!

[Boogie-woogie]

Oh, before the war and for some time afterward Mr. and Mrs. Massa understood the colored folks so well that they had a washerwoman they paid $1.50 a week and a cook they paid $1.75 a week and a butler they paid $2.25 a week and it was mighty lucky for these colored folks that the washerwoman was the cook's mother and the butler was the cook's husband because this enabled the three of them to live cozily in the fifth one-room shack from the left on the other side of the railroad tracks and thus pay $0.85 less a week for rent than the total of their combined salaries.

[Boogie-woogie]

Oh, and over and above the total of their combined salaries Mrs. Massa every other week gave the cook a ham bone outright and Mr. Massa every other month gave the butler a whole quarter of a dollar extra right out of a clear sky. It was manna, Mammy! Manna!

[Boogie-woogie]

Oh, but after the war had been going along for a while the butler, whose name was Charles F. Parker, came to Mr. Massa and told him he was going to quit because he had been offered a job as a counterman in the cafeteria of a defense plant at a salary of $15 a week plus three meals a day and Mr. Massa understood the colored folks so well he told Charles F. Parker that up to then he (Mr. Massa) had been able through influence to persuade the local draft board not to draft him (Charles F. Parker) but that if he (Charles F. Parker) quit his job as butler he (Mr. Massa) would have to persuade the draft board to go ahead and draft him (Charles F. Parker). Swing low, sweet Lincoln!

[Boogie-woogie]

Oh, but then Charles F. Parker told Mr. Massa that as he (Charles F. Parker) understood the situation after conversations with the draft board he (Charles F. Parker) had already been classed as 4-F owing to a number of physical disabilities, including chronic hoecake poisoning, and that therefore he thought he would take the job at the defense-plant cafeteria but with all due respect to Mr. Massa, etc. and etc. Hit that hoecake, boys! Hit it!

[Boogie-woogie]

Oh, so Mr. and Mrs. Massa saw the straws in the wind, saw which way the wind was blowing, and also recognized the trend of the time, so they took another tack, changed face, turned over new leaves, and each gave Charles F. Parker fifteen cents as a bonus and wished him success in his new job and raised the washerwoman (Esther G. Henderson) from $1.50 a week to $1.75 a week and raised the cook (Mrs. Charles F. Parker) from $1.75 a week to $1.85 a week with the understanding that Mrs. Esther G. Henderson would help out Mrs. Charles F. Parker in the kitchen and that Mrs. Charles F. Parker would wait on the table. Pass the hominy grits, boys! Pass it!

[Boogie-woogie]

Oh, but at the end of the first week under the new arrangement Mrs. Charles F. Parker came to Mrs. Massa and said she was going to quit because she had been offered a job as cook at the defense-plant cafeteria at a salary of $22.50 per week plus three meals a day and Mrs. Massa jus' had to cry. Weep some mo', my lady, oh, weep some mo'!

[Boogie-woogie]

Oh, and then the washerwoman (Esther G. Henderson) came to Mrs. Massa and said she was going to quit because she was eighty-two years old and her back ached and her daughter and son-in-law were going to support her for nothing, and Mrs. Massa jus' had to cry some mo'!

[Boogie-woogie]

Oh, and then one day a week after that Mr. and Mrs. Massa were walking back home after a dinner at the Old Southern Greek Chophouse and they saw Charles F. Parker and Mrs. Charles F. Parker and Esther G. Henderson coming out of the colored section of a movie house after having seen a Technicolored feature featuring Jack Benny and Mr. and Mrs. Massa noticed that Charles F. Parker had on a new suit and looked happy and that Mrs. Charles F. Parker had on a new dress and looked happy and that Esther G. Henderson had on a new shawl and looked happy and moreover was still laughing at the jokes Jack Benny had made inside the movie house and Mr. and Mrs. Massa saw the three of them go into a three-room stucco bungalow where Esther G. Henderson had a room all to herself and Mr. and Mrs. Charles F. Parker had a room all to themselves and then Mr. and Mrs. Massa looked at each other understandingly and tears came into the eyes of Mrs. Massa and Mr. Massa put his hand on her shoulder and said to her softly, "Nevah you mind, there'll be a reckonin' one of these days!"

[Boogie-woogie]

Oh, and so Mr. and Mrs. Massa finally closed up the house in old So Forth and old So On and came to New York and leased a suite at the Savoy-Plaza and the Savoy-Netherlands and the Savoy-So Forth and the Savoy-So On and any time you want to listen day or night as well as any time you don't want to listen day or night they will tell you for hours without stopping how they understand the colored people like no other white folks on earth understand colored folks and how the war and high wages are jus' ruinin' everything down in old So Forth and old So On and how never you mind there's goin' to be a reckonin' one of these days. Reckon twice and hit it again, boys! Hit it!

[Boogie-woogie]

Oh, and the bones of Mr. and Mrs. Massa are not growing cold and their heads are not bending low and no angel voices are calling to them and if nobody will carry them back to old So Forth and old So On, oh, then . . .

[Boogie-woogie]

Let's fix us a julep and kick us a houn'
(Sing "Yassah! Yassah! Yassah!")
And let's dig a place in de col', col' groun'
For Mr. and Mrs. Massa!

(1943)

From

CASS TIMBERLANE
by Sinclair Lewis

As he came up the black-and-white marble walk to the bulbous carriage-porch, a black kitten, an entire stranger, was sitting on a step. It said "meow," not whiningly but in a friendly mood, as between equals, and it looked at Cass in a way that dared him to invite it in for a drink.

He was a lover of cats, and he had had none since the ancient and misanthropic Stephen had died, six months before. He had a lively desire to own this little black clown, all black, midnight black, except for its sooty yellow eyes. It would play on the faded carpets when he came home from the court room to the still loneliness that, in the old house, was getting on his nerves.

"Well, how are you, my friend?" he said.

The kitten said she was all right. And about some cream now—?

"Kitten, I can't steal you from some child who's out looking for you. It wouldn't be right to invite you in."

The kitten did not answer anything so naive and prudish. It merely said, with its liquid and trusting glance, that Cass was its god, beyond all gods. It frisked, and dabbled at a fly with its tiny black paw, and looked up at him to ask, "How's that?"

"You are a natural suborner of perjury and extremely sweet," admitted Cass, as he scooped it up and took it through the huge oak door, down the dim hallway to the spacious kitchen and to Mrs. Higbee, his cook-general.

Mrs. Higbee was sixty years old, and what is known as "colored," which meant that she was not quite so dark of visage as Webb Wargate after his annual Florida tanning. She was graceful and sensible and full of love and loyalty. She was in no way a comic servant; she was like any other wholesome Middle-Class American, with an accent like that of any other emigree from Ohio. It must be said that Mrs. Higbee was not singularly intelligent; only slightly more intelligent than Mrs. Boone Havock or Mrs. Webb Wargate; not more than twice as intelligent as Mrs. Vincent Osprey. She was an Episcopalian, and continued to be one, for historic reasons, though she was not greatly welcomed in the more fashionable temples of that faith. Judge Timberlane depended on her good sense rather more than he did on that of George Hame or his friend Christabel Grau.

Mrs. Higbee took the black kitten, tickled it under the chin, and remarked, "Our cat?"

"I'm afraid so. I've stolen it."

"Well, I understand a black cat is either very good luck or very bad luck, I forget which, so we can take a chance on it. What's its name?"

"What is it? A her?"

"Let's see. Um, I think so."

"How about 'Cleo'? You know—from Cleopatra. The Egyptians worshiped cats, and Cleopatra was supposed to be thin and dark and uncanny, like our kitten."

But he was not thinking of Queen Cleopatra. He was thinking of Jinny Marshland, and the thought was uneasy with him.

"All right, Judge. You, Cleo, I'm going to get those fleas off you right away tomorrow, and no use your kicking."

Cass marveled, "Has she got fleas?"

"Has—she—got—fleas! Judge, don't you ever take a real good look at females?"

"Not often. Oh, Mrs. Higbee, you know I'm dining out tonight—at Dr. Drover's."

"Yes. You'll get guinea hen. And that caramel ice cream. And Miss Grau. You won't be home early."

"Anything else I ought to know about the party?"

"Not a thing. . . . Will you look at that Cleo! She knows where the refrigerator is, already!"

(1945)

From

THE MEMBER OF THE WEDDING
Carson McCullers

When they began the second round of that last dinner, it was past five o'clock, and nearing twilight. It was the time of afternoon when in the old days, sitting with the red cards at the table, they would sometimes begin to criticize the Creator. They would judge the work of God, and mention the ways how they would improve the world. And Holy Lord God John Henry's voice would rise up happy and high and strange, and his world was a mixture of delicious and freak, and he did not think in global terms: the sudden long arm that could stretch from here to California, chocolate dirt and rains of lemonade, the extra eye seeing a thousand miles, a hinged tail that could be let down as a kind of prop to sit on when you wished to rest, the candy flowers.

But the world of the Holy Lord God Berenice Sadie Brown was a different world, and it was round and just and reasonable. First, there would be no separate coloured people in the world, but all human beings would be light brown colour with blue eyes and black hair. There would be no coloured people and no white people to make the coloured people feel cheap and sorry all through their lives. No coloured people, but all human men and ladies and children as one loving family on the earth. And when Berenice spoke of this first principle her voice was a strong deep song that soared and sang in beautiful dark tones leaving an echo in the corner of the room that trembled for a long time until silence.

No war, said Berenice. No stiff corpses hanging from the Europe trees and no Jews murdered anywhere. No war, and the young boys leaving home in army suits, and no wild cruel Germans and Japanese. No war in the whole world, but peace in all countries everywhere. Also, no starving. To begin with, the real Lord God had made free air and free rain and free dirt for the benefit of all. There would be free food for every human mouth, free meals and two pounds of fatback a week, and after that each able-bodied person would work for whatever else he wished to eat or own. No killed Jews and no hurt coloured people. No war and no hunger in the world. And, finally, Ludie Freeman would be alive.

The world of Berenice was a round world, and the old Frankie would listen to the strong deep singing voice, and she would agree with Berenice. But the old Frankie's world was the best of the three worlds. She agreed with Berenice about the main laws of her creation, but she added many things: an aeroplane and a motor-cycle to each person, a world club with certificates and badges, and a better law of gravity. She did not completely agree with Berenice about the war: and sometimes she said she would have one War Island in the world where those who wanted to could go, and fight or donate blood, and she might go for a while as a WAC in the Air Corps. She also changed the seasons, leaving out summer altogether, and adding much snow. She planned it so that people could instantly change back and forth from boys to girls, whichever way they felt like and wanted. But Berenice would argue with her about this, insisting that the law of human sex was exactly right just as it was and could in no way be improved. And then John Henry West would very likely add his two cents' worth about this time, and think that people ought to be half boy and half girl, and when the old Frankie threatened to take him to the Fair and sell him to the Freak Pavilion, he would only close his eyes and smile.

So the three of them would sit there at the kitchen table and criticize the Creator and the work of God. Sometimes their voices crossed and the three worlds twisted. The Holy Lord God John Henry West. The Holy Lord God Berenice Sadie Brown. The Holy Lord God Frankie Addams. The worlds at the end of the long stale afternoons.

* * * * *

Berenice had a very strong long right arm, and when F. Jasmine passed her the next time as she was running around the table, this arm reached out and snatched her by the petticoat so quickly that she was caught up with a jerk that made her bones crack and her teeth rattle.

"*Is* you gone raving wild?" she asked. The long arm pulled F. Jasmine closer and wrapped around her waist. "You sweating like a mule. Lean down and let me feel your forehead. Is you got a fever?"

F. Jasmine pulled one of Berenice's plaits and pretended she was going to saw it off with the knife.

"You trembling," said Berenice. "I truly believe you took a fever walking around in that sun today. Baby, you sure you ain't sick?"

"Sick?" asked F. Jasmine. "Who, me?"

"Set here in my lap," said Berenice. "And rest a minute."

F. Jasmine put the knife on the table and settled down on Berenice's lap. She leaned back and put her face against Berenice's neck; her face was sweaty and Berenice's neck was sweaty also, and they both smelled salty and sour and sharp. Her right leg was flung across Berenice's knee, and it was trembling— but when she steadied her toes on the floor, her leg did not tremble any more. John Henry shuffled towards them in the high-heeled shoes and crowded up jealous and close to Berenice. He put his arm around Berenice's head and held on to her ear. Then after a moment he tried to push F. Jasmine out of her lap, and he pinched F. Jasmine with a mean and tiny little pinch.

"Leave Frankie alone," said Berenice. "She ain't bothered you."

He made a fretting sound: "I'm sick."

"Now no, you ain't. Be quiet and don't grudge your cousin a little bit of love."

"Old mean bossy Frankie," he complained in a high sad voice.

"What she doing so mean right now? She just laying here wore out."

F. Jasmine rolled her head and rested her face against Berenice's shoulder. She could feel Berenice's soft big ninnas against her back, and her soft wide stomach, her warm solid legs. She had been breathing very fast, but after a minute her breath slowed down so that she breathed in time with Berenice; the two of them were close together as one body, and Berenice's stiffened hands were clasped around F. Jasmine's chest. Their backs were to the window, and before them the kitchen was now almost dark. It was Berenice who finally sighed and started the conclusion of that last queer conversation.

"I think I have a vague idea what you were driving at," she said. "We all of us somehow caught. We born this way or that way and we don't know why. But we caught anyhow. I born Berenice. You born Frankie. John Henry born John Henry. And maybe we wants to widen and bust free. But no matter what we do we still caught. Me is me and you is you and he is he. We each one of us somehow caught all by ourself. Is that what you was trying to say?"

"I don't know," F. Jasmine said. "But I don't want to be caught."

"Me neither," said Berenice. "Don't none of us. I'm caught worse than you is."

F. Jasmine understood why she had said this, and it was John Henry who asked in his child voice: "Why?"

"Because I am black," said Berenice. "Because I am coloured. Everybody is caught one way or another. But they done drawn completely extra bounds around all coloured people. They done squeezed us off in one corner by ourself. So we caught that firstway I was telling you, as all human beings is caught. And we caught as coloured people also. Sometimes a boy like Honey feel like he just can't breathe no more. He feel like he got to break something or break himself. Sometimes it just about more than we can stand."

"I know it," F. Jasmine said. "I wish Honey could do something."

"He just feels desperate like."

"Yes," F. Jasmine said. "Sometimes I feel like I want to break something, too. I feel like I wish I could just tear down the whole town."

"So I have heard you mention," said Berenice. "But that won't help none. The point is that we all caught. And we try in one way or another to widen ourself free. For instance, me and Ludie. When I was with Ludie, I didn't feel so caught. But then Ludie died. We go around trying one thing or another, but we caught anyhow."

The conversation made F. Jasmine almost afraid. She lay there close to Berenice and they were breathing very slowly. She could not see John Henry, but she could feel him; he had climbed up on the back rungs of the chair and was hugging Berenice's head. He was holding her ears, for in a moment Berenice said: "Candy, don't wrench my ears like that. Me and Frankie ain't going to float up through the ceiling and leave you."

Water dropped slowly into the kitchen sink and the rat was knocking behind the wall.

"I believe I realize what you were saying," F. Jasmine said. "Yet at the same time you almost might use the word loose instead of caught. Although they are two opposite words. I mean you walk around and you see all the people. And to me they look loose."

"Wild, you mean?"

"Oh, no!" she said. "I mean you don't see what joins them up together. You don't know where they all came from, or where they're going to. For instance, what made anybody ever come to this town in the first place? Where did all these people come from and what are they going to do? Think of all those soldiers."

"They were born," said Berenice. "And they going to die."

F. Jasmine's voice was thin and high. "I know," she said. "But what is it all about? People loose and at the same time caught. Caught and loose. All these people and you don't know what joins them up. There's bound to be some sort of reason and connexion. Yet somehow I can't seem to name it. I don't know."

"If you did you would be God," said Berenice. "Didn't you know that?"

"Maybe so."

"We just know so much. Then beyond that we don't know no more."

"But I wish I did." Her back was cramped and she stirred and stretched herself on Berenice's lap, her long legs sprawled out beneath the kitchen table. "Anyway, after we leave Winter Hill I won't have to worry about things any more."

"You don't have to now. Nobody requires you to solve the riddles of the world." Berenice took a deep meaning breath and said: "Frankie, you got the sharpest set of human bones I ever felt."

This was a strong hint for F. Jasmine to stand up. She would turn on the light, then take one of the cup cakes from the stove, and go out to finish her business in the town. But for a moment longer she lay there with her face pressed close to Berenice's shoulder. The sounds of the summer evening were mingled and long-drawn.

"I never did say just what I was talking about," she said finally. "But there's this. I wonder if you have ever thought about this. Here we are—right now, this minute is passing. And it will never come again. Never in all the world. When it is gone it is gone. No power on earth could bring it back again. It is gone. Have you ever thought about that?"

Berenice did not answer, and the kitchen was now dark. The three of them sat silent, close together, and they could feel and hear each other's breaths. Then suddenly it started, though why and how they did not know; the three of them began to cry. They started at exactly the same moment, in the way that often on these summer evenings they would suddenly start a song. Often in the dark, that August, they would all at once begin to sing a Christmas carol, or a song like the Slitbelly Blues. Sometimes they knew in advance that they would sing, and they would agree on the tune among themselves.

Or again, they would disagree and start off on three different songs at once, until at last the tunes began to merge and they sang a special music that the three of them made up together. John Henry sang in a high wailing voice, and no matter what he named his tune, it sounded always just the same: one high trembling note that hung like a musical ceiling over the rest of the song. Berenice's voice was dark and definite and deep, and she rapped the offbeats with her heel. The old Frankie sang up and down the middle space between John Henry and Berenice, so that their three voices were joined, and the parts of the song were woven together.

Often they would sing like this and their tunes were sweet and queer in the August kitchen after it was dark. But never before had they suddenly begun to cry; and though their reasons were three different reasons, yet they started at the same instant as though they had agreed together. John Henry was crying because he was jealous, though later he tried to say he cried because of the rat behind the wall. Berenice was crying because of their talk about coloured people, or because of Ludie, or perhaps because F. Jasmine's bones were really sharp. F. Jasmine did not know why she cried, but the reason she named was the crew-cut and the fact that her elbows were so rusty. They cried in the dark for about a minute. Then they stopped as suddenly as they had begun. The unaccustomed sound had quieted the rat behind the wall.

"Get up from there," said Berenice. They stood around the kitchen table and F. Jasmine turned on the light. Berenice scratched her head and sniffled a little. "We certainly is a gloomy crowd. Now I wonder what started that."

The light was sudden and sharp after the darkness. F. Jasmine ran the faucet of the sink and put her head beneath the stream of water. And Berenice wiped off her face with a dishrag and patted her plaits before the mirror. John Henry stood like a little old woman dwarf, wearing the pink hat with the plume, and the high-heel shoes. The walls of the kitchen were crazy drawn and very bright. The three of them blinked at each other in the light as though they were three strangers or three ghosts. Then the front door opened and F. Jasmine heard her father trudging slowly down the hall. Already the moths were at the window, flattening their wings against the screen, and the final kitchen afternoon was over at last.

(1946)

From

A WIFE OF NASHVILLE
by Peter Taylor

The Lovells' old cook Sarah had quit to get married in the spring, and they didn't have anybody else for a long time—for several months, that is. It was during the depression, and when a servant quit, people in Nashville (and even people out at Thornton, where the Lovells came from) tried to see how long they could go before they got another. All through the summer, there would be knocks on the Lovells' front door or on the wooden porch floor, by the steps. And when one of the children or their mother went to the door, some Negro man or woman would be standing there, smiling and holding out a piece of paper. A recommendation it was supposed to be, but the illegible note scribbled with a blunt lead pencil was something no white person could have written if he had tried. If Helen Ruth, the children's mother, went to the door, she always talked awhile to whoever it was, but she hardly ever even looked at the note held out to her. She would give a piece of advice or say to meet her around at the back door for a handout. If one of the boys—there were three Lovell boys, and no girls—went to the door, he always brought the note in to Helen Ruth, unless John R., their father, was at home, sick with his back ailment. Helen Ruth would shake her head and say to tell whoever it was to go away, go away! "Tell him to go back home," she said once to the oldest boy, who was standing in the sun-parlor doorway with a smudged scrap of paper in his hand. "Tell him if he had any sense, he never would have left the country."

"He's probably not from the country, Mother."

"They're all from the country," Helen Ruth said. "When they knock on the porch floor like that, they're bound to be from the country, and they're better off at home, where somebody cares something about them. I don't care anything about them any more than you do."

But one morning Helen Ruth hired a cheerful-looking and rather plump, light-complexioned young Negress named Jess McGehee, who had come knocking on the front-porch floor just as the others had. Helen Ruth talked to her at the front door for a while; then she told her to come around to the kitchen, and they talked there for nearly an hour. Jess stayed to fix lunch and supper, and after she had been there a few days, the family didn't know how they had ever got along without her.

In fact, Jess got on so well with the Lovells that Helen Ruth even decided to let her come and live on the place, a privilege she had never before allowed a servant of hers. Together, she and Jess moved all of John R.'s junk—a grass duck-hunting outfit, two mounted stags' heads, an outboard motor, and so on—from the little room above the garage into the attic of the house. John R. lent Jess the money for the down payment on a "suit" of furniture, and Jess moved in. "You would never know she was out there," Helen Ruth told her friends. "There is never any rumpus. And her room! It's as clean as yours or mine."

Jess worked for them for eight years. John R. got so one of his favorite remarks was "The honeymoon is over, but this is the real thing this time." Then he would go on about what he called Helen Ruth's "earlier affairs." The last one before Jess was Sarah, who quit to get married and go to Chicago at the age of sixty-eight. She was with them for six years and was famous for her pies and her banana dishes. Before Sarah, there was Carrie. Carrie had been with them when the two younger boys were born, and it was she who had once tried to persuade Helen Ruth not to go to the hospital but to let her act as midwife. She had quit them after five years, to become an undertaker. And before Carrie there was Jane Blakemore, the very first of them all, whom John R. and Helen Ruth had brought with them from Thornton to Nashville when they married. She lasted less than three years; she quit soon after John R., Jr., was born, "because, she said, the baby made her nervous. "It's an honorable record," John R. would say. "Each of them was better than the one before, and each one stayed with us longer. It proves that experience is the best teacher."

(1949)

ETHNIC PRIDE
Ethnic Heroes

The features were rather prominent and well defined. The rich olive complexion, the grave, pensive countenance, proclaimed a proud descent from the only true American—the Indian.

Mourning Dove
Cogewea the Half-Blood

There where she sips her wine, her copper
    brow
Is itself the sunset. Her eyes are lifted now,
Her eyes are evening-stars.

Witter Bynner
A Beautiful Mexican

There was a veil upon you, Pocahontas,
    bride—
O princess whose brown lap was virgin May;
And bridal flanks and eyes hid tawny pride.

Hart Crane
The Dance

From

DELMAR OF PIMA
by Hamlin Garland

The county seat of Pima was an adobe Mexican town, so far as its exterior went, and hugged close under the semicircle formed by the turbid flow of the Rio Perco on the left and the deep arroyo on the right, wherein Medicine Creek lost itself. The houses looked to be dens of animals—and the life that went on within them was often too cruel and too shameless for any beast to have a share in it.

Andrew Delmar approached the river from the south, and having been a long time on the road, was glad of the gleam of water and the sight of a town. His little wagon train was heavily laden with goods bought on credit in Santa Fé, and it was his intention to set up a grocery in San Felipe if he should safely arrive there.

As he drew down to the river bank he came upon a bridge spanning the river, and at one end thereof stood a gate and a small hut.

"I wonder what this means?" he said in Spanish to José, who drove the team next to him.

"It is a toll-bridge, boss."

"Oh, I don't think so," Delmar replied.

At this moment a formidable person appeared at the door of the hut and advanced to meet the train. He wore a wide white hat and a big revolver swung at his hip. His belt was well filled with cartridges.

"Good evenin', gentlemen," said he.

"Good evening. Is that a toll-bridge?" asked Delmar.

"You bet it is," was the decided reply.

"How much toll?"

The gate-keeper eyed the loads critically. "Fifteen dollars," he finally said.

Delmar turned his head and said in Spanish: "How about the river, José? it looks low. I believe we can ford it."

"I think so, too, boss."

Delmar turned his team and was moving away when the gate-keeper called out: "Don't you go to fording that river. I'll hold you up for the fifteen just the same. This bridge is a mighty accommodation ten months in the year, and you can't——"

"That's all right," said Delmar. "It don't accommodate me just now. Go on, Jack."

Delmar at this time was about thirty-five years old, and tall and thin; but his dark gray eyes had a keen hawk-like stare which could make a man feel uncomfortable. He carried two fine revolvers frankly ready for use, and the gate-keeper retired for reënforcements. Delmar put his teams into the shallow river, whose sandy bottom he found to be hard and smooth. As he emerged from the water on the town-side the gate-keeper, reënforced by another influential citizen of the town, confronted him.

"You'd better pony up the metal," he said menacingly. "We don't allow no funny business about it."

"Get out of my way," replied Delmar, and his hand fell with a swift flirt upon his revolver. "You'll repent any gun-play you start with me." There was something in his tone which ended the controversy, for the moment at least. The two tax-gatherers retired, muttering threats.

"We'll make this town hot for you."

"That's all right," he replied; "I'm used to a hot climate."

Delmar was a natural-born politician, and before he had covered his goods with a roof he had possessed himself of the situation in the county. First of all, the cattle element ("The Cowmen") held every office and controlled every election. Cowboys were privileged to "shoot up" the town and have roaring times without regard to the "greasers" or ordinary citizens. Law was for them license and the restraint to their opponents. To kill a Mexican was reprehensible, but not criminal. To stampede a herd of cattle through a drove of sheep was considered a useful, practical joke. It tended to keep the sheepherders humble, and diminished the number of sheep who destroyed the range for cattle. Secondly, this element was "Democratic," and considered itself the aristocracy of the county in contradistinction to the Mexican, or "greaser" population.

In the eyes of these cattle barons and their retainers the greaser was a nuisance. He was given to cultivating the soil along the river-beds, and might be seen any day wading like a snipe in the red mud of his irrigating ditches. They were getting too plenty anyhow and needed to be discouraged. They interfered with the water-rights, and were coming to be so infernal sharp as to argue their rights, saying, "We have as good a claim to the government range as you cattlemen."

The Mexicans, as a matter of fact, knew very little about American politics or any other kind, but they were "agin the government," so far as they knew it. They collected, therefore, under the Republican banner, and made persistent but ineffectual efforts to gain their rights in the county. Numerically they were considerably in the lead, but as the cattlemen controlled all the election machinery, numbers did not count. At the time when Delmar crossed the river and became a citizen of Felipe, the cattlemen were calm and complacent in despotic control of the county.

Delmar at once lined up with the Mexicans. He was half-Spanish, and spoke the Mexican dialect perfectly; but he was also a shrewd trader and ambitious to rule. It was his opportunity, and he seized upon it. His two drivers went out among the Mexicans at once, telling them of Delmar's parentage, and that his sympathies were with them and against the cattlemen, and also that he was going into the sheep business himself. They also spread a knowledge of his reputation as a pistol-shot, and enumerated the men in Albuquerque County who had tried to "snuff him out" and failed.

As a result of this work, and by virtue of his own engaging manner, Delmar did a roaring trade from the start. He bought wool and sold goods, "catching 'em goin' and comin'," as the saying is. He was attentive, alert, and smiling, and withal exact in his dealings. He said frankly, "I'm here to make money, but I'll give you as good a deal as any other merchant and treat you like men, but right there I stop. I'm not selling goods for my health. What I say I'll do, you may bank on, and I'm on your side in this fight against the cattle interest."

He invited leading citizens among the Mexicans to his house, and was hearty and unaffected with every man, woman, and child. The women chattered for hours about him, and came at last to trust him absolutely.

After a careful study of the situation Delmar said to a group of influential Mexicans, "What you want to do first is to get your votes counted."

This remark he made dispassionately, but he was considerably more insistent on the election day which followed. Not a single Republican vote appeared in the count of his voting precinct, though a dozen were known to have voted for the Republican candidate.

After the vote was announced, Delmar walked up to the desk behind which the judges sat smoking comfortably.

"Howdy, gentlemen?" said he.

"Howdy, Delmar? Come in."

"No, thank you. I just called to know where my Republican vote is. I voted the straight ticket, and it does not appear in the returns."

The chairman looked amused. "Is that so? Well, you know how it is— one vote that way—it must have got lost in the shuffle."

This pleased the other judges, and they laughed together most heartily.

With a deadly earnestness which stopped their gaping mouths in a distorted grin, Delmar said, "Gentlemen, at the next election my vote will not get lost in the shuffle. Good-night."

In the months which followed he set to work quietly to organize the Mexican vote, and a year later, at the head of seventy-five men, he marched to the polls, and walking up to the window, thrust his head in, and without greeting said:

"Gentlemen, last year my Republican vote got lost in the shuffle. I don't think it will this time."

The judges were insolent. "How are you going to help yourself?"

"I'm going to see that you count it," replied Delmar. He took a ticket and read it aloud to his men and to all the judges. He then handed it in and said, "I here deposit my vote. If that ballot does not appear on the returns I shall hold every man of you personally responsible for its loss."

He then called up his Mexican supporters one by one and read their ballots. One by one they deposited their ballots, and when they had finished, Delmar said:

"Seventy-six Republican ballots must appear in the returns or you will answer for them." The judges sat in silence, too amazed to formulate a sentence.

As the time for closing the polls came, Delmar was present, and the clerk said with insolent inflection:

"It is customary to clear the room during the counting of the ballots. Mr. Delmar, you must retire."

"This is a public room, and as I have no representative on your board I shall stay."

"Clear the room," called the chairman angrily.

Delmar stepped to the door and threw it open. Twenty swart and resolute Mexicans, armed and ready for battle, filed into the room, ominously silent, their eyes on their leader.

Delmar, calm with the calmness of the rattlesnake, walked toward the window and said: "Go on with your count, and if every one of those seventy-six ballots does not appear in the returns, we'll kill every man of you right where you sit. You can't count us out the way you do the niggers in Arkansas."

With trembling fingers the judges went on with their counting, and the Mexican vote was returned in full.

"Gentlemen, I am obliged to you. Before another election comes I shall make arrangements to have every other polling place in the county guarded, and I here publicly announce myself a candidate for the office of sheriff. If the Democrats of this county want war, they can have it to their complete satisfaction."

(1902)

From

FRECKLES
by Gene Stratton-Porter

"Why don't you sing as you did a week ago? Answer me that, please?"

Freckles smiled confusedly at the Angel, who sat on one of his fancy seats playing his accompaniment on her banjo.

"You are a fraud," she said. "Here you went last week and led me to think that there was the making of a great singer in you, and now you are sing-ing—do you know how badly you are singing?"

"Yis," said Freckles meekly. "I'm thinking I'm too happy to be singing well to-day. The music don't come right only when I'm lonesome and sad. The world's for being all sunshine at prisint, for among you and Mr. McLean and the Bird Woman I'm after being *that* happy that I can't keep me thoughts on me notes. It's more than sorry I am to be disappointing you. Play it over, and I'll be beginning again, and this time I'll hold hard."

"Well," said the Angel, disgustedly, "it seems to me that if I had all the things to be proud of that you have, I'd lift up my head and sing!"

"And what is it I've to be proud of, ma'am?" politely inquired Freckles.

"Why a whole worldful of things," cried the Angel, explosively. "For one thing, you can be good and proud over the way you've kept the timber-thieves out of this lease, and the trust your father has in you. You can be proud that you've never even once disappointed him or failed in what he believed you could do. You can be proud over the way every one speaks of you with trust and honour, and about how brave of heart and strong of body you are. I heard a big man say a few days ago that the Limberlost was full of disagreeable things—positive dangers, unhealthy as it could be, and that since the memory of the first settlers it has been a rendezvous for runaways, thieves, and murderers. This swamp is named for a man that got lost here and wandered around 'till he starved. That man I was talking with said he wouldn't take your job for a thousand dol-lars a month—in fact, he said he wouldn't have it for any money, and you've never missed a day or lost a tree. Proud! Why, I should think you would just parade around about proper over that!

"And you can always be proud that you are born an Irishman. My father is Irish, and if you want to see him just get up and strut, give him a teeny opening to enlarge on his race. He says that if the Irish had decent territory they'd lead the world. He says they've always been handicapped by lack of space and of fertile soil. He says if Ireland had been as big and fertile as Indiana, why, England wouldn't ever have had the upper hand. She'd just be a little appendage. Fancy England an appendage! He says Ireland has the finest orators and the keenest statesmen in Europe to-day, and when England wants to fight, with whom does she fill her trenches? Irishmen, of course! Ireland has the greenest grass and trees, the finest stones and lakes, and they've jaunting-cars. I don't know just exactly what they are, but Ireland has all there are, any-way. They've a lot of great actors, and a few singers, and there never was a sweeter poet than one of theirs. You should hear my father recite 'Dear Harp of My Country.' He does it this way.''

The Angel rose, made an elaborate old-time bow, and holding up the banjo, recited in clipping feet and metre, with rhythmic swing and a touch of brogue that was simply irresistible:

"Dear harp of my country" [The Angel ardently clasped the banjo],

"In darkness I found thee" [She held it up to the light],

"The cold chain of silence had hung o'er thee long" [She muted the strings with her rosy palm];

"Then proudly, my own Irish harp, I unbound thee" [She threw up her head and swept a ringing harmony];

"And gave all thy chords to light, freedom, and song" [She crashed into the notes of the accompaniment she had been playing for Freckles].

"That's what you want to be thinking of!" she cried. "Not darkness, and lonesomeness, and sadness, but 'light, freedom, and song.' I can't begin to think off-hand of all the big, splendid things an Irishman has to be proud of; but whatever they are, they are all yours, and you are a part of them. I just despise that 'saddest-when-I-sing' business. You can sing! Now you go over there and do it! Ireland has had her statesmen, warriors, actors, and poets; now you be her voice! You stand right out there before the cathedral door, and I'm going to come down the aisle playing that accompaniment, and when I stop in front of you—you sing!''

The Angel's face wore an unusual flush. Her eyes were flashing and she was palpitating with earnestness.

She parted the bushes and disappeared. Freckles, straight as a young pine, and with the tenseness of a war-horse scenting battle, stood waiting. Presently, before he saw she was there, she was coming down the aisle toward him, play-ing compellingly, and rifts of light were touching her with golden glory. Frec-kles stood as if transfixed. The blood rioted in his veins.

The cathedral was majestically beautiful, from arched dome of frescoed gold, green, and blue in never-ending shades and harmonies, to the mosaic aisle she trod, richly inlaid in choicest colours, and gigantic pillars that were God's handiwork, fashioned and perfected down through ages of sunshine and rain. But the fair young face and divinely moulded form of the Angel were His most perfect work of all. Never had she looked so surpassingly beautiful. She was smiling encouragingly now, and as she came toward him she struck the chords full and strong.

The heart of poor Freckles almost burst with dull pain and his great love for her. In his desire to fulfil her expectations he forgot everything else, and when she reached his initial chord he was ready. He literally burst forth:

"Three little leaves of Irish green,
    United on one stem,
Love, truth, and valour do they mean,
    They form a magic gem."

The Angel's eyes widened curiously and her lips fell apart. A heavier colour swept into her cheeks. She had intended to arouse him. She had succeeded with a vengeance. She was too young to know that in the effort to rouse a man, women frequently kindle fires that they can neither quench nor control. Freckles was looking out over her head now and singing that song, as it had never been sung before, for her alone; and instead of her helping him, as she had intended, he was carrying her with him on the waves of his voice, away, away into a world she knew not of. When he struck into the chorus, wide-eyed and panting, she was swaying toward him and playing for dear life to keep up.

"Oh, do you love? Oh, say you love,
You love the shamrock green!"

At the last note, Freckles' voice died away and his eyes fastened on the Angel's. He had given his best and his all. He fell on his knees and folded his arms across his breast. The Angel, as if magnetised, walked straight down the aisle to him, and running her fingers into the crisp masses of his red hair, tilted his head back and laid her lips on his forehead.

Then she stepped back and faced him. "Good boy!" she said, in a voice that wavered from the throbbing of her shaken heart. "Dear boy! I knew you could do it! I knew it was in you! Freckles, when you go out into the world, if you can face a great audience and sing like that, just once, you will be immortal, and anything you want will be yours."

"Anything?" gasped Freckles.

"Anything," said the Angel.

(1904)

O BLACK AND UNKNOWN BARDS
by James Weldon Johnson

O black and unknown bards of long ago,
How came your lips to touch the sacred fire?
How, in your darkness, did you come to know
The power and beauty of the minstrel's lyre?
Who first from midst his bonds lifted his eyes?
Who first from out the still watch, lone and long,
Feeling the ancient faith of prophets rise
Within his dark-kept soul, burst into song?

Heart of what slave poured out such melody
As "Steal away to Jesus"? On its strains
His spirit must have nightly floated free,
Though still about his hands he felt his chains.
Who heard great "Jordan roll"? Whose starward eye
Saw chariot "swing low"? And who was he
That breathed that comforting, melodic sigh,
"Nobody knows de trouble I see"?

What merely living clod, what captive thing,
Could up toward God through all its darkness grope,
And find within its deadened heart to sing
These songs of sorrow, love and faith, and hope?
How did it catch that subtle undertone,
That note in music heard not with the ears?
How sound the elusive reed so seldom blown,
Which stirs the soul or melts the heart to tears.

Not that great German master in his dream
Of harmonies that thundered amongst the stars
At the creation, ever heard a theme
Nobler than "Go down, Moses." Mark its bars
How like a mighty trumpet-call they stir
The blood. Such are the notes that men have sung
Going to valorous deeds; such tones there were
That helped make history when Time was young.

There is a wide, wide wonder in it all,
That from degraded rest and servile toil
The fiery spirit of the seer should call
These simple children of the sun and soil.
O black slave singers, gone, forgot, unfamed,
You—you alone, of all the long, long line
Of those who've sung untaught, unknown, unnamed,
Have stretched out upward, seeking the divine.

You sang not deeds of heroes or of kings;
No chant of bloody war, no exulting paean
Of arms-won triumphs; but your humble strings
You touched in chord with music empyrean.
You sang far better than you knew; the songs
That for your listeners' hungry hearts sufficed
Still live,—but more than this to you belongs:
You sang a race from wood and stone to Christ.

(1917)

From

THE CHINESE NIGHTINGALE
by Vachel Lindsay

A Song in Chinese Tapestries

"How, how," he said. "Friend Chang," I said,
"San Francisco sleeps as the dead—
Ended license, lust and play:
Why do you iron the night away?
Your big clock speaks with a deadly sound,
With a tick and a wail till dawn comes round.
While the monster shadows glower and creep,
What can be better for man than sleep?"

"I will tell you a secret," Chang replied;
"My breast with vision is satisfied,
And I see green trees and fluttering wings,
And my deathless bird from Shanghai sings."

Then he lit five firecrackers in a pan.
"Pop, pop," said the firecrackers, "cra-cra-crack."
He lit a joss stick long and black.
Then the proud gray joss in the corner stirred;
On his wrist appeared a gray small bird,
And this was the song of the gray small bird:
"Where is the princess, loved forever,
Who made Chang first of the kings of men?"

And the joss in the corner stirred again;
And the carved dog, curled in his arms, awoke,
Barked forth a smoke-cloud that whirled and broke.
It piled in a maze round the ironing-place,
And there on the snowy table wide
Stood a Chinese lady of high degree,
With a scornful, witching, tea-rose face. . . .
Yet she put away all form and pride,
And laid her glimmering veil aside
With a childlike smile for Chang and for me.

The walls fell back, night was aflower,
The table gleamed in a moonlit bower,
While Chang, with a countenance carved of stone,
Ironed and ironed, all alone.
And thus she sang to the busy man Chang:
"Have you forgotten . . .
Deep in the ages, long, long ago,
I was your sweetheart, there on the sand—
Storm-worn beach of the Chinese land?
We sold our grain in the peacock town—
Built on the edge of the sea-sands brown—
Built on the edge of the sea-sands brown. . . .

When all the world was drinking blood
From the skulls of men and bulls
And all the world had swords and clubs of stone,
We drank our tea in China beneath the sacred spice-trees,
And heard the curled waves of the harbor moan.
And this gray bird, in Love's first spring,
With a bright-bronze breast and a bronze-brown wing,
Captured the world with his carolling.
Do you remember, ages after,
At last the world we were born to own?
You were the heir of the yellow throne—

The world was the field of the Chinese man
And we were the pride of the Sons of Han?
We copied deep books and we carved in jade,
And wove blue silks in the mulberry shade. . . ."
"I remember, I remember
That Spring came on forever,
That Spring came on forever,"
Said the Chinese nightingale.

My heart was filled with marvel and dream,
Though I saw the western street-lamps gleam,
Though dawn was bringing the western day,
Though Chang was a laundryman ironing away. . . .
Mingled there with the streets and alleys,
The railroad-yard and the clock-tower bright,
Demon clouds crossed ancient valleys;
Across wide lotus-ponds of light
I marked a giant firefly's flight.

(1917)

TO THE WHITE FIENDS
by Claude McKay

Think you I am not fiend and savage too?
Think you I could not arm me with a gun
And shoot down ten of you for every one
Of my black brothers murdered, burnt by you?
Be not deceived, for every deed you do
I could match—out-match: am I not Afric's son,
Black of that black land where black deeds are done?
But the Almighty from the darkness drew
My soul and said: Even thou shalt be a light
Awhile to burn on the benighted earth,
Thy dusky face I set among the white
For thee to prove thyself of higher worth;
Before the world is swallowed up in night,
To show thy little lamp: go forth, go forth!

(1919)

From

MAMBA'S DAUGHTERS
by DuBose Heyward

Slowly the light in the big auditorium commenced to ebb, dimming the modern decorations and endowing them with a mysterious beauty, then plunging the audience into interstellar night. The slow throb of music filled the dark, then the curtain of the final act drew up on a stage of swirling mists and vague half-lights. Instantly the mood of the play was re-established, fixing the watchers in attitudes of rigid expectancy.

Dawn again, but no longer the red of an old despair. A thin essential radiance breathed upward behind the massed towers of a metropolis. It gathered strength, spraying out like the corona of an aurora, gilding the towers, then dominating them. The music caught the mood of the sky. The arresting dissonances, the sharp syncopations of the early acts, were no longer individually evident but seemed to merge into a broader irresistible current of sound. The rhythm, too, was no longer a thing separate. It became a force as indistinguishable and pervasive as the life current. It was a fundamental law that moved light, music, the sway of the crowd, the passage of time, in a concerted and inevitable progression. The artificial declamations of operatic convention were gone. The cast was reduced to two elemental forces. The crowd with its heavy mass rhythms and reiterated choruses was the body, and the single transcendent mezzo-soprano that soared above it was the spirit, aspiring, daring, despairing, lifting again. The movement became faster. The voice commenced to lift the chorus from its inertia and carry it along on short, daring flights. Then, in a final acceleration, the scene soared toward its tremendous climax. The light, the movement, the music, merged into a sweeping crescendo, the chorus sprang from its lethargy, while the voice of the woman climbed triumphantly above it until it shook the air like a storm of beating wings. Then the curtain shot downward.

When Wentworth recovered from his trancelike absorption the house was applauding; the large negro chorus was taking a curtain call. The demands of the audience became deafening. Lissa's great hour! She advanced to the footlights and bowed. Now, in the full light she was plainly visible for the first time, a mulatto, a little above medium height, and of superb proportions. Wentworth noticed that she wore no make-up except a slight darkening of the lips that made them seem fuller, more deliberately negroid. This struck him as significant. From the light bronze of her face her eyes looked out, large, expressive, and extraordinarily brilliant—Mamba's eyes—yes, and Hagar's. Now, for the first time, he noticed that she appeared self-conscious, anxious to be away. She bowed for the second time, and without waiting for the curtain, withdrew among the chorus.

But the audience would not let it rest at that. They got to their feet and cheered. They kept the clamour going with a sort of mad persistence. After five minutes of it the curtain was seen to move, rising slowly on a bright vacant stage.

Lissa stepped from the wings, and the clamour plunged into silence. The trace of embarrassed self-consciousness was gone. She seemed detached, oblivious of both herself and her audience. The conductor rose and looked up to her for his cue. Apparently she did not see him, for she gave no sign. Instead she stopped where she was just out of the wings, and unaccompanied commenced to sing the National Anthem of the American Negro.

Apparently most of the audience had never heard of it. Wentworth never had. From the first note he was aware of an absolutely new sensation. Against his perception beat the words of James Weldon Johnson's inspiring poem swept forward in the marching rhythm of Rosamond Johnson's music:

"Lift every voice and sing
Till earth and heaven ring,
Ring with the harmonies of Liberty;
Let our rejoicing rise
High as the list'ning skies,
Let it resound loud as the rolling sea.
Sing a song full of faith that the dark past has taught us,
Sing a song full of the hope that the present has brought us;
Facing the rising sun of our new day begun,
Let us march on till victory is won."

Wentworth, listening, felt suddenly the impact of something tremendously and self-consciously racial; something that had done with apologies for being itself, done with imitations, reaching back into its own origin, claiming its heritage of beauty from the past.

On the stage, as the song progressed toward its conclusion, the singer commenced to sway—sway as Mamba always did toward the end of a spiritual. Only in this young voice to which art had brought discipline there was a difference. It wasted nothing in hysteria, but released the full torrent of its pent emotion into the words and music. Now she was singing the final stanza:

"God of our weary years,
God of our silent tears,
Thou who hast brought us thus far on the way;
Thou who hast by Thy might
Led us into the light,
Keep us ever in the path, we pray.
Lest our feet stray from the places, our God, where we met   Thee,
Lest our hearts, drunk with the wine of the world, we forget   Thee;

Shadowed beneath Thy hand,
May we forever stand.
True to our God,
True to our native land.''

The song ceased, and the curtain descended. In the auditorium the audience paid it the tribute of a breathless silence. Then they rose quietly and filed out into the street.

(1929)

From

LAUGHING BOY
by Oliver La Farge

Laughing Boy went off alone to wrestle with gods: Slim Girl turned to loneliness as a tried friend and counsellor. To be with herself, complete to herself, that was familiar reality; distraction and strangeness was to be among many, to consult. On a high place she sat down to think, not facing the greatness of the desert, but where she could look on her gathered people, made small and impersonal below her. Long habit and self-training had made her cool and contained; she did not like to admit that she had need of mere emotion, and when she did allow herself a luxury of feeling, it had to be where none could spy on her. It was not that she would make any demonstration; she just did not want to be looked at when she was not quite mistress of herself. Now her isolated, high position put a physical difference between her impulses and those of the people in the valley, making them visibly superior. She lit a cigarette and relaxed.

If she did not watch out, she would love this man. She did not intend to love any one; had she not learned enough of that? He was necessary to her; he was the perfect implement delivered to her hands; he was an axe with which to hew down the past; he was a light with which to see her way back to her people, to the good things of her people. She held him up against the past, matrons and teachers at school, platitudes and well-meaning lies. And now, for all their care and training and preaching, she was ''going back to the blanket,'' because under the blanket were the things worth while, and all the rest was hideous. With her knowledge and experience, with what the Americans had taught her, she would lead this man, and make for them both the most perfect life that could be made—with an Indian, a long-haired, heathen Indian, a blanket Indian, a Navajo, the names thrown out like an insult in the faces of those who bore them, of her own people, Denné, The People, proud as she was proud, and clear of heart as she could never be.

There were to be no mistakes, and no chances. She could tie this man to her as surely as any prisoner; she would follow her clear plan to its victorious end. She had conquered herself, she had conquered circumstance; emerging from the struggle not American, not Indian, mistress of herself. Now from the Americans she took means, and in the Indians would achieve her end. Not such an amazing end, perhaps, but strange enough for her: a home in the Northern desert, and children, in a place where the agent's men never came to snatch little children from their parents and send them off to school. They would be Navajo, all Navajo, those children, when the time came. This was her revenge, that all the efforts of all those very different Americans to drag her up or to drag her down into the American way, in the end would be only tools to serve a Navajo end.

It made her happy to think of that man. Laughing Boy. He was more than just what that name implied; one felt the warrior under the gaiety, and by his songs and his silver, he was an artist. All Navajo, even to his faults, he would teach her the meaning of those oft-repeated phrases, *"bik'é hojoni*, the trail of beauty''; through him she would learn the content, and she would provide the means.

Yes, this was her man, as though he had been made expressly for her, strong, straight, gay, a little stubborn. He had character, she would develop it. And she would bind him. There would be no second wife in her hogahn.

"Patience," she told herself; "you are not in the Northern desert yet. You have a long road to travel yet, full of ambushes."

She had no intention of herding sheep and slaving away her youth in a few years of hard labour, herding sheep, hoeing corn, packing firewood, growing square across the hips and flat in the face and heavy in the legs. No; she had seen the American women. First there was money; the Americans must serve her a little while yet; then, after that, the unmapped cañons, and the Indians who spoke no English.

She sat perfectly still, looking at nothing and hating Americans. She had not turned herself loose like this in a long time. Some young man, far below, was singing a gay song about the owl that turned her thoughts to Laughing Boy; she relaxed and smiled. This was something happy to think of. He came like the War God in the song, she thought, and began to sing it haltingly, not sure of the exact words—

"Now Slayer of Enemy Gods, alone I see him coming;
Down from the skies, alone I see him coming.
His voice sounds all about. *Lé-é!*
His voice sounds, divine. *Lé-é!"*

That is he, she thought, Slayer of Enemy Gods. He would be shocked to hear me say it, to hear a woman sing that song.

She went on to the formal ending, "In beauty it is finished, in beauty it is finished," then changed it, "In beauty it is begun. In beauty it is begun. Thanks."

That is a good religion, as good as Christianity. I wonder if I can learn to believe in it? One needs some religion. At least, I can get good out of its ideas. If he is that god, what am I? White Shell Woman? Changing Woman, perhaps. I must mould and guide this War God I have made. I must not let him get away from me. None of the bad things must happen; I must make no mistakes. I am not a Navajo, nor am I an American, but the Navajos are my people.

(1929)

JEW

by Karl Shapiro

The name is immortal but only the name, for the rest
Is a nose that can change in the weathers of time or persist
Or die out in confusion or model itself on the best.

But the name is a language itself that is whispered and hissed
Through the houses of ages, and ever a language the same,
And ever and ever a blow on our heart like a fist.

And this last of our dream in the desert, O curse of our name,
Is immortal as Abraham's voice in our fragment of prayer
Adonai, Adonai, for our bondage of murder and shame!

And the word for the murder of God will cry out on the air
Though the race is no more and the temples are closed of our will
And the peace is made fast on the earth and the earth is made fair;

Our name is impaled in the heart of the world on a hill
Where we suffer to die by the hands of ourselves, and to kill.

(1943)

THE STRONG SWIMMER
by William Rose Benét

I have a story fit to tell,
In head and heart a song;
A burning blue Pacific swell;
A raft that was towed along.

Out in the bloody Solomon Isles
Destroyer *Gregory* gone;
Ocean that kills for all her smiles,
And darkness coming on.

The *Gregory*'s raft bobbed on the tide
Loaded with wounded men.
Ensign and seaman clung her side.
Seaward she drifted then.

A mess-attendant, a Negro man,
Mighty of chest and limb,
Spoke up: "I'll tow you all I can
As long as I can swim."

Naked, he wound his waist with a line;
Slipped smoothly overside,
Where the red bubble tells the brine
That sharks have sheared the tide.

"I'm goin' to tow this old craft in
Since we ain't got not one oar,"
He breathed, as the water lapped his chin;
And he inched that raft ashore.

Strongly he stroked, and long he hauled—
No breath for any song.
His wounded mates clung close, appalled.
He towed that raft along.

Clear to the eye the darkening swell
Where glimmering dangers glide;
The raft of sailors grimed from Hell
Afloat on a smoky tide—

And a dark shoulder and muscled arm
Lunging, steady and strong.
The messman, their brother, who bears a charm,
Is towing their raft along.

He gasped, *"Just say if I'm goin' right!"*
Yes, brother, right you are!
Danger of ocean or dark of night,
You steer by one clear star.

Six hours crawled by. . . . A barge in sight
With the raft just off the shore. . . .
The messman coughed, "Sure, I'm all right."
He was just as he was before.

And all that they knew was they called him "French"—
Not quite a name to sing.
Green jungle hell or desert trench,
No man did a braver thing.

He's burned a story in my brain
Set in my heart a song.
He and his like, by wave and main,
World without end—*and not in vain*—
Are towing this world along!

(1944)

From

LETTER TO THE FRONT
by Muriel Rukeyser

To be a Jew in the twentieth century
Is to be offered a gift. If you refuse,
Wishing to be invisible, you choose
Death of the spirit, the stone insanity.
Accepting, take full life, full agonies:
Your evening deep in labyrinthine blood
Of those who resist, fail, and resist; and God
Reduced to a hostage among hostages.

The gift is torment. Not alone the still
Torture, isolation; or torture of the flesh.
That may come also. But the accepting wish,
The whole and fertile spirit as guarantee
For every human freedom, suffering to be free,
Daring to live for the impossible.

(1944)

DARK SYMPHONY
by Melvin B. Tolson

I   ALLEGRO MODERATO

Black Crispus Attucks taught
          Us how to die
Before white Patrick Henry's bugle breath
Uttered the vertical
          Transmitting cry:
"Yea, give me liberty, or give me death."

And from that day to this
        Men black and strong
For Justice and Democracy have stood,
Steeled in the faith that Right
        Will conquer Wrong
And Time will usher in one brotherhood.

No Banquo's ghost can rise
        Against us now
And say we crushed men with a tyrant's boot
Or pressed the crown of thorns
        On Labor's brow,
Or ravaged lands and carted off the loot.

II LENTO GRAVE

The centuries-old pathos in our voices
Saddens the great white world,
And the wizardry of our dusky rhythms
Conjures up shadow-shapes of ante-bellum years:

Black slaves singing *One More River to Cross*
In the torture tombs of slave ships,
Black slaves singing *Steal Away to Jesus*
In jungle swamps,
Black slaves singing *The Crucifixion*
In slave pens at midnight,
Black slaves singing *Swing Low, Sweet Chariot*
In cabins of death,
Black slaves singing *Go Down, Moses*
In the canebrakes of the Southern Pharaohs.

III ANDANTE SOSTENUTO

They tell us to forget
The Golgotha we tread . . .
We who are scourged with hate,
A price upon our head.
They who have shackled us
Require of us a song,
They who have wasted us
Bid us o'erlook the wrong.

They tell us to forget
Democracy is spurned.
They tell us to forget
The Bill of Rights is burned.
Three hundred years we slaved,
We slave and suffer yet:
Though flesh and bone rebel,
They tell us to forget!

Oh, how can we forget
Our human rights denied?
Oh, how can we forget
Our manhood crucified?
When Justice is profaned
And plea with curse is met,
When Freedom's gates are barred,
Oh, how can we forget?

IV *TEMPO PRIMO*

The New Negro strides upon the continent
In seven league boots . . .
The New Negro
Who sprang from the vigor-stout loins
Of Nat Turner, gallows-martyr for Freedom,
Of Joseph Cinquez, Black Moses of the Amistad Mutiny,
Of Frederick Douglass, oracle of the Catholic Man,
Of Sojourner Truth, eye and ear of Lincoln's legions,
Of Harriet Tubman, St. Bernard of the Underground Railroad.

V *LARGHETTO*

None in the Land can say
To us black men Today:
You send the tractors on their bloody path,
And create Oakies for *The Grapes of Wrath*.
You breed the slum that breeds a *Native Son*
To damn the good earth Pilgrim Fathers won.

None in the Land can say
To us black men Today:

You dupe the poor with rags-to-riches tales,
And leave the workers empty dinner pails.
You stuff the ballot box, and honest men
Are muzzled by your demogogic din.

None in the Land can say
To us black men Today:
You smash stock markets with your coined blitzkriegs
And make a hundred million guinea pigs.
You counterfeit our Christianity,
And bring contempt upon Democracy.

None in the Land can say
To us black men Today:
You prowl when citizens are fast asleep,
And hatch Fifth Column plots to blast the deep
Foundations of the State and leave the Land
A vast Sahara with a Fascist brand.

None in the Land can say
To us black men Today:
You send flame-gutting tanks, like swarms of flies,
And plump a hell from dynamiting skies.
You fill machine-gunned towns with rotting dead—
A No Man's Land where children cry for bread.

VI   TEMPO DI MARCIA

Out of abysses of Illiteracy,
Through labyrinths of Lies,
Across wastelands of Disease . . .
We advance!

Out of dead-ends of Poverty,
Through wildernesses of Superstition,
Across barricades of Jim Crowism . . .
We advance!

With the Peoples of the World . . .
We advance!

                                        (1944)

FREDERICK DOUGLASS
by Robert Hayden

When it is finally ours, this freedom, this liberty, this beautiful
and terrible thing, needful to man as air,
usable as earth; when it belongs at last to all,
when it is truly instinct, brain matter, diastole, systole,
reflex action; when it is finally won; when it is more
than the gaudy mumbo jumbo of politicians:
this man, this Douglass, this former slave, this Negro
beaten to his knees, exiled, visioning a world
where none is lonely, none hunted, alien,
this man, superb in love and logic, this man
shall be remembered. Oh, not with statues' rhetoric,
not with legends and poems and wreaths of bronze alone,
but with the lives grown out of his life, the lives
fleshing his dream of the beautiful, needful thing.

                                                    (1949)

THE SOUTHERN SCENE

There are single acres in Europe that house more first-rate men than all the states south of the Potomac; there are probably single square miles in America.

> H. L. Mencken
> The Sahara of the Bozart

The Dixie Pike has grown from a goat path in Africa.

> Jean Toomer
> *Cane*

St. Peter said, "Well,
    You got back quick.
How's de devil? An' what's
    His latest trick?"

An Slim say, "Peter,
    I really cain't tell,
The place was Dixie
    That I took for hell."

Then Peter say, "You must
    Be crazy, I vow,
Where'n hell dja think Hell *was*,
    Anyhow?

> Sterling A. Brown
> Slim in Hell

From

NAPOLEON JACKSON
by Ruth McEnery Stuart

The picture of the family group of Rose Ann, washerwoman, as gathered almost any day at her cabin door, was a pictorial expression of the great story of her life—its romance, its tragedy, and, fortunately for all concerned, its comedy.

Rose Ann was, as already introduced, and as she herself would have told you, a washerwoman—"not none o' yo' fancy laund'esses, but jes a plain grass-bleachin', sun-dryin', clair-starch-in', muscle-polishin' washerwoman." Would there were more of her kind!

She was fat, black, maternal; and as she stood among her piccaninnies before her tubs, in character, even to the turning up of her faded skirt from her bare feet, it was gratifying to see that she was alive and happy.

The group of children, a dog or two, and a maternal cat,—also in character,—slept, played, quarreled, or frolicked about her feet, and on the grass-plot beyond her wash-bench. The smaller children were nearly naked, taking the group in midsummer; a baby of less than a year, who disputed a bone with a playful pup, was quite so.

This much of the picture might have been duplicated, excepting as to unimportant details, at any one of a dozen cabin doors within a mile of Rose Ann's. A note of apparent discord comes in with the father of the family, the gentleman in starched linen, if you please, who, in an attitude of elegant leisure, reclined in the easy-chair at the washer's right—somewhat apart from the group, but near enough to his spouse for comfortable conversation.

This personage—there are some who are always, by grace of a certain innate distinction, "personages" in any group of persons—this personage, then, was, so he was introduced, "Mr. Napoleon Jackson, Esquire," and he was, as seen at a glance, a man of color, of leisure, of family, and of parts. As to color, Napoleon, or 'Poleon familiarly, was so deeply endowed as to be almost colorless, which is to say, he was black. He was as nearly black, that is, as any man or crow was ever known to be. The highest expression of the pure African is by no means a forbidding type. Far from it. Of course the familiar "types," which alone are really typical, are of other sorts. But Napoleon was an exception. If there had been any room for the suspicion, any slight deflection of color admitting a ray of doubt, one would have said, with small feeling of hazard, that he was part Indian. But that was simply because of his slender and great proportions, the straight lines defining his supple figure, and the high bridge of his nose, to which feature his amiable face chiefly owed its dignity.

It takes more than polished linen, plush easy-chairs, and muscular relaxation to express the real inborn spirit of repose. It is true that the only creases in Napoleon's duck trousers were those which told of easy risings and sittings, and that his cuffs, which were polished until they were as fine as celluloid, generally went "all unbroke" back to Rose Ann's tubs, but the lordly grace of the man was a thing apart from either raiment or incidental setting. That it was somewhat heightened in effect by the chair of crimson plush in which he lounged cannot be denied. This resplendent article, of which more anon, was of the pattern known as the Morris chair, with an adjustable back.

*   *   *   *   *

The back of the Morris chair was lowered by means of a brass rod and a series of notches. About the hour when the morning-glories began to twist up their cups, leaving the blood of the cypress stars to catch the upmoving sun, Rose Ann's habit was to slip the rod back a notch or two behind her lord, for this was his usual napping-time. Not that he always slept. For there were mornings when he seemed to enjoy whatever he saw in the canopy above his head, and occasionally he would call Rose Ann's attention to a tragedy or comedy of life there which might have been a reflection of that enacting below, though neither he nor she would ever have discovered it. He-birds are often mighty fine gentlemen, if you please, and there are plush rockers galore in nature's greenery chambers for such as they when their pleasure may be to tilt upon their perches while they bask in the adoration of their dutifully sitting mates. What is the difference, a nest or a tub, to typify the conserving partner—the home-maker?

And some of these feathered fellows are, even as was Napoleon, fine, able-bodied types. And many are songbirds, too, as was he.

Rose Ann was a magnetic woman, as most thoroughly vitalized people are—most, but not all. Some there be who thrive as air-plants, ever luxuriant, but detached, self-contained. But our woman was not of this class. Rather was she of those who, rooted to the soil by a thousand live fibers, grow, thrive, blossom, and bloom, not to speak of bearing, for the joy of all such as come in contact with them. It was her part of life—life abundant, warm, sweet to the possessor. It needed that God should send a woman like this as mate to the man in the chair; that is, if he be mated at all. And surely, if physical perfection and a gentle heart count for aught, it were a pity to have him wasted. Perhaps it would better be said, for the sake of the few space-blind, who know not how to read between the lines, that Napoleon had never in his life been known to do any kind of work—that the situation, which has already been described as interpretative, was not an incident or a phase of his being. It was its very essence.

Such a life was, of course, open to criticism, and, equally of course, it got it. But since Rose Ann had, according to her oft-declared defense, known just what she was doing when she married him, and since it was her pleasure, perhaps even her pride, to labor for her lord's leisure,—in other words, to pit her tubs against his chair,—and since there was neither lean nor hungry one between the two, and while there was joy in the song by which she washed, as well as impetus to industry in its stirring measure, it would seem that criticism may have been vain and sympathy wasted.

"Well, I married for love, an' I got it," she was wont to exclaim to such of her neighbors as were indiscreet enough to challenge her conjugal loyalty. And she generally added, often flapping a wet garment between her palms for emphasis, "An' *I'm happy in it!*"

Then, if the guest were of an insistent turn, or if Rose Ann happened to be herself in a voluble mood, she would enter more deeply into the subject in this wise:

"Of co'se, when I married 'Poleon, I knowed he was n't to say de 'dustriousest man in de worl', an' I ain't got no right to complain. He did n't *work* whilst he was *co'tin'* me an' *stop* arter he got *married*. No, sir. He co'ted me settin' down fannin' 'isself or layin' in de clover whilst I flung de hoe. An' I swapped off de hoe for love an' duty arter I got married, 'ca'se a wash-bench is better 'n a potato-hill to raise chillen roun'. No, I know it ain't none o' his fault. He *can't* work, 'ca'se his mammy she *marked* him so. She had been overworked befo' he was born, an' she marked her chile for *rest*."

(1902)

From

FOLLOWING THE COLOUR LINE
by Ray Stannard Baker

Another case shows one of the strange relationships which grow out of Southern conditions. An old white man, much agitated and very pale, was brought before the judge. With him came a much younger, comely appearing woman. Both were well dressed and looked respectable—so much so, indeed, that there was a stir of interest and curiosity among the spectators. Why had they been arrested? As they stood in front of the judge's desk, the old man hung his head, but the woman looked up with such an expression, tearless and tragic, as I hope I shall not have to see again.

"What's the charge?" asked the judge.

"Adultery," said the officer.

The woman winced, the old man did not look up.

The judge glanced from one to the other in surprise.

"Why don't you get married?" he asked.

"The woman," said the officer, "is a nigger."

She was as white as I am, probably an octoroon; I could not have distinguished her from a white person, and she deceived even the experienced eye of the judge.

"Is that so?" asked the judge.

The man continued to hang his head, the woman looked up; neither said a word. It then came out that they had lived together as man and wife for many years and that they had children nearly grown. One of the girls—and a very bright, ambitious girl—as I learned later, was a student in Atlanta University, a Negro college, where she was supported by her father, who made good wages as a telegraph operator. Some neighbour had complained and the man and woman were arrested.

"Is this all true?" asked the judge.

Neither said a word.

"You can't marry under the Georgia law," said the judge; "I'll have to bind you over for trial in the county court."

They were led back to the prisoners' rooms. A few minutes later the bailiff came out quickly and said to the judge:

"The old man has fallen in a faint."

Not long afterward they half led, half carried him out across the court room.

(1908)

From

THE SOUTHERNER
by Walter Hines Page

When we were to start home I felt like picking up forgotten threads of old things, and I said to Uncle Ephraim that we would go and see Sam.

"Sam who?"

"Sam who used to belong to us."

"Sam what run away? I thought he done gone or was daid, or som't'in' happen ter him."

"He's teaching."

"Sam a-teachin' school? Whar'd he git his larnin'?"

For Sam was now a teacher in a large school for Negro youth. In the pamphlet of explanation of the school, he appeared as "Samuel Worth, Teacher of Building."

It was Saturday when we arrived. Professor Worth (Is "dat what we got ter call Sam, Mars' Littlenick?") showed us the workshops of the school. Here were young men learning carpentry; here were others learning shoe-making; and others, harness-making; others were laying bricks; others were learning to shoe horses; others to plan and to build houses (this was Professor Worth's own department). The young women were taught to cook, to sew, to do fine laundry work, to care for poultry, to nurse the sick. There was a farm where both sexes worked, and a dairy where women were taught to make butter. And at night they had lessons from books.

And there was not a white man on the premises. All this work was done by coloured men and women.

"Now dat's de way ter larn de young folks ter be some account," Uncle Ephraim said.

Saturday night the custom was for all the students to gather in the great hall, a large auditorium of which Sam was the architect, and to sing the plantation melodies. Professor Worth was the leader of the singing as well as the teacher of building. They insisted that Uncle Ephraim and I should sit on the platform. In they came, six hundred of them, more than half being half-white. After the reading of a chapter from the Bible and a brief prayer, which all recited, the singing of the religious songs and plantation melodies was begun.

That mighty chorus of six hundred voices sent the rolling old refrains up to the rafters.

They sang, "O Lord, What a Mornin'."

I saw tears come to Uncle Ephraim's eyes.

"Let 'em sing dat ag'in, suh, if you please," said the old man; and again, even louder and more melodiously, the Heavens were rolled up as a scroll, and the Great Day was come!

Here was a reason, as I had found a reason among the white folk, why we who are born here ever feel the call of the land to serve the people. Here were the fundamental crudities exposed. Here were three hundred half-white faces before me—three hundred tragedies—the white man calling out in every one of them to the life of his kinsmen and the black man holding him to the plane of the African. And here was the African, now through the tutelage of slavery, trying to become an independent, full-grown man—all children in civilization, not yet understanding, nor yet understood, pulling upward against odds that must be endured rather than resented, a patient race, with need of all its patience, a humour-loving people, with need of all their humour, a melodious folk, with need of all their music for consolation—pulling up, pulling up, and here at least rising by the best way, the way of trained industry; and yet their very songs were the songs of slavery. But it was a music such as the master race had not developed. The pathos of it would move even old Stringweather to tears, if he could see and hear it in his long home.

Yet a more pathetic fact was that not one of the Stringweathers or their like or their dupes would ever have such an experience, for not one of them would ever visit such a school, nor even believe the truthful reports that were made of it.

I must make an address to the students, they told me; and the Principal introduced me. I do not know what I said—no matter; for something far more important happened when I sat down.

Without invitation or warning, Uncle Ephraim arose. He was feeble, but he hobbled to the centre of the platform, his white head a fitting crown of his great black stature; and he looked down from his height of ninety years. He turned to the Principal and bowed.

There was a long silence. Something in his motion recalled my grandfather. He said nothing, and the silence became intense.

He bowed again.

Was the old man getting a glimpse at last, before he should go, of the great problem of which he was a part, and of which he had never been aware?

At last he began to speak:

"I wants ter say, suh, I is er ol' man, done pas' de years er de prophets, an' I'll soon be gwine ter de odder sho'.

"Before I goes, whar I'll see de gret men of dem gret ol' times—Mars' Henry Clay and my ol' Marster and Mars' Lawd Gawd A'mighty hisself—I'se much obleeged ter hear dem gret ol' songs and ter see yer a-fetchin' up dese young fo'ks here ter do deir hones' wuk. Now I bids yer far-well."

I looked at Sam, who sat motionless. But presently he awoke and beckoned to the congregation to rise, and again they all sang, six hundred strong:

"O Lord, What a Mornin'."

(1909)

From

THE AUTOBIOGRAPHY OF
AN EX-COLOURED MAN
by James Weldon Johnson

The next morning I got out of the car at Jacksonville with a stiff and aching body. I determined to ask no more porters, not even my benefactor, about stopping places; so I found myself on the street not knowing where to go. I walked along listlessly until I met a coloured man who had the appearance of a preacher. I asked him if he could direct me to a respectable boarding-house for coloured people. He said that if I walked along with him in the direction he was going, he would show me such a place: I turned and walked at his side. He proved to be a minister, and asked me a great many direct questions about myself. I answered as many as I saw fit to answer; the others I evaded or ignored. At length we stopped in front of a frame-house, and my guide informed me that it was the place. A woman was standing in the doorway, and he called to her saying that he had brought her a new boarder. I thanked him for his trouble, and after he had urged upon me to attend his church while I was in the city, he went on his way.

I went in and found the house neat and not uncomfortable. The parlour was furnished with cane-bottomed chairs, each of which was adorned with a white crocheted tidy. The mantel over the fireplace had a white crocheted cover; a marble-topped centre table held a lamp, a photograph album and several trinkets, each of which was set upon a white crocheted mat. There was a cottage organ in a corner of the room, and I noted that the lamp-racks upon it were covered with white crocheted mats. There was a matting on the floor, but a white crocheted carpet would not have been out of keeping. I made arrangements with the landlady for my board and lodging; the amount was, I think, three dollars and a half a week. She was a rather fine-looking, stout, brown-skin woman of about forty years of age. Her husband was a light-coloured Cuban, a man about one half her size, and one whose age could not be guessed from his appearance. He was small in size, but a handsome black moustache and typical Spanish eyes redeemed him from insignificance.

I was in time for breakfast, and at the table I had the opportunity to see my fellow boarders. There were eight or ten of them. Two, as I afterwards learned, were coloured Americans. All of them were cigar-makers and worked in one of the large factories—cigar-making is one trade in which the colour line is not drawn. The conversation was carried on entirely in Spanish, and my ignorance of the language subjected me to more alarm than embarrassment. I had never heard such uproarious conversation; everybody talked at once, loud exclamations, rolling *"carambas,"* menacing gesticulations with knives, forks, and spoons. I looked every moment for the clash of blows. One man was emphasizing his remarks by flourishing a cup in his hand, seemingly forgetful of the fact that it was nearly full of hot coffee. He ended by emptying it over what was, relatively, the only quiet man at the table excepting myself, bringing from him a volley of language which made the others appear dumb by comparison. I soon learned that in all of this clatter of voices and table utensils they were discussing purely ordinary affairs and arguing about mere trifles, and that not the least ill feeling was aroused. It was not long before I enjoyed the spirited chatter and *badinage* at the table as much as I did my meals—and the meals were not bad.

I spent the afternoon in looking round the town. The streets were sandy, but were well shaded by fine oak-trees and far preferable to the clay roads of Atlanta. One or two public squares with green grass and trees gave the city a touch of freshness. That night after supper I spoke to my landlady and her husband about my intentions. They told me that the big winter hotels would not open for two months. It can easily be imagined what effect this news had on me. I spoke to them frankly about my financial condition and related the main fact of my misfortune in Atlanta. I modestly mentioned my ability to teach music and asked if there was any likelihood of my being able to get some scholars. My landlady suggested that I speak to the preacher who had shown me her house; she felt sure that through his influence I should be able to get up a class in piano. She added, however, that the coloured people were poor, and that the general price for music lessons was only twenty-five cents. I noticed that the thought of my teaching white pupils did not even remotely enter her mind. None of this information made my prospects look much brighter.

The husband, who up to this time had allowed the woman to do most of the talking, gave me the first bit of tangible hope; he said that he could get me a job as a "stripper" in the factory where he worked, and that if I succeeded in getting some music pupils, I could teach a couple of them every night, and so making a living until something better turned up. He went on to say that it would not be a bad thing for me to stay at the factory and learn my trade as a cigar-maker, and impressed on me that, for a young man knocking about the country, a trade was a handy thing to have. I determined to accept his offer and thanked him heartily. In fact, I became enthusiastic, not only because I saw a way out of my financial troubles, but also because I was eager and curious over the new experience I was about to enter. I wanted to know all about the cigar-making business. This narrowed the conversation down to the husband and myself, so the wife went in and left us talking.

He was what is called a *regalia* workman, and earned from thirty-five to forty dollars a week. He generally worked a sixty-dollar job; that is, he made cigars for which he was paid at the rate of sixty dollars per thousand. It was impossible for him to make a thousand in a week because he had to work very carefully and slowly. Each cigar was made entirely by hand. Each piece of filler and each wrapper had to be selected with care. He was able to make a bundle of one hundred cigars in a day, not one of which could be told from the others by any difference in size or shape, or even by any appreciable difference in weight. This was the acme of artistic skill in cigar-making. Workmen of this class were rare, never more than three or four in one factory, and it was never necessary for them to remain out of work. There were men who made two, three and four hundred cigars of the cheaper grades in a day; they had to be very fast in order to make decent week's wages. Cigar-making was a rather independent trade; the men went to work when they pleased and knocked off when they felt like doing so. As a class the workmen were careless and improvident; some very rapid makers would not work more than three or four days out of the week, and there were others who never showed up at the factory on Mondays. "Strippers" were the boys who pulled the long stems from the tobacco leaves. After they had served at that work for a certain time they were given tables as apprentices.

All of this was interesting to me; and we drifted along in conversation until my companion struck the subject nearest his heart, the independence of Cuba. He was an exile from the island, and a prominent member of the Jacksonville Junta. Every week sums of money were collected from juntas all over the country. This money went to buy arms and ammunition for the insurgents. As the man sat there nervously smoking his long, "green" cigar, and telling me of the Gomezes, both the white one and the black one, of Maceo and Bandera, he grew positively eloquent. He also showed that he was a man of considerable education and reading. He spoke English excellently, and frequently surprised me by using words one would hardly expect from a foreigner. The first one of this class of words he employed almost shocked me, and I never forgot it; 'twas "ramify." We sat on the piazza until after ten o'clock. When we arose to go in to bed, it was with the understanding that I should start in the factory on the next day.

I began work the next morning seated at a barrel with another boy, who showed me how to strip the stems from the leaves, to smooth out each half leaf, and to put the "rights" together in one pile, and the "lefts" together in another pile on the edge of the barrel. My fingers, strong and sensitive from their long training, were well adapted to this kind of work, and within two weeks I was accounted the fastest "stripper" in the factory. At first the heavy odour of the tobacco almost sickened me, but when I became accustomed to it, I liked the smell. I was now earning four dollars a week, and was soon able to pick up a couple more by teaching a few scholars at night, whom I had secured through the good offices of the preacher I had met on my first morning in Jacksonville.

At the end of about three months, through my skill as a "stripper" and the influence of my landlord, I was advanced to a table and began to learn my trade; in fact, more than my trade; for I learned not only to make cigars, but also to smoke, to swear, and to speak Spanish. I discovered that I had a talent for languages as well as for music. The rapidity and ease with which I acquired Spanish astonished my associates. In a short time I was able not only to understand most of what was said at the table during meals, but to join in the conversation. I bought a method for learning the Spanish language, and with the aid of my landlord as a teacher, by constant practice with my fellow workmen, and by regularly reading the Cuban newspapers and finally some books of standard Spanish literature which were at the house, I was able in less than a year to speak like a native. In fact, it was my pride that I spoke better Spanish than many of the Cuban workmen at the factory.

After I had been in the factory a little over a year, I was repaid for all the effort I had put forth to learn Spanish by being selected as "reader." The "reader" is quite an institution in all cigar factories which employ Spanish-speaking workmen. He sits in the centre of the large room in which the cigar-makers work and reads to them for a certain number of hours each day all the important news from the papers and whatever else he may consider would be interesting. He often selects an exciting novel and reads it in daily instalments. He must, of course, have a good voice, but he also must have a reputation among the men for intelligence, for being well posted and having in his head a stock of varied information. He is generally the final authority on all arguments which arise, and in a cigar factory these arguments are many and frequent, ranging from the respective and relative merits of rival baseball clubs to the duration of the sun's light and energy—cigar-making is a trade in which talk does not interfere with work. My position as "reader" not only released me from the rather monotonous work of rolling cigars, and gave me something more in accord with my tastes, but also added considerably to my income. I was now earning about twenty-five dollars a week, and was able to give up my peripatetic method of giving music lessons. I hired a piano and taught only those who could arrange to take their lessons where I lived. I finally gave up teaching entirely, as what I made scarcely paid for my time and trouble. I kept the piano, however, in order to keep up my own studies, and occasionally I played at some church concert or other charitable entertainment.

Through my music teaching and my not absolutely irregular attendance at church I became acquainted with the best class of coloured people in Jacksonville. This was really my entrance into the race. It was my initiation into what I have termed the freemasonry of the race. I had formulated a theory of what it was to be coloured; now I was getting the practice. The novelty of my position caused me to observe and consider things which, I think, entirely escaped the young men I associated with; or, at least, were so commonplace to them as not to attract their attention. And of many of the impressions which came to me then I have realized the full import only within the past few years, since I have had a broader knowledge of men and history, and a fuller comprehension of the tremendous struggle which is going on between the races in the South.

It is a struggle; for though the black man fights passively, he nevertheless fights; and his passive resistance is more effective at present than active resistance could possibly be. He bears the fury of the storm as does the willow-tree.

It is a struggle; for though the white man of the South may be too proud to admit it, he is, nevertheless, using in the contest his best energies; he is devoting to it the greater part of his thought and much of his endeavour. The South today stands panting and almost breathless from its exertions.

And how the scene of the struggle has shifted! The battle was first waged over the right of the Negro to be classed as a human being with a soul; later, as to whether he had sufficient intellect to master even the rudiments of learning; and today it is being fought out over his social recognition.

I said somewhere in the early part of this narrative that because the coloured man looked at everything through the prism of his relationship to society as a *coloured* man, and because most of his mental efforts ran through the narrow channel bounded by his rights and his wrongs, it was to be wondered at that he has progressed so broadly as he has. The same thing may be said of the white man of the South; most of his mental efforts run through one narrow channel; his life as a man and a citizen, many of his financial activities, and all of his political activities are impassably limited by the ever present "Negro question." I am sure it would be safe to wager that no group of Southern white men could get together and talk for sixty minutes without bringing up the "race question." If a Northern white man happened to be in the group, the time could be safely cut to thirty minutes. In this respect I consider the conditions of the whites more to be deplored than that of the blacks. Here, a truly great people, a people that produced a majority of the great historic Americans from Washington to Lincoln, now forced to use up its energies in a conflict as lamentable as it is violent.

(1912)

From

THE SAHARA OF THE BOZART
by H. L. Mencken

What is needed down there, before the vexatious public problems of the region may be intelligently approached, is a survey of the population by competent ethnologists and anthropologists. The immigrants of the North have been studied at great length, and anyone who is interested may now apply to the Bureau of Ethnology for elaborate data as to their racial strains, their stature and cranial indices, their relative capacity for education, and the changes that they undergo under American *Kultur*. But the older stocks of the South, and particularly the emancipated and dominant poor white trash, have never been investigated scientifically, and most of the current generalizations about them are probably wrong. For example, the generalization that they are purely Anglo-Saxon in blood. This I doubt very seriously. The chief strain down there, I believe, is Celtic rather than Saxon, particularly in the hill country. French blood, too, shows itself here and there, and so does Spanish, and so does German. The last-named entered from the northward, by way of the limestone belt just east of the Alleghenies. Again, it is very likely that in some parts of the South a good many of the plebeian whites have more than a trace of Negro blood. Interbreeding under concubinage produced some very light half-breeds at an early day, and no doubt appreciable numbers of them went over into the white race by the simple process of changing their abode. Not long ago I read a curious article by an intelligent Negro, in which he stated that it is easy for a very light Negro to pass as white in the South on account of the fact that large numbers of Southerners accepted as white have distinctly negroid features. Thus it becomes a delicate and dangerous matter for a train conductor or a hotel-keeper to challenge a suspect. But the Celtic strain is far more obvious than any of these others. It not only makes itself visible in physical stigmata—*e.g.,* leanness and dark coloring—but also in mental traits. For example, the religious thought of the South is almost precisely identical with the religious thought of Wales. There is the same naïve belief in an anthropomorphic Creator but little removed, in manner and desire, from an evangelical bishop; there is the same submission to an ignorant and impudent sacerdotal tyranny, and there is the same sharp contrast between doctrinal orthodoxy and private ethics. Read Caradoc Evans's ironical picture of the Welsh Wesleyans in his preface to "My Neighbors," and you will be instantly reminded of the Georgia and Carolina Methodists. The most booming sort of piety, in the South, is not incompatible with the theory that lynching is a benign institution. Two generations ago it was not incompatible with an ardent belief in slavery.

It is highly probable that some of the worst blood of western Europe flows in the veins of the Southern poor whites, now poor no longer. The original strains, according to every honest historian, were extremely corrupt. Philip Alexander Bruce (a Virginian of the old gentry) says in his "Industrial History of Virginia in the Seventeenth Century" that the first native-born generation was largely illegitimate. "One of the most common offenses against morality committed in the lower ranks of life in Virginia during the Seventeenth Century," he says, "was bastardy." The mothers of these bastards, he continues, were chiefly indentured servants, and "had belonged to the lowest class in their native country." Fanny Kemble Butler, writing of the Georgia poor whites of a century later, described them as "the most degraded race of human beings claiming an Anglo-Saxon origin that can be found on the face of the earth—filthy, lazy, ignorant, brutal, proud, penniless savages." The Sunday-school and the chautauqua, of course, have appreciably mellowed the descendants of these "savages," and their economic progress and rise to political power have done perhaps even more, but the marks of their origin are still unpleasantly plentiful. Every now and then they produce a political leader who puts their secret notions of the true, the good and the beautiful into plain words, to the amazement and scandal of the rest of the country. That amazement is turned into downright incredulity when news comes that his platform has got him high office, and that he is trying to execute it.

In the great days of the South the line between the gentry and the poor whites was very sharply drawn. There was absolutely no intermarriage. So far as I know there is not a single instance in history of a Southerner of the upper class marrying one of the bondwomen described by Mr. Bruce. In other societies characterized by class distinctions of that sort it is common for the lower class to be improved by extra-legal crosses. That is to say, the men of the upper class take women of the lower class as mistresses, and out of such unions spring the extraordinary plebeians who rise sharply from the common level, and so propagate the delusion that all other plebeians would do the same thing if they had the chance—in brief, the delusion that class distinctions are merely economic and conventional, and not congenital and genuine. But in the South the men of the upper classes sought their mistresses among the blacks, and after a few generations there was so much white blood in the black women that they were considerably more attractive than the unhealthy and bedraggled women of the poor whites. This preference continued into our own time. A Southerner of good family once told me in all seriousness that he had reached his majority before it ever occurred to him that a white woman might make quite as agreeable a mistress as the octaroons of his jejune fancy. If the thing has changed of late, it is not the fault of the Southern white man, but of the Southern mulatto women. The more sightly yellow girls of the region, with improving economic opportunities, have gained self-respect, and so they are no longer as willing to enter into concubinage as their grand-dams were.

As a result of this preference of the Southern gentry for mulatto mistresses there was created a series of mixed strains containing the best white blood of the South, and perhaps of the whole country. As another result the poor whites went unfertilized from above, and so missed the improvement that so constantly shows itself in the peasant stocks of other countries. It is a commonplace that nearly all Negroes who rise above the general are of mixed blood, usually with the white predominating. I know a great many Negroes, and it would be hard for me to think of an exception. What is too often forgotten is that this white blood is not the blood of the poor whites but that of the old gentry. The mulatto girls of the early days despised the poor whites as creatures distinctly inferior to Negroes, and it was thus almost unheard of for such a girl to enter into relations with a man of that submerged class. This aversion was based upon a sound instinct. The Southern mulatto of today is a proof of it. Like all other half-breeds he is an unhappy man, with disquieting tendencies toward anti-social habits of thought, but he is intrinsically a better animal than the pure-blooded descendant of the old poor whites, and he not infrequently demonstrates it. It is not by accident that the Negroes of the South are making faster progress, culturally, than the masses of the whites. It is not by accident that the only visible esthetic activity in the South is in their hands. No Southern composer has ever written music so good as that of half a dozen white-black composers who might be named. Even in politics, the Negro reveals a curious superiority. Despite the fact that the race question has been the main political concern of the Southern whites for two generations, to the practical exclusion of everything else, they have contributed nothing to its discussion that has impressed the rest of the world so deeply and so favorably as three or four books by Southern Negroes.

(1920)

THE MERRY-GO-ROUND
by Julia Peterkin

I

A white man came from nobody knew where with a merry-go-round and set it up in the vacant lot across from the village depot. Every evening when work on the plantations was over the gay music sounded clear in the still air, and the darkies flocked down to the village and rode out all the money they had. Then they stayed on a while to listen to the merry tunes.

Flaming gasoline torches lighted the tent, and fiery looking bay and black and gray horses rocked and challenged riders to come try them; and gilded chariots shone bright.

The man's name was Carson. He was white, for his skin was fair, but no such white man had ever been in these parts before. Except for his white skin he seemed black as any of the folks that rode on the merry-go-round.

Maum Mary Parker cooked his meals and took them to his tent. He offered to go to her house to eat, but she refused to allow this.

"No, I rudder fetch yo' victuals here to yo'," she said.

He offered to pay her well if she'd let him sleep in the soft looking, quilt-covered bed that he could see through the open window.

"No," she said. "No white man ain' nebber yet sleep in no bed o' mine, an' I know I ain't gwine sta't wid you."

He laughed and spat on the ground.

"All right, Aunty, but my money's good as anybody's. I'm sure it's as good as any these white folks round here's got, if they've got any."

"You eat yo' dinner; I'm waitin' on dem t'ings, an' keep yo' mout' off my white folks."

He laughed again.

"Some folks, eh?"

II

Jesse Weeks worked at the oil mill for good wages. He was strong as a mule and muscled like an ox. He was well fed, for Maum Mary fed him, and besides her good meals he often carried sweet potatoes to the mill and dipped them in the smoking hot oil that dripped from the press. Nothing in the world was better, except sometimes ash cake dipped in that same hot oil for gravy.

Jesse worked at the press ten hours a day, then went home to Maum Mary's, washed up, dressed, and was ready to take Meta, Maum Mary's daughter, to a dance or a party. Now they rode on the merry-go-round every night. One night they'd choose a chariot; another night white horses side by side. Meta sat modestly sidewise as she had seen white ladies sit on real horses. Another night they'd ride bay horses, or black.

They'd be married Thanksgiving with a big wedding. Maum Mary was already saving up eggs for the cakes. For 'twas something in these days to raise a girl and marry her off without anybody's ever having said anything against her.

The first time Carson smiled at Meta she was confused. She dropped a curtsey in return and said respectfully,

"Good evenin', sir."

He laughed, looking at her with bold, appraising eyes.

The next night when Jesse left Meta and went over to the parcher to buy a sack of peanuts, Carson walked over by her and said with a smile,

"You look like you're scared to speak to me. What's the matter with you? Is he got you under the hack?" indicating Jesse, who was returning.

"No, sir," answered Meta in an embarrassed way. She was not altogether certain of his words, for his r's rolled strangely.

Next morning Meta went to the village store, and Carson was lounging on the counter inside.

"Won't you have a dope?" he asked her.

The clerk glanced up at him quickly, but Meta appeared not to hear, and nothing more was said.

When the girl stepped out of the door, Carson got down off the counter and stood in the door and watched her cross the railroad track, then on the path up the hill.

Maum Mary was late getting the clothes in off the line that evening. The washing was a big one.

"Meta, you run on an' take da' white man's supper to him. I ain' likes to sen' yo', but jus' leab de dishes wid him till in de mornin', an' hurry on back."

Carson took the pan from the girl and untied the white cloth that covered it. Chicken, biscuits, hominy, gravy.

"Your ma is some cook, girl. I'll get fat staying here. But what makes you treat me so cold?"

Meta turned away and started home.

"Ma say she'll git de dishes in de mornin'."

"Hold on, what's your hurry? I've got a book of tickets here for you to ride out. Wait a minute, let me get 'em for you."

But Meta was gone.

III

Jesse cut a step or two to the jazzy music, then asked Meta gaily, a little later,

"What'll we ride tonight?"

"Le's ride one o' them gol' chariots. I declare tha's de sweetes' ridin' I ever ride," declared Meta in her gentle voice.

When the ride was over and a pair of horses had been tried to see which was really the better, Jesse went to the parcher for peanuts. Carson saw him go and came at once to where Meta stood waiting.

"What made you run off so? Whyn't you wait and get the tickets? You must think I want to eat you or something. Why, a girl like you!"

He didn't finish his sentence, for Jesse landed a terrific blow on his jaw, and followed it quickly with another.

A crowd gathered around them uncertain what to do. "You all lef' Jesse 'lone, he knows what he'd do. Dat ain' no white gentleman." One of the older men watched the fight with interest until Carson was soundly beaten, then he took Jesse's arm in a firm grip.

"You done gi' him enough, Jesse. Quit now."

Meta's voice was full of excitement as they walked home up the hill.

"I'm sho glad you done it, Jesse, but I was dat scared!"

But Maum Mary shook her head in disapproval.

"You better mine, boy. It don' do to trifle wid strange white men."

Next morning, before day, somebody knocked on the door of the shed-room where Jesse slept. He jumped up quickly, for the gasoline torches had made him dream of fire. Maybe the oil mill was afire!

He opened the door, saying excitedly,

"What you want?"

Carson's pistol gleamed in the starlight.

"Gawd!" said Jesse as it flashed and he fell, shot through, in the door-way.

The stillness was rent with the shrieks of Meta and Maum Mary. The news spread like wild-fire—Carson had shot Jesse. By dawn, hundreds of negroes filled the village street. Men and women were armed with hoes and rakes, axes and guns. Where was Carson? He was not in the tent where he slept.

The clerk in the village store had already dressed and gone downstairs, from the room where he slept, to the telephone. When he got Central, he said,

"Will you please telephone all the gentlemen around here and tell them that this merry-go-round fellow down here has shot Jesse Weeks? The niggers are pretty well stirred up, and they'd all better come help me get him off on the eight o'clock train."

By sunrise one of the plantation owners on horseback, with a gun on his shoulder, came riding down the hill into the village.

"What are all you niggers doin' here this time o' day?" he asked as he rode through the crowd.

"Good mornin', Cap'n," they answered politely and touched their hats.

"You'd better go on home, all of you. If Sheriff Hill has to come up here this mornin' there'll be trouble for somebody."

There were indistinct mutterings as he hitched his horse to a tree in front of the store and went upstairs to the clerk's room. Soon three more gentlemen rode up, hitched their horses and went upstairs, then two more. At last, nine horses were hitched outside.

Maum Hannah cooked for the clerk upstairs and lived in a cabin back of the store. She came out of her door with a great pot of steaming coffee that left a trail of fragrance behind it.

"One o' you niggers come open dis door fo' me," she commanded.

When it was done she went up the stairs talking to herself.

The eight o'clock train blew at the river bridge three miles away. There was a hush. Then steps sounded on the stairway, slow ready steps. Ten men came down—no, eleven. In the hollow square they formed at the door was a man with his hat pulled down over his eyes. Another man joined them, the village policeman. He was black, but he upheld the law whenever it was possible.

They walked slowly across the street to the depot, as with the dead, and reached it just as the train stopped. Two men stepped aboard; then Carson; then two more. The train started and the four men got off the rear end of it.

"Looks like you-all are having a picnic out here," said the conductor to the others who were standing outside.

"No, nothing like that," one of them answered.

The white men mounted their horses and rode up the hill toward home. The black people stood around talking in low tones. One of them came over to the policeman and talked a minute, and the policeman walked on down the street in another direction. Soon there was a shout and the tent over the merry-go-round was in flames. Horses and chariots stood still and burned to charred wood, they that had been so gay and swift!

IV

Carson left the train at the first large station it reached. He went to the station lunch counter, got a sandwich and a cup of coffee, then went across the street where he saw a sign "Board and Lodging." He took a room and went to bed.

When he awoke, the day was almost over. A new moon showed clear through the window. He stretched his limbs, yawned, then got up and washed his face in the china basin. He looked in the glass at his bruised cheek, smoothed his hair with his hands, put on his coat and went downstairs to the sidewalk.

With his hands in his pockets, he looked around. A cotton mill was over on the hill beyond the depot. Not far from it was a large tent. It was no merry-go-round tent. He'd go take a look at it.

He walked through its open door and a red-faced, stockily built man with a black moustache greeted him.

"Well, brother, how do you do?"

Carson's quick eyes took in the Bible on the table, the organ on one side, the hymn books.

"I'm down and out," he answered gloomily. "I thought I'd come talk to you."

"That's right, that's right. Cast your burden on the Lord, brother, it's the only way to salvation."

"But I'm out of a job," said Carson.

"Well, according to John 6:27, 'Labor not for the meat that perisheth.' What's your business, brother?"

Carson hesitated.

"I wish I could get work here with you. I'm mighty handy with a tent. You ought to see me take one down and put it up."

"You know anything about music?"

"I know it from A to Z," Carson answered confidently.

"I've been thinking about getting a regular fellow to go around and help me, but collections haven't been much lately."

"I tell you," said Carson. "You try me. I'll work for my board till you see if I give satisfaction. You won't be out anything much that way."

"How about them gas lights; can you light them?"

"Just watch me."

That night Carson rose from the congregation and gave a remarkable testimony of his salvation from sin. Next morning he practised faithfully on the organ until he could play a number of the hymns to be sung during the services.

"That's right, you got to put pep in 'em," approved the preacher.

Carson soon developed into a fine exhorter, and followed the sermons with a moving appeal to sinners to turn from sin. It was a steadier business than his former one; more exciting, too.

Jesse did not die. He's only crippled. He has crutches, and drags both feet together when he walks. He makes baskets and fish traps and chair bottoms out of split hickory.

Meta and Maum Mary take in washing still, and all together they make a living. Maum Mary is careful to take a part of their earnings to pay the preacher.

"Preachers is de servants ob Gawd, Meta, we 'bliged to take care of 'em or de world 'ud git too full o' sin."

(1921)

From

BIRTHRIGHT

by T. S. Stribling

At Cairo, Illinois, the Pullman-car conductor asked Peter Siner to take his suit-case and traveling-bag and pass forward into the Jim Crow car. The request came as a sort of surprise to the negro. During Peter Siner's four years in Harvard the segregation of black folk on Southern railroads had become blurred and reminiscent in his mind; now it was fetched back into the sharp distinction of the present instant. With a certain sense of strangeness, Siner picked up his bags, and saw his own form, in the car mirrors, walking down the length of the sleeper. He moved on through the dining-car, where a few hours before he had had dinner and talked with two white men, one an Oregon apple-grower, the other a Wisconsin paper-manufacturer. The Wisconsin man had furnished cigars, and the three had sat and smoked in the drawing-room, indeed, had discussed this very point; and now it was upon him.

At the door of the dining-car stood the porter of his Pullman, a negro like himself, and Peter mechanically gave him fifty cents. The porter accepted it silently, without offering the amenities of his whisk-broom and shoe-brush, and Peter passed on forward.

Beyond the dining-car and Pullmans stretched twelve day-coaches filled with less-opulent white travelers in all degrees of sleepiness and dishabille from having sat up all night. The thirteenth coach was the Jim Crow car. Framed in a conspicuous place beside the entrance of the car was a copy of the Kentucky state ordinance setting this coach apart from the remainder of the train for the purposes therein provided.

The Jim Crow car was not exactly shabby, but it was unkept. It was half filled with travelers of Peter's own color, and these passengers were rather more noisy than those in the white coaches. Conversation was not restrained to the undertones one heard in the other day-coaches or the Pullmans. Near the entrance of the car two negroes in soldiers' uniforms had turned a seat over to face the door, and now they sat talking loudly and laughing the loose laugh of the half intoxicated as they watched the inflow of negro passengers coming out of the white cars.

The windows of the Jim Crow car were shut, and already it had become noisome. The close air was faintly barbed with the peculiar, penetrating odor of dark, sweating skins. For four years Peter Siner had not known that odor. Now it came to him not so much offensively as with a queer quality of intimacy and reminiscence. The tall, carefully tailored negro spread his wide nostrils, vacillating whether to sniff it out with disfavor or to admit it for the sudden mental associations it evoked.

It was a faint, pungent smell that played in the back of his nose and somehow reminded him of his mother, Caroline Siner, a thick-bodied black woman whom he remembered as always bending over a wash-tub. This was only one unit of a complex. The odor was also connected with negro protracted meetings in Hooker's Bend, and the Harvard man remembered a lanky black preacher waving long arms and wailing of hell-fire, to the chanted groans of his dark congregation; and he, Peter Siner, had groaned with the others. Peter had known this odor in the press-room of Tennessee cotton-gins, over a river packet's boilers, where he and other roustabouts were bedded, in bunk-houses in the woods. It also recalled a certain octoroon girl named Ida May, and an intimacy with her which it still moved and saddened Peter to think of. Indeed, it resurrected innumerable vignettes of his life in the negro village in Hooker's Bend; it was linked with innumerable emotions, this pungent, unforgettable odor that filled the Jim Crow car.

Somehow the odor had a queer effect of appearing to push his conversation with the two white Northern men in the drawing-room back to a distance, an indefinable distance of both space and time.

The negro put his suitcase under the seat, hung his overcoat on the hook, and placed his hand-bag in the rack overhead; then with some difficulty he opened a window and sat down by it.

A stir of travelers in the Cairo station drifted into the car. Against a broad murmur of hurrying feet, moving trucks, and talking there stood out the thin, flat voice of a Southern white girl calling good-by to some one on the train. Peter could see her waving a bright parasol and tiptoeing. A sandwich boy hurried past, shrilling his wares. Siner leaned out, with fifteen cents, and signaled to him. The urchin hesitated, and was about to reach up one of his wrapped parcels, when a peremptory voice shouted at him from a lower car. With a sort of start the lad deserted Siner and went trotting down to his white customer. A moment later the train bell began ringing, and the Dixie Flier puffed deliberately out of the Cairo station and moved across the Ohio bridge into the South.

Half an hour later the blue-grass fields of Kentucky were spinning outside of the window in a vast green whirlpool. The distant trees and houses moved forward with the train, while the foreground, with its telegraph poles, its culverts, section-houses, and shrubbery, rushed backward in a blur. Now and then into the Jim Crow window whipped a blast of coal smoke and hot cinders, for the engine was only two cars ahead.

Peter Siner looked out at the interminable spin of the landscape with a certain wistfulness. He was coming back into the South, into his own country. Here for generations his forebears had toiled endlessly and fruitlessly, yet the fat green fields hurtling past him told with what skill and patience their black hands had labored.

The negro shrugged away such thoughts, and with a certain effort replaced them with the constructive idea that was bringing him South once more. It was a very simple idea. Siner was returning to his native village in Tennessee to teach school. He planned to begin his work with the ordinary public school at Hooker's Bend, but, in the back of his head, he hoped eventually to develop an institution after the plan of Tuskeegee or the Hampton Institute in Virginia.

To do what he had in mind, he must obtain aid from white sources, and now, as he traveled southward, he began conning in his mind the white men and white women he knew in Hooker's Bend. He wanted first of all to secure possession of a small tract of land which he knew adjoined the negro schoolhouse over on the east side of the village.

Before the negro's mind the different villagers passed in review with that peculiar intimacy of vision that servants always have of their masters. Indeed, no white Southerner knows his own village so minutely as does any member of its colored population. The colored villagers see the whites off their guard and just as they are, and that is an attitude in which no one looks his best. The negroes might be called the black recording angels of the South. If what they know should be shouted aloud in any Southern town, its social life would disintegrate. Yet it is a strange fact that gossip seldom penetrates from the one race to the other.

So Peter Siner sat in the Jim Crow car musing over half a dozen villagers in Hooker's Bend. He thought of them in a curious way. Although he was now a B. A. of Harvard University, and although he knew that not a soul in the little river village, unless it was old Captain Renfrew, could construe a line of Greek and that scarcely two had ever traveled farther north than Cincinnati, still, as Peter recalled their names and foibles, he involuntarily felt that he was telling over a roll of the mighty. The white villagers came marching through his mind as beings austere, and the very cranks and quirks of their characters somehow held that austerity. There were the Brownell sisters, two old maids, Molly and Patti, who lived in a big brick house on the hill. Peter remembered that Miss Molly Brownell always doled out to his mother, at Monday's wash-day dinner, exactly one biscuit less than the old negress wanted to eat, and she always paid her in old clothes. Peter remembered, a dozen times in his life, his mother coming home and wondering in an impersonal way how it was that Miss Molly Brownell could skimp every meal she ate at the big house by exactly one biscuit. It was Miss Brownell's thin-lipped boast that she understood negroes. She had told Peter so several times when, as a lad, he went up to the big house on errands. Peter Siner considered this remembrance without the faintest feeling of humor, and mentally removed Miss Molly Brownell from his list of possible subscribers. Yet, he recalled, the whole Brownell estate had been reared on negro labor.

Then there was Henry Hooker, cashier of the village bank. Peter knew that the banker subscribed liberally to foreign missions; indeed, at the cashier's behest, the white church of Hooker's Bend kept a paid missionary on the upper Congo. But the banker had sold some village lots to the negroes, and in two instances, where a streak of commercial phosphate had been discovered on the properties, the lots had reverted to the Hooker estate. There had been in the deed something concerning a mineral reservation that the negro purchasers knew nothing about until the phosphate was discovered. The whole matter had been perfectly legal.

A hand shook Siner's shoulder and interrupted his review. Peter turned, and caught an alcoholic breath over his shoulder, and the blurred voice of a Southern negro called out above the rumble of the car and the roar of the engine:

" 'Fo' Gawd, ef dis ain't Peter Siner I's been lookin' at de las' twenty miles, an' not knowin' him wid sich skeniptious clo'es on! Wha you fum, nigger?''

Siner took the enthusiastic hand offered him and studied the heavily set, powerful man bending over the seat. He was in a soldier's uniform, and his broad nutmeg-colored face and hot black eyes brought Peter a vague sense of familiarity; but he never would have identified his impression had he not observed on the breast of the soldier's uniform the Congressional military medal for bravery on the field of battle. Its glint furnished Peter the necessary clew. He remembered his mother's writing him something about Tump Pack going to France and getting "crowned" before the army. He had puzzled a long time over what she meant by "crowned" before he guessed her meaning. Now the medal aided Peter in reconstructing out of this big umber-colored giant the rather spindling Tump Pack he had known in Hooker's Bend.

Siner was greatly surprised, and his heart warmed at the sight of his old playmate.

"What have you been doing to yourself, Tump?" he cried, laughing, and shaking the big hand in sudden warmth. "You used to be the size of a dime in a jewelry store."

"Been in 'e army, nigger, wha I's been fed," said the grinning brown man, delightedly. "I sho is picked up, ain't I?"

"And what are you doing here in Cairo?"

"Tryin' to bridle a lil white mule." Mr. Pack winked a whisky-brightened eye jovially and touched his coat to indicate that some of the "white mule" was in his pocket and had not been drunk.

"How'd you get here?"

"Wucked my way down on de St. Louis packet an' got paid off at Padjo [Paducah, Kentucky]; 'n 'en I thought I'd come on down heah an' roll some bones. Been hittin' 'em two days now, an' I sho come putty nigh bein' cleaned; but I put up lil Joe heah, an' won 'em all back, 'n 'en some." He touched the medal on his coat, winked again, slapped Siner on the leg, and burst into loud laughter.

Peter was momentarily shocked. He made a place on the seat for his friend to sit. "You don't mean you put up your medal on a crap game, Tump?"

"Sho do, black man." Pack became soberer. "Dat's one o' de great benefits o' bein' dec'rated. Dey ain't a son uv a gun on de river whut kin win lil Joe; dey all tried it."

A moment's reflection told Peter how simple and natural it was for Pack to prize his military medal as a good-luck piece to be used as a last resort in crap games. He watched Tump stroke the face of his medal with his fingers.

"My mother wrote me about your getting it, Tump. I was glad to hear it."

The brown man nodded, and stared down at the bit of gold on his barrel-like chest.

"Yas-suh, dat 'uz guv to me fuh bravery. You know whut a skeery lil nigger I wuz roun' Hooker's Ben'; well, de sahgeant tuk me an' he drill ever' bit o' dat right out 'n me. He gimme a baynit an' learned me to stob dummies wid it over at Camp Oglethorpe, until he felt lak I had de heart to stob anything; 'n 'en he sont me acrost. I had to git a new pair breeches ever' three weeks, I growed so fas'." Here he broke out into his big loose laugh again, and renewed the alcoholic scent around Peter.

"And you made good?"

"Sho did, black man, an', 'fo' Gawd, I 'serve a medal ef any man ever did. Dey gimme dish-heah fuh stobbin fo' white men wid a baynit. 'Fo' Gawd, nigger, I never felt so quare in all my born days as when I wuz a-jobbin' de livers o' dem white men lak de sahgeant tol' me to." Tump shook his head, bewildered, and after a moment added, "Yas-suh, I never wuz mo' surprised in all my life dan when I got dis medal fuh stobbin' fo' white men."

Peter Siner looked through the Jim Crow window at the vast rotation of the Kentucky landscape on which his forebears had toiled; presently he added soberly:

"You were fighting for your country, Tump. It was war then; you were fighting for your country."

(1922)

From

TOUCOUTOU
by Edward Laroque Tinker

Two days had seen Bazile Bujac on the road to recovery but still very weak. Claircine could not quite decide whether to attribute his cure to her prayers or to her incantations, though deep down in her heart she inclined to the belief that it was the power of voodoo that had saved his life. Exhausted by her days and nights of ceaseless nursing, she went to get a little sleep; leaving Toucoutou with her patient.

Bazile, who had the ravenous hunger peculiar to those recovering from yellow fever, begged the child to bring him the rest of the red beans and rice left from her lunch. Claircine, of course, would have known better, but little Toucoutou merely did as she was told.

The heavy food eaten before the veins in the stomach had had time to recover their normal tone proved too much for his weakened blood vessels and he was suddenly taken with an internal hemorrhage. Toucoutou ran screaming for Claircine, but by the time she got there he was dead—a dreadful sight as he lay on the bed, his skin a deep yellow approaching green, and blood oozing from his nose and running from the corners of his mouth over the bedclothes.

For Claircine the world seemed to have stopped. She sobbed and groaned with all the emotional abandon characteristic of the negro side of her ancestry.

As she recovered from her first paroxysm of grief the memory of that terrible cry, "Bring out yo' dead!" cut into her consciousness. She knew that in that sweltering heat interments could not be delayed, for with deaths averaging a thousand a week, the few embalmers worked only for the very rich; so she realized that if her Bazile was not to be thrown wrapped in a sheet into that frightful human offal wagon, she must act quickly.

She sent Toucoutou, red eyed and frightened, scurrying to get Madame Rigaud to stay with the body, meanwhile putting on the black dress that forms part of every Creole wardrobe, even the poorest, against just such an emergency.

When Madame arrived, sympathetic and voluble, Claircine took Toucoutou by the hand and hurried rapidly to Gossiron's over on Rampart, through streets just beginning to show signs of life with the cooling coming of sunset. Just as she arrived the hearse drawn by its team of sweat-greyed blacks was driving in. The office was filled by overwrought men and women who clamored around a small fat Creole, clad in the traditional uniform of his profession—a black frock coat and tie. His hands flew around his head in rapid incoördinated gestures as he shouted, "Non! Non! c'est impossíble. I hav' no more coffin. My men are exhaust'." Claircine recognized among the besiegers Madame Giron the wife of the confiseur. She remembered now having heard their daughter had died. Well if Madame Giron could obtain no help, rich as she was, how was she, Claircine, going to get any attention?

As she sat hopelessly in the background, she thought of an Irishman she had once nursed through a bad attack of dengue fever. Yes, she was sure now, it was Dennis Shea and he was one of Gossiron's drivers. If she could only find him. Still holding Toucoutou by the hand, she slipped quietly through a side door into the stable. There was something comforting about the pleasant smell of horses as she walked between the long lines of stalls to a yard in the back and there discovered the man she was looking for sitting in his shirt sleeves on a box, smoking a comforting pipe, his high silk hat pushed on the back of his head. When she told him of Bujac's death he was all quick Irish sympathy and said, "Now listen, I know there ain't a coffin in town but don't ye worry. It ain't Dennis Shea that will let them early morning birds take annybody of yours to his last bed. I ain't fergot how ye saved me from that kind of a ride mesilf. Now ye go home an' don't harry yesilf. After I've had me supper I know where there's some good boards in a fince, an' I'll fetch thim over an' make ye as fine a coffin as any carpinter. Thin in the mornin' I'll sneak me carriage out early widout the boss knowin' an' drive ye to the graveyard."

"Yes, but a priest I mus' have," wailed Claircine, "his soul mus' not stay in the Purgatoire."

"Lave it to me," replied the good-hearted Dennis, "lave it to me an' I'll git Father Flynn, as good an Irishman as ever drained a dram, to stop an' say a prayer."

Claircine went home heartened, and after she had given Toucoutou her supper and put her to bed, she began the grewsome task of preparing her man for burial. Her work was lightened by the arrival of Dennis, who came staggering under a load of boards with saw, hammer and nails in a bag over his shoulder. He helped her get the corpse into its clothes and then went out to the kitchen to begin his grim job of carpentry.

Claircine knelt beside the bed where she had watched so many hours and prayed the Virgin that the soul of Bazile should soon go through Purgatory to Heaven; and, holding his cold hand in both of hers, she buried her face in the bedclothes and sobbed desperately. The sound of hammering in the other room brought her back to realities and she went out to the kitchen to drip some coffee to cheer Dennis in his work.

The next morning Claircine and the child were dressed and ready when Dennis drove up with Father Flynn inside his carriage. Toucoutou in a little white dress with a piece of black ribbon around her arm opened the door for them and stood wide-eyed and frightened by the side of the older woman as the Father, standing at the head of the coffin, read something she could not understand from a little black book. Then the two men picked up the rough wooden box, some of the planks of which still bore traces of the yellow-green stain that had protected them when they had been part of a fence. They staggered out to the carriage and propped it up on end on the box seat. Father Flynn said a few perfunctory words advising resignation to the Will of God and hurried away to other duties. Dennis helped the woman and child into the carriage and then climbed up onto the box seat and started off.

As they drove out Claircine sat stiff and bolt upright, her face taut. The nervous way she picked at the handkerchief in her lap showed how hard she was fighting to keep herself in hand. Toucoutou, with all a child's curiosity, could not resist looking out of the window, and what she saw remained indelibly fixed in her mind. She never forgot the man walking along the sidewalk with a coffin, child's size, balanced on his shoulder and water streaming from his eyes; or the black hearses dripping disinfectant like carbolic tears; or the pockmarked negro pushing a wheelbarrow loaded with an overhanging coffin, followed by a black frocked frightened white woman with a child in her arms; or the boys driving dumpcarts, piled high with corpses, who beat their spavined mules to a gallop; or the old woman and the young man tugging together at a child's wagon on which was precariously perched a full sized casket.

People and vehicles got thicker and thicker as they neared the cemetery. The road was just one ghastly funeral procession two and a half miles long. Dennis had to walk his horses. The heat became so intense he pushed his beaver to the back of his head, and, taking off his coat, hung it over the end of the coffin. Toucoutou could see great lazy columns of smoke trailing black into the skies like enormous streamers of crepe pinned to the clouds. They came from fires of tar burnt in the graveyards as a preventive of infection. But nothing could kill the stench of the tainted air.

The impromptu hearse and mourners' carriage, all in one, stopped near the gates, around which clustered withered old men and greasy women of all colors selling sweetmeats and bellywash; some with their candies on little tables, others with baskets on their arms wandering through the crowd calling their wares.

Lazy green bottle flies, gorged and lethargic, swarmed everywhere, even over the "dainties" of the vendors who made futile attempts to brush them off with fly whips made from strips of gaily colored paper fastened on the end of sticks.

The child sitting in the carriage caught jumbled phrases over the ceaseless humming of the mob:

"Pralines! Pralines!"

"Bel calas tou' chaud!"

"Damn shame yellow jack got him."

"Bel pain patate."

"Creme à la Vanille!"

"God! what a stink!"

People kept ebbing in and out of the gates, their expressions harassed, pitiful, frightened, nauseated, sad,—or worst of all, with the terrible vacant stare of the morbidly curious. One gesture was common to them all, however, each and everyone held his handkerchief to his nose. Here and there moved grave-diggers, recruited from the vilest types of black and white laborers, who were easily recognizable because the lower part of their faces were swathed in cheap cheesecloth soaked with camphor.

Dennis picked out an Irishman from among them and beckoning him over, offered him two bits to lend a hand with the coffin.

The man only laughed brutally and answered, "What do ye think I'm in this stink-hole for? Sure an' I wouldn't raise me hand fer less than two dollars an' in there they're paying five dollars an hour to bury th' stiffs an all the whisky ye can guzzle besides."

"It's a hell of a way to treat another Irishman an' him dead," said Dennis as he glanced at Claircine to see if she had overheard his lie.

"Why didn't ye say so at furst?" said the man, "I'll take the two bits then."

Together they lifted the coffin down and Dennis opened the carriage door and helped his passengers out. Then the two men took opposite ends of the pine box and walked heavily into the graveyard with their burden. Claircine followed with only her harried nervous eyes showing above the handkerchief she held to her face, while Toucoutou, horror-stricken, clung to her skirts and openly sobbed with fear.

Inside were sights that would have nauseated far more callous people. Coffins were stacked in piles of fifty under the hot, torrid sun, many of them burst open with the swelling corruption within. Terrible dark trickles oozed from the broken sides and flies feasted everywhere. The stench was almost insupportable. An occasional whiff of carbolic acid came as a blessed relief. Workmen were digging a shallow trench not two feet deep because the water lay so near the surface. They stopped frequently, swore and passed a bottle from hand to hand, lifting the cloths from their mouths to be able to drink. The molasses rum had its effect and one man broke into an obscene song current in the lowest bawdy houses. Another, at the end of the ditch, cursed as his pick met an obstruction and he kicked some human bones from the trench with a brutal, "Room for yo' betters! God damn ye!" Zizi Bidonnier drove in with his grisly load and his helpers shoveled the corpses into the fosse like so much manure, there the grave-diggers pushed them around with their mattocks and kicked them into position so that they would take up the least possible room. There were grim glimpses of stark bodies or lemon-yellow staring faces as the coverings of the cadavers became disarranged under this treatment. They filled what was left of the space with others from the pile of bursting coffins and covered them with loosely-heaped clods of earth, through the interstices of which flies found their way to lay their ovaria in the putrescent mass and raise more countless swarms of flies. The workmen threw a few shovels' full of lime over the hundred foot long trench and considered their job finished.

What was evidently the interment of a person of consequence was taking place over in a corner. The family slaves were employed in digging a deep grave and were up to their waists in water. When the coffin was put in, it floated and wouldn't go down to the bottom. This did not find the party unprepared for an auger was produced and holes were bored in the top of the coffin. The two slaves then stood on either end balancing by holding each other's hands, and the casket sank slowly down in the grave with ghastly gurgles of escaping air.

No wonder New Orleans was known up and down the river as the "Wet Grave."

Meanwhile Dennis' helper had gotten tools from somewhere and they were both sweatingly engaged in digging a shallow hole. They dropped the coffin in and threw some earth on top, while Claircine stood by gray-pale and staring eyed. When it was over the kindly old Irishman led her unresisting back to the carriage through all the horrors she no longer saw. As they drove off she shuddered miserably in one corner of the carriage while Toucoutou huddled in the other. She was weeping quietly.

(1928)

From

THE SOUND AND THE FURY
by William Faulkner

Along toward ten oclock I went up front. There was a drummer there. It was a couple of minutes to ten, and I invited him up the street to get a coca-cola. We got to talking about crops.

"There's nothing to it," I says, "Cotton is a speculator's crop. They fill the farmer full of hot air and get him to raise a big crop for them to whipsaw on the market, to trim the suckers with. Do you think the farmer gets anything out of it except a red neck and a hump in his back? You think the man that sweats to put it into the ground gets a red cent more than a bare living," I says. "Let him make a big crop and it wont be worth picking; let him make a small crop and he wont have enough to gin. And what for? so a bunch of damn eastern jews, I'm not talking about men of the jewish religion," I says, "I've known some jews that were fine citizens. You might be one yourself," I says.

"No," he says, "I'm an American."

"No offense," I says. "I give every man his due, regardless of religion or anything else. I have nothing against jews as an individual," I says. "It's just the race. You'll admit that they produce nothing. They follow the pioneers into a new country and sell them clothes."

"You're thinking of Armenians," he says, "aren't you. A pioneer wouldn't have any use for new clothes."

"No offense," I says. "I dont hold a man's religion against him."

"Sure," he says, "I'm an American. My folks have some French blood, why I have a nose like this. I'm an American, all right."

"So am I," I says. "Not many of us left. What I'm talking about is the fellows that sit up there in New York and trim the sucker gamblers."

"That's right," he says. "Nothing to gambling, for a poor man. There ought to be a law against it."

"Dont you think I'm right?" I says.

"Yes," he says, "I guess you're right. The farmer catches it coming and going." ·

"I know I'm right," I says. "It's a sucker game, unless a man gets inside information from somebody that knows what's going on. I happen to be associated with some people who're right there on the ground. They have one of the biggest manipulators in New York for an adviser. Way I do it," I says, "I never risk much at a time. It's the fellow that thinks he knows it all and is trying to make a killing with three dollars that they're laying for. That's why they are in the business."

Then it struck ten. I went up to the telegraph office. It opened up a little, just like they said. I went into the corner and took out the telegram again, just to be sure. While I was looking at it a report came in. It was up two points. They were all buying. I could tell that from what they were saying. Getting aboard. Like they didn't know it could go but one way. Like there was a law or something against doing anything but buying. Well, I reckon those eastern jews have got to live too. But I'll be damned if it hasn't come to a pretty pass when any damn foreigner that cant make a living in the country where God put him, can come to this one and take money right out of an American's pockets. It was up two points more. Four points. But hell, they were right there and knew what was going on. And if I wasn't going to take the advice, what was I paying them ten dollars a month for. I went out, then I remembered and came back and sent the wire. "All well. Q writing today."

"Q?" the operator says.

"Yes," I says, "Q. Cant you spell Q?"

"I just asked to be sure," he says.

"You send it like I wrote it and I'll guarantee you to be sure," I says. "Send it collect."

"What you sending, Jason?" Doc Wright says, looking over my shoulder. "Is that a code message to buy?"

"That's all right about that," I says. "You boys use your own judgment. You know more about it than those New York folks do."

"Well, I ought to," Doc says, "I'd a saved money this year raising it at two cents a pound."

Another report came in. It was down a point.

"Jason's selling," Hopkins says. "Look at his face."

"That's all right about what I'm doing," I says. "You boys follow your own judgment. Those rich NewYork jews have got to live like everybody else," I says.

(1929)

From

INCHIN' ALONG
by Welbourn Kelley

The dogwood buds were swelling with sap and he had only a few days to spare when he got into his bateau and rowed across the river and walked along the trail to Mist' Henry's house—the huge white house with towering white columns, which Mist' Henry's father had built with money made from breeding and selling slaves. Dink, as was proper, approached the house from the rear and then he went around to the side of the house where Mist' Henry had his office, built so it was accessible from the outside and so the nigger share-croppers would not have to enter it by going through the house proper.

Mist' Henry was nearing sixty; he was tall, well built; his hair was white but his mustache, which drooped a little at the ends, was still brown.

"Well, Dink," said Mist' Henry, "I hear you are getting along all right on the place I sold you."

Mist' Henry seemed neither pleased nor displeased.

"Yessuh, Mist' Henry," Dink replied. "I made a good crop las' yeah an' I'm 'bout ready to start plantin' again."

"I hear you've got a baby in the family, too—Lige's wife, Osie, was telling me about it. . . . Too bad those things have to happen."

"Yessuh, Mist' Henry—sho is."

"Well, Dink, what can I do for you?"

"I come to see yo' 'bout some lan', Mist' Henry. Yo' got some lan' over nex' to my place—like dat yo' sol' me befo'—an' I thought maybe I could buy it fum yo' an' clear it up when I didn' have nothin' else to do."

Mist' Henry seemed faintly surprised. "Did you make a lot of money on your crops last year, Dink?" he inquired.

"Yessuh, Mist' Henry—I sho did make a lot, fuh me. An' I cain' do nothin' wid it 'less'n somebody wanta sell me some lan' what dey don' wanta use deyse'fs.''

Mist' Henry's surprise turned into faint amusement. "What would you do with more land, Dink?''

The question left Dink in a stall because he was afraid he would give the wrong answer.

"You've got thirty acres of land in cultivation now and thirty acres of land are plenty for one man. What would you do with more land if you had more?''

Dink sensed disapproval in Mist' Henry's tone and he knew that an explanation was expected of him. "Look like I'm gonta have some mo' chillun, Mist' Henry,'' he said. "Chillun sho do eat a heap. . . . Maybe when dey grow up I'll have some he'p to work mo' lan', kin I git some mo'.''

"No, Dink,'' Mist' Henry decided judicially. "You're making money on the land you have. I'm glad to see that you're getting along all right, and all that. But this part of the country is different from other parts, and there is no need of setting an example. . . . I don't know whether I should have sold you any land in the first place.''

"Yessuh, Mist' Henry,'' said Dink, his voice agreeing in a manner which was wholly automatic.

Well, Mist' Henry would sell him no more land, that was certain. He had the money and he wanted more land. He had only one other hope. His land was bounded on the one side by Mist' Henry's and on the other by old Judge Hudson's. If Mist' Henry would sell him no land, maybe Judge Hudson would. Judge Hudson, who lived in Harrodsville and presided over the Circuit Court, was at least eighty years old. And people said old Judge Hudson had been acting queerly of late, with the queerness which often accompanies old age. Maybe Judge Hudson would sell him some land.

Arrived in Harrodsville, Dink found Judge Hudson also amused at his offer to buy land. But Judge Hudson, prone to talk lengthily and, to Dink, unintelligibly, seemed to be amused more at himself than at Dink.

"So Hen Weatherby wouldn't sell you any more land?'' the old man inquired, his eyes twinkling in a secret manner.

"Nawsuh, Cap'm Judge,'' Dink answered. "He say I don' need no mo' lan'.''

"He tell you this was a white man's country?''

"Nawsuh—he didn' tell me dat.''

Judge Hudson, who was small and wrinkled and pink, sat musing, silently amused. Judge Hudson wore a linen shirt the front of which was pleated; his suit was of plain black broadcloth; his black string of a bow tie was knotted in a flowing manner; Judge Hudson's eyes were weak and watery but seemed always to be looking through you.

"I don't suppose you ever heard of Appomatox, did you?'' the old man asked of a sudden.

"Yessuh, I has," Dink assured him. "Dat whah us got turnt loose in de wah wid de Nawthe'ners. My ol' pappy fowt in it, 'longside of Mist' Henry's pappy."

"That's a nice little slice of irony for you," Judge Hudson observed: "Your father, at his master's side, fighting on the wrong side of a cause espoused in his name. And I'm doubtful as to whether he was not right—fighting against those who fought for his freedom. I mean, I'm doubtful—God knows—as to whether the issue was really ever changed any, except in name. Well, well. Maybe, the whole thing will have to be gone through with again, different the next time in that the niggers won't have any white friends. We won't live to see it, though—probably it will be only a moral battle."

"Yessuh," Dink assured the judge in a hopeful voice. "If'n yo' got some mo' lan' yo' don' want, Cap'm Judge, I thought maybe I could buy it fum yo'."

Judge Hudson's soliloquy began again.

"Commendable of purpose," he said, "but errant as to direction. What Hen Weatherby didn't say was that he's got much more land than he has money and that he's got much more of stupidity which he calls pride than of either. Hen didn't mind a nigger neighbor as long as the nigger was *his* nigger. . . . Well, well. Times are going to change but when that time comes perhaps there will be no Hen Weatherbys to suffer. . . . The trouble with the South is that it loves its *nigger* and kicks hell out of its *niggers*. And that's how the change will come about: Some day the South will quit loving its nigger because it will no longer be able to kick hell out of its niggers. . . . And the North—either utter disregard or tolerance with contempt. . . ."

Dink was sure the old judge was crazy. He did not understand what the judge was talking about but he dared not interrupt the old man's ramblings. Besides, so far he had not heard a refusal.

"I'm going to sell you some land, Dink," Judge Hudson decided at last. "You're a hard-working nigger who knows his place and who deserves to get along. I know I am not much longer for this world and God knows what will become of what I leave behind me."

"Thank yo', Cap'm Judge," Dink said, bowing low in gratitude. "I sho do thank yo'."

Judge Hudson got down to business. "I've got nearly a section of the same land Hen Weatherby sold you last year. It's mostly uncleared but the timber on it isn't worth much. You can have all you want at five dollars an acre."

Dink began a rapid count on hs fingers and, simultaneously, in his head. . . . Twenty nickels in a dollar, using comparative mathematics, figured out to twenty acres of land at five dollars an acre for each of his hundred dollars. After an interminable and involved process, he determined his financial position.

"Yessuh, Cap'm Judge," he said at last. "I buys a hund'ed an' fawty acres."

"A hundred and forty acres!" Judge Hudson gasped. "Well now, after all, that's a lot of land for a nigger. No, Dink, I don't believe it would be to your benefit to own that much land. You would get some money ahead and become reckless of your surroundings—I've seen it happen before. I'll let you have sixty acres, though, because I believe you know your place and have got it in you to get ahead."

"Yessuh, Cap'm Judge."

"And now," Judge Hudson concluded, "this is my advice to you, the advice of an old man: Work hard and save your money, but no matter how much money you save, never forget who and what you are—a nigger. Stay on friendly terms with the white people—you know how to do that—and you can go as far as your ability will allow. Disregard those rules and, whether they're fair or unfair, your reward will be a swinging limb."

"Thank yo', Cap'm Judge," said Dink.

And Dink knew that Judge Hudson was right. If you lived on a white man's place the white man would see that you had a house and plenty of the food which you had raised. If you got sick he would come and look after you himself if no doctor were available. But if you didn't show him the respect due a white man from a nigger, he would hit you on the head with an ax-handle and say, "There, you black son-of-a-bitch—let that be a lesson to you."

Of course the white man took ample pay for what he did for you, out of the crop you made. And, come to think of it, it didn't matter whether you lived on his place or not when it came to how you acted in his presence.

But Dink had his land, anyway; and as he trudged along homeward his voice rose in a song that was at once a chant of victory and a profession of humility. He sang:

Just-a inchin' along,
Just-a inchin' along,
Just-a inchin' along like a po' inch-worm—
'Twell de Lawd come an' git me by an' by.
Yes, oh, Lawd!
'Twell de Lawd take me home on high.

(1932)

A SUMMER TRAGEDY
by Arna Bontemps

Old Jeff Patton, the black share farmer, fumbled with his bow tie. His fingers trembled and the high stiff collar pinched his throat. A fellow loses his hand for such vanities after thirty or forty years of simple life. Once a year, or maybe twice if there's a wedding among his kinfolks, he may spruce up; but generally fancy clothes do nothing but adorn the wall of the big room and feed the moths. That had been Jeff Patton's experience. He had not worn his stiff-bosomed shirt more than a dozen times in all his married life. His swallow-tailed coat lay on the bed beside him, freshly brushed and pressed, but it was as full of holes as the overalls in which he worked on weekdays. The moths had used it badly. Jeff twisted his mouth into a hideous toothless grimace as he contended with the obstinate bow. He stamped his good foot and decided to give up the struggle.

"Jennie," he called.

"What's that, Jeff?" His wife's shrunken voice came out of the adjoining room like an echo. It was hardly bigger than a whisper.

"I reckon you'll have to he'p me wid this heah bow tie, baby," he said meekly. "Dog if I can hitch it up."

Her answer was not strong enough to reach him, but presently the old woman came to the door, feeling her way with a stick. She had a wasted, dead-leaf appearance. Her body, as scrawny and gnarled as a string bean, seemed less than nothing in the ocean of frayed and faded petticoats that surrounded her. These hung an inch or two above the tops of her heavy unlaced shoes and showed little grotesque piles where the stockings had fallen down from her negligible legs.

"You oughta could do a heap mo' wid a thing like that'n me—beingst as you got yo' good sight."

"Looks like I oughta could,' he admitted. "But my fingers is gone democrat on me. I get all mixed up in the looking glass an' can't tell wicha way to twist the devilish thing."

Jennie sat on the side of the bed and old Jeff Patton got down on one knee while she tied the bow knot. It was a slow and painful ordeal for each of them in this position. Jeff's bones cracked, his knee ached, and it was only after a half dozen attempts that Jennie worked a semblance of a bow into the tie.

"I got to dress maself now," the old woman whispered. "These is ma old shoes an' stockings, and I ain't so much as unwrapped ma dress."

"Well, don't worry 'bout me no mo', baby," Jeff said. "That 'bout finishes me. All I gotta do now is slip on that old coat'n ves' an' I'll be fixed to leave.''

Jennie disappeared again through the dim passage into the shed room. Being blind was no handicap to her in that black hole. Jeff heard the cane placed against the wall beside the door and knew that his wife was on easy ground. He put on his coat, took a battered top hat from the bedpost and hobbled to the front door. He was ready to travel. As soon as Jennie could get on her Sunday shoes and her old black silk dress, they would start.

Outside the tiny log house, the day was warm and mellow with sunshine. A host of wasps were humming with busy excitement in the trunk of a dead sycamore. Gray squirrels were searching through the grass for hickory nuts and blue jays were in the trees, hopping from branch to branch. Pine woods stretched away to the left like a black sea. Among them were scattered scores of log houses like Jeff's, houses of black share farmers. Cows and pigs wandered freely among the trees. There was no danger of loss. Each farmer knew his own stock and knew his neighbor's as well as he knew his neighbor's children.

Down the slope to the right were the cultivated acres on which the colored folks worked. They extended to the river, more than two miles away, and they were today green with the unmade cotton crop. A tiny thread of a road, which passed directly in front of Jeff's place, ran through these green fields like a pencil mark.

Jeff, standing outside the door, with his absurd hat in his left hand, surveyed the wide scene tenderly. He had been forty-five years on these acres. He loved them with the unexplained affection that others have for the countries to which they belong.

The sun was hot on his head, his collar still pinched his throat, and the Sunday clothes were intolerably hot. Jeff transferred the hat to his right hand and began fanning with it. Suddenly the whisper that was Jennie's voice came out of the shed room.

"You can bring the car round front whilst you's waitin'," it said feebly. There was a tired pause; then it added, "I'll soon be fixed to go."

"A'right, baby," Jeff answered. "I'll get it in a minute."

But he didn't move. A thought struck him that made his mouth fall open. The mention of the car brought to his mind, with new intensity, the trip he and Jennie were about to take. Fear came into his eyes; excitement took his breath. Lord, Jesus!

"Jeff . . . O Jeff," the old woman's whisper called.

He awakened with a jolt. "Hunh, baby?"

"What you doin'?"

"Nuthin. Jes studyin'. I jes been turnin' things round'n round in ma mind."

"You could be gettin' the car," she said.

"Oh yes, right away, baby."

He started round to the shed, limping heavily on his bad leg. There were three frizzly chickens in the yard. All his other chickens had been killed or stolen recently. But the frizzly chickens had been saved somehow. That was fortunate indeed, for those curious creatures had a way of devouring "Poison" from the yard and in that way protecting against conjure and black luck and spells. But even the frizzly chickens seemed now to be in a stupor. Jeff thought they had some ailment; he expected all three of them to die shortly.

The shed in which the old T-model Ford stood was only a grass roof held up by four corner poles. It had been built by tremulous hands at a time when the little rattletrap car had been regarded as a peculiar treasure. And, miraculously, despite wind and downpour it still stood.

Jeff adjusted the crank and put his weight upon it. The engine came to life with a sputter and bang that rattled the old car from radiator to taillight. Jeff hopped into the seat and put his foot on the accelerator. The sputtering and banging increased. The rattling became more violent. That was good. It was good banging, good sputtering and rattling, and it meant that the aged car was still in running condition. She could be depended on for this trip.

Again Jeff's thought halted as if paralyzed. The suggestion of the trip fell into the machinery of his mind like a wrench. He felt dazed and weak. He swung the car out into the yard, made a half turn and drove around to the front door. When he took his hands off the wheel, he noticed that he was trembling violently. He cut off the motor and climbed to the ground to wait for Jennie.

A few minutes later she was at the window, her voice rattling against the pane like a broken shutter.

"I'm ready, Jeff."

He did not answer, but limped into the house and took her by the arm. He led her slowly through the big room, down the step and across the yard.

"You reckon I'd oughta lock the do'?" he asked softly.

They stopped and Jennie weighed the question. Finally she shook her head.

"Ne' mind the do'," she said. "I don't see no cause to lock up things."

"You right," Jeff agreed. "No cause to lock up."

Jeff opened the door and helped his wife into the car. A quick shudder passed over him. Jesus! Again he trembled.

"How come you shaking so?" Jennie whispered.

"I don't know," he said.

"You mus' be scairt, Jeff."

"No, baby, I ain't scairt."

He slammed the door after her and went around to crank up again. The motor started easily. Jeff wished that it had not been so responsive. He would have liked a few more minutes in which to turn things around in his head. As it was, with Jennie chiding him about being afraid, he had to keep going. He swung the car into the little pencil-mark road and started off toward the river, driving very slowly, very cautiously.

Chugging across the green countryside, the small battered Ford seemed tiny indeed. Jeff felt a familiar excitement, a thrill, as they came down the first slope to the immense levels on which the cotton was growing. He could not help reflecting that the crops were good. He knew what that meant, too; he had made forty-five of them with his own hands. It was true that he had worn out nearly a dozen mules, but that was the fault of old man Stevenson, the owner of the land. Major Stevenson had the odd notion that one mule was all a share farmer needed to work a thirty-acre plot. It was an expensive notion, the way it killed mules from overwork, but the old man held to it. Jeff thought it killed a good many share farmers as well as mules, but he had no sympathy for them. He had always been strong, and he had been taught to have no patience with weakness in men. Women or children might be tolerated if they were puny, but a weak man was a curse. Of course, his own children—

Jeff's thought halted there. He and Jennie never mentioned their dead children any more. And naturally he did not wish to dwell upon them in his mind. Before he knew it, some remark would slip out of his mouth and that would make Jennie feel blue. Perhaps she would cry. A woman like Jennie could not easily throw off the grief that comes from losing five grown children within two years. Even Jeff was still staggered by the blow. His memory had not been much good recently. He frequently talked to himself. And, although he had kept it a secret, he knew that his courage had left him. He was terrified by the least unfamiliar sound at night. He was reluctant to venture far from home in the daytime. And that habit of trembling when he felt fearful was now far beyond his control. Sometimes he became afraid and trembled without knowing what had frightened him. The feeling would just come over him like a chill.

The car rattled slowly over the dusty road. Jennie sat erect and silent, with a little absurd hat pinned to her hair. Her useless eyes seemed very large, very white in their deep sockets. Suddenly Jeff heard her voice, and he inclined his head to catch the words.

"Is we passed Delia Moore's house yet?" she asked.

"Not yet," he said.

"You must be drivin' mighty slow, Jeff."

"We might just as well take our time, baby."

There was a pause. A little puff of steam was coming out of the radiator of the car. Heat wavered above the hood. Delia Moore's house was nearly half a mile away. After a moment Jennie spoke again.

"You ain't really scairt, is you, Jeff?"

"Nah, baby, I ain't scairt."

"You know how we agreed—we gotta keep on goin'."

Jewels of perspiration appeared on Jeff's forehead. His eyes rounded, blinked, became fixed on the road.

"I don't know," he said with a shiver. "I reckon it's the only thing to do."

"Hm."

A flock of guinea fowls, pecking in the road, were scattered by the passing car. Some of them took to their wings; others hid under bushes. A blue jay, swaying on a leafy twig, was annoying a roadside squirrel. Jeff held an even speed till he came near Delia's place. Then he slowed down noticeably.

Delia's house was really no house at all, but an abandoned store building converted into a dwelling. It sat near a crossroads, beneath a single black cedar tree. There Delia, a cattish old creature of Jennie's age, lived alone. She had been there more years than anybody could remember, and long ago had won the disfavor of such women as Jennie. For in her young days Delia had been gayer, yellower and saucier than seemed proper in those parts. Her ways with menfolks had been dark and suspicious. And the fact that she had had as many husbands as children did not help her reputation.

"Yonder's old Delia," Jeff said as they passed.

"What she doin'?"

"Jes sittin' in the do'," he said.

"She see us?"

"Hm," Jeff said. "Musta did."

That relieved Jennie. It strengthened her to know that her old enemy had seen her pass in her best clothes. That would give the old she-devil something to chew her gums and fret about, Jennie thought. Wouldn't she have a fit if she didn't find out? Old evil Delia! This would be just the thing for her. It would pay her back for being so evil. It would also pay her, Jennie thought, for the way she used to grin at Jeff—long ago when her teeth were good.

The road became smooth and red, and Jeff could tell by the smell of the air that they were nearing the river. He could see the rise where the road turned and ran along parallel to the stream. The car chugged on monotonously. After a long silent spell, Jennie leaned against Jeff and spoke.

"How many bale o' cotton you think we got standin'?" she said.

Jeff wrinkled his forehead as he calculated.

" 'Bout twenty-five, I reckon."

"How many you make las' year?"

"Twenty-eight," he said. "How come you ask that?"

"I's jes thinkin'," Jennie said quietly.

"It don't make a speck o' difference though," Jeff reflected. "If we get much or if we get little, we still gonna be in debt to old man Stevenson when he gets through counting up agin us. It's took us a long time to learn that."

Jennie was not listening to these words. She had fallen into a trance-like meditation. Her lips twitched. She chewed her gums and rubbed her gnarled hands nervously. Suddenly she leaned forward, buried her face in the nervous hands and burst into tears. She cried aloud in a dry cracked voice that suggested the rattle of fodder on dead stalks. She cried aloud like a child, for she had never learned to suppress a genuine sob. Her slight old frame shook heavily and seemed hardly able to sustain such violent grief.

"What's the matter, baby?" Jeff asked awkwardly. "Why you cryin' like all that?"

"I's jes thinkin'," she said.

"So you the one what's scairt now, hunh?"

"I ain't scairt, Jeff. I's jes thinkin' 'bout leavin' eve'thing like this—eve'thing we been used to. It's right sad-like."

Jeff did not answer, and presently Jennie buried her face again and cried.

The sun was almost overhead. It beat down furiously on the dusty wagon-path road, on the parched roadside grass and the tiny battered car. Jeff's hands, gripping the wheel, became wet with perspiration; his forehead sparkled. Jeff's lips parted. His mouth shaped a hideous grimace. His face suggested the face of a man being burned. But the torture passed and his expression softened again.

"You mustn't cry, baby," he said to his wife. "We gotta be strong. We can't break down."

Jennie waited a few seconds, then said, "You reckon we oughta do it, Jeff? You reckon we oughta go 'head an' do it, really?"

Jeff's voice choked; his eyes blurred. He was terrified to hear Jennie say the thing that had been in his mind all morning. She had egged him on when he had wanted more than anything in the world to wait, to reconsider, to think things over a little longer. Now she was getting cold feet. Actually there was no need of thinking the question through again. It would only end in making the same painful decision once more. Jeff knew that. There was no need of fooling around longer.

"We jes as well to do like we planned," he said. "They ain't nothin' else for us now—it's the bes' thing."

Jeff thought of the handicaps, the near impossibility, of making another crop with his leg bothering him more and more each week. Then there was always the chance that he would have another stroke, like the one that had made him lame. Another one might kill him. The least it could do would be to leave him helpless. Jeff gasped—Lord, Jesus! He could not bear to think of being helpless, like a baby, on Jennie's hands. Frail, blind Jennie.

The little pounding motor of the car worked harder and harder. The puff of steam from the cracked radiator became larger. Jeff realized that they were climbing a little rise. A moment later the road turned abruptly and he looked down upon the face of the river.

"Jeff."

"Is that the water I hear?"

"Hm. Tha's it."

"Well, which way you goin' now?"

"Down this-a way," he said. "The road runs 'long 'side o' the water a lil piece."

She waited a while calmly. Then she said, "Drive faster."

"A'right, baby," Jeff said.

The water roared in the bed of the river. It was fifty or sixty feet below the level of the road. Between the road and the water there was a long smooth slope, sharply inclined. The slope was dry, the clay hardened by prolonged summer heat. The water below, roaring in a narrow channel, was noisy and wild.

"Jeff."

"Hunh?"

"How far you goin'?"

"Jes a lil piece down the road."

"You ain't scairt, is you, Jeff?"

"Nah, baby," he said trembling. "I ain't scairt."

"Remember how we planned it, Jeff. We gotta do it like we said. Brave-like."

"Hm."

Jeff's brain darkened. Things suddenly seemed unreal, like figures in a dream. Thoughts swam in his mind foolishly, hysterically, like little blind fish in a pool within a dense cave. They rushed, crossed one another, jostled, collided, retreated and rushed again. Jeff soon became dizzy. He shuddered violently and turned to his wife.

"Jennie, I can't do it. I can't." His voice broke pitifully.

She did not appear to be listening. All the grief had gone from her face. She sat erect, her unseeing eyes wide open, strained and frightful. Her glossy black skin had become dull. She seemed as thin, as sharp and bony, as a starved bird. Now, having suffered and endured the sadness of tearing herself away from beloved things, she showed no anguish. She was absorbed with her own thoughts, and she didn't even hear Jeff's voice shouting in her ear.

Jeff said nothing more. For an instant there was light in his cavernous brain. The great chamber was, for less than a second, peopled by characters he knew and loved. They were simple, healthy creatures, and they behaved in a manner that he could understand. They had quality. But since he had already taken leave of them long ago, the remembrance did not break his heart again. Young Jeff Patton was among them, the Jeff Patton of fifty years ago who went down to New Orleans with a crowd of country boys to the Mardi Gras doings. The gay young crowd, boys with candy-striped shirts and rouged-brown girls in noisy silks, was like a picture in his head. Yet it did not make him sad. On that very trip Slim Burns had killed Joe Beasley—the crowd had been broken up. Since then Jeff Patton's world had been the Greenbriar Plantation. If there had been other Mardi Gras carnivals, he had not heard of them. Since then there had been no time; the years had fallen on him like waves. Now he was old, worn out. Another paralytic stroke (like the one he had already suffered) would put him on his back for keeps. In that condition, with a frail blind woman to look after him, he would be worse off than if he were dead.

Suddenly Jeff's hands became steady. He actually felt brave. He slowed down the motor of the car and carefully pulled off the road. Below, the water of the stream boomed, a soft thunder in the deep channel. Jeff ran the car onto the clay slope, pointed it directly toward the stream and put his foot heavily on the accelerator. The little car leaped furiously down the steep incline toward the water. The movement was nearly as swift and direct as a fall. The two old black folks, sitting quietly side by side, showed no excitement. In another instant the car hit the water and dropped immediately out of sight.

A little later it lodged in the mud of a shallow place. One wheel of the crushed and upturned little Ford became visible above the rushing water.

(1933)

RUNAGATE NIGGERS
by William March

Lafe Rockett's wife began talking as soon as Uncle Elbert arrived and eased himself into the wicker chair on the porch: "I don't know what this country's coming to, when they put law-abiding citizens like Lafe in jail for no reason!"

Uncle Elbert rocked, rubbed his chin, and said: "If you want me to help Lafe out of his trouble, you'd better tell me what happened, Birdie."

"It really began last winter, Uncle Elbert, when Lafe put a nigger couple named Sam and Aphie to farm his cutover land near Milden, and no niggers ever got better treatment from a white man than those two did. Lafe advanced 'em their vittles and rented 'em a mule, but from the first those two niggers was always complaining. They said the land was so pore and stumpy that nobody could make a crop on it without some fertilizer. Sam said the only thing that growed well on that land was the squash and collards that Aphie raised.

"Well, things went on like that, with them niggers complaining that they didn't have enough to live on, and Lafe advancing meal and side meat now and then, until the cotton they'd planted was forming bolls. Lafe used to ride out regular to look at the cotton, and even though it was pindling, because of them niggers being so worthless, he figgered the crop would just about pay for the vittles he'd laid out and the rent owing to him.

"Uncle Elbert, Lafe treated them niggers as fair as anybody could, but they was just no-account. This'll give you some idea: Last spring Aphie wanted a dog for company, so Lafe gave her a hound puppy. Well, sir, when Lafe seen that hound three months ago, he said the sight of it made him want to cry. It was nothing but skin and bones. He said he couldn't understand how anybody could treat a dog like that. Sam said the reason was because they hadn't had nothing to eat all summer themselves, except collards and squash, and that a hound wouldn't eat squash or greens."

"I haven't got no use for folks that treat their dogs sorry," said Uncle Elbert. He shook his head.

"Things might have been all right," continued Birdie, "except for that rainy spell in September. It started just when the cotton was made and ready to be picked, and it lasted three weeks, nearabout. When it was over, Sam and Aphie's whole crop was soured and rotted in the bolls. After that, it looked like those two niggers was hanging around our kitchen all the time, begging for vittles. There wasn't much Lafe could do, but to show you how fair he acted, he said he'd let 'em stay on another year, if they found a way to feed themselves. By that time they'd have all the stumps out, and could make a better crop. He even said he might advance some fertilizer next spring if things worked out well."

Birdie laughed bitterly and wiped her mouth. "We found out later what a sly one that Aphie is, and how she was working behind Lafe's back all the time she was begging him for vittles. You see, Uncle Elbert, she had a sister cooking for some white folks in Chicago, so when Aphie got old Mrs. Todd to write a hard-luck letter to this here sister, she answered right off and sent what money she'd saved up, telling Sam and Aphie to come on to Chicago. That next day Mrs. Todd read the letter to Aphie and told her how to cash the money order.

"Well, Sam and Aphie must have had a guilty conscience, and when they ran away they didn't go to Milden to cash that money order or take the train there, because they knowed Lafe would hear about it, sure, and stop 'em. Instead, they lit out one night to walk to Lippincott, twenty miles away. It might have worked, at that, except the Pritchett boy seen 'em on the road, figgered out what was going on, and told Lafe. He also knowed about Aphie's letter, because Mrs. Todd was his aunt, so when Lafe found out about that, he did what anybody would: He wired the deputy sheriff at Lippincott to watch for two niggers carrying bundles and leading a hound and to hold them until he got there.

"Lafe said, when he got back from Lippincott, that he and the niggers and the sheriff all got to the depot about the same time. Sam and Aphie had already cashed the money order and were buying tickets when the sheriff put the handcuffs on 'em. It provoked Lafe right smart to see those niggers spending money they rightly owed him, so he lost his temper, like anybody would, and started hitting Sam and Aphie with a strap he happened to have with him at the time. But the story that he chained 'em to a tree when he got 'em home is a pure lie! He only *said* he'd do it, if they run off owing him money again, to show off before that woman at the depot. . . .

"You see, Uncle Elbert, when the trouble started, there was a young white woman standing on the platform who seen the whole thing, and when Lafe started hitting the niggers, she opened her camera and took pictures of it. She even followed the men back of the depot and talked with Lafe and the sheriff, laughing and joking. She asked Lafe how it happened, and he told her the whole story, just as I've told it to you; but the woman shook her head and said she didn't believe that part about sending the telegram. That was too smart to think of, she said, and she thought Lafe was making that part up.

"Well, sir, by that time she'd told her name and Lafe and the sheriff had told theirs, and they were all laughing and talking together in the friendliest way, so the sheriff took out the telegram and showed it to her, to prove Lafe was right. So this woman said she'd like to keep the telegram for a souvenir and put it in her purse. The train pulled in about that time and the woman shook hands and got on board. . . . Well, like you've already guessed, she went straight to Washington and turned the photos and the telegram over to the government, and yesterday two Federal men arrested Lafe and the deputy sheriff on a peonage charge and took 'em to jail."

Lafe's wife was quiet for a moment, rocking back and forth. "I declare," she said bitterly, "I don't see how any white woman could go back on her own race that-a-way! I don't see how anybody could be so low-down!"

Uncle Elbert spat over the rail and wiped his chin slowly.

"I been figgering things over all yesterday and today," continued Birdie, "and the more I think, the more disgusted I am with this here country and the way things are run. Things have come to a pretty pass when a man can't catch his own runagate niggers!"

Uncle Elbert spoke thoughtfully: "Lafe got him a lawyer yet?"

Birdie said: "For two cents I'd move out of this country and go some place where people still enjoy liberty. That's how disgusted I am with this here country, and I don't much keer who knows it, either!"

(1938)

From

YOU CAN'T GO HOME AGAIN
by Thomas Wolfe

He came from an old and distinguished family, and, like all his male ancestors for one hundred years or more, he had been trained in the profession of the law. For a single term he had been a police court magistrate, and from then on was known as "Judge" Bland. But he had fallen grievously from the high estate his family held. During the period of George Webber's boyhood he still professed to be a lawyer. He had a shabby office in a disreputable old building which he owned, and his name was on the door as an attorney, but his living was earned by other and more devious means. Indeed, his legal skill and knowledge had been used more for the purpose of circumventing the law and defeating justice than in maintaining them. Practically all his "business" was derived from the Negro population of the town, and of this business the principal item was usury.

On the Square, in his ramshackle two-story building of rusty brick, was "the store." It was a second-hand furniture store, and it occupied the ground floor and basement of the building. It was, of course, nothing but a blind for his illegal transactions with the Negroes. A hasty and appalled inspection of the mountainous heap of ill-smelling junk which it contained would have been enough to convince one that if the owner had to depend on the sale of his stock he would have to close his doors within a month. It was incredible. In the dirty window was a pool table, taken as brutal tribute from some Negro billiard parlor. But what a pool table! Surely it had not a fellow in all the relics in the land. Its surface was full of lumps and dents and ridges. Not a pocket remained without a hole in the bottom big enough to drop a baseball through. The green cloth covering had worn through or become unfixed in a dozen places. The edges of the table and the cloth itself were seared and burnt with the marks of innumerable cigarettes. Yet this dilapidated object was by all odds the most grandiose adornment of the whole store.

As one peered back into the gloom of the interior he became aware of the most fantastic collection of nigger junk that was ever brought together in one place. On the street floor as well as in the basement it was piled up to the ceiling, and all jumbled together as if some gigantic steam-shovel had opened its jaws and dumped everything just as it was. There were broken-down rocking chairs, bureaus with cracked mirrors and no bottoms in the drawers, tables with one, two, or three of their legs missing, rusty old kitchen stoves with burnt-out grates and elbows of sooty pipe, blackened frying pans encased in the grease of years, flat irons, chipped plates and bowls and pitchers, washtubs, chamber pots, and a thousand other objects, all worn out, cracked, and broken.

What, then, was the purpose of this store, since it was filled with objects of so little value that even the poorest Negroes could get slight use from them? The purpose, and the way Judge Rumford Bland used it, was quite simple:

A Negro in trouble, in immediate need of money to pay a police court fine, a doctor's bill, or some urgent debt, would come to see Judge Bland. Sometimes he needed as little as five or ten dollars, occasionally as much as fifty dollars, but usually it was less than that. Judge Bland would then demand to know what security he had. The Negro, of course, had none, save perhaps a few personal possessions and some wretched little furniture—a bed, a chair, a table, a kitchen stove. Judge Bland would send his collector, bulldog, and chief lieutenant—a ferret-faced man named Clyde Beals—to inspect these miserable possessions, and if he thought the junk important enough to its owner to justify the loan, he would advance the money, extracting from it, however, the first installment of his interest.

From this point on, the game was plainly and flagrantly usurious. The interest was payable weekly, every Saturday night. On a ten-dollar loan Judge Bland extracted interest of fifty cents a week; on a twenty-dollar loan, interest of a dollar a week; and so on. That is why the amount of the loans was rarely as much as fifty dollars. Not only were the contents of most Negro shacks worth less than that, but to pay two dollars and a half in weekly interest was beyond the capacity of most Negroes, whose wage, if they were men, might not be more than five or six dollars a week, and if they were women—cooks or house-servants in the town—might be only three or four dollars. Enough had to be left them for a bare existence or it was no game. The purpose and skill of the game came in lending the Negro a sum of money somewhat greater than his weekly wage and his consequent ability to pay back, but also a sum whose weekly interest was within the range of his small income.

Judge Bland had on his books the names of Negroes who had paid him fifty cents or a dollar a week over a period years, on an original loan of ten or twenty dollars. Many of these poor and ignorant people were unable to comprehend what had happened to them. They could only feel mournfully, dumbly, with the slavelike submissiveness of their whole training and conditioning, that at some time in the distant past they had got their money, spent it, and had their fling, and that now they must pay perpetual tribute for that privilege. Such men and women as these would come to that dim-lit place of filth and misery on Saturday night, and there the Judge himself, black-frocked, white-shirted, beneath one dingy, fly-specked bulb, would hold his private court:

"What's wrong, Carrie? You're two weeks behind in your payments. Is fifty cents all you got this week?"

"It doan seem lak it was three weeks. Musta slipped up somewheres in my countin'."

"You didn't slip up. It's three weeks. You owe a dollar fifty. Is this all you got?"

With sullen apology: "Yassuh."

"When will you have the rest of it?"

"Dey's a fellah who say he gonna give me—"

"Never mind about that. Are you going to keep up your payments after this or not?"

"Dat's whut Ah wuz sayin'. Jus' as soon as Monday come, an' dat fel-lah—"

Harshly: "Who you working for now?"

"Doctah Hollandah—"

"You cooking for him?"

Sullenly, with unfathomable Negro mournfulness: "Yassuh."

"How much is he paying you?"

"Three dollahs."

"And you mean you can't keep up? You can't pay fifty cents a week?"

Still sullen, dark, and mournful, as doubtful and confused as jungle depths of Africa: "Doan know. . . . Seem lak a long time since Ah started payin' up—"

Harshly, cold as poison, quick as a striking snake: "You've never started paying up. You've paid nothing. You're only paying interest, and behind in that."

And still doubtfully, in black confusion, fumbling and fingering and bringing forth at last a wad of greasy little receipts from the battered purse: "Doan know, seem lake Ah got enough of dese to've paid dat ten dollahs up long ago. How much longer does Ah have to keep on payin'?"

"Till you've got ten dollars. . . . All right, Carrie: here's your receipt. You bring that extra dollar in next week."

Others, a little more intelligent than Carrie, would comprehend more clearly what had happened to them, but would continue to pay because they were unable to get together at one time enough money to release them from their bondage. A few would have energy and power enough to save their pennies until at last they were able to buy back their freedom. Still others, after paying week by week and month by month, would just give up in despair and would pay no more. Then, of course, Clyde Beals was on them like a vulture. He nagged, he wheedled, and he threatened; and if, finally, he saw that he could get no more money from them, he took their household furniture. Hence the chaotic pile of malodorous junk which filled the shop.

Why, it may be asked, in a practice that was so flagrantly, nakedly, and unashamedly usurious as this, did Judge Rumford Bland not come into collision with the law? Did the police not know from what sources, and in what ways, his income was derived?

They knew perfectly. The very store in which this miserable business was carried on was within twenty yards of the City Hall, and within fifty feet of the side entrance to the town calaboose, up whose stone steps many of these same Negroes had time and again been hauled and mauled and hurled into a cell. The practice, criminal though it was, was a common one, winked at by the local authorities, and but one of many similar practices by which unscrupulous white men all over the South feathered their own nests at the expense of an oppressed and ignorant people. The fact that such usury was practiced chiefly against "a bunch of niggers" to a large degree condoned and pardoned it in the eyes of the law.

Moreover, Judge Rumford Bland knew that the people with whom he dealt would not inform on him. He knew that the Negro stood in awe of the complex mystery of the law, of which he understood little or nothing, or in terror of its brutal force. The law for him was largely a matter of the police, and the police was a white man in a uniform, who had the power and authority to arrest him, to beat him with his fist or with a club, to shoot him with a gun, and to lock him up in a small, dark cell. It was not likely, therefore, that any Negro would take his troubles to the police. He was not aware that he had any rights as a citizen, and that Judge Rumford Bland had violated those rights; or, if he was aware of rights, however vaguely, he was not likely to ask for their protection by a group of men at whose hands he had known only assault, arrest, and imprisonment.

(1940)

From

ON A FLORIDA KEY
by E. B. White

FEBRUARY 1941

I am writing this in a beach cottage on a Florida key. It is raining to beat the cars. The rollers from a westerly storm are creaming along the shore, making a steady boiling noise instead of the usual intermittent slap. The Chamber of Commerce has drawn the friendly blind against this ugliness and is busy getting out some advance notices of the style parade which is to be held next Wednesday at the pavilion. The paper says cooler tomorrow.

*   *   *   *   *

This morning I read in the paper of an old Negro, one hundred-and-one years old, and he was boasting of the quantity of whiskey he had drunk in his life. He said he had once worked in a distillery and they used to give him half a gallon of whiskey a day to take home, which kept him going all right during the week, but on weekends, he said, he would have to buy a gallon extry, to tide him over till Monday.

In the kitchen cabinet is a bag of oranges for morning juice. Each orange is stamped "Color Added." The dyeing of an orange, to make it orange, is man's most impudent gesture to date. It is really an appalling piece of effrontery, carrying the clear implication that Nature doesn't know what she is up to. I think an orange, dyed orange, is as repulsive as a pine cone painted green. I think it is about as ugly a thing as I have ever seen, and it seems hard to believe that here, within ten miles, probably, of the trees that bore the fruit, I can't buy an orange that somebody hasn't smeared with paint. But I doubt that there are many who feel that way about it, because fraudulence has become a national virtue and is well thought of in many circles. In the last twenty-four hours, I see by this morning's paper, 136 cars of oranges have been shipped. There are probably millions of children today who have never seen a natural orange—only an artifically colored one. If they should see a natural orange they might think something had gone wrong with it.

There are two moving picture theaters in the town to which my key is attached by a bridge. In one of them colored people are allowed in the balcony. In the other, colored people are not allowed at all. I saw a patriotic newsreel there the other day which ended with a picture of the American flag blowing in the breeze, and the words: one nation indivisible, with liberty and justice for all. Everyone clapped, but I decided I could not clap for liberty and justice (for all) while I was in a theater from which Negroes had been barred. And I felt there were too many people in the world who think liberty and justice for all means liberty and justice for themselves and their friends. I sat there wondering what would happen to me if I were to jump up and say in a loud voice: "If you folks like liberty and justice so much, why do you keep Negroes from this theater?" I am sure it would have surprised everybody very much and it is the kind of thing I dream about doing but never do. If I had done it I suppose the management would have taken me by the arm and marched me out of the theater, on the grounds that it is disturbing the peace to speak up for liberty just as the feature is coming on. When a man is in the South he must do as the Southerners do; but although I am willing to call my wife "sugar" I am not willing to call a colored person a nigger.

Northerners are quite likely to feel that Southerners are bigoted on the race question, and Southerners almost invariably figure that Northerners are without any practical experience and therefore their opinions aren't worth much. The Jim Crow philosophy of color is unsatisfying to a Northerner, but is regarded as sensible and expedient to residents of towns where the Negro population is as large as or larger than the white. Whether one makes a practical answer or an idealistic answer to a question depends partly on whether one is talking in terms of one year, or ten years, or a hundred years. It is, in other words, conceivable that the Negroes of a hundred years from now will enjoy a greater degree of liberty if the present restrictions on today's Negroes are not relaxed too fast. But that doesn't get today's Negroes in to see Hedy Lamarr.

I have to laugh when I think about the sheer inconsistency of the Southern attitude about color: the Negro barred from the movie house because of color, the orange with "color added" for its ultimate triumph. Some of the cities in this part of the State have fête days to commemorate the past and advertise the future, and in my mind I have been designing a float that I would like to enter in the parades. It would contain a beautiful Negro woman riding with the other bathing beauties and stamped with the magical words, Color Added.

(1941)

From

LET US NOW PRAISE FAMOUS MEN
by James Agee

They came into the Coffee Shoppe while we were finishing breakfast, and Harmon introduced the other, whose name I forget, but which had a French sound. He was middle-sized and dark, beginning to grizzle, with the knotty, walnut kind of body and a deeply cut, not unkindly monkey's face. He wore dark trousers, a starched freshly laundered white collarless shirt, and a soft yellow straw hat with a band of flowered cloth. His shoes were old, freshly blacked, not polished; his suspenders were nearly new, blue, with gold lines at the edge. He was courteous, casual, and even friendly, without much showing the element of strain: Harmon let him do the talking and watched us from behind the reflecting lenses of his glasses. People in the street slowed as they passed and lingered their eyes upon us. Walker said it would be all right to make pictures, wouldn't it, and he said, Sure, of course, take all the snaps you're a mind to; that is, if you can keep the niggers from running off when they see a camera. When they saw the amount of equipment stowed in the back of our car, they showed that they felt they had been taken advantage of, but said nothing of it.

Harmon drove out with Walker, I with the other, up a loose wide clay road to the northwest of town in the high glittering dusty sunday late morning heat of sunlight. The man I drove with made steady conversation, in part out of nervous courtesy, in part as if to forestall any questions I might ask him. I was glad enough of it; nearly all his tenants were negroes and no use to me, and I needed a rest from asking questions and decided merely to establish myself as even more easygoing, casual, and friendly than he was. It turned out that I had not been mistaken in the French sound of his name; ancestors of his had escaped an insurrection of negroes in Haiti. He himself, however, was entirely localized, a middling well-to-do landowner with a little more of the look of the direct farmer about him than the average. He was driving a several-years-old tan sedan, much the sort of car a factory worker in a northern city drives, and was pointing out to me how mean the cotton was on this man's land, who thought he could skimp by on a low grade of fertilizer, and how good it was along this pocket and high lift, that somehow caught whatever rain ran across this part of the country, though that was no advantage to cotton in a wet year or even an average; it was good in a drowt year like this one, though; his own cotton, except for a stretch of it along the bottom, he couldn't say yet it was going to do either very good or very bad; here we are at it, though.

A quarter of a mile back in a flat field of short cotton a grove of oaks spumed up and a house stood in their shade. Beyond, as we approached, the land sank quietly away toward woods which ran tendrils along it, and was speckled near and far with nearly identical two-room shacks, perhaps a dozen, some in the part shade of chinaberry bushes, others bare to the brightness, all with the color in the sunlight and frail look of the tissue of hornets' nests. This nearest four-room house we were approaching was the foreman's. We drew up in the oak shade as the doors of this house filled. They were negroes. Walker and Harmon drew up behind us. A big iron ring hung by a chain from the low branch of an oak. A heavy strip of iron leaned at the base of the tree. Negroes appeared at the doors of the two nearest tenant houses. From the third house away, two of them were approaching. One was in clean overalls; the other wore black pants, a white shirt, and a black vest unbuttoned.

Here at the foreman's home we had caused an interruption that filled me with regret: relatives were here from a distance, middle-aged and sober people in their sunday clothes, and three or four visiting children, and I realized that they had been quietly enjoying themselves, the men out at the far side of the house, the women getting dinner, as now, by our arrival, they no longer could. The foreman was very courteous, the other men were non-committal, the eyes of the women were quietly and openly hostile; the landlord and the foreman were talking. The foreman's male guests hovered quietly and respectfully in silence on the outskirts of the talk until they were sure what they might properly do, then withdrew to the far side of the house, watching carefully to catch the landowner's eyes, should they be glanced after, so that they might nod, smile, and touch their foreheads, as in fact they did, before they disappeared. The two men from the third house came up; soon three more came, a man of forty and a narrow-skulled pair of sapling boys. They all approached softly and strangely until they stood within the shade of the grove, then stayed their ground as if floated, their eyes shifting upon us sidelong and to the ground and to the distance, speaking together very little, in quieted voices: it was as if they had been under some sort of magnetic obligation to approach just this closely and to show themselves. The landlord began to ask of them through the foreman, How's So-and-So doing, all laid by? Did he do that extra sweeping I told you?— and the foreman would answer, Yes sir, yes sir, he do what you say to do, he doin all right; and So-and-So shifted on his feet and smiled uneasily while, uneasily, one of his companions laughed and the others held their faces in the blank safety of deafness. And you, you ben doin much coltn lately, you horny old bastard?—and the crinkled, old, almost gray-mustached negro who came up tucked his head to one side looking cute, and showed what was left of his teeth, and whined, tittering, Now Mist So-and-So, you know I'm settled down, married-man, you wouldn't—and the brutal negro of forty split his face in a villainous grin and said, He too *ole*, Mist So-and-So, he don't got no sap lef in him; and everyone laughed, and the landowner said, These yer two yere, colts yourn ain't they?—and the old man said they were, and the landowner said, Musta found *them* in the woods, strappin young niggers as that; and the old man said, No sir, he got the both of them lawful married, Mist So-and-So; and the landowner said that eldest on em looks to be ready for a piece himself, and the negroes laughed, and the two boys twisted their beautiful bald gourd-like skulls in a unison of shyness and their faces were illumined with maidenly smiles of shame, delight and fear; and meanwhile the landowner had loosened the top two buttons of his trousers, and he now reached his hand in to the middle of the forearm, and, squatting with bent knees apart, clawed, scratched and rearranged his genitals.

But now three others stood in the outskirts who had been sent for by a running child; they were young men, only twenty to thirty, yet very old and sedate; and their skin was of that sootiest black which no light can make shine and with which the teeth are blue and the eyeballs gold. They wore pressed trousers, washed shoes, brilliantly starched white shirts, bright ties, and carried newly whited straw hats in their hands, and at their hearts were pinned the purple and gilded ribbons of a religious and burial society. They had been summoned to sing for Walker and for me, to show us what nigger music is like (though we had done all we felt we were able to spare them and ourselves this summons), and they stood patiently in a stiff frieze in the oak shade, their hats and their shirts shedding light, and were waiting to be noticed and released, for they had been on their way to church when the child caught them; and now that they were looked at and the order given they stepped forward a few paces, not smiling, and stopped in rigid line, and, after a constricted exchange of glances among themselves, the eldest tapping the clean dirt with his shoe, they sang. It was as I had expected, not in the mellow and euphonious Fisk Quartette style, but in the style I have heard on records by Mitchell's Christian Singers, jagged, tortured, stony, accented as if by hammers and cold-chisels, full of a nearly paralyzing vitality and iteration of rhythm, the harmonies constantly splitting the nerves; so that of western music the nearest approach to its austerity is in the first two centuries of polyphony. But here it was entirely instinctual; it tore itself like a dance of sped plants out of three young men who stood sunk to their throats in land, and whose eyes were neither shut nor looking at anything; the screeching young tenor, the baritone, stridulant in the height of his register, his throat tight as a fist, and the bass, rolling the iron wheels of his machinery, his hand clenching and loosening as he tightened and relaxed against the spraining of his ellipses: and they were abruptly silent; totally wooden; while the landowner smiled coldly. There was nothing to say. I looked them in the eyes with full and open respect and said, that was fine. Have you got time to sing us another? Their heads and their glances collected toward a common center, and restored, and they sang us another, a slow one this time; I had a feeling, through their silence before entering it, that it was their favorite and their particular pride; the tenor lifted out his voice alone in a long, plorative line that hung like fire on heaven, or whistle's echo, sinking, sunken, along descents of a modality I had not heard before, and sank along the arms and breast of the bass as might a body sunken from a cross; and the baritone lifted a long black line of comment; and they ran in a long and slow motion and convolution of rolling as at the bottom of a stormy sea, voice meeting voice as ships in dream, retreated, met once more, much woven, digressions and returns of time, quite tuneless, the bass, over and over, approaching, drooping, the same declivity, the baritone taking over, a sort of metacenter, murmuring along monotones between major and minor, nor in any determinable key, the tenor winding upward like a horn, a wire, the flight of a bird, almost into full declamation, then failing it, silencing; at length enlarging, the others lifting, now, alone, lone, and largely, questioning, alone and not sustained, in the middle of space, stopped; and now resumed, sunken upon the bosom of the bass, the head declined; both muted, droned; the baritone makes his comment, unresolved, that is a question, all on one note: and they are quiet, and do not look at us, nor at anything.

The landlord objected that that was too much howling and too much religion on end and how about something with some life to it, they knew what he meant, and then they could go.

They knew what he meant, but it was very hard for them to give it just now. They stiffened in their bodies and hesitated, several seconds, and looked at each other with eyes ruffled with worry; then the bass nodded, as abruptly as a blow, and with blank faces they struck into a fast, sassy, pelvic tune whose words were loaded almost beyond translation with comic sexual metaphor; a refrain song that ran like a rapid wheel, with couplets to be invented, progressing the story; they sang it through four of the probably three dozen turns they knew, then bit it off sharp and sharply, and for the first time, relaxed out of line, as if they knew they had earned the right, with it, to leave.

Meanwhile, and during all this singing, I had been sick in the knowledge that they felt they were here at our demand, mine and Walker's, and that I could communicate nothing otherwise; and now, in a perversion of self-torture, I played my part through. I gave their leader fifty cents, trying at the same time, through my eyes, to communicate much more, and said I was sorry we had held them up and that I hoped they would not be late; and he thanked me for them in a dead voice, not looking me in the eye, and they went away, putting their white hats on their heads as they walked into the sunlight.

(1941)

AND/OR

by Sterling A. Brown

For safety's sake, though he is a lieutenant in the army now and may never come back to the South, let us call him Houston. He was short and frail, with a dark brown sensitive face. I first met him at the FEPC hearings in Birmingham when, on short acquaintance, he revealed to me how he was burned up by conditions in Dixie. To judge from his twang, he was southern-born, and he was Tuskegee trained, but he had the rather dicty restaurant on edge when he went into his tirades. The brown burghers, some of them a bit jittery anyway at FEPC and especially at the influx of a bunch of young "foreign" and radical Negroes into dynamite-loaded Birmingham, eyed him carefully over their glasses of iced tea.

I ran into him again in the small Alabama town where he was teaching. He was still quite a talker, in his high-pitched voice with a quaver in it—though he didn't quaver in other respects. He was brimming over with facts and consequent bitterness, deeper than I expected in a graduate of Tuskegee. To him, as to so many college men, the Negro's great need was the ballot. He had made a thoughtful study of the disenfranchising techniques and political shenanigans of Alabama in general. He laughed sardonically at the Negro's being asked to interpret such "constitutional" questions as "What is *non compos mentis* when it is applied to a citizen in legal jeopardy?" But he knew also how deeply engraved was the symbol at the head of the Democratic column on the official ballot used in all elections in Alabama: a rooster with the words "White Supremacy" arched over its head, and the words under it: "For the Right." White supremacy was well symbolized by the rooster, he thought; and he was afraid that Negro purposefulness was too well symbolized by a chicken. And a chicken with pip, lethargic, gaping, and trembling. He was determined to vote himself, and he told me with gusto the tragicomedy, at times the farce, of his experiences with the county board of registrars.

Knowing the ropes, Houston's first strategic step to get the vote was to buy a radio at a white store and charge it. This was his first charge account in the town, but it meant a possible white sponsor to vouch for him when the polls opened. Two weeks later he applied to the Board of Registrars. He was asked, "Do you have three hundred dollars worth of taxable property?"

Houston said no, but added that he understood that the property qualification was alternative to the literacy qualification. He was told that he was wrong: he had to have three hundred dollars worth of property or forty acres of land. That seemed to end the matter as far as the Board was concerned. Houston waited a few minutes and then asked if he would be permitted to make out an application. He was granted permission with the warning that the Board would have to pass on his case, and that as he did not have the property qualification, the chances were against him. He was also told that he needed two residents of the town to vouch for his character. He named the merchant from whom he had bought the radio and a clothing merchant.

When approached, the first merchant said that he would be glad to go over and sign, but that he couldn't leave his store just then. He would go over late that afternoon. Houston thanked him. The next day he telephoned the merchant, who hadn't quite managed it the day before but would try to get over some time that day. Houston thanked him again. The next day the merchant hadn't seen his way clear, either, things being so busy, but he gave his word that he wouldn't let the polls close on Houston. Three days later, the merchant told Houston that he had just got tied up and the polls had closed. A week later, Houston went to the store and paid the balance on the radio. The merchant said that he was sorry; he just hadn't been able to get around to doing that little favor, but he gave his word again that he would be glad indeed to go over when the polls opened again. Yessir, glad. That would be just the next month, Houston told him.

When the polls opened the next month, Houston called the merchant, who made an appointment with him for "about 2 P.M." At the store on the dot, Houston was told that the merchant was out of town. Yessir, a quick trip.

Houston then applied to the second merchant, with whom he had had even more dealings, but on a cash basis. The runaround here was also efficient. He didn't know Houston well enough "to take an oath about his character," but he promised that if men at the Post Office and Bank said O.K., he would vouch for him. Every time the Post Office superintendent called, the merchant was out. Finally, the banker caught him, and the appointment was made.

"I understand you have an application for R. T. Houston, who has been working out at the school for the last three years or so." The board informed the merchant that investigation showed that Houston did not have either three hundred dollars worth of property or forty acres of land. The merchant said, "Oh, I don't know anything about that." He wanted to get out of there quick. Houston stated again his understanding about the alternative literacy qualification.

"It doesn't make any difference whether you graduated from Harvard. If you don't have the property, you can't register," the merchant offered. Houston remembered that he seemed to cheer up, saying it.

The merchant and Houston left the office, Houston thanking him for his time, and the merchant saying jocularly, "Well, you got to get your three hundred dollars worth of property or forty acres of land somewhere. What are you going to do?"

"I'm going to register," said Houston. "There is a provision in the Constitution for having your qualifications determined." Houston was partly compensated for the long runaround by the look of amazement on the merchant's face.

With two other colleagues, both acquainted with the law, Houston approached the Board again to thresh out the matter of qualifications. The registrar, a woman, stated that somebody else had asked the same question and that she had "marked it in the book." She was told that the property qualification was an alternative.

"No," she said, "you must have the property."

"When was the amendment passed making both qualifications necessary?"

This question was ignored. In triumph, the registrar read the second qualification. ". . . owner or husband of woman who is owner . . . of forty acres of land, or personal property or real estate assessed . . . at value of three hundred dollars or more," etc.

She was then asked to read the first qualification. She complied, hesitantly. Another registrar horned in: "This board will have to pass on you, and we register who we want to register."

The first qualification set up the requirement of "reading and writing any article of the Constitution of the United States in the English language . . ." and of being "regularly engaged in some lawful employment the twelve months next preceding the time they offer to register . . . etc." The word linking this to the second qualification is *or*.

On being asked what the word *or* meant, the registrar said that it meant *in addition to*, based on an interpretation from the Attorney General. Houston and his colleagues asked for this ruling, but it was not produced. Instead the three troublemakers were shunted across the hall to the Probate Judge's office. The Judge was asked point blank if "or" in the state constitution meant "and." The Judge replied point-blank that it did. "You must have both the property as well as the literacy qualification," he said. The registrars got their ruling from the Attorney General; the Judge knew nothing of any law that had been made. Questioned closely on whether all the list of voters owned three hundred dollars worth of property, the judge hedged. He complained that his questioners were only trying to get him into an argument with the Board of Registrars.

"What steps should we take to get an interpretation of the disputed passage?" was the straw breaking the camel's back.

"Find out for yourself," the Judge yelled, and stormed out of his office.

A few hours later, while preparing papers for an appeal to the Circuit Court to clarify the problem of qualification, Houston learned that the Board of Registrars had been busy telephoning him. Another call, unidentified but "from someone in touch with the Judge," informed Houston that he would get his registration papers.

When he walked into the office, there was a decided stir. One of the women on the Board said, "Here he is now." The spokesman of the Board was polite. "We decided to let you register," he said.

"Thank you very much," said Houston. The certificate was signed and dated as of the preceding day, when the Judge had ruled on "And/Or."

Houston was told that it would be wise to get two good people of the town to vouch for him.

He named colleagues of his at the school.

"We mean white people," said the registrar. "Don't you know two good white people?"

"Nossir," said Houston politely. "I don't know two good white people . . . to vouch for me."

(1946)

Index of Authors, Titles and Ethnic Groups

Page numbers for ethnic groups refer to selections in which there is some significant representation.